Shojo Beat

Skip·Beat!

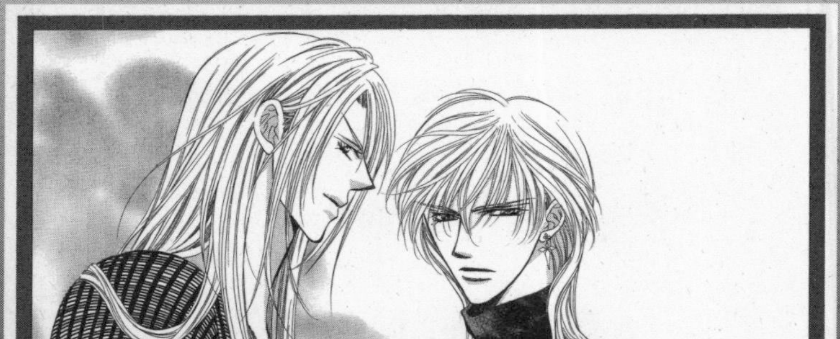

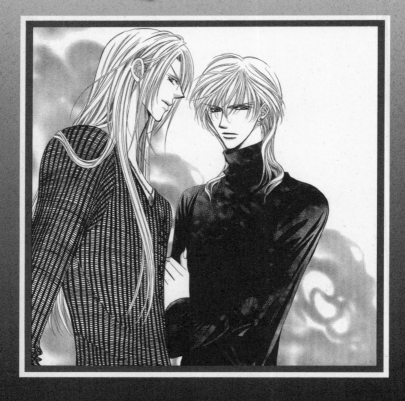

17

Story & Art by Yoshiki Nakamura

Skip·Beat!

Volume 17

CONTENTS

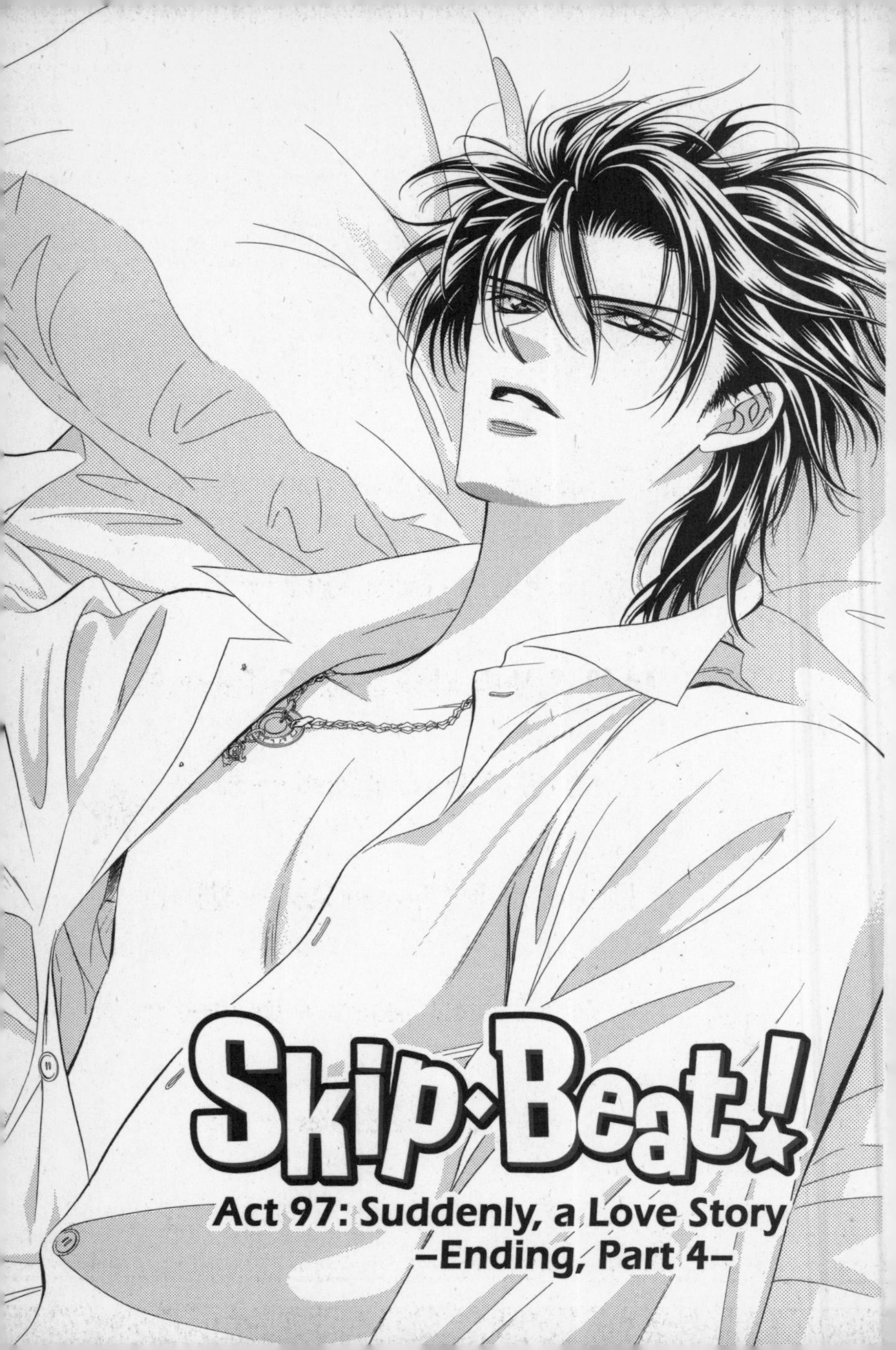
Skip·Beat!
Act 97: Suddenly, a Love Story
–Ending, Part 4–

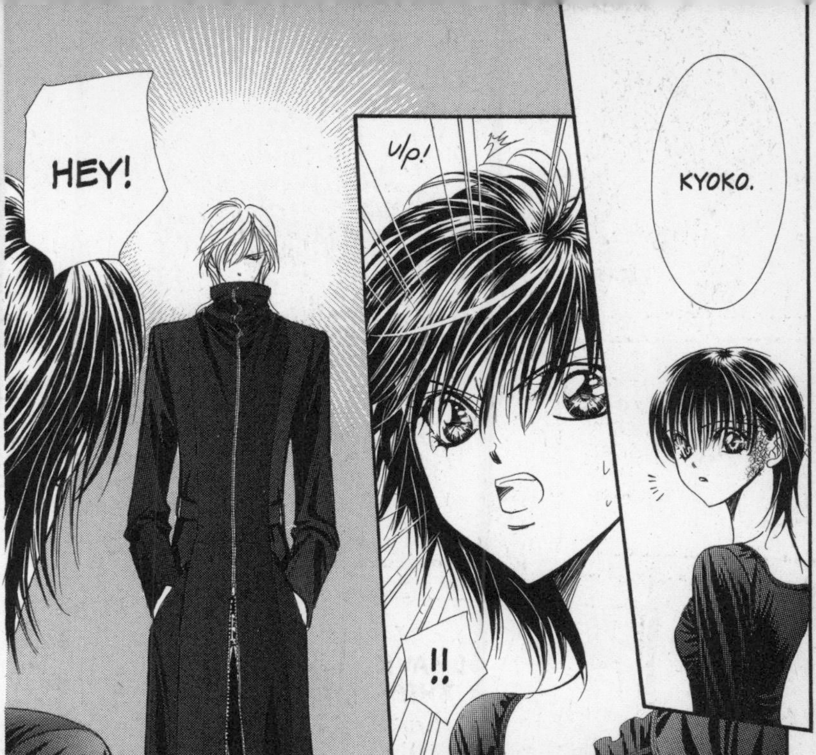
KYOKO.
u/p!
!!
H...
HEY!

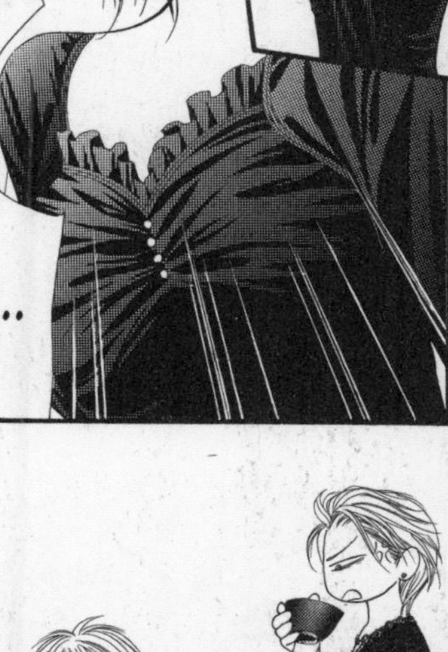

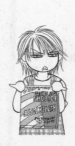

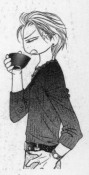

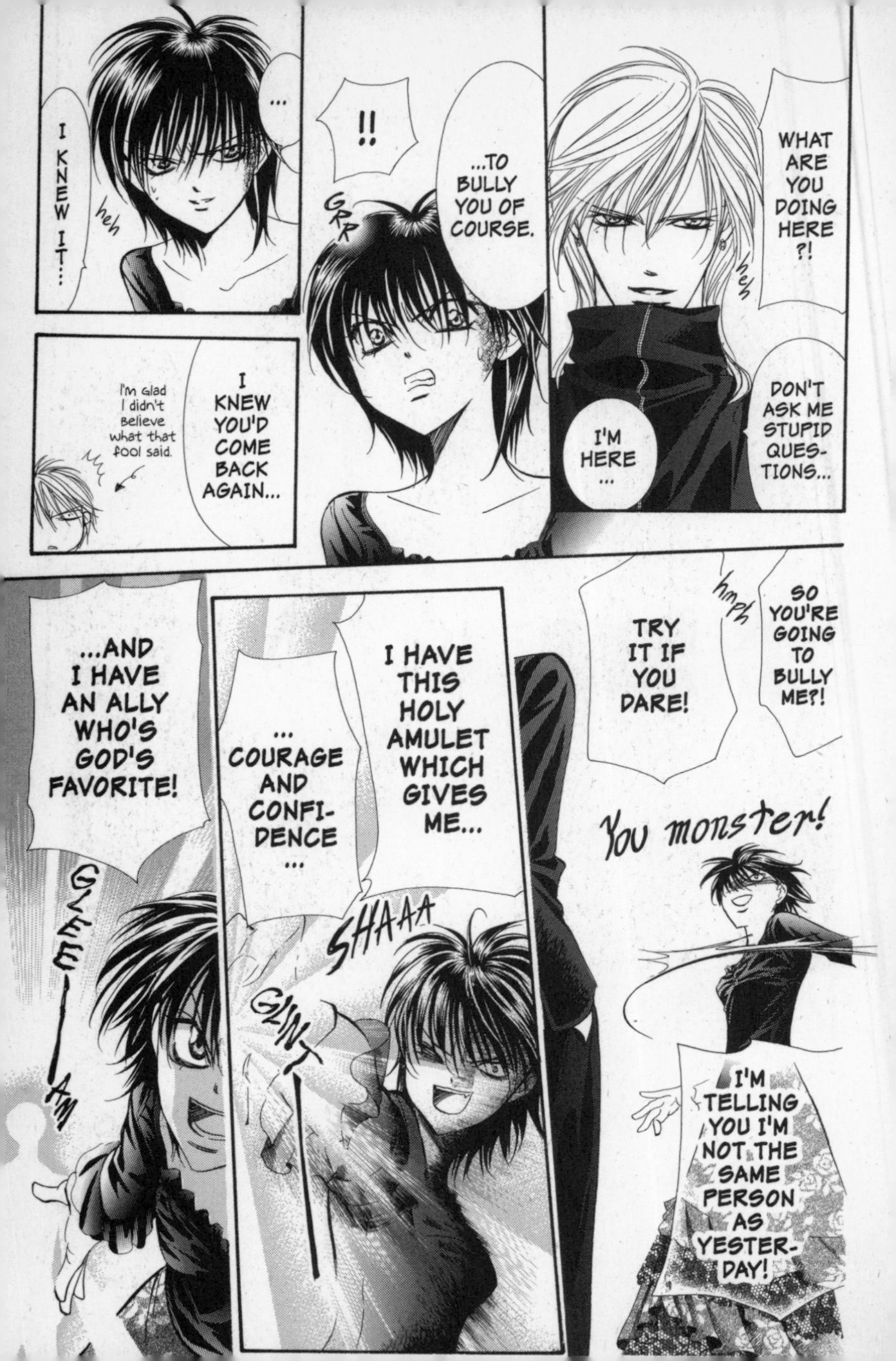
WHAT ARE YOU DOING HERE?!
heh
DON'T ASK ME STUPID QUES-TIONS...
I'M HERE ...
...TO BULLY YOU OF COURSE.
!!
GRR
...
I KNEW IT...
heh
I KNEW YOU'D COME BACK AGAIN...
I'm Glad I didn't Believe what that fool said.
SO YOU'RE GOING TO BULLY ME?!
hmph
TRY IT IF YOU DARE!
You monster!
I'M TELLING YOU I'M NOT THE SAME PERSON AS YESTER-DAY!
I HAVE THIS HOLY AMULET WHICH GIVES ME...
... COURAGE AND CONFI-DENCE ...
SHAAA
GLINT
...AND I HAVE AN ALLY WHO'S GOD'S FAVORITE!
GLEE—AM

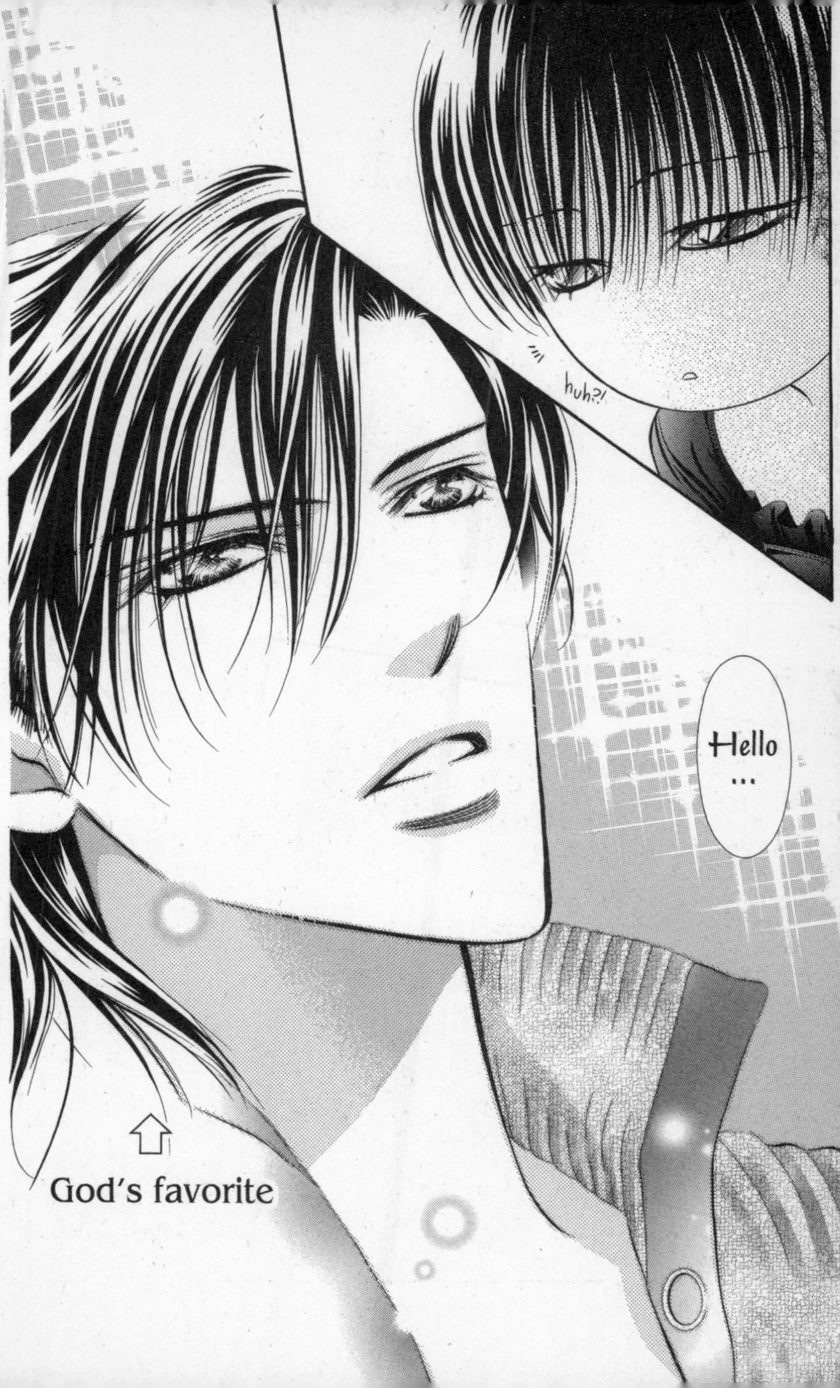
huh?!
Hello ...
God's favorite

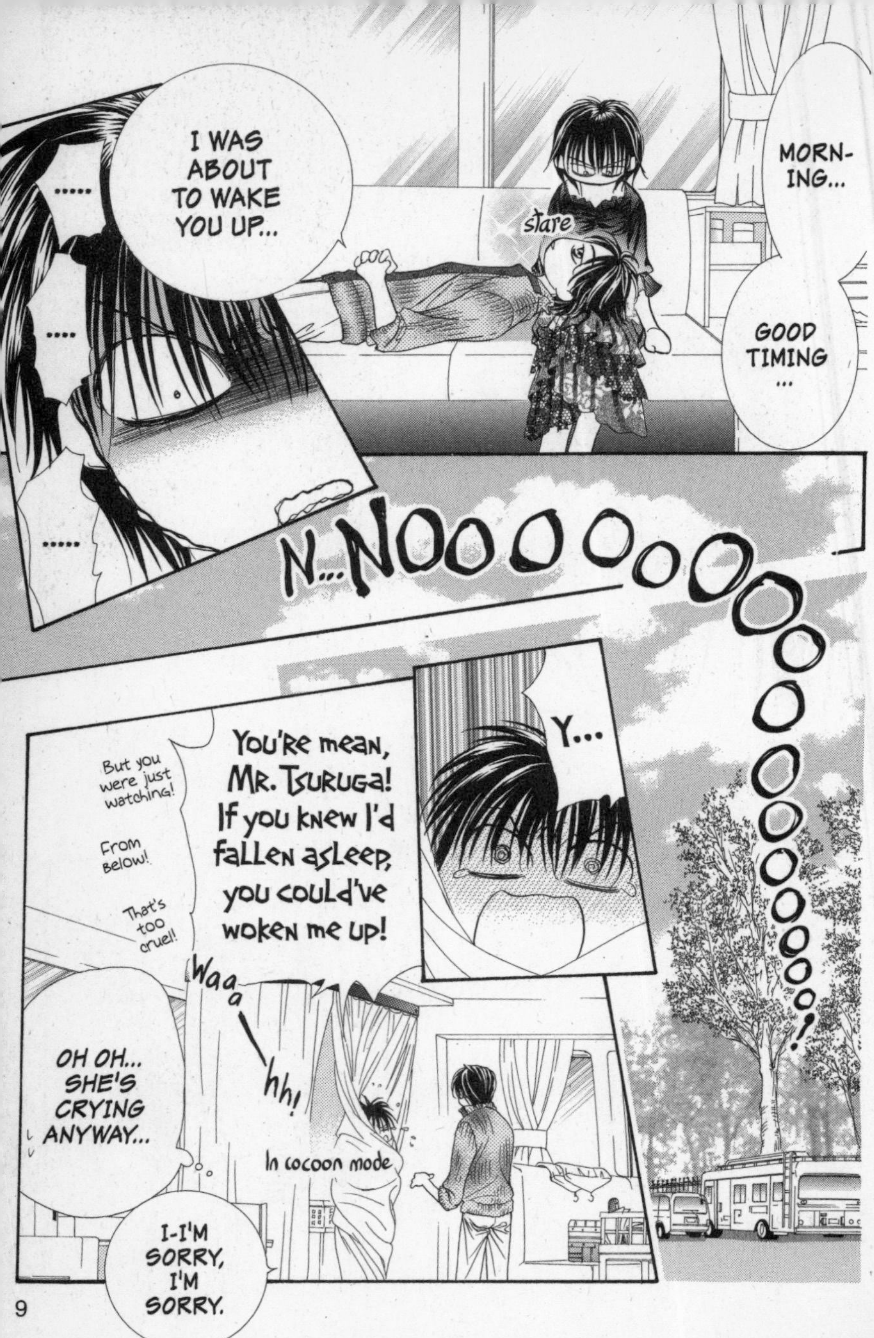
MORN-ING...
GOOD TIMING...
stare
I WAS ABOUT TO WAKE YOU UP...
......
......
......
N...NOOOOOOOOOOOOOOOOOO!
Y...
You're mean, Mr. Tsuruga! If you knew I'd fallen asleep, you could've woken me up!
But you were just watching!
From below!
That's too cruel!
Waaaahh!
In cocoon mode
OH OH... SHE'S CRYING ANYWAY...
I-I'M SORRY, I'M SORRY.

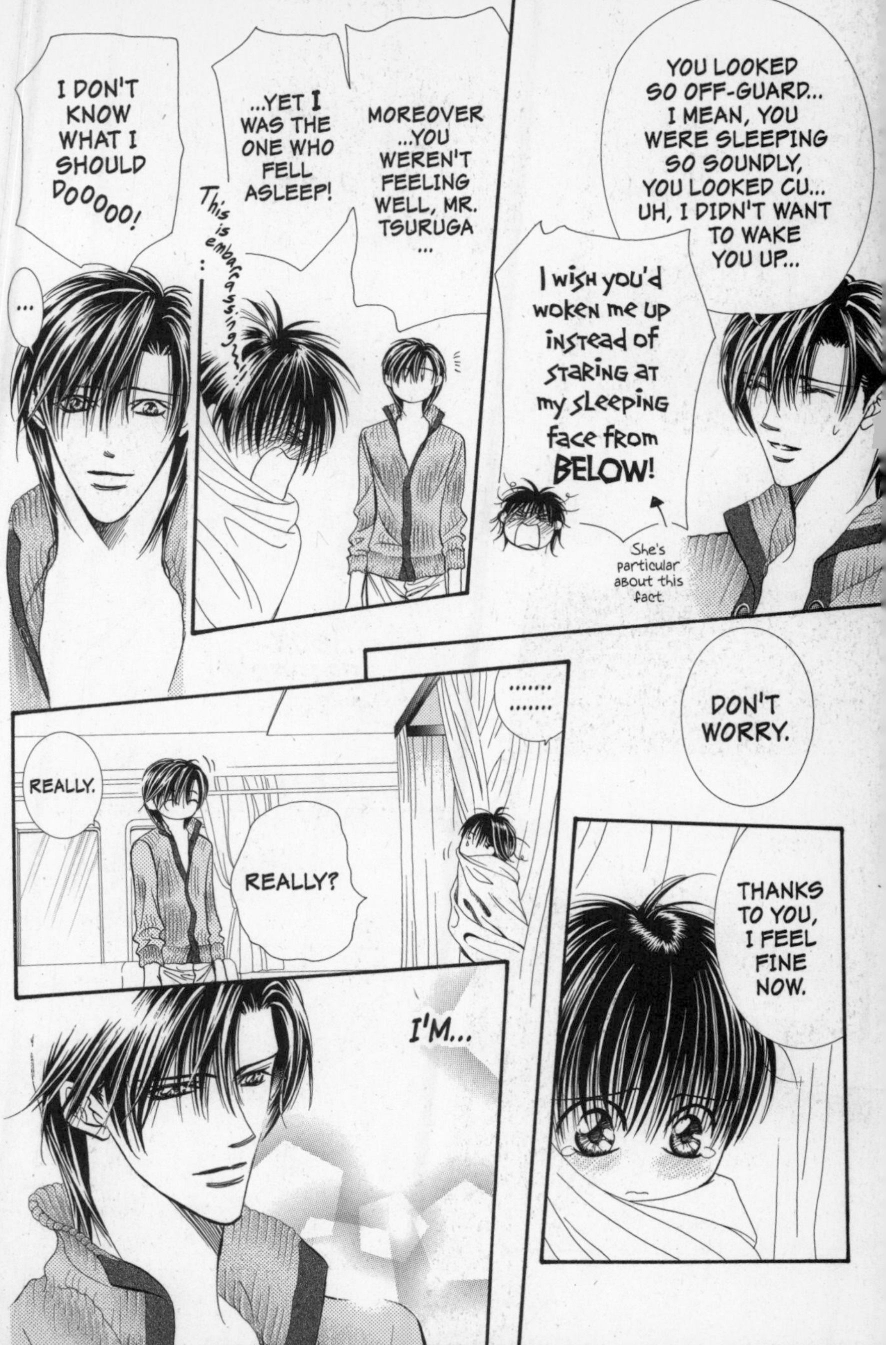

YOU LOOKED SO OFF-GUARD... I MEAN, YOU WERE SLEEPING SO SOUNDLY, YOU LOOKED CU... UH, I DIDN'T WANT TO WAKE YOU UP...
I wish you'd woken me up instead of staring at my sleeping face from BELOW!
She's particular about this fact.
MOREOVER ...YOU WEREN'T FEELING WELL, MR. TSURUGA ...
...YET I WAS THE ONE WHO FELL ASLEEP!
This is embarrassing...
I DON'T KNOW WHAT I SHOULD DOOOOOO!
...
DON'T WORRY.
....
....
REALLY?
REALLY.
THANKS TO YOU, I FEEL FINE NOW.
I'M...

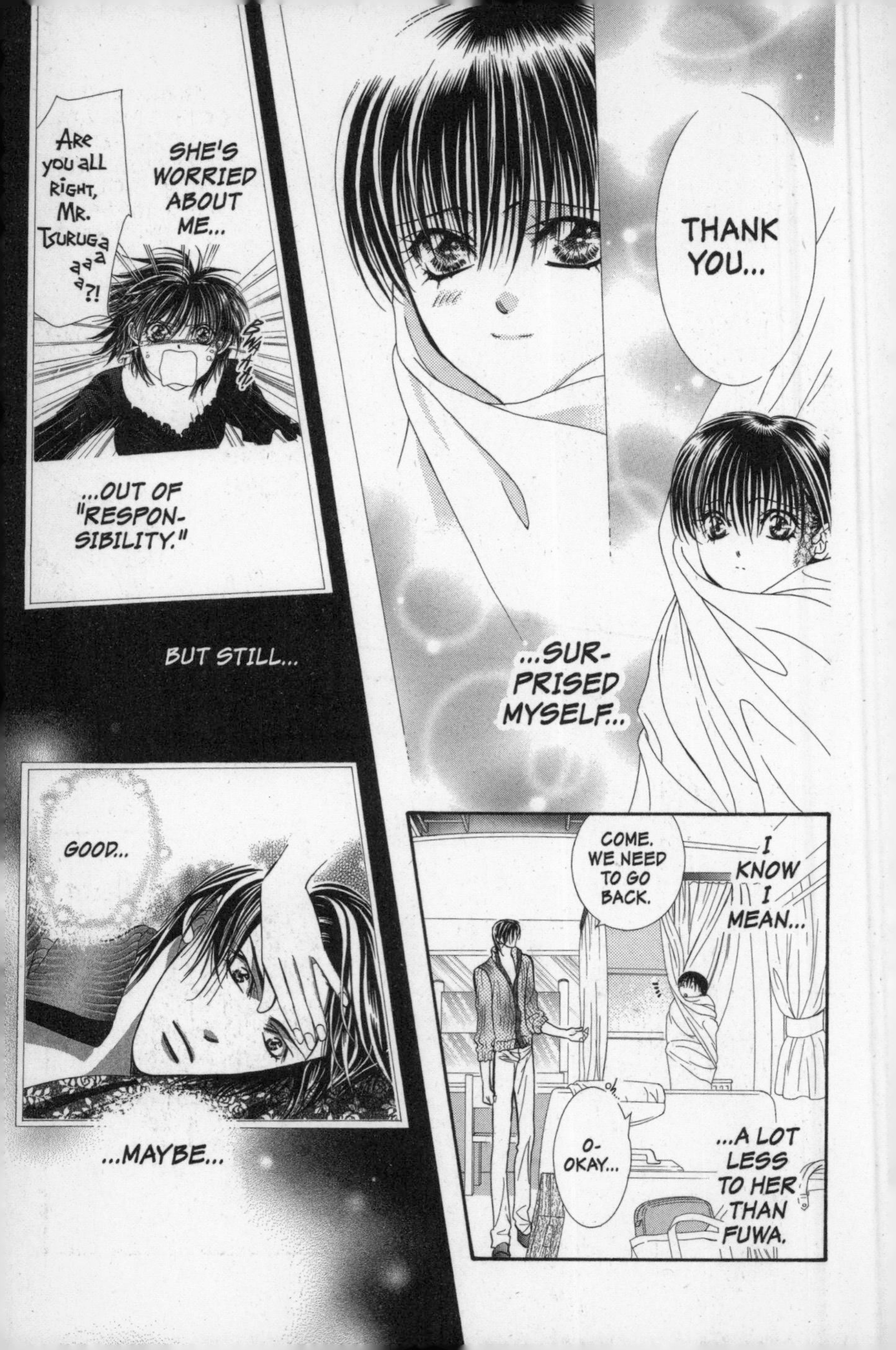
THANK YOU...
...SUR-PRISED MYSELF...
SHE'S WORRIED ABOUT ME...
Are you all right, Mr. Tsurugaaaaa?!
...OUT OF "RESPON-SIBILITY."
BUT STILL...
COME. WE NEED TO GO BACK.
I KNOW I MEAN...
oh...
O-OKAY...
...A LOT LESS TO HER THAN FUWA.
GOOD...
...MAYBE...

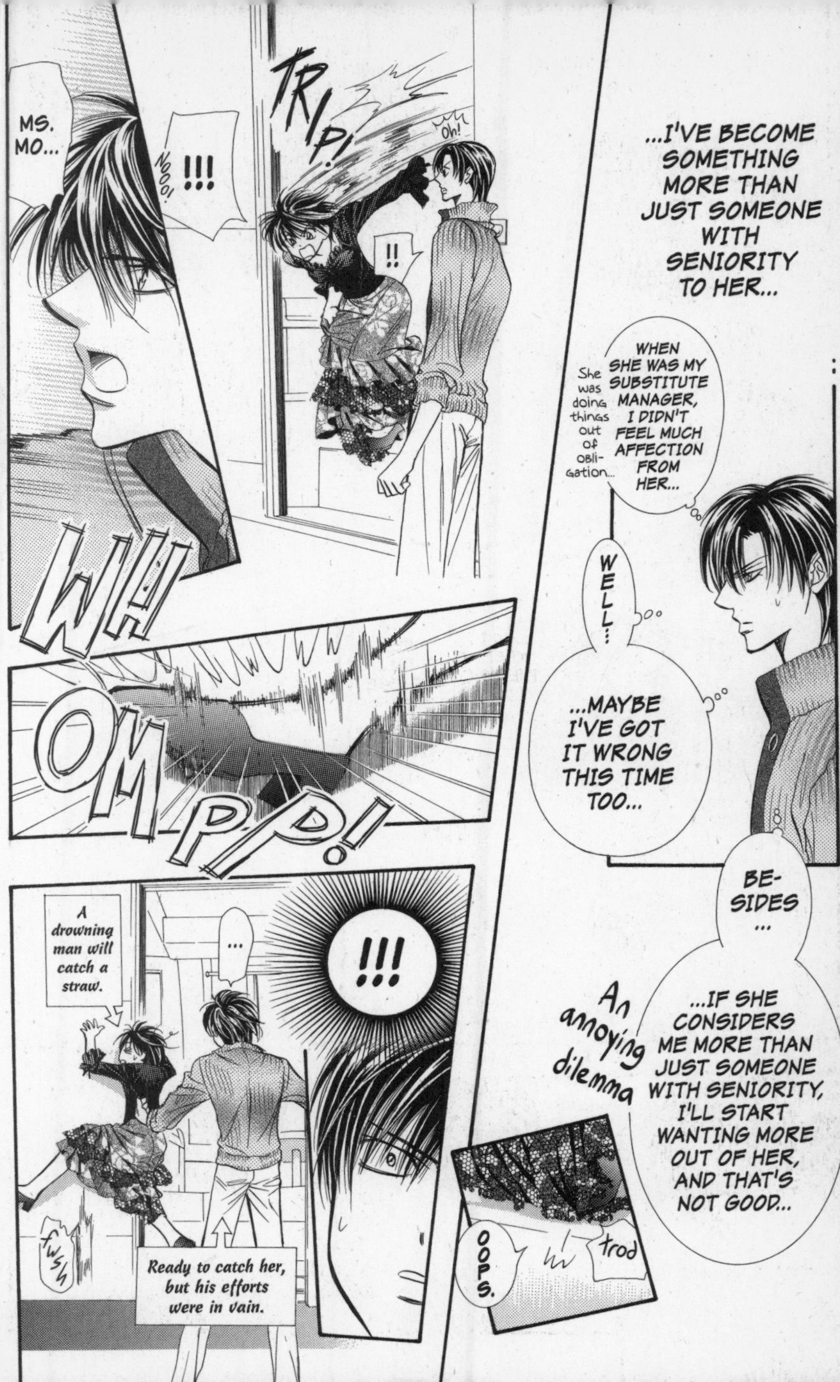
...I'VE BECOME SOMETHING MORE THAN JUST SOMEONE WITH SENIORITY TO HER...
WHEN SHE WAS MY SUBSTITUTE MANAGER, I DIDN'T FEEL MUCH AFFECTION FROM HER...
She was doing things out of obli-gation...
WELL...
...MAYBE I'VE GOT IT WRONG THIS TIME TOO...
BE-SIDES...
...IF SHE CONSIDERS ME MORE THAN JUST SOMEONE WITH SENIORITY, I'LL START WANTING MORE OUT OF HER, AND THAT'S NOT GOOD...
An annoying dilemma
trod
OOPS.
TRIP!
Oh!
!!
MS. MO...
NOOO!
!!!
WHOMPP!
!!!
A drowning man will catch a straw.
...
Ready to catch her, but his efforts were in vain.
fwsh

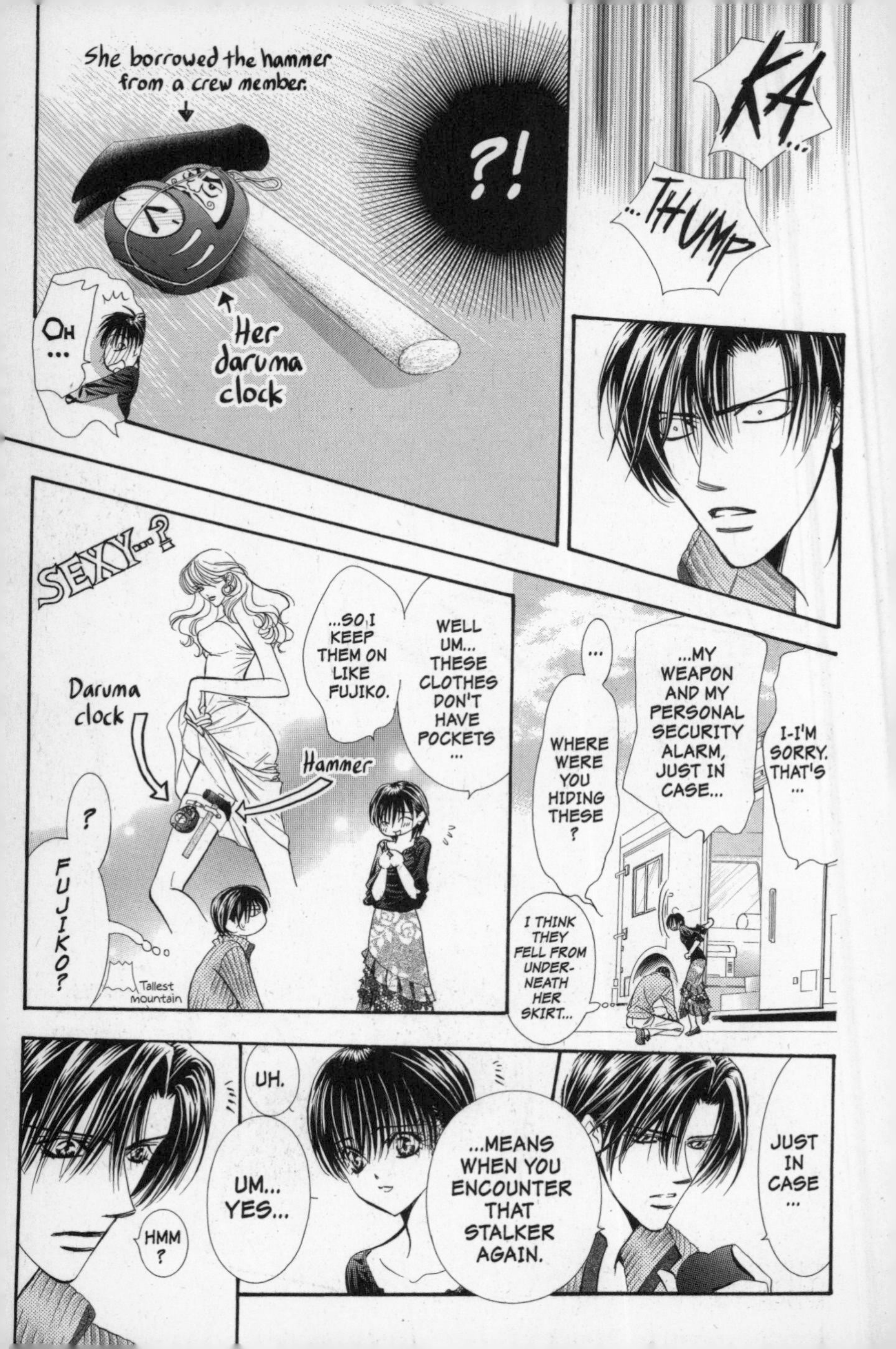
KA...
...THUMP
?!
She borrowed the hammer from a crew member.
Her daruma clock
OH ...
I-I'M SORRY. THAT'S ...
...MY WEAPON AND MY PERSONAL SECURITY ALARM, JUST IN CASE...
...
WHERE WERE YOU HIDING THESE?
I THINK THEY FELL FROM UNDERNEATH HER SKIRT...
SEXY...?
WELL UM... THESE CLOTHES DON'T HAVE POCKETS ...
...SO I KEEP THEM ON LIKE FUJIKO.
Hammer
Daruma clock
? FUJIKO?
Tallest mountain
JUST IN CASE ...
...MEANS WHEN YOU ENCOUNTER THAT STALKER AGAIN.
UH.
UM... YES...
HMM?

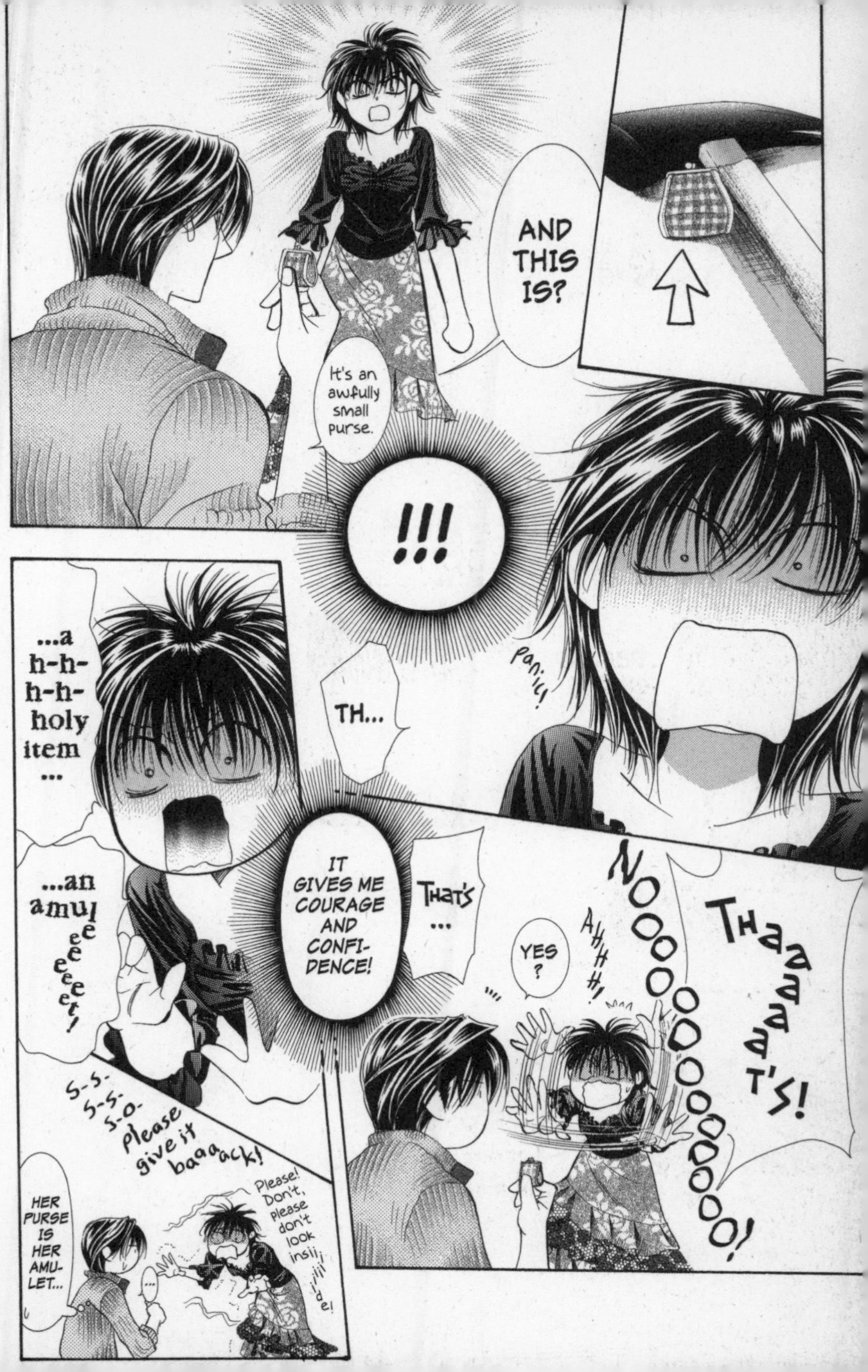
AND THIS IS?
It's an awfully small purse.
!!!
Panic!
TH...
Thaaaaat's!
NOOOOOOOOOOOOOOO!
AHHH!
YES?
That's...
IT GIVES ME COURAGE AND CONFIDENCE!
...a h-h-h-h-holy item...
...an amuleeeeeet!
S-S-S-S-S-O- please give it baaaack!
Please! Don't, please don't look insiiiiide!
...
HER PURSE IS HER AMULET...

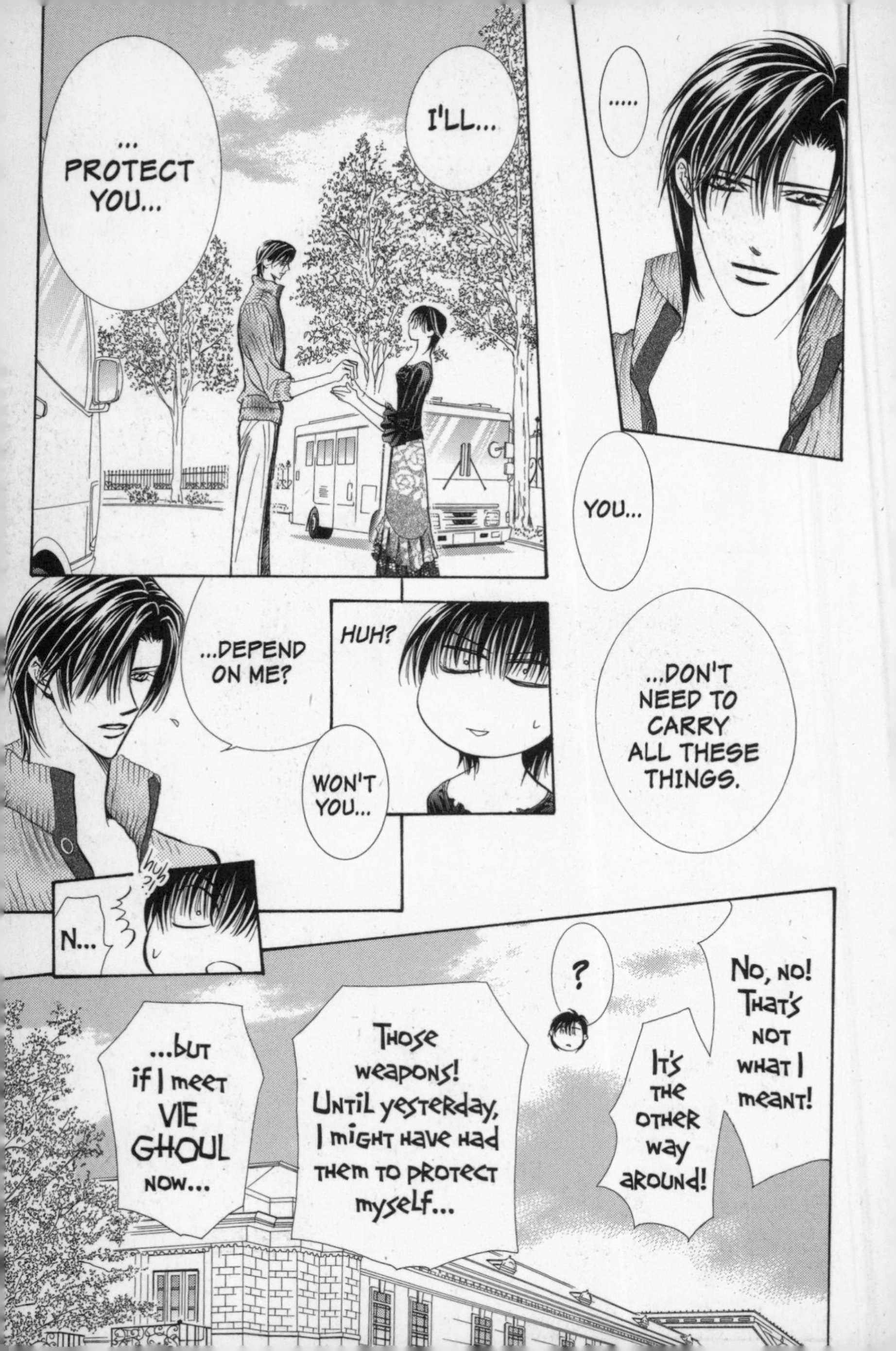
.....
I'LL...
...PROTECT YOU...
YOU...
...DON'T NEED TO CARRY ALL THESE THINGS.
HUH?
WON'T YOU...
...DEPEND ON ME?
huh?!
N...
?
No, no! That's not what I meant!
It's the other way around!
Those weapons! Until yesterday, I might have had them to protect myself...
...but if I meet VIE GHOUL now...

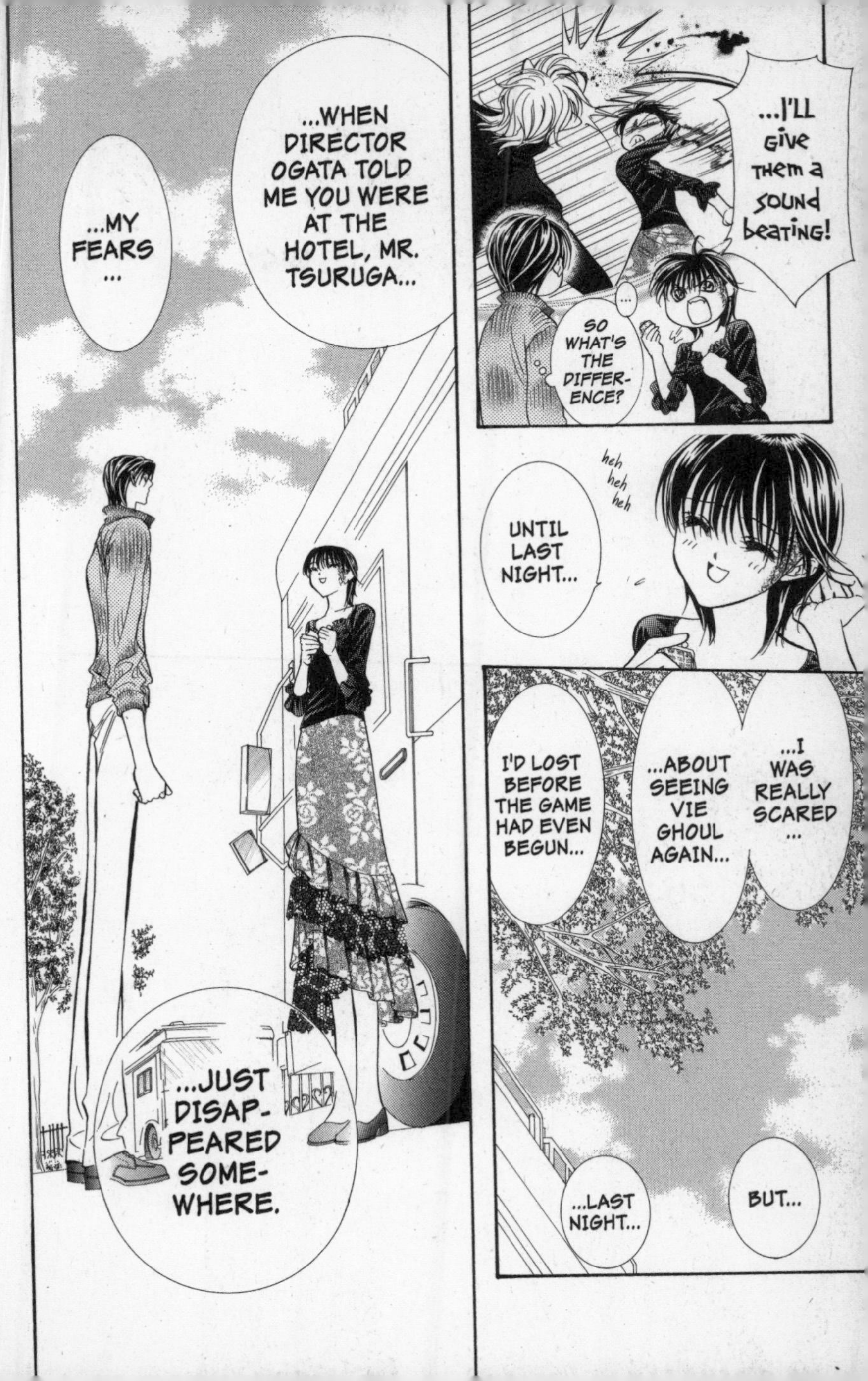
...I'LL GIVE THEM A SOUND BEATING!
...
SO WHAT'S THE DIFFER-ENCE?
heh heh heh
UNTIL LAST NIGHT...
...I WAS REALLY SCARED ...
...ABOUT SEEING VIE GHOUL AGAIN...
I'D LOST BEFORE THE GAME HAD EVEN BEGUN...
BUT...
...LAST NIGHT...
...WHEN DIRECTOR OGATA TOLD ME YOU WERE AT THE HOTEL, MR. TSURUGA...
...MY FEARS ...
...JUST DISAP-PEARED SOME-WHERE.

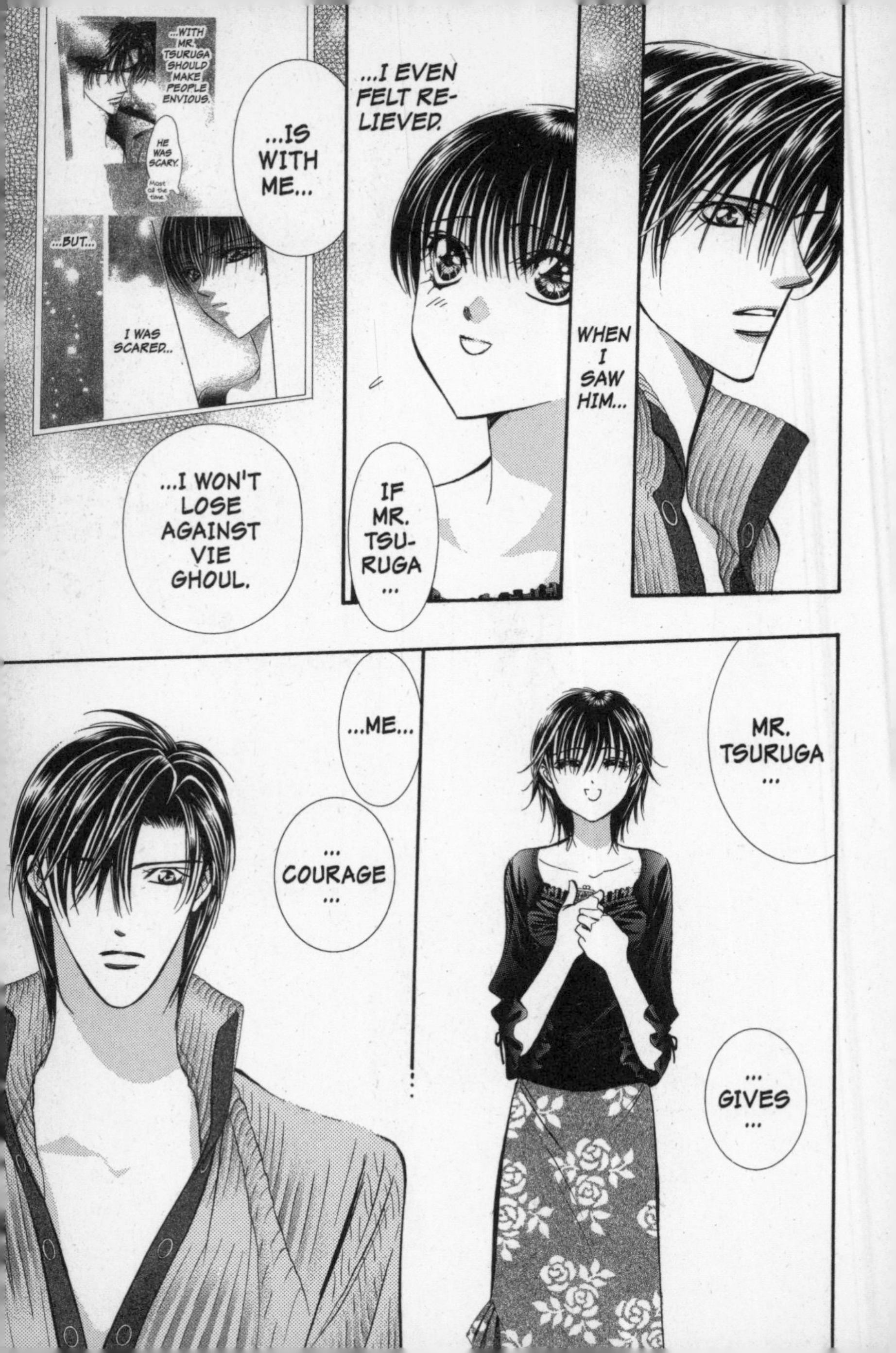

WHEN I SAW HIM...
...I EVEN FELT RE-LIEVED.
IF MR. TSU-RUGA ...
...IS WITH ME...
...WITH MR. TSURUGA SHOULD MAKE PEOPLE ENVIOUS.
HE WAS SCARY.
Most of the time.
...BUT...
I WAS SCARED...
...I WON'T LOSE AGAINST VIE GHOUL.
MR. TSURUGA ...
... GIVES ...
...ME...
... COURAGE ...

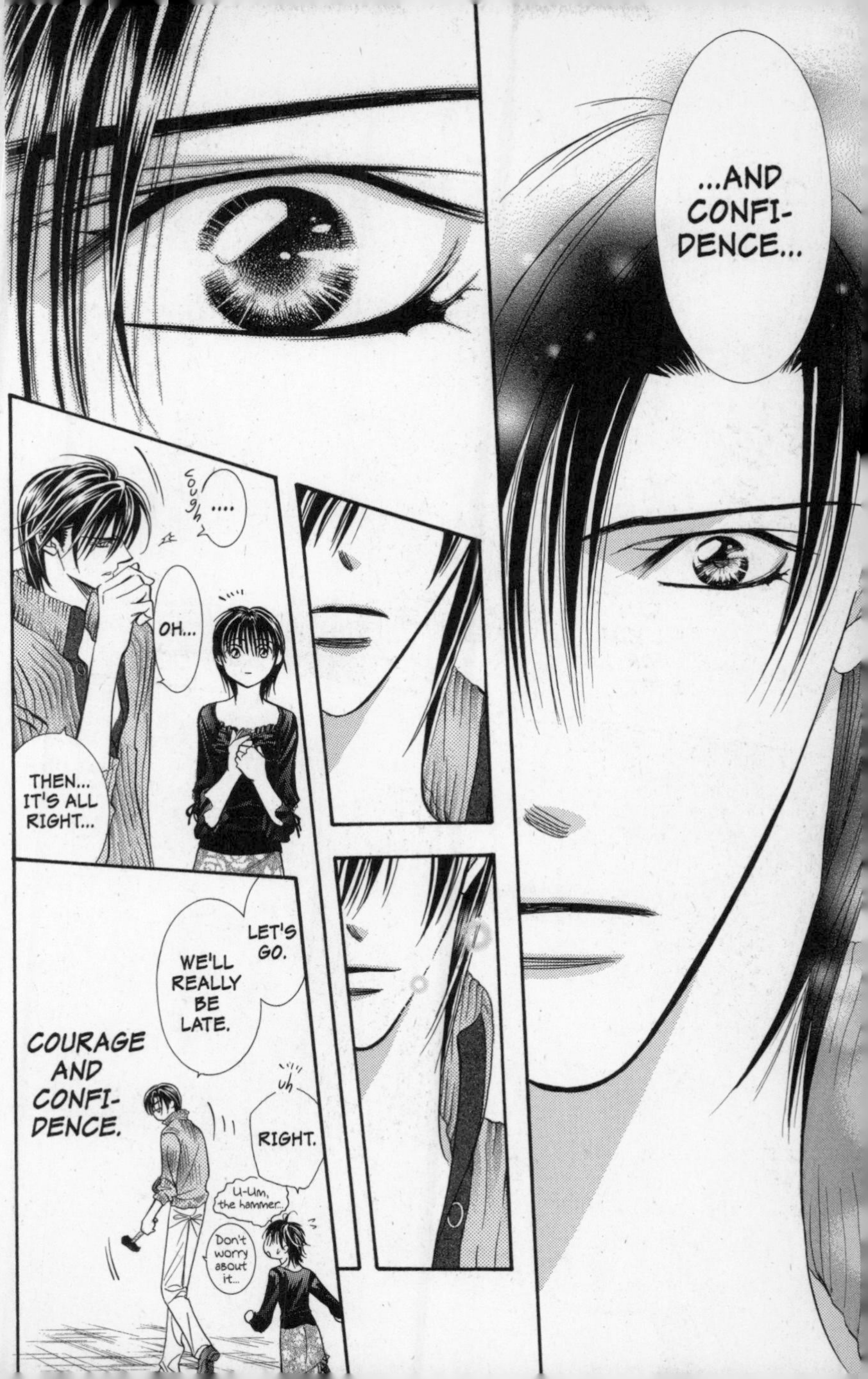
...AND CONFIDENCE...
....
cough
OH...
THEN... IT'S ALL RIGHT...
LET'S GO.
WE'LL REALLY BE LATE.
COURAGE AND CONFIDENCE.
uh
RIGHT.
U-Um, the hammer...
Don't worry about it...

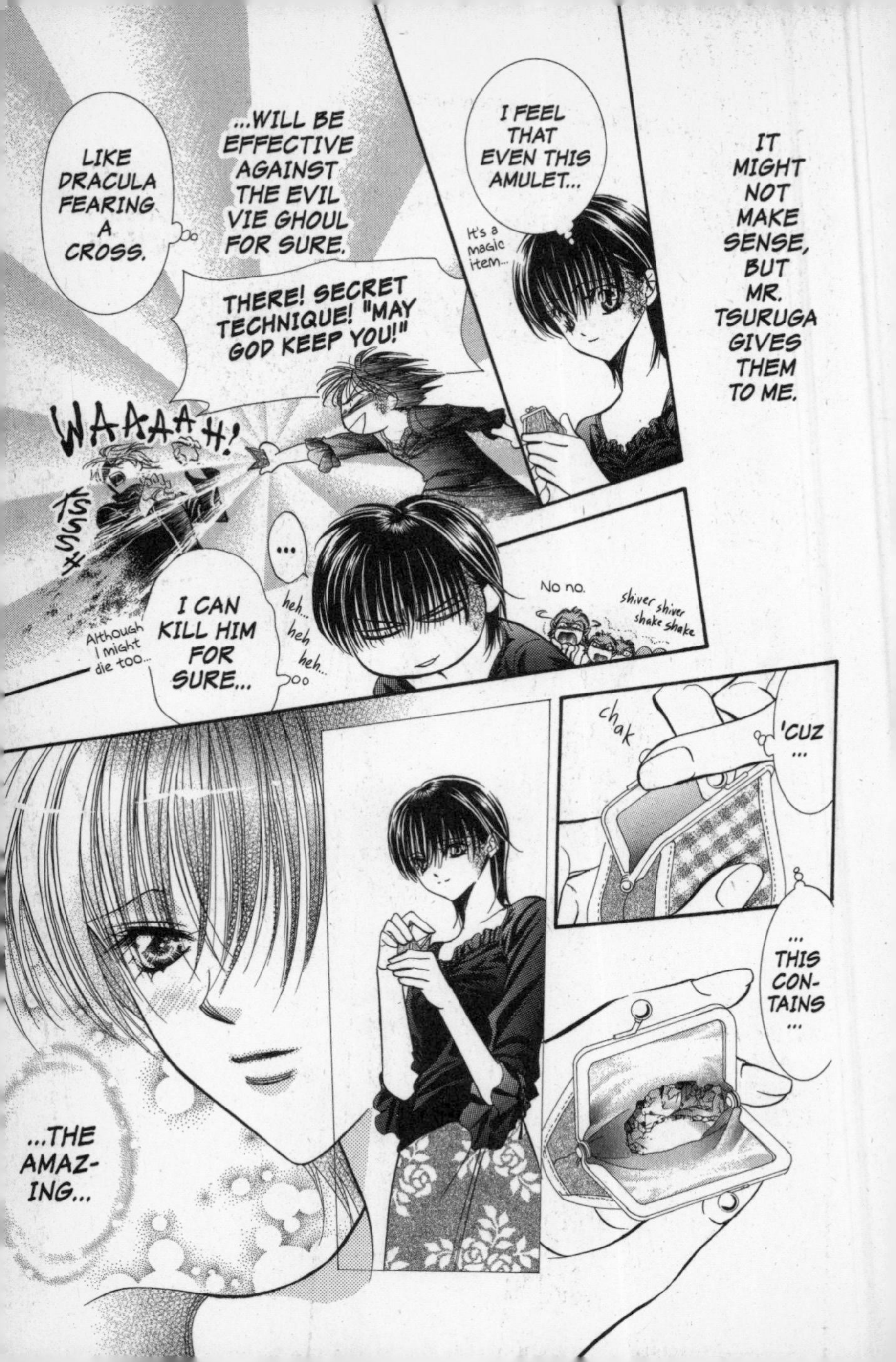
IT MIGHT NOT MAKE SENSE, BUT MR. TSURUGA GIVES THEM TO ME.
I FEEL THAT EVEN THIS AMULET...
It's a magic item...
...WILL BE EFFECTIVE AGAINST THE EVIL VIE GHOUL FOR SURE.
LIKE DRACULA FEARING A CROSS.
THERE! SECRET TECHNIQUE! "MAY GOD KEEP YOU!"
WAAAAH!
TSSSH
...
No no.
shiver shiver shake shake
heh... heh... heh...
I CAN KILL HIM FOR SURE...
Although I might die too...
'CUZ...
chak
...THIS CONTAINS...
...THE AMAZING...

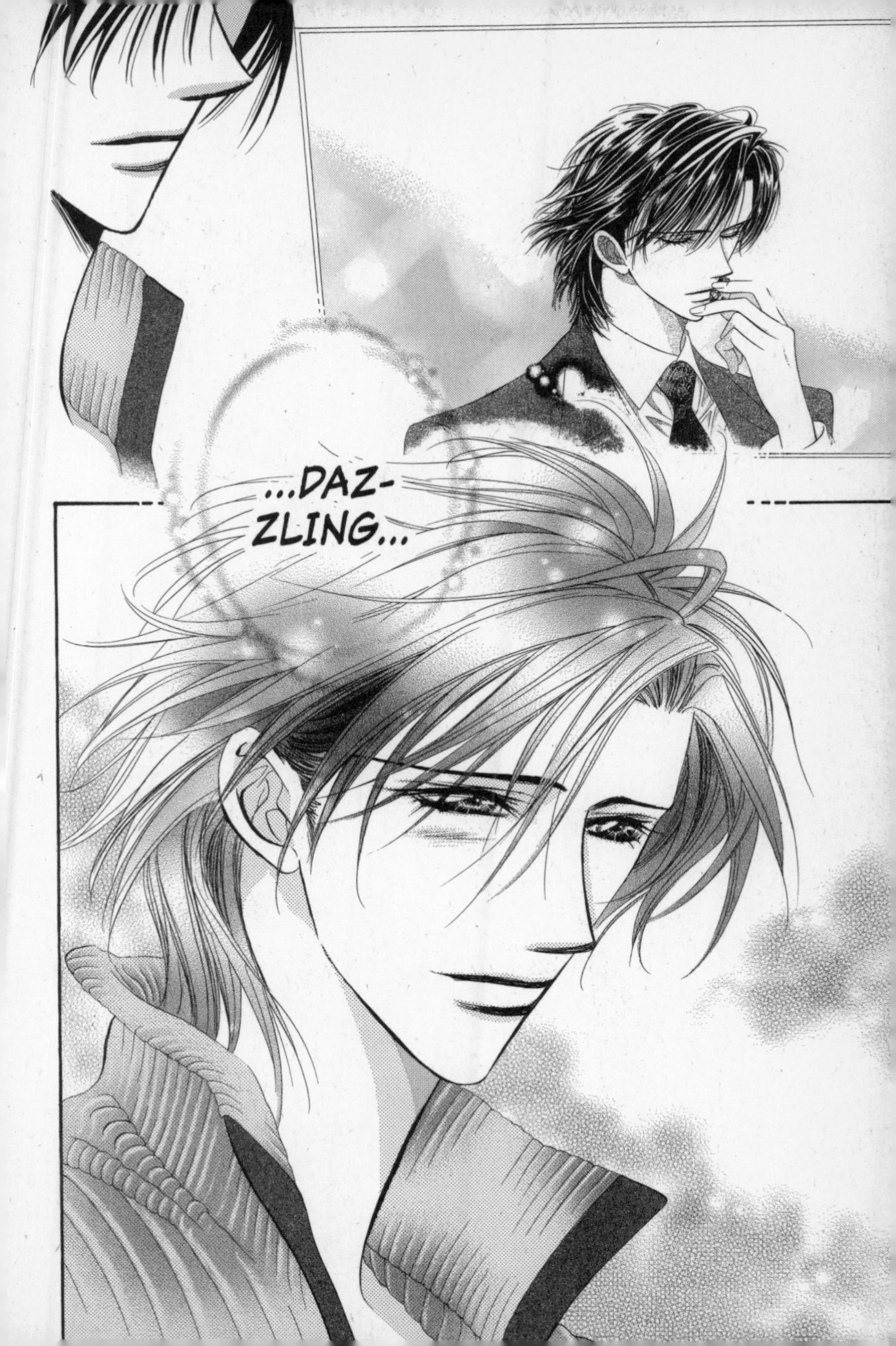
...DAZ-
ZLING...

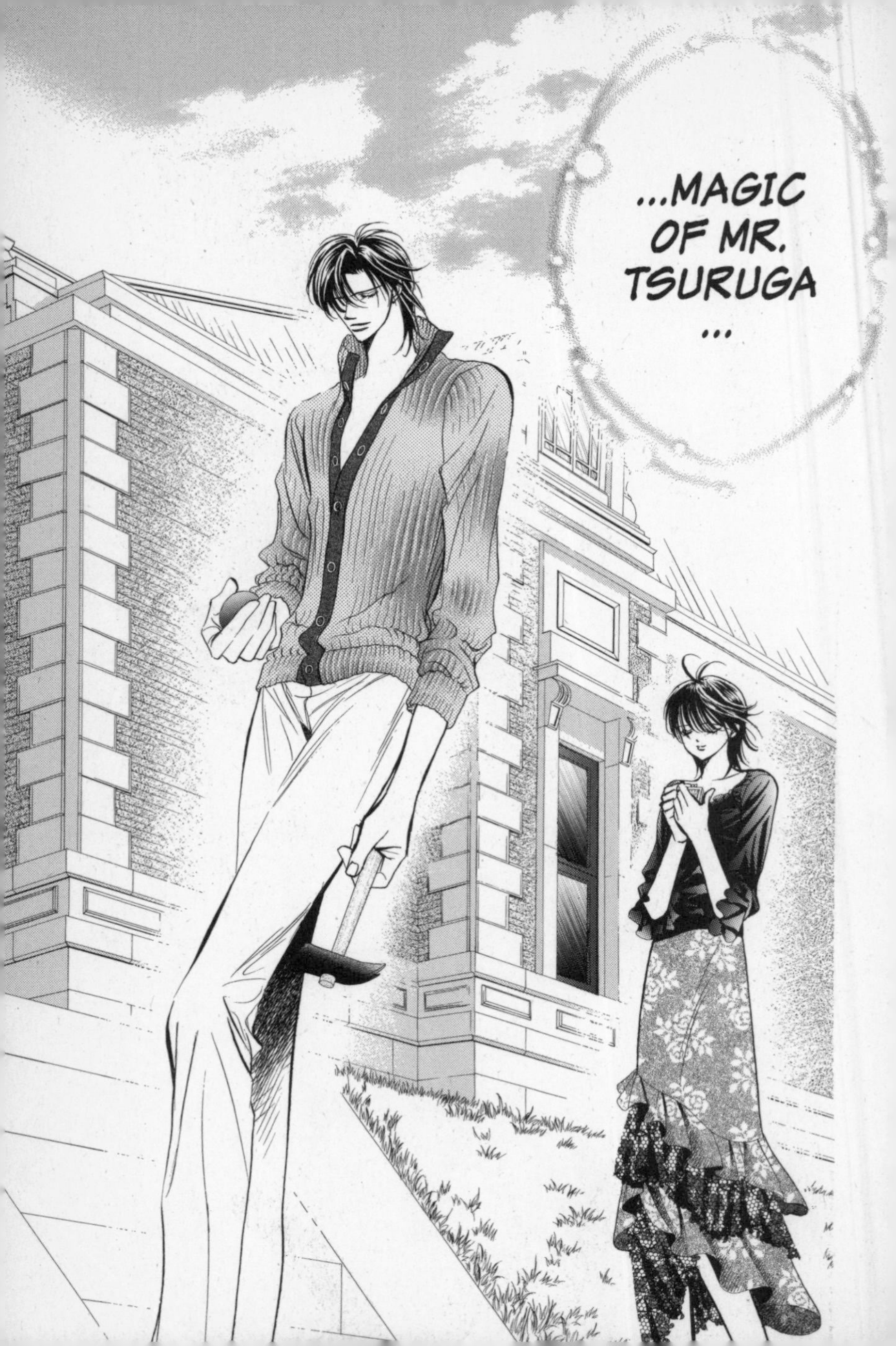
...MAGIC OF MR. TSURUGA ...

I can't do it anymore.
The agreement is over.

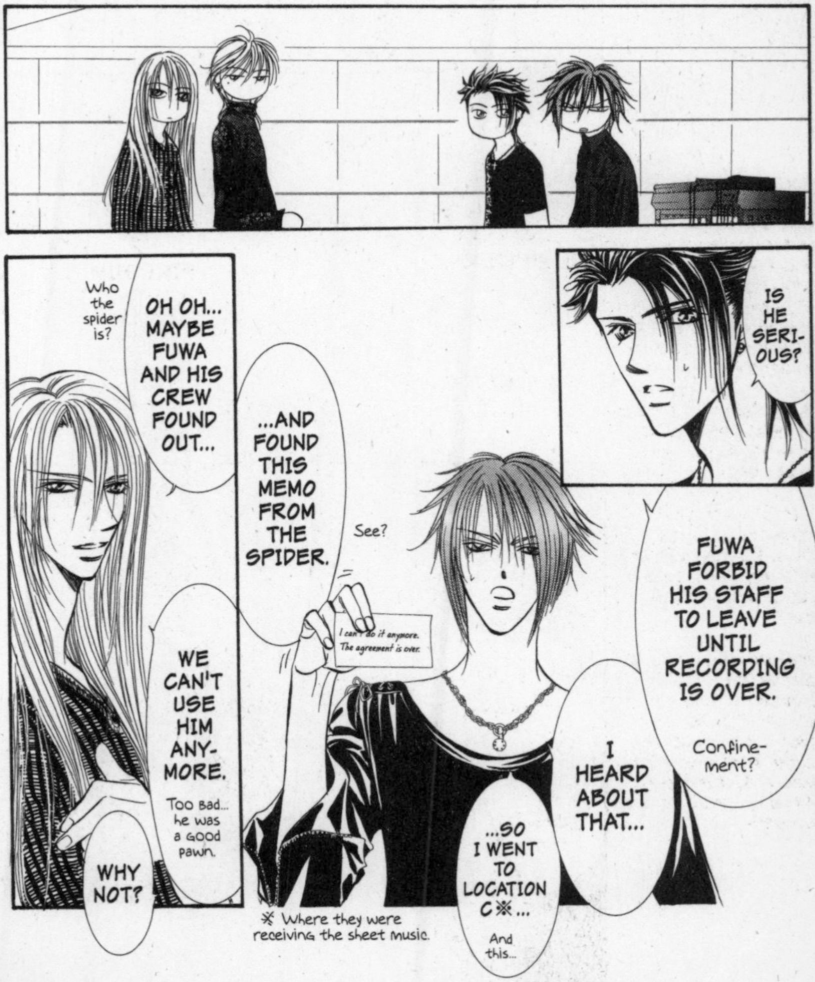

IS HE SERIOUS?
FUWA FORBID HIS STAFF TO LEAVE UNTIL RECORDING IS OVER.
Confinement?
I HEARD ABOUT THAT...
...SO I WENT TO LOCATION C※...
And this...
See?
...AND FOUND THIS MEMO FROM THE SPIDER.
I can't do it anymore. The agreement is over.
OH OH... MAYBE FUWA AND HIS CREW FOUND OUT...
Who the spider is?
WE CAN'T USE HIM ANYMORE.
Too bad... he was a good pawn.
WHY NOT?
※ Where they were receiving the sheet music.

Miroku (drums)

Probably the most scheming member. He's 19.

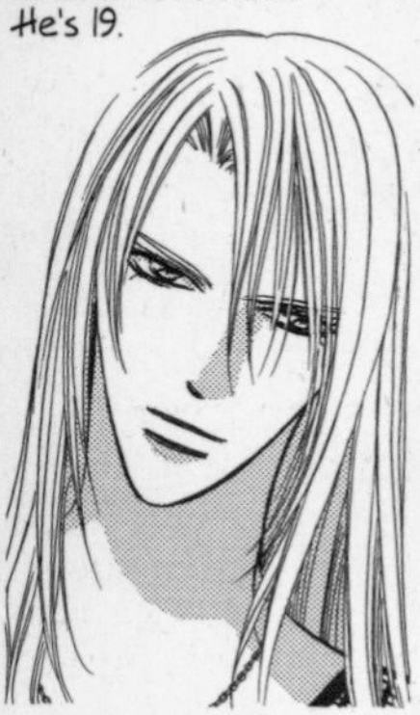

When he appeared in Act 80, I hadn't decided on the personalities of the members other than Reino. Miroku was awfully androgynous back then... well...they were trying to win against Sho, so I felt that the band should contain different types of guys...But now, both his body and face have become very masculine...(well...I have more fun drawing it that way...)

In Act 81, when I put Miroku beside Reino, the way the two met and their relationship zoomed through my brain in an instant...

Therefore, when I thought about their past (which won't be revealed to anyone) Miroku's name popped out naturally...He was the first one to be named, and I didn't think he'd end up appearing this frequently...

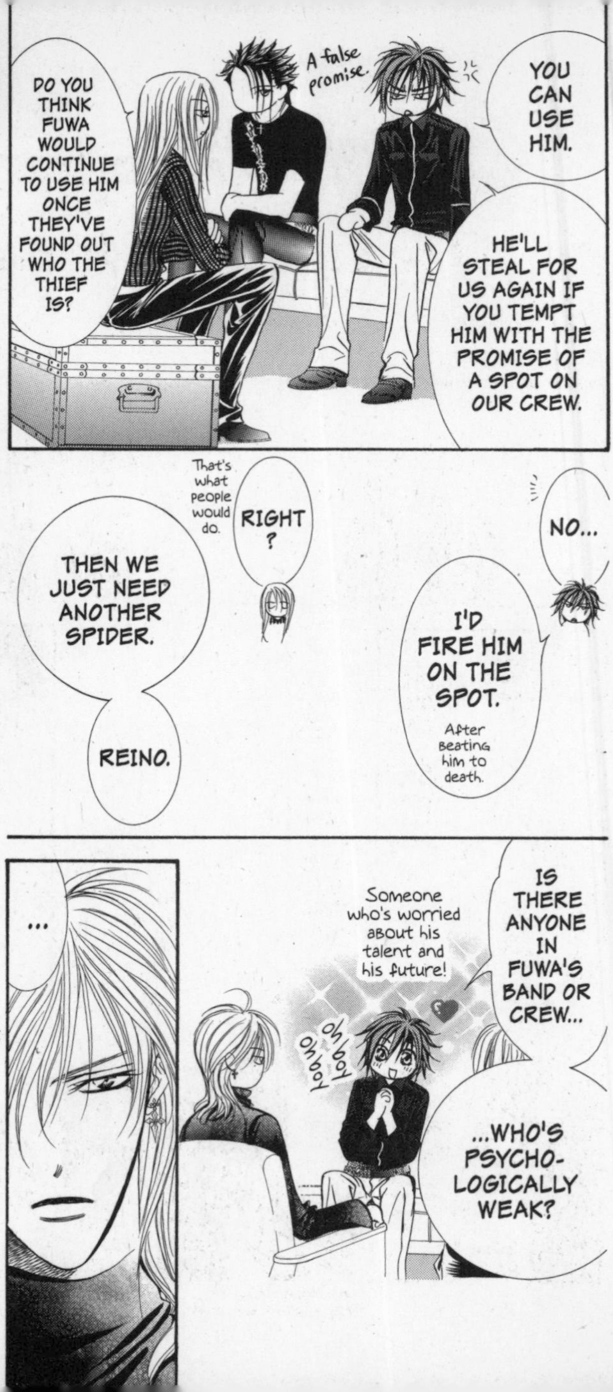
YOU CAN USE HIM.
HE'LL STEAL FOR US AGAIN IF YOU TEMPT HIM WITH THE PROMISE OF A SPOT ON OUR CREW.
A false promise.
DO YOU THINK FUWA WOULD CONTINUE TO USE HIM ONCE THEY'VE FOUND OUT WHO THE THIEF IS?
NO...
I'D FIRE HIM ON THE SPOT.
After beating him to death.
RIGHT?
That's what people would do.
THEN WE JUST NEED ANOTHER SPIDER.
REINO.
IS THERE ANYONE IN FUWA'S BAND OR CREW...
Someone who's worried about his talent and his future!
oh boy oh boy
...WHO'S PSYCHOLOGICALLY WEAK?
...

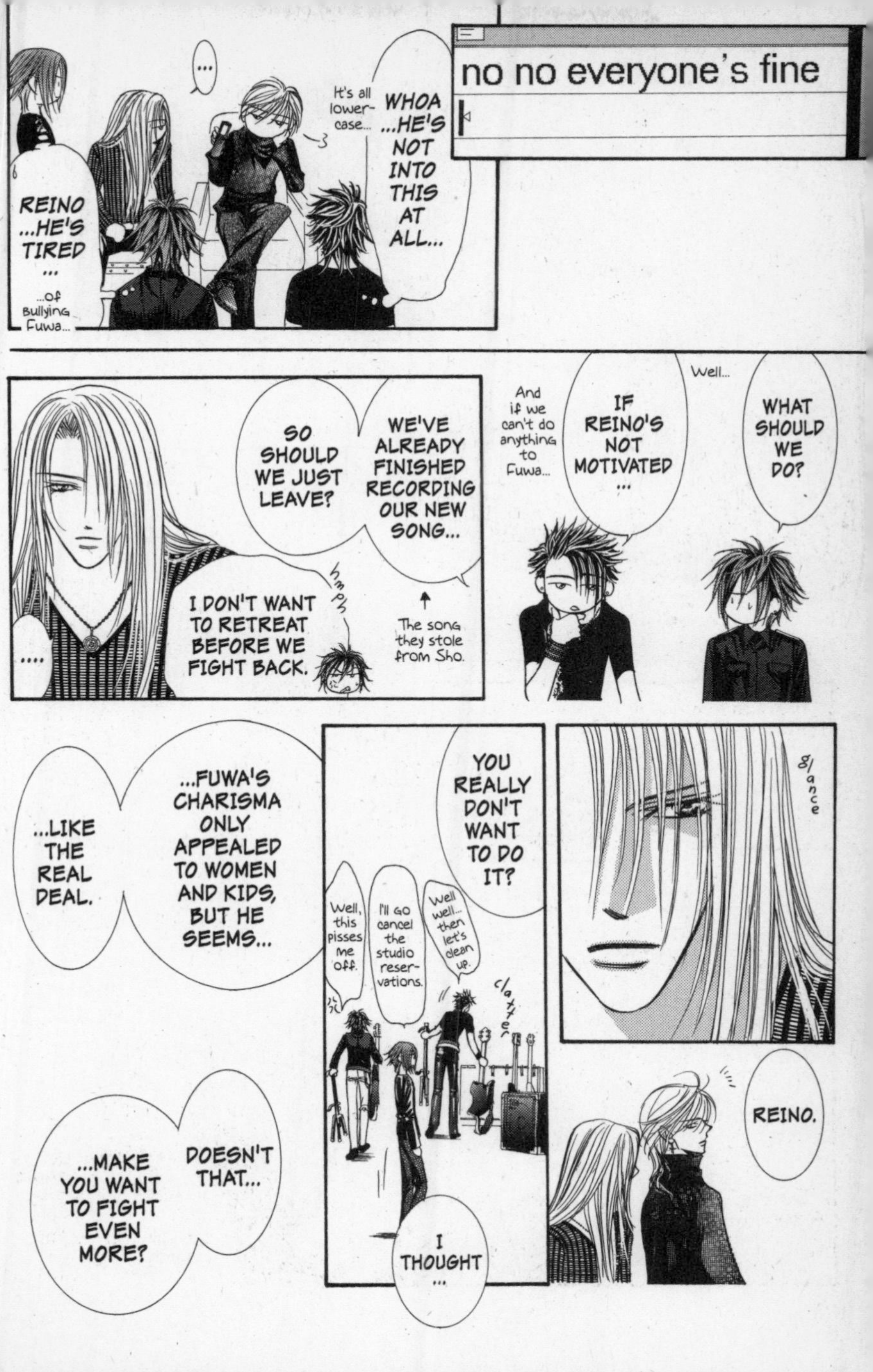
no no everyone's fine
WHOA ...HE'S NOT INTO THIS AT ALL...
It's all lower-case...
...
REINO ...HE'S TIRED ...
...of Bullying Fuwa...
WHAT SHOULD WE DO?
Well...
IF REINO'S NOT MOTIVATED ...
And if we can't do anything to Fuwa...
WE'VE ALREADY FINISHED RECORDING OUR NEW SONG...
SO SHOULD WE JUST LEAVE?
The song they stole from Sho.
hmph
I DON'T WANT TO RETREAT BEFORE WE FIGHT BACK.
....
glance
REINO.
YOU REALLY DON'T WANT TO DO IT?
Well well... then let's clean up.
I'll go cancel the studio reser-vations.
Well, this pisses me off.
clatter
I THOUGHT ...
...FUWA'S CHARISMA ONLY APPEALED TO WOMEN AND KIDS, BUT HE SEEMS...
...LIKE THE REAL DEAL.
DOESN'T THAT...
...MAKE YOU WANT TO FIGHT EVEN MORE?

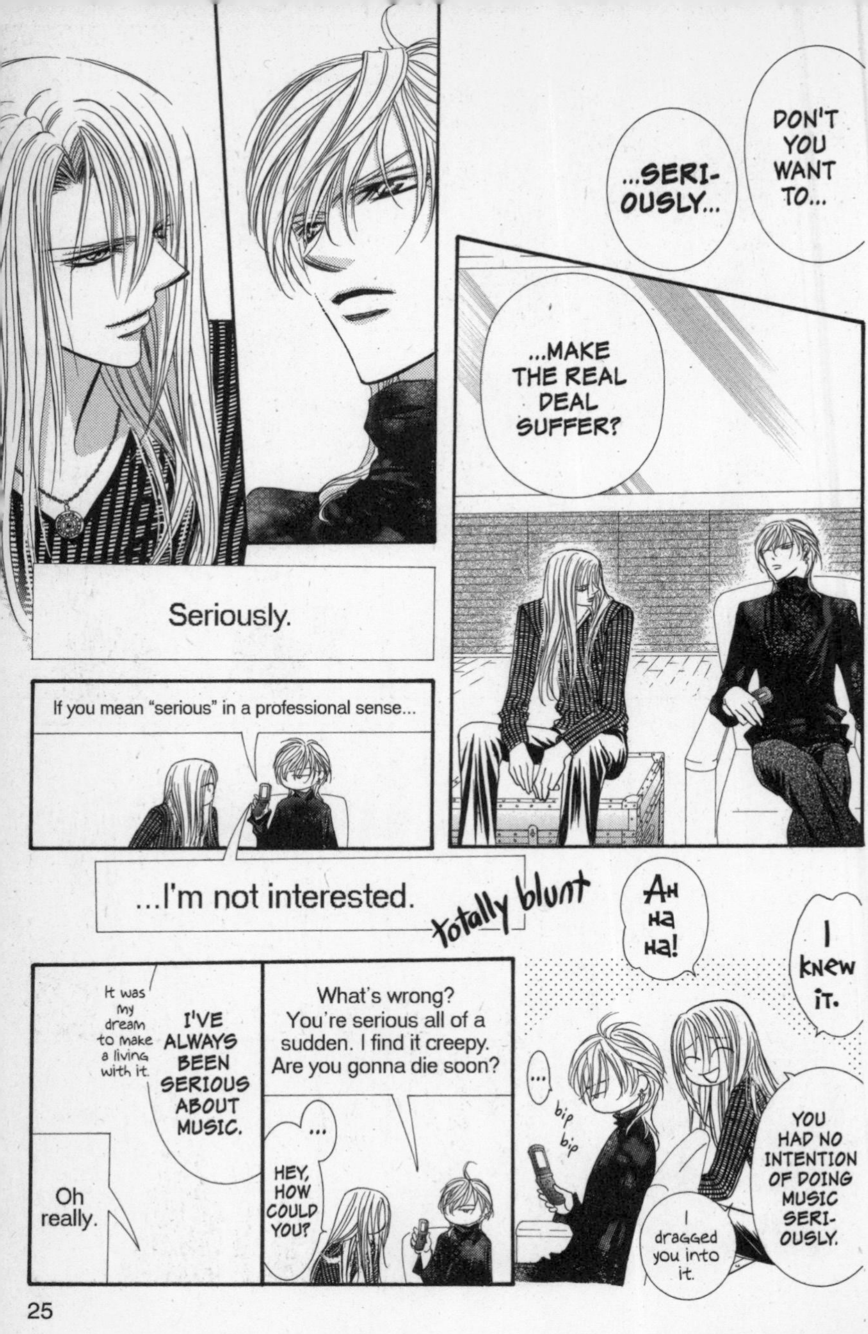
DON'T YOU WANT TO...
...SERI-OUSLY...
...MAKE THE REAL DEAL SUFFER?
Seriously.
If you mean "serious" in a professional sense...
...I'm not interested.
totally blunt
AH HA HA!
I KNEW IT.
YOU HAD NO INTENTION OF DOING MUSIC SERI-OUSLY.
I dragged you into it.
...
bip bip
What's wrong? You're serious all of a sudden. I find it creepy. Are you gonna die soon?
...
HEY, HOW COULD YOU?
I'VE ALWAYS BEEN SERIOUS ABOUT MUSIC.
It was my dream to make a living with it.
Oh really.

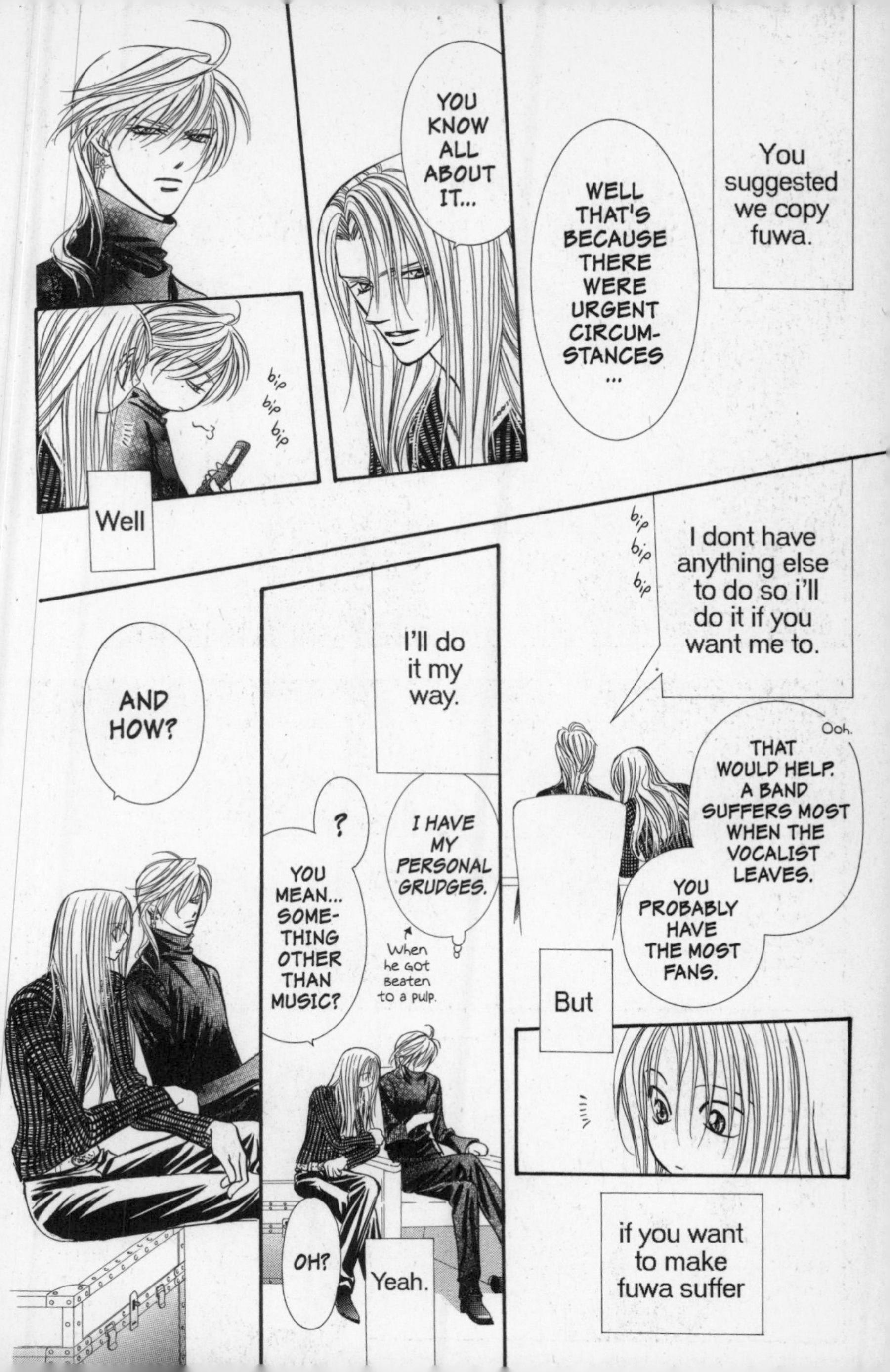

You suggested we copy fuwa.
WELL THAT'S BECAUSE THERE WERE URGENT CIRCUM-STANCES...
YOU KNOW ALL ABOUT IT...
bip bip bip
Well
bip bip bip
I dont have anything else to do so i'll do it if you want me to.
Ooh.
THAT WOULD HELP. A BAND SUFFERS MOST WHEN THE VOCALIST LEAVES.
YOU PROBABLY HAVE THE MOST FANS.
But
if you want to make fuwa suffer
I'll do it my way.
I HAVE MY PERSONAL GRUDGES.
When he got beaten to a pulp.
?
YOU MEAN... SOME-THING OTHER THAN MUSIC?
OH?
Yeah.
AND HOW?

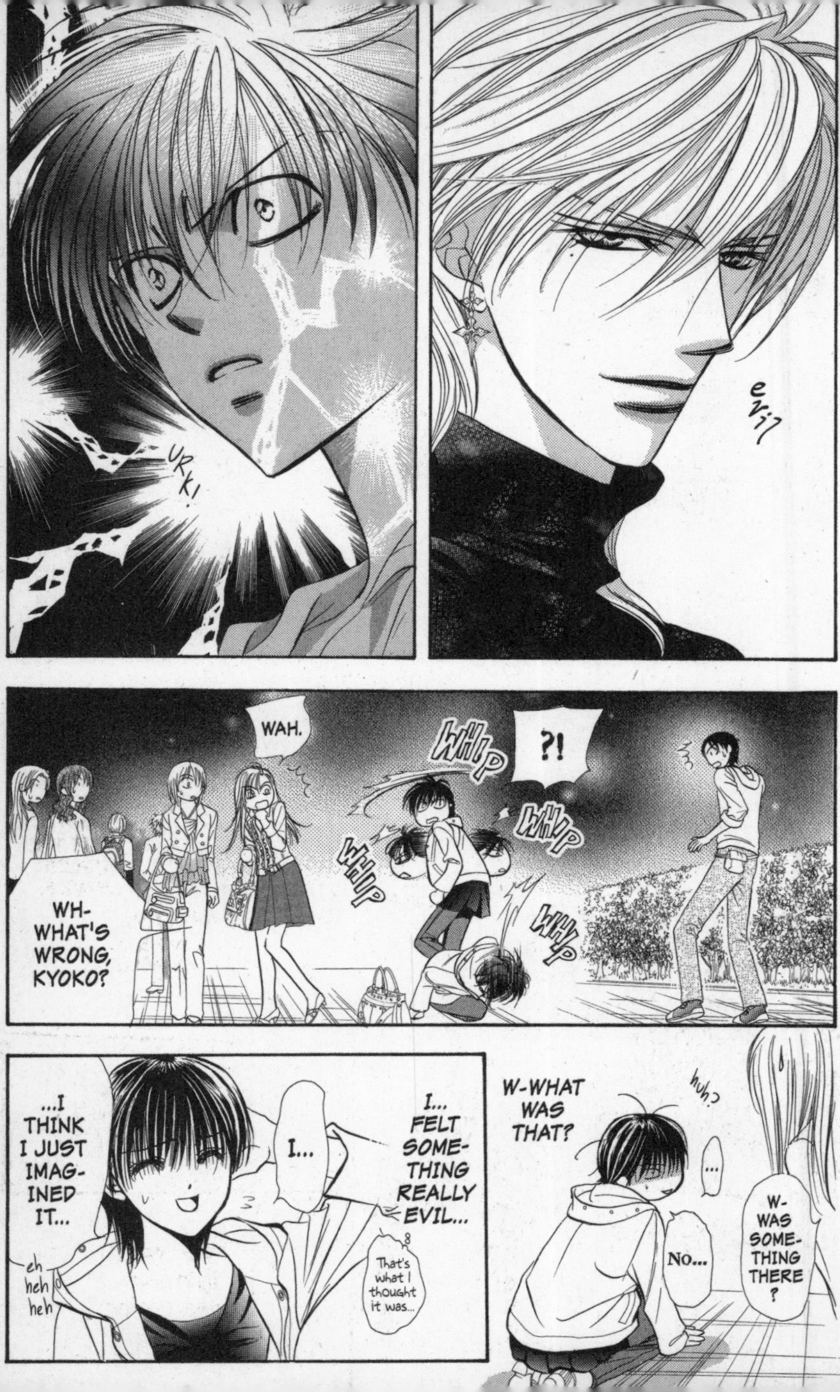
evil
URK!
?!
WHIP
WHIP
WHIP
WHIP
WAH.
WH-WHAT'S WRONG, KYOKO?
huh?
W-WHAT WAS THAT?
...
W-WAS SOMETHING THERE?
No...
I... FELT SOMETHING REALLY EVIL...
I...
That's what I thought it was...
...I THINK I JUST IMAGINED IT...
eh heh heh

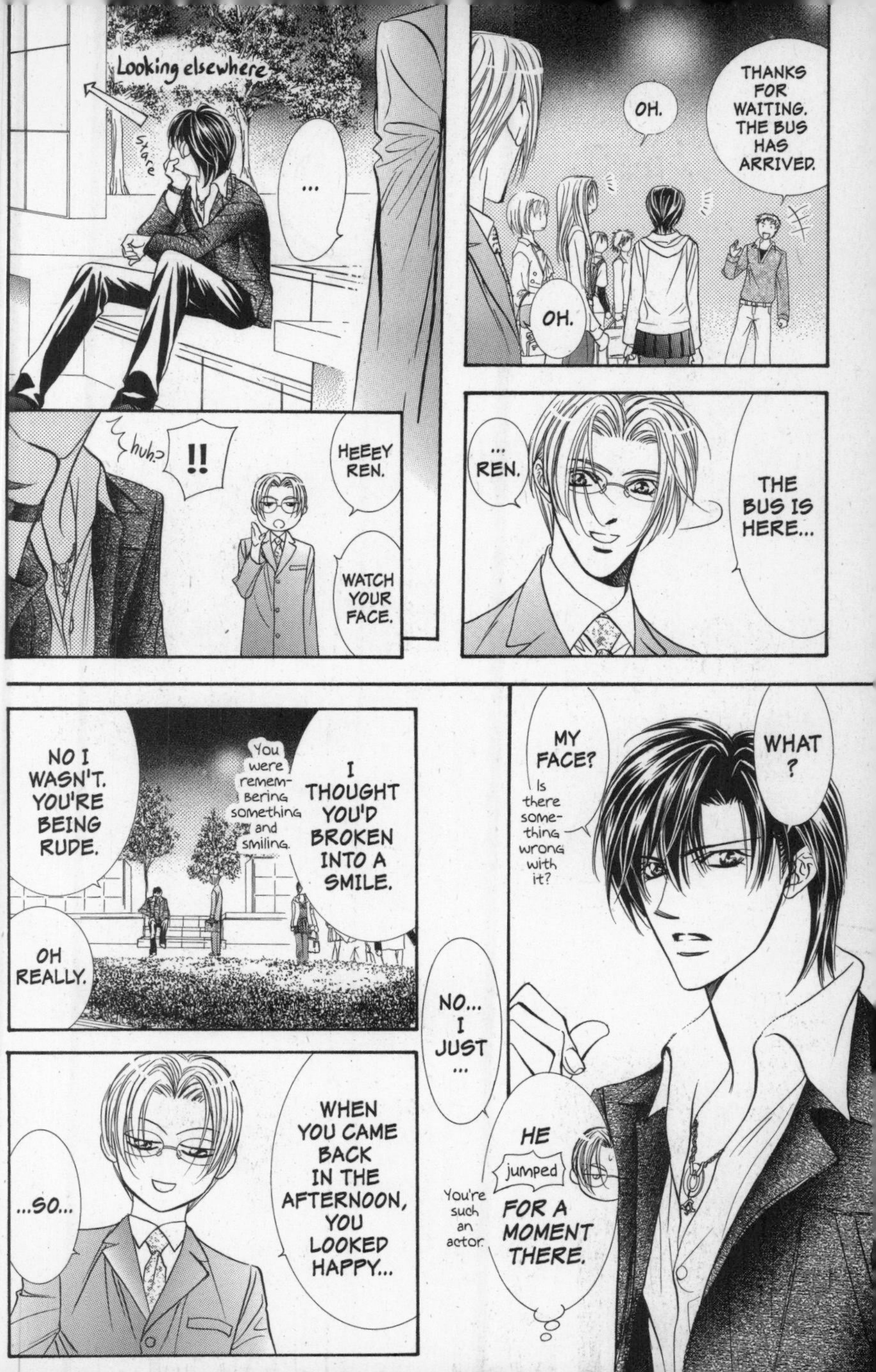
THANKS FOR WAITING. THE BUS HAS ARRIVED.
OH.
OH.
Looking elsewhere
Stare
...
... REN.
THE BUS IS HERE...
HEEEY REN.
WATCH YOUR FACE.
huh?
!!
WHAT ?
MY FACE?
Is there something wrong with it?
NO... I JUST ...
HE jumped FOR A MOMENT THERE.
You're such an actor.
I THOUGHT YOU'D BROKEN INTO A SMILE.
You were remembering something and smiling.
NO I WASN'T. YOU'RE BEING RUDE.
OH REALLY.
WHEN YOU CAME BACK IN THE AFTERNOON, YOU LOOKED HAPPY...
...SO...

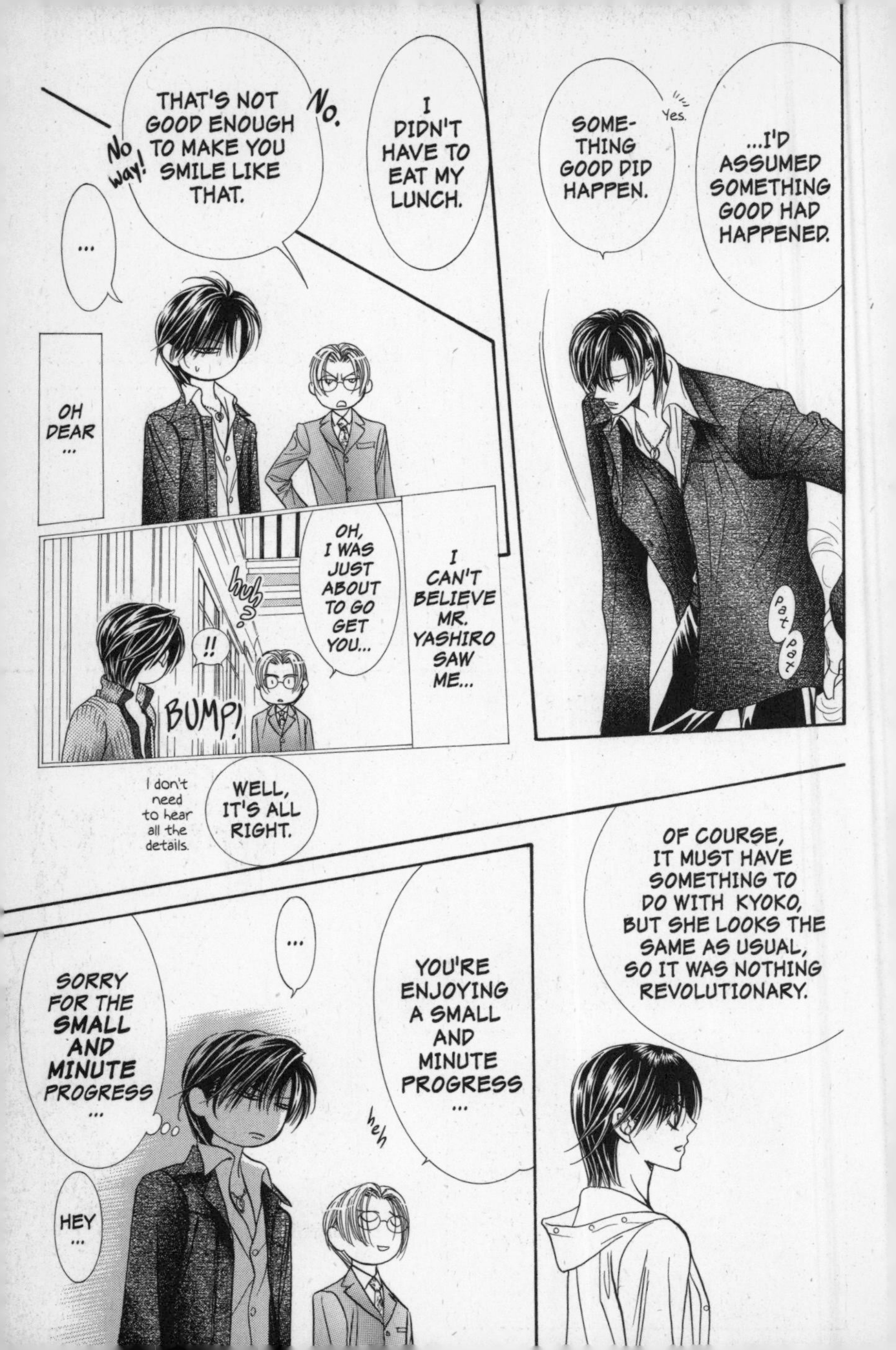
...I'D ASSUMED SOMETHING GOOD HAD HAPPENED.
SOME-THING GOOD DID HAPPEN.
Yes.
Pat pat
I DIDN'T HAVE TO EAT MY LUNCH.
No.
THAT'S NOT GOOD ENOUGH TO MAKE YOU SMILE LIKE THAT.
No way!
...
OH DEAR...
I CAN'T BELIEVE MR. YASHIRO SAW ME...
OH, I WAS JUST ABOUT TO GO GET YOU...
huh?
!!
BUMP!
WELL, IT'S ALL RIGHT.
I don't need to hear all the details.
OF COURSE, IT MUST HAVE SOMETHING TO DO WITH KYOKO, BUT SHE LOOKS THE SAME AS USUAL, SO IT WAS NOTHING REVOLUTIONARY.
YOU'RE ENJOYING A SMALL AND MINUTE PROGRESS...
heh
...
SORRY FOR THE SMALL AND MINUTE PROGRESS...
HEY...

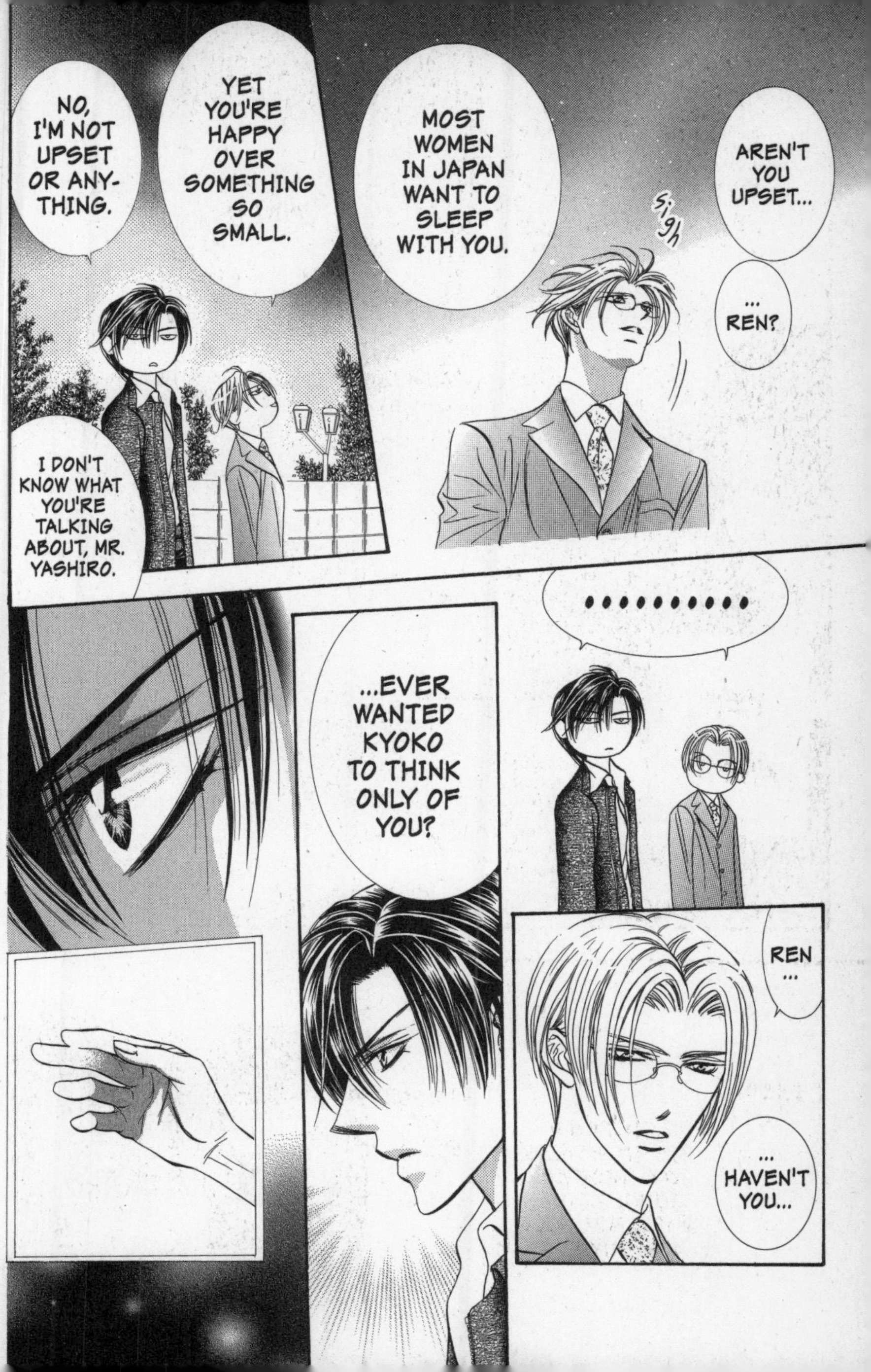
AREN'T YOU UPSET...
... REN?
Sigh
MOST WOMEN IN JAPAN WANT TO SLEEP WITH YOU.
YET YOU'RE HAPPY OVER SOMETHING SO SMALL.
NO, I'M NOT UPSET OR ANY-THING.
I DON'T KNOW WHAT YOU'RE TALKING ABOUT, MR. YASHIRO.
....
REN ...
... HAVEN'T YOU...
...EVER WANTED KYOKO TO THINK ONLY OF YOU?

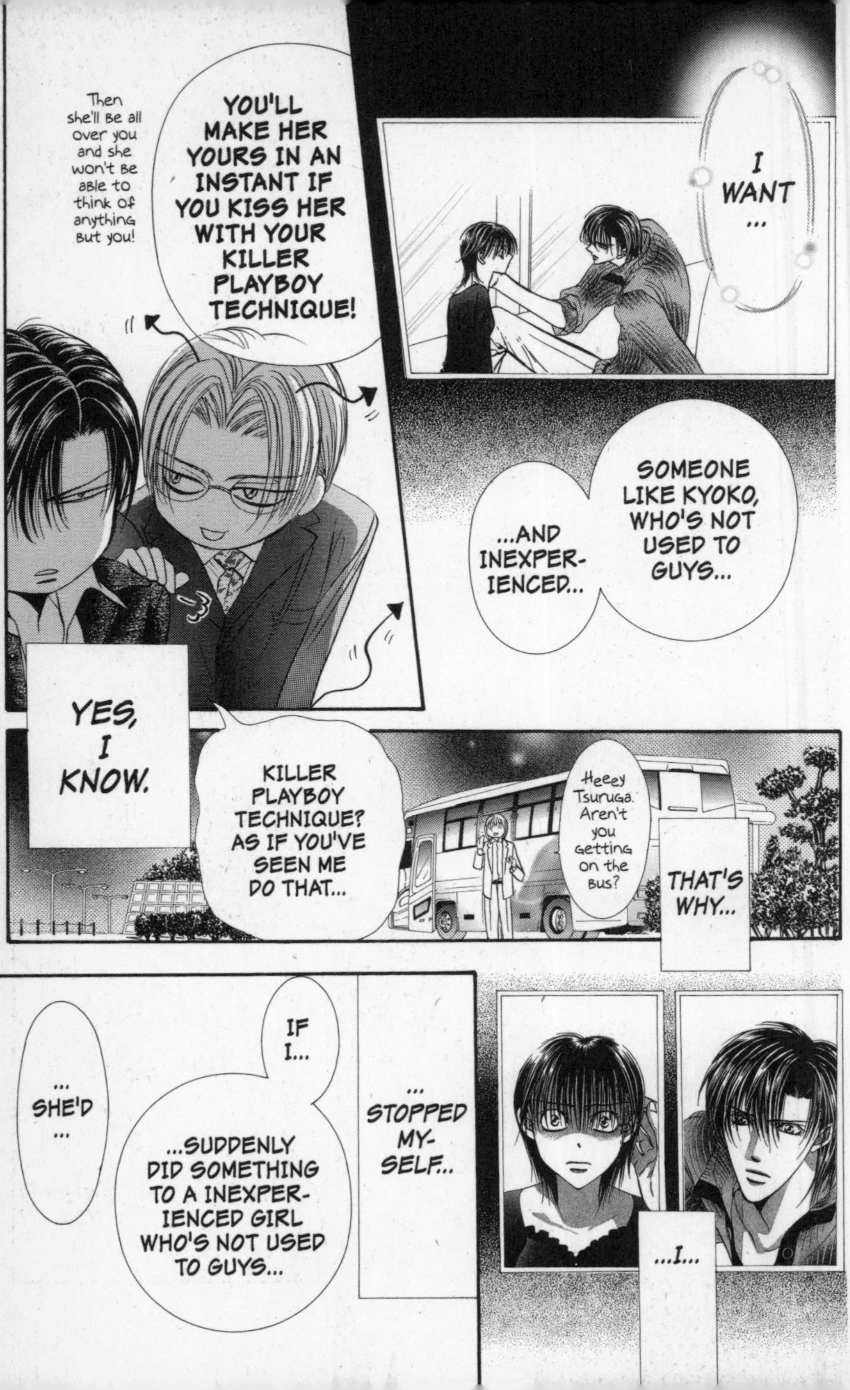
I WANT ...
SOMEONE LIKE KYOKO, WHO'S NOT USED TO GUYS...
...AND INEXPER-IENCED...
YOU'LL MAKE HER YOURS IN AN INSTANT IF YOU KISS HER WITH YOUR KILLER PLAYBOY TECHNIQUE!
Then she'll Be all over you and she won't Be able to think of anything But you!
THAT'S WHY...
Heeey Tsuruga. Aren't you getting on the Bus?
KILLER PLAYBOY TECHNIQUE? AS IF YOU'VE SEEN ME DO THAT...
YES, I KNOW.
...I...
... STOPPED MY-SELF...
IF I...
...SUDDENLY DID SOMETHING TO A INEXPER-IENCED GIRL WHO'S NOT USED TO GUYS...
... SHE'D ...

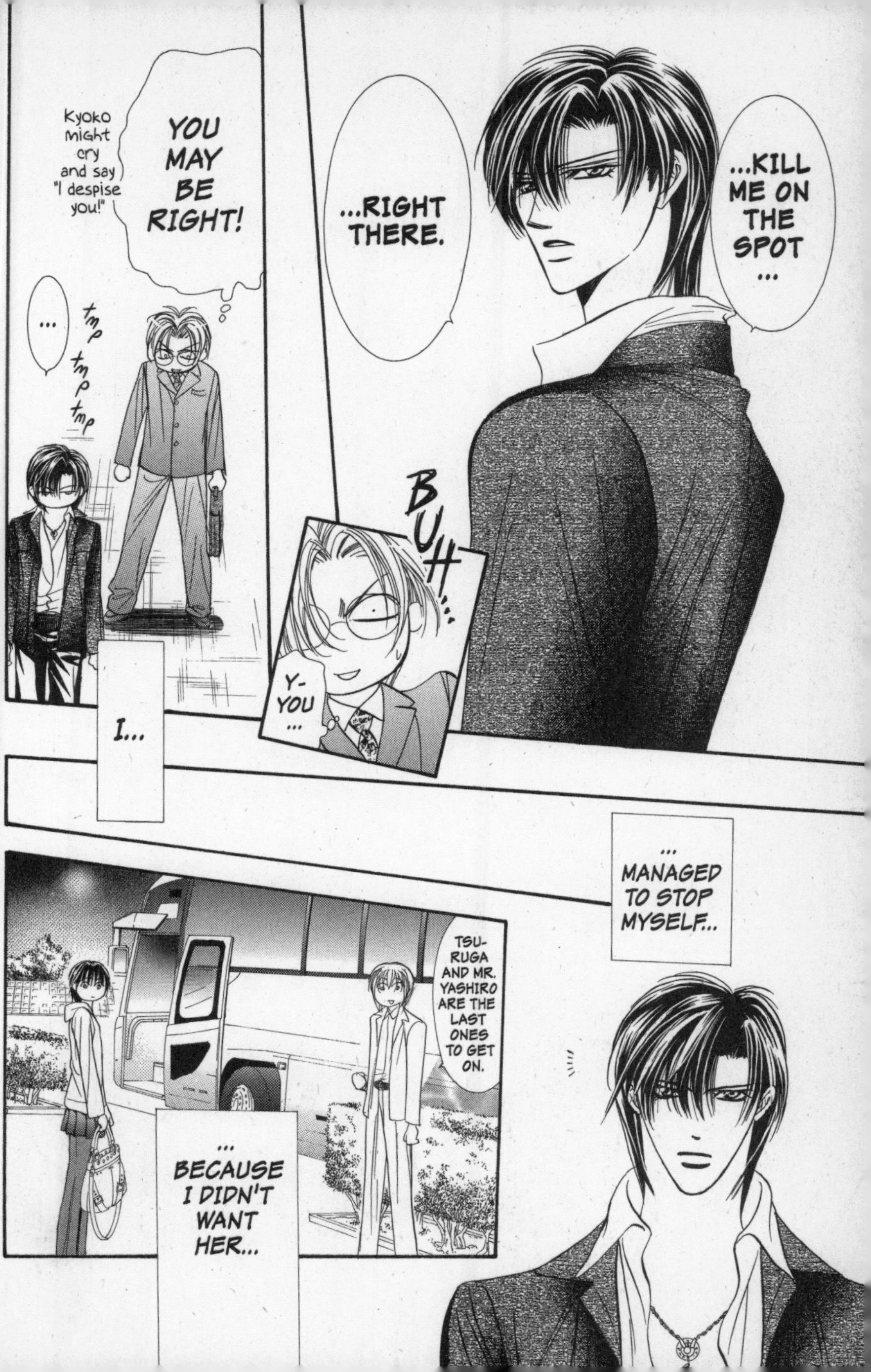
...KILL ME ON THE SPOT...
...RIGHT THERE.
BUH...
Y-YOU...
YOU MAY BE RIGHT!
Kyoko might cry and say "I despise you!"
...
tmp tmp tmp
I...
...MANAGED TO STOP MYSELF...
TSU-RUGA AND MR. YASHIRO ARE THE LAST ONES TO GET ON.
...BECAUSE I DIDN'T WANT HER...

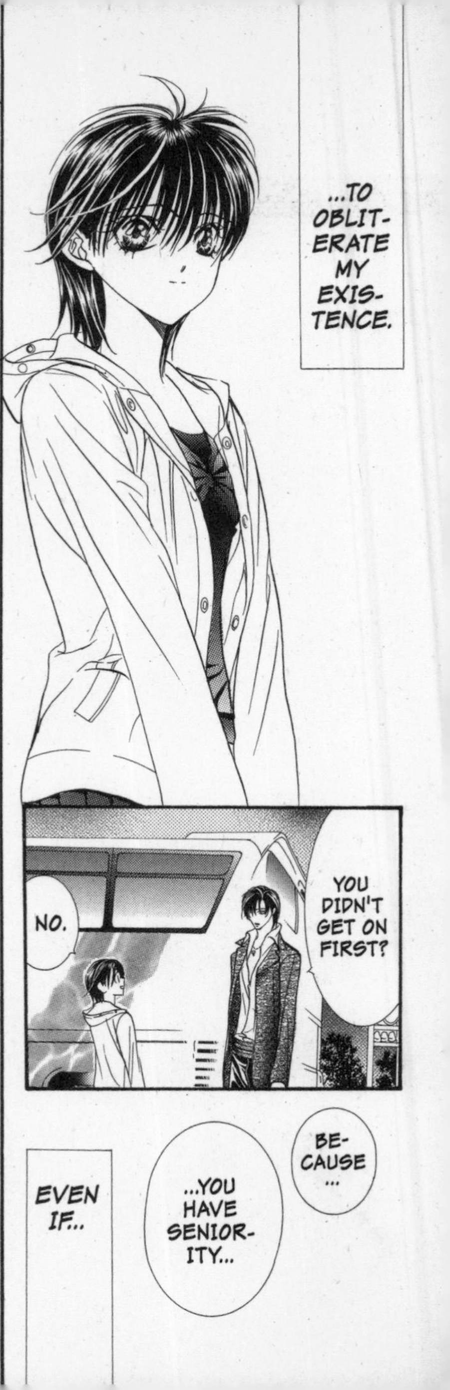
...TO OBLIT- ERATE MY EXIS- TENCE.
YOU DIDN'T GET ON FIRST?
NO.
BE- CAUSE ...
...YOU HAVE SENIOR- ITY...
EVEN IF...

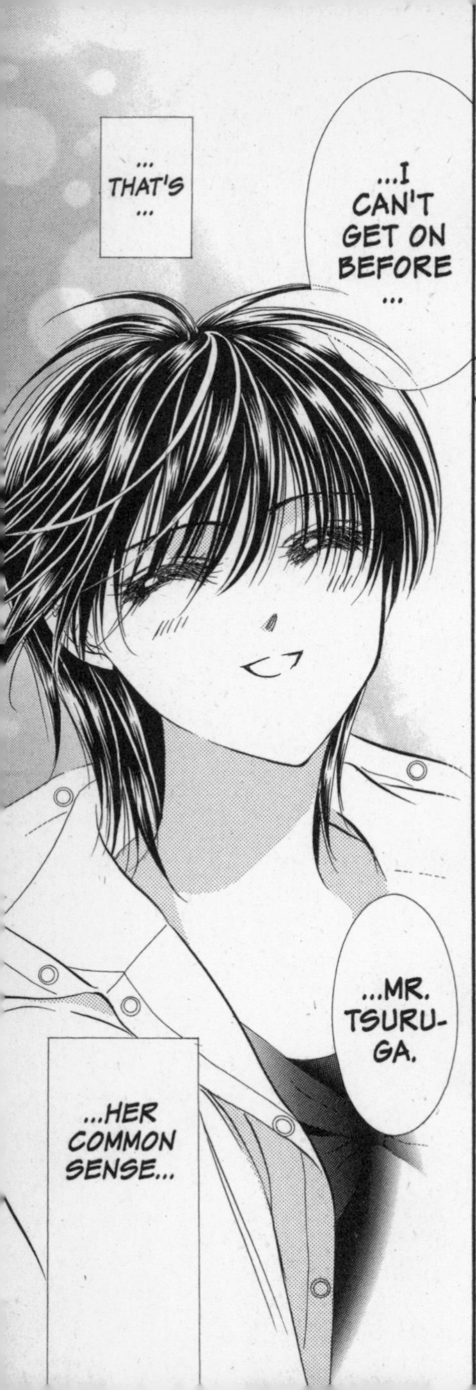
...I CAN'T GET ON BEFORE ...
... THAT'S ...
...MR. TSURU- GA.
...HER COMMON SENSE...

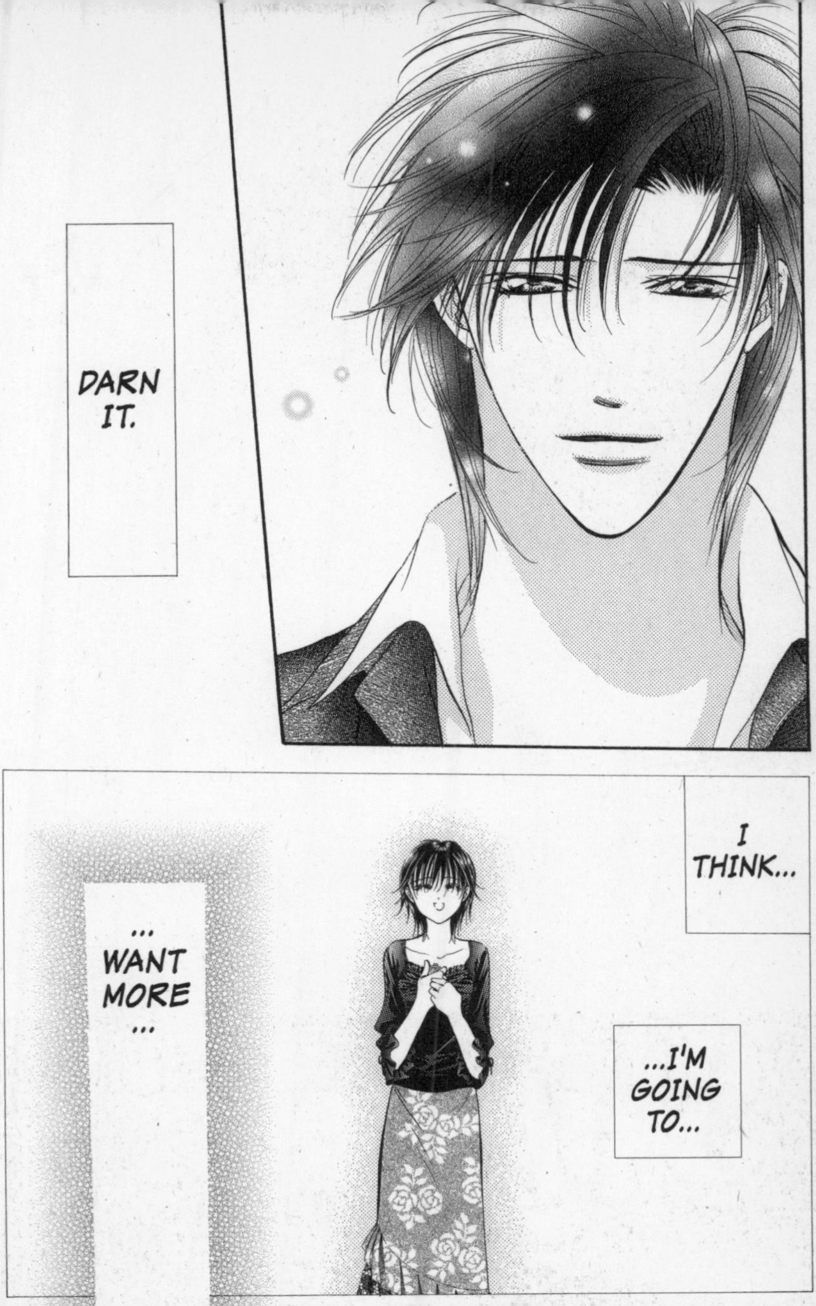
DARN IT.
I THINK...
...I'M GOING TO...
...WANT MORE...

End of Act 97

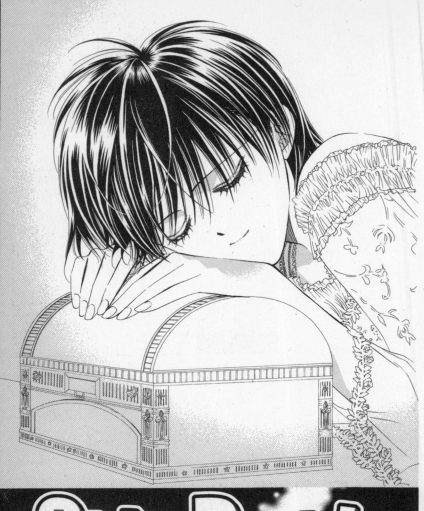

Skip·Beat!

Act 98: Suddenly, a Love Story
–Ending, Part 5–

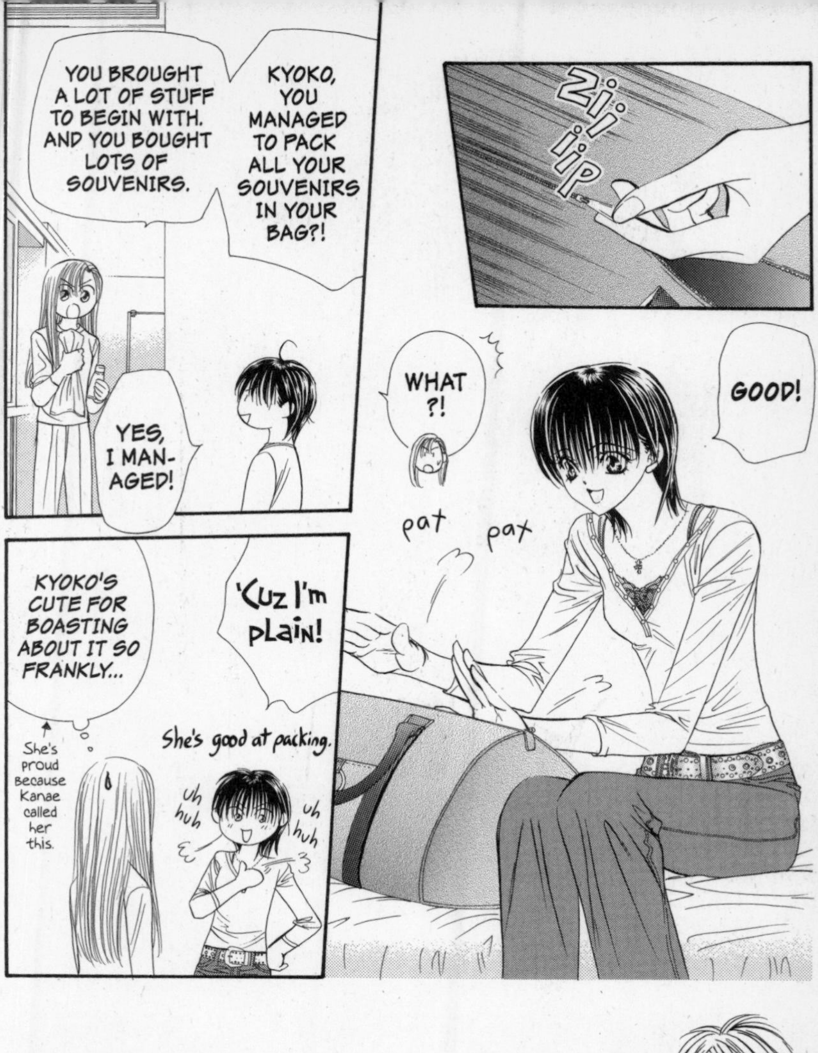
ZIIIP
GOOD!
WHAT?!
pat
pat
KYOKO, YOU MANAGED TO PACK ALL YOUR SOUVENIRS IN YOUR BAG?!
YOU BROUGHT A LOT OF STUFF TO BEGIN WITH. AND YOU BOUGHT LOTS OF SOUVENIRS.
YES, I MAN-AGED!
'CUZ I'M PLAIN!
KYOKO'S CUTE FOR BOASTING ABOUT IT SO FRANKLY...
She's good at packing.
She's proud because Kanae called her this.
uh huh
uh huh

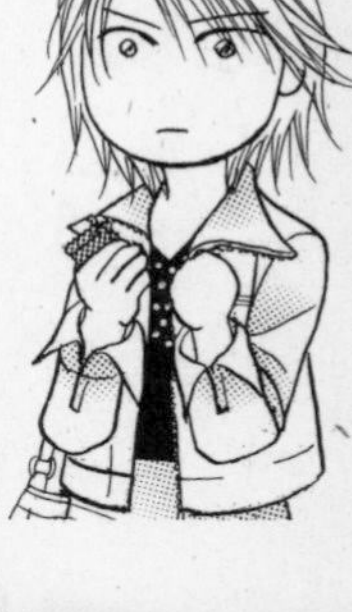

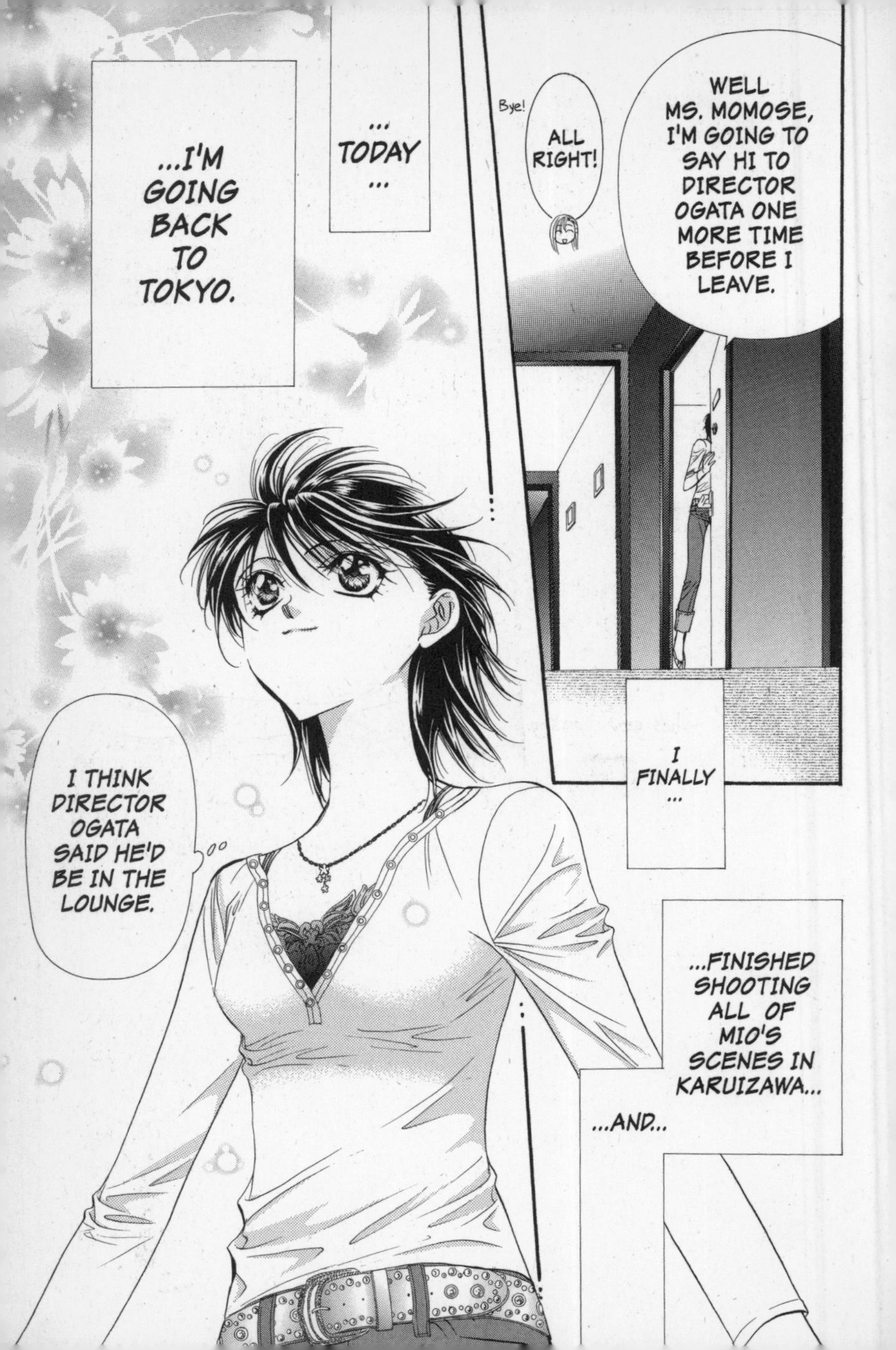
WELL MS. MOMOSE, I'M GOING TO SAY HI TO DIRECTOR OGATA ONE MORE TIME BEFORE I LEAVE.
Bye!
ALL RIGHT!
I FINALLY...
...FINISHED SHOOTING ALL OF MIO'S SCENES IN KARUIZAWA...
...AND...
...TODAY...
...I'M GOING BACK TO TOKYO.
I THINK DIRECTOR OGATA SAID HE'D BE IN THE LOUNGE.

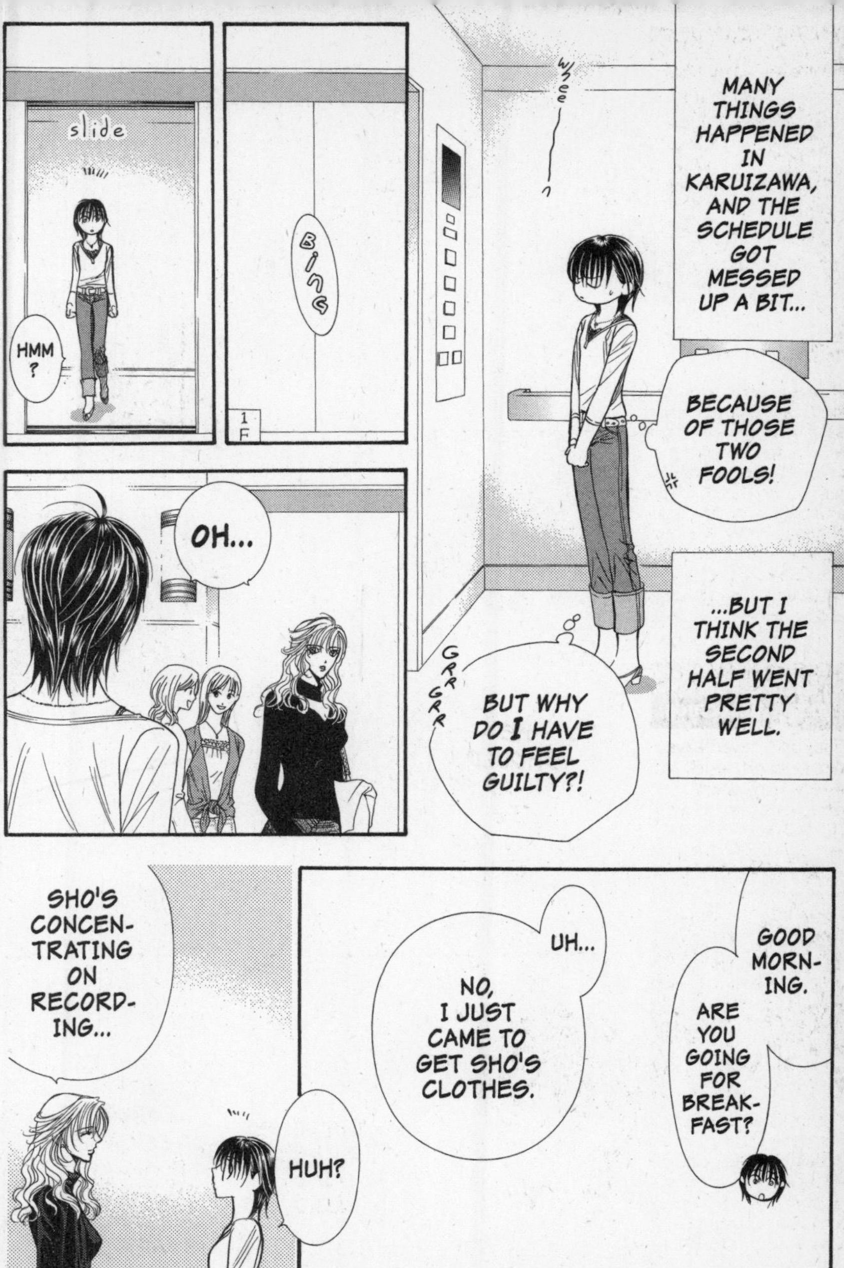
MANY THINGS HAPPENED IN KARUIZAWA, AND THE SCHEDULE GOT MESSED UP A BIT...
wheee
BECAUSE OF THOSE TWO FOOLS!
...BUT I THINK THE SECOND HALF WENT PRETTY WELL.
GRR GRR
BUT WHY DO I HAVE TO FEEL GUILTY?!
BING
1F
slide
HMM?
OH...
GOOD MORNING.
ARE YOU GOING FOR BREAKFAST?
UH...
NO, I JUST CAME TO GET SHO'S CLOTHES.
SHO'S CONCENTRATING ON RECORDING...
HUH?

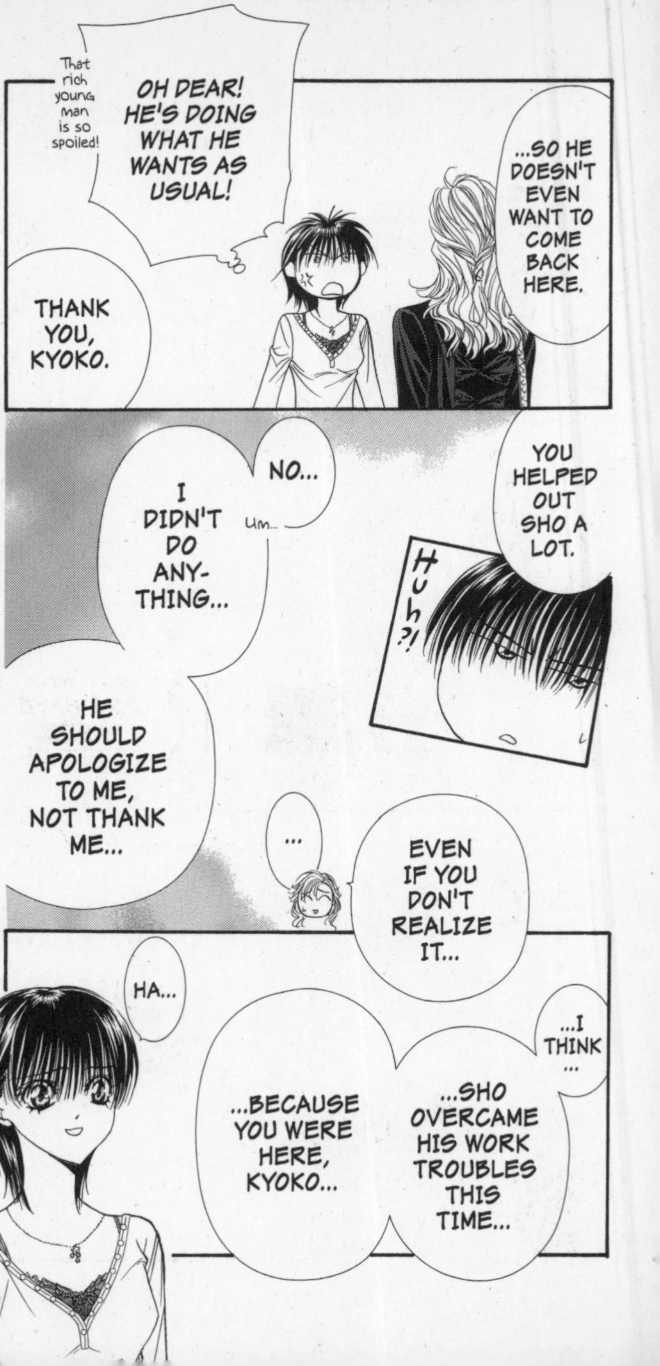
...SO HE DOESN'T EVEN WANT TO COME BACK HERE.
OH DEAR! HE'S DOING WHAT HE WANTS AS USUAL!
That rich young man is so spoiled!
THANK YOU, KYOKO.
Huh?!
YOU HELPED OUT SHO A LOT.
NO...
Um...
I DIDN'T DO ANYTHING...
HE SHOULD APOLOGIZE TO ME, NOT THANK ME...
...
EVEN IF YOU DON'T REALIZE IT...
...SHO OVERCAME HIS WORK TROUBLES THIS TIME...
...BECAUSE YOU WERE HERE, KYOKO...
...I THINK...
HA...

Shizuru (Bass)

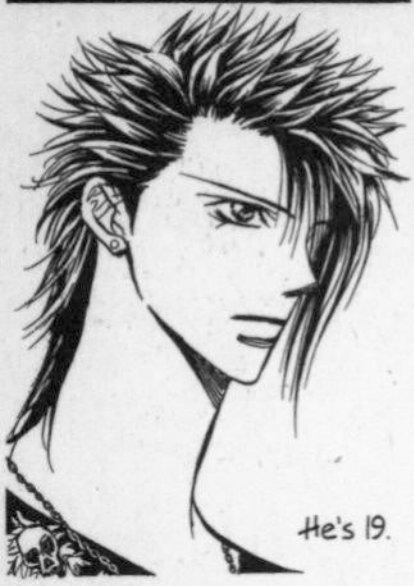
He's 19.

He was there just to fill in the band. And he plays bass. That makes it seem like he doesn't stand out much. (I'm sorry. That's just my impression as an amateur. ☺) That's how I thought I drew him, but somehow, by the end of the "Love Story" arc, it became fun drawing him, and I grew to like him...

The others (Guitar) (Keyboards)

They don't even have first names...which means that I really don't care about them.

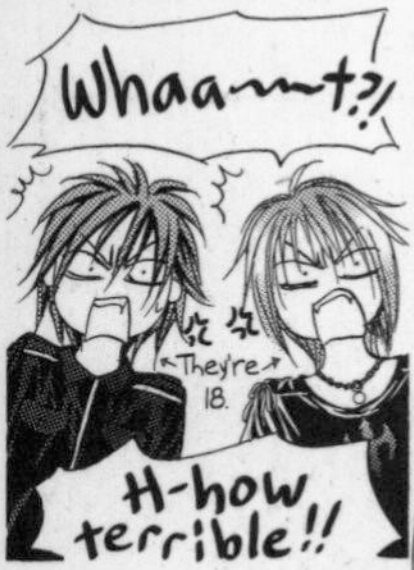
Whaa—t?!
They're 18.
H-how terrible!!

The ones who were treated relatively well (besides Reino) faded into the background... I wonder if a day will come when the poor guys will be named...

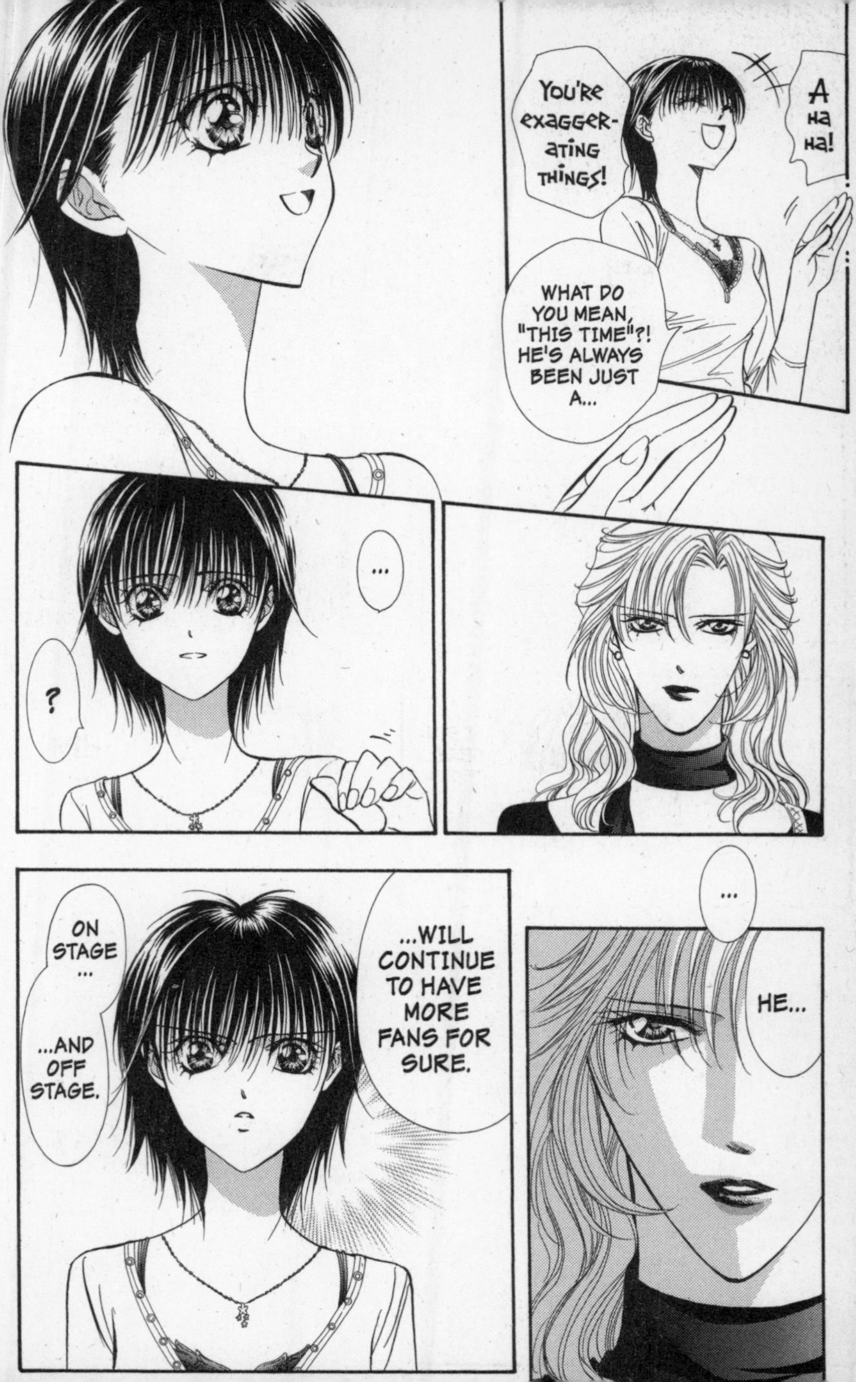
A ha ha!
You're exaggerating things!
WHAT DO YOU MEAN, "THIS TIME"?! HE'S ALWAYS BEEN JUST A...
...
?
...
HE...
ON STAGE...
...AND OFF STAGE.
...WILL CONTINUE TO HAVE MORE FANS FOR SURE.

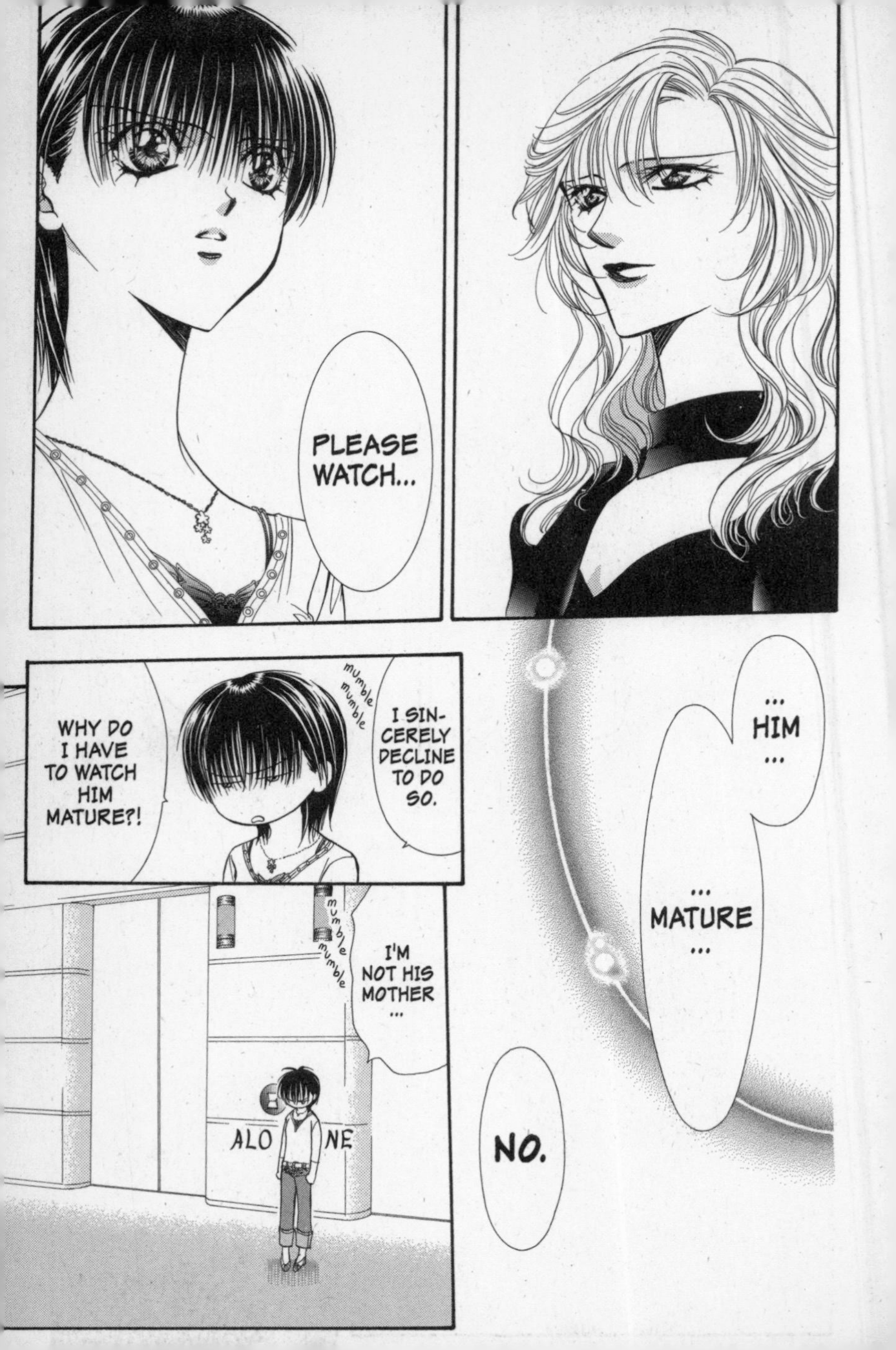
PLEASE WATCH...
...HIM...
...MATURE...
NO.
mumble mumble
I SINCERELY DECLINE TO DO SO.
WHY DO I HAVE TO WATCH HIM MATURE?!
mumble mumble
I'M NOT HIS MOTHER...
ALONE

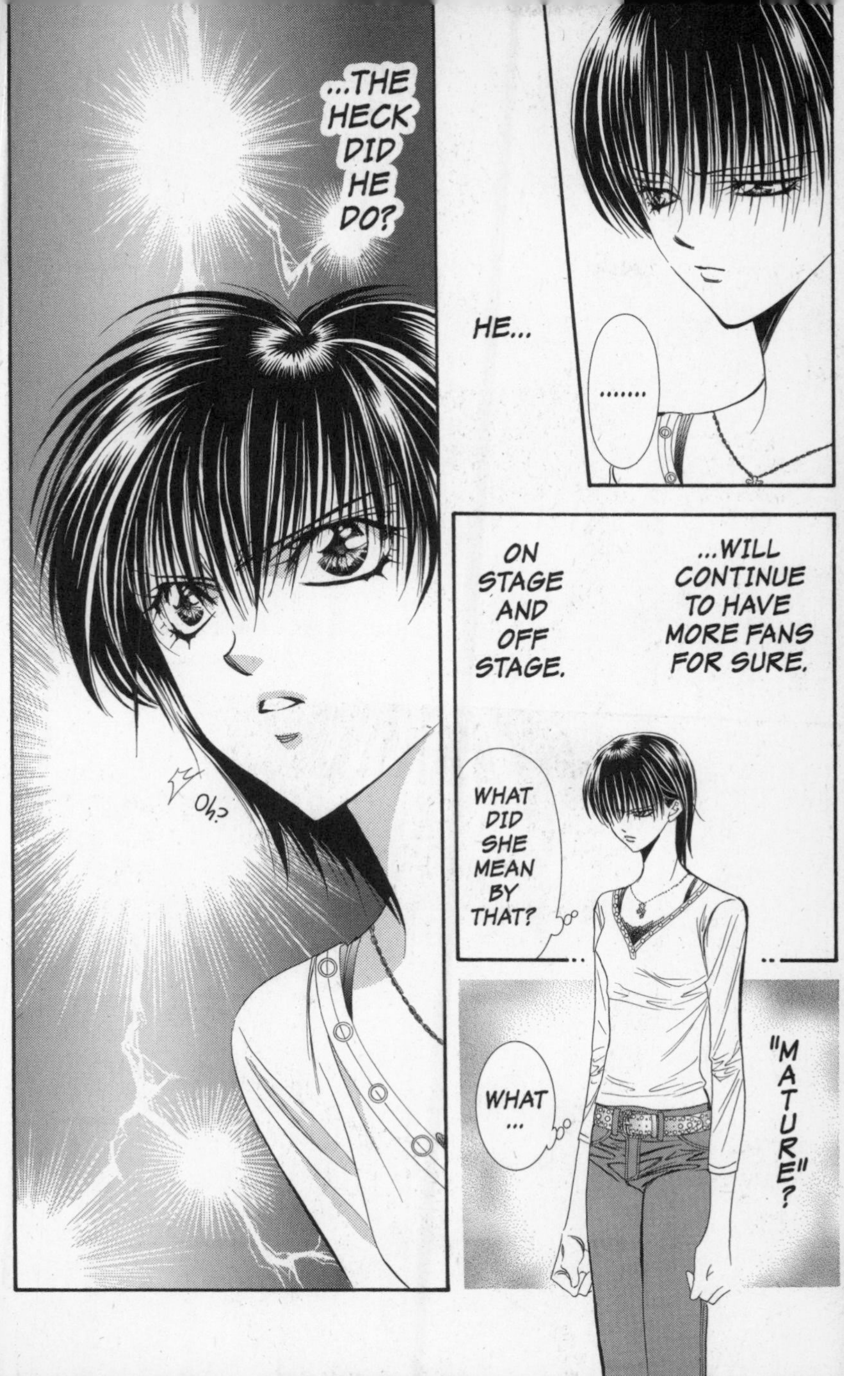
....
HE...
...WILL CONTINUE TO HAVE MORE FANS FOR SURE.
ON STAGE AND OFF STAGE.
WHAT DID SHE MEAN BY THAT?
"MATURE"?
WHAT...
...THE HECK DID HE DO?
Oh?

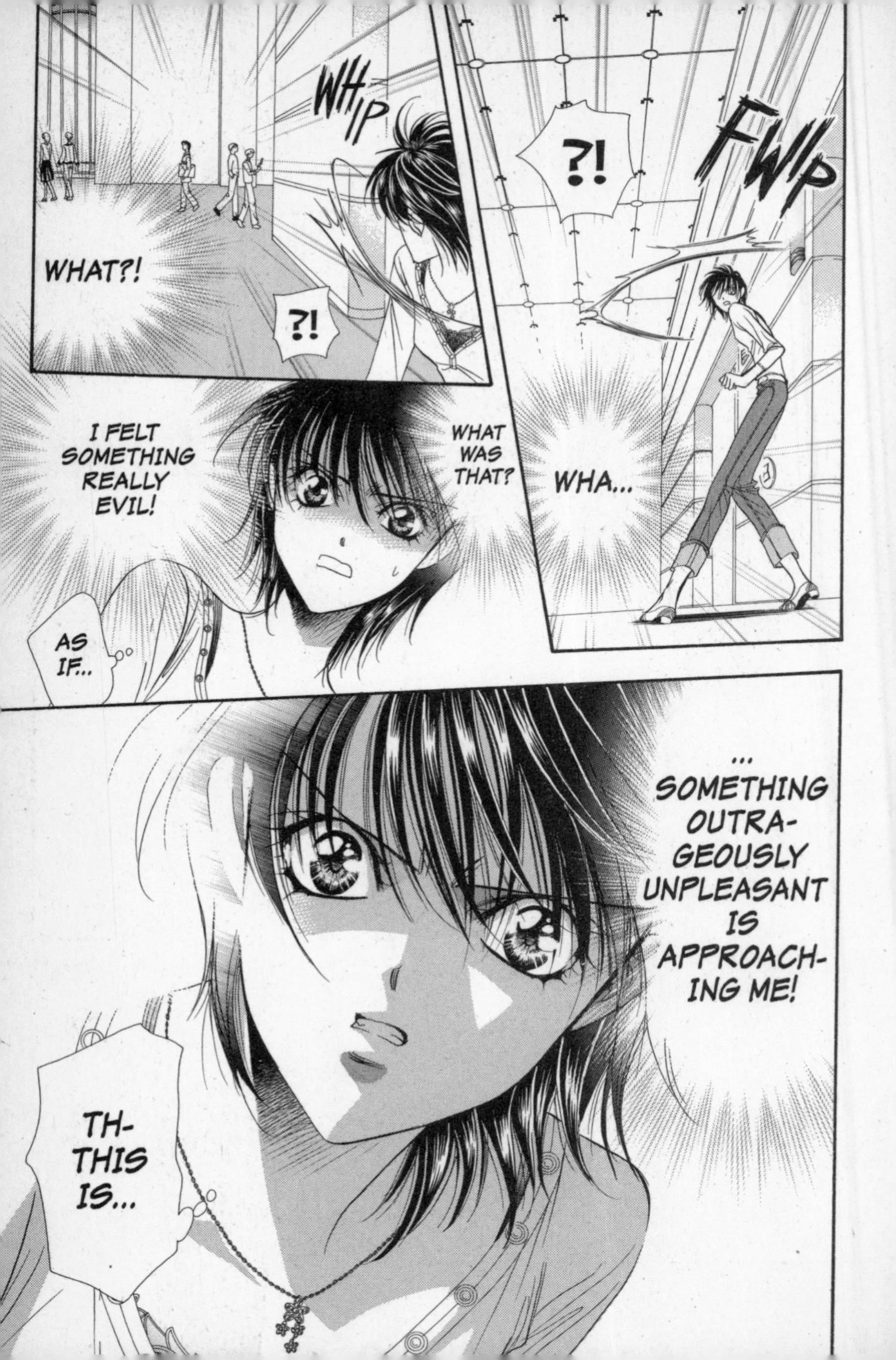
FWIP
?!
WHA...
WHIP
WHAT?!
?!
WHAT WAS THAT?
I FELT SOMETHING REALLY EVIL!
AS IF...
...SOMETHING OUTRA-GEOUSLY UNPLEASANT IS APPROACH-ING ME!
TH-THIS IS...

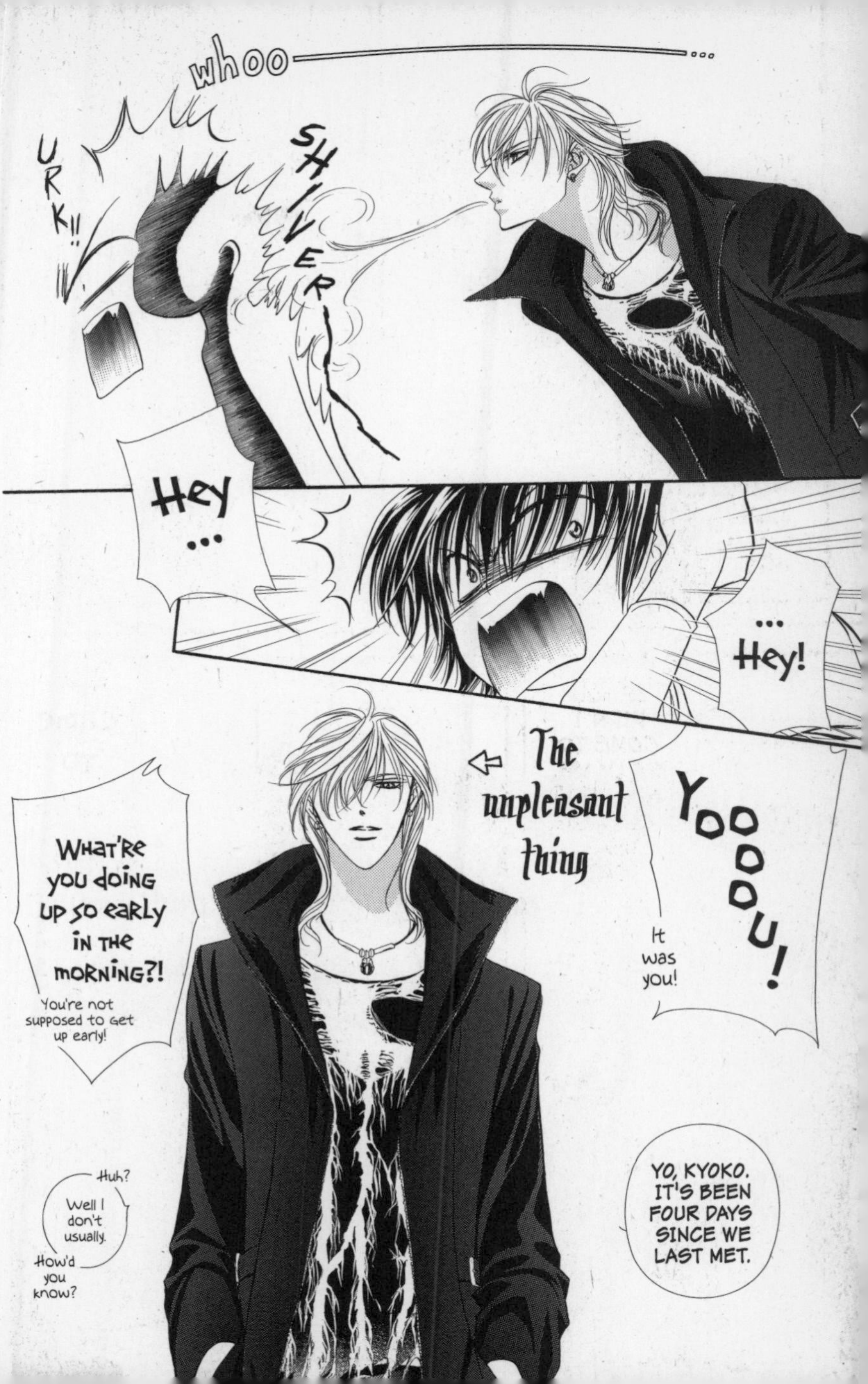
whoo———...
SHIVER
URK!!
Hey...
...Hey!
YOOOOU!
It was you!
The unpleasant thing
WHAT'RE YOU DOING UP SO EARLY IN THE MORNING?!
You're not supposed to get up early!
YO, KYOKO. IT'S BEEN FOUR DAYS SINCE WE LAST MET.
Huh?
Well I don't usually.
How'd you know?

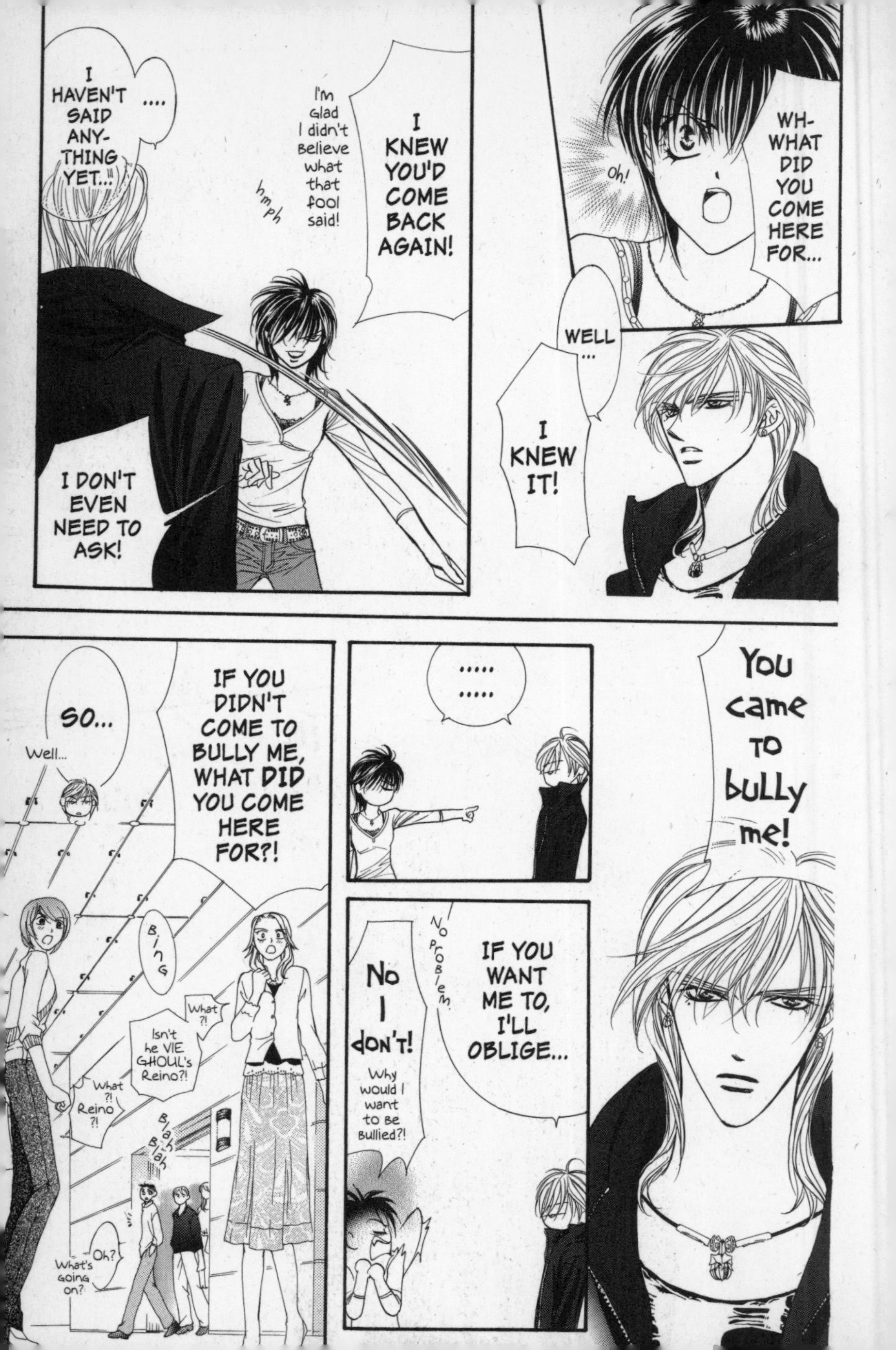

WH-WHAT DID YOU COME HERE FOR...
Oh!
WELL...
I KNEW IT!
I KNEW YOU'D COME BACK AGAIN!
I'm Glad I didn't Believe what that fool said!
hmph
I HAVEN'T SAID ANYTHING YET...
....
I DON'T EVEN NEED TO ASK!
You came to bully me!
.....
.....
IF YOU WANT ME TO, I'LL OBLIGE...
No problem
No I don't!
Why would I want to be Bullied?!
SO...
Well...
IF YOU DIDN'T COME TO BULLY ME, WHAT DID YOU COME HERE FOR?!
Bing
What?!
Isn't he VIE GHOUL's Reino?!
What?! Reino?!
Blah Blah
Oh?
What's going on?

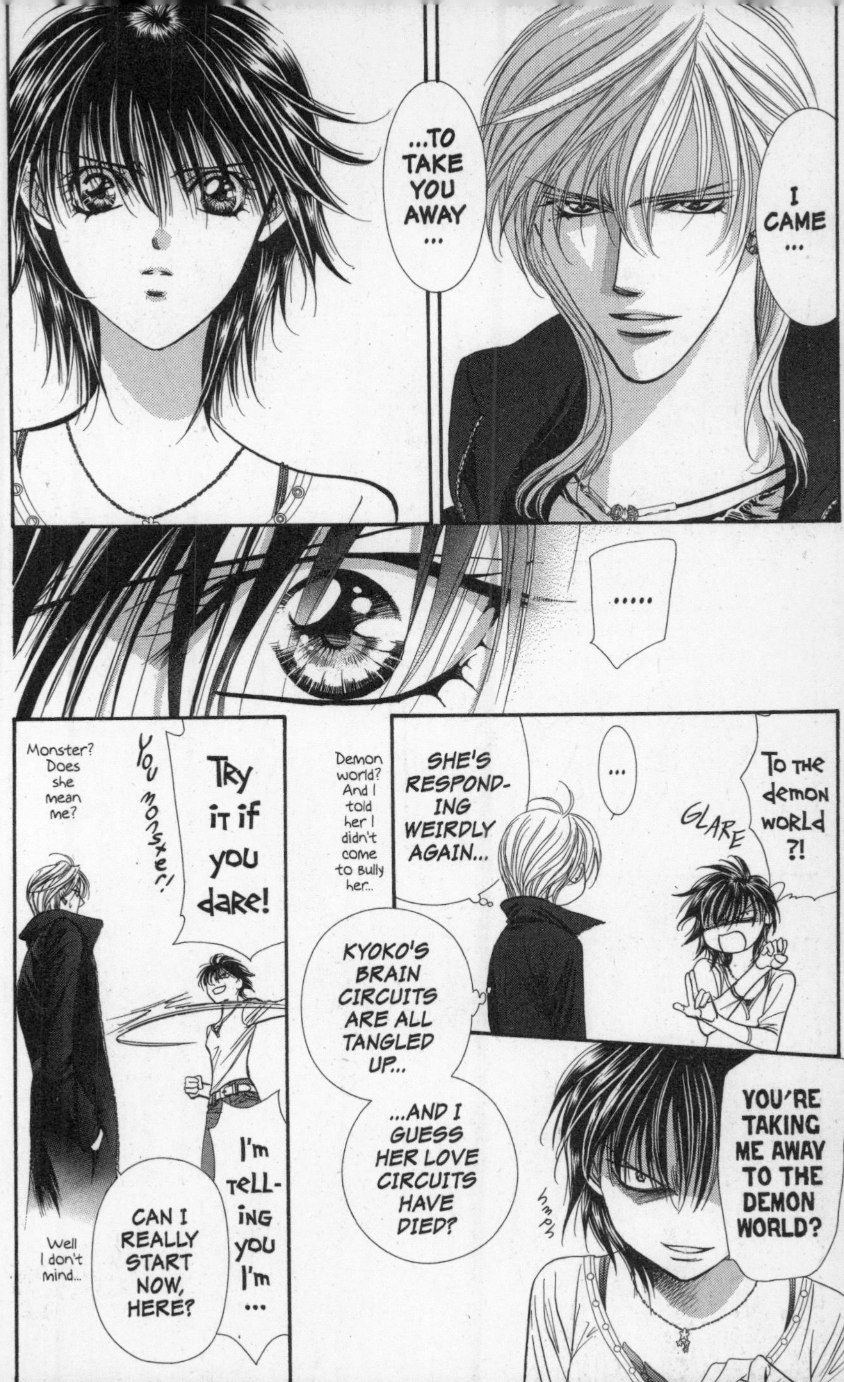
I CAME ...
...TO TAKE YOU AWAY ...
......
To the demon world ?!
GLARE
...
SHE'S RESPONDING WEIRDLY AGAIN...
Demon world? And I told her I didn't come to bully her...
YOU'RE TAKING ME AWAY TO THE DEMON WORLD?
hmph
KYOKO'S BRAIN CIRCUITS ARE ALL TANGLED UP...
...AND I GUESS HER LOVE CIRCUITS HAVE DIED?
Try it if you dare!
You monster!
Monster? Does she mean me?
I'm telling you I'm ...
CAN I REALLY START NOW, HERE?
Well I don't mind...

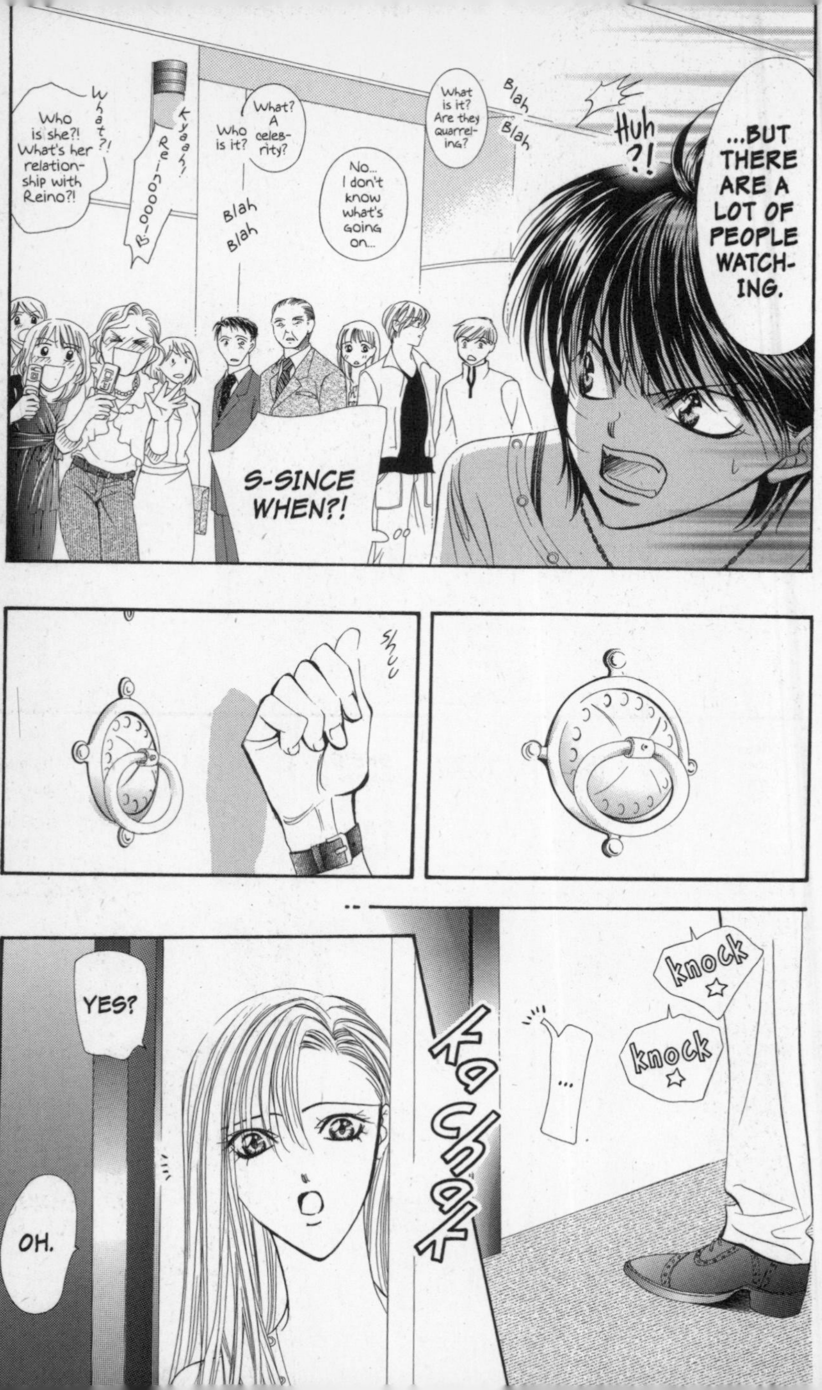
...BUT THERE ARE A LOT OF PEOPLE WATCHING.
HUH?!
Blah Blah
What is it? Are they quarrel-ing?
What? A celeb-rity?
Who is it?
No... I don't know what's going on...
Blah Blah
Kyaah! Rei-nooo
B_oooo
What?!
Who is she?! What's her relation-ship with Reino?!
S-SINCE WHEN?!
shu
knock ☆
knock ☆
...
ka chak
YES?
OH.

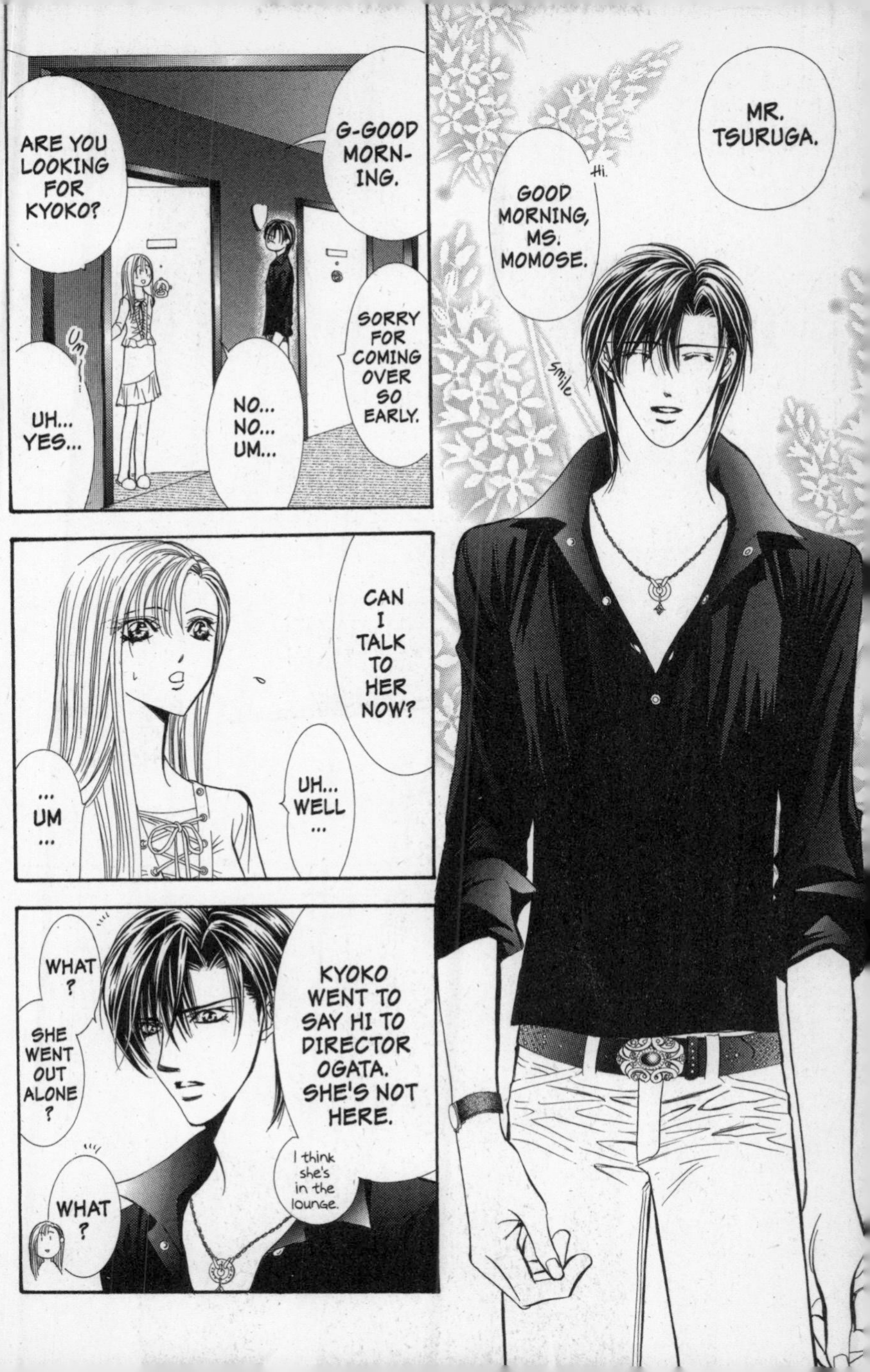
MR. TSURUGA.
Hi.
GOOD MORNING, MS. MOMOSE.
Smile
G-GOOD MORNING.
ARE YOU LOOKING FOR KYOKO?
SORRY FOR COMING OVER SO EARLY.
NO... NO... UM...
Um
UH... YES...
CAN I TALK TO HER NOW?
UH... WELL ...
... UM ...
KYOKO WENT TO SAY HI TO DIRECTOR OGATA. SHE'S NOT HERE.
I think she's in the lounge.
WHAT? SHE WENT OUT ALONE?
WHAT?

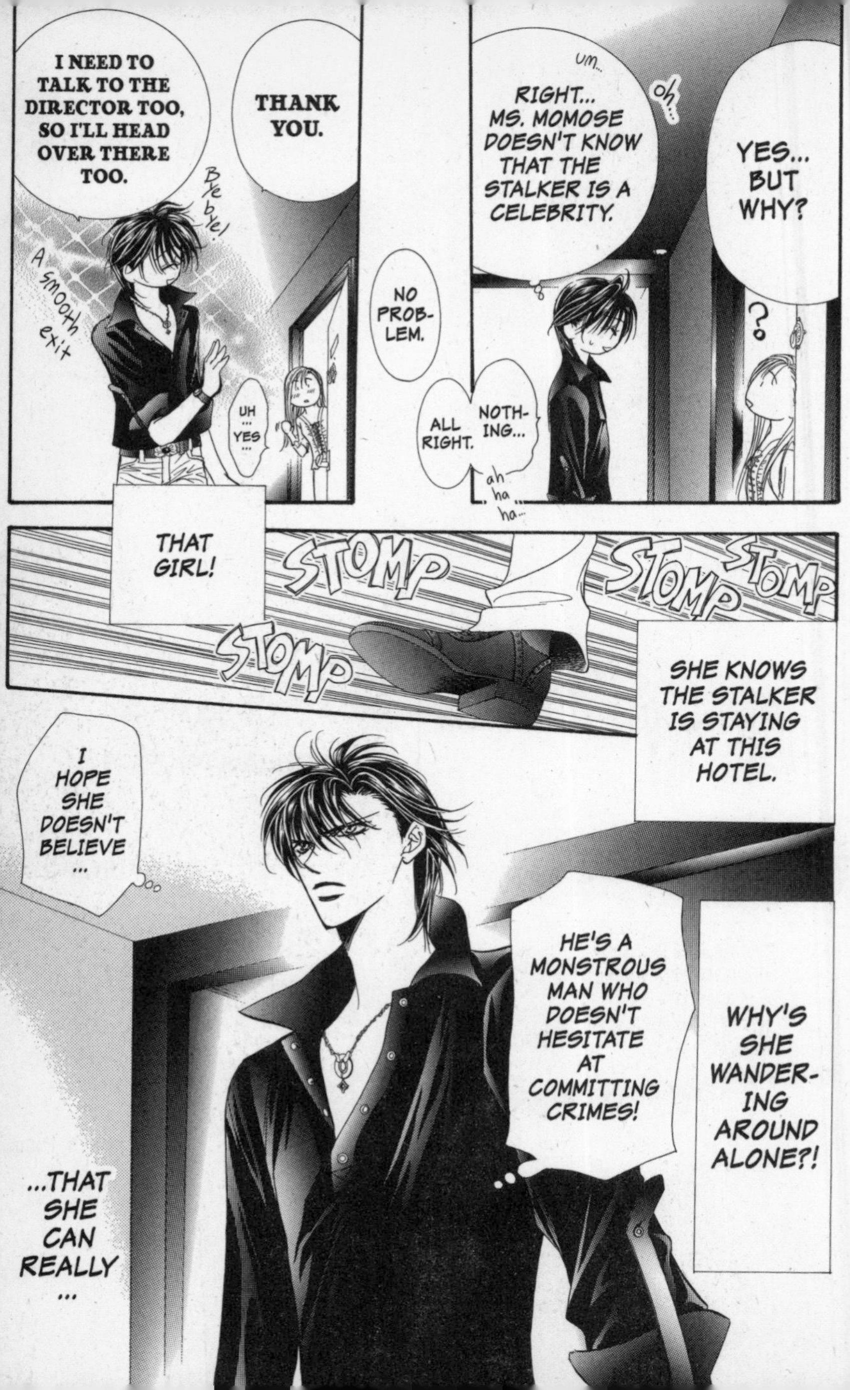
YES... BUT WHY?
?
oh...
um...
RIGHT... MS. MOMOSE DOESN'T KNOW THAT THE STALKER IS A CELEBRITY.
NOTHING...
ALL RIGHT.
ah ha ha...
THANK YOU.
I NEED TO TALK TO THE DIRECTOR TOO, SO I'LL HEAD OVER THERE TOO.
NO PROBLEM.
Bye bye!
A smooth exit
UH... YES...
STOMP
STOMP
STOMP
STOMP
THAT GIRL!
SHE KNOWS THE STALKER IS STAYING AT THIS HOTEL.
WHY'S SHE WANDER-ING AROUND ALONE?!
HE'S A MONSTROUS MAN WHO DOESN'T HESITATE AT COMMITTING CRIMES!
I HOPE SHE DOESN'T BELIEVE...
...THAT SHE CAN REALLY...

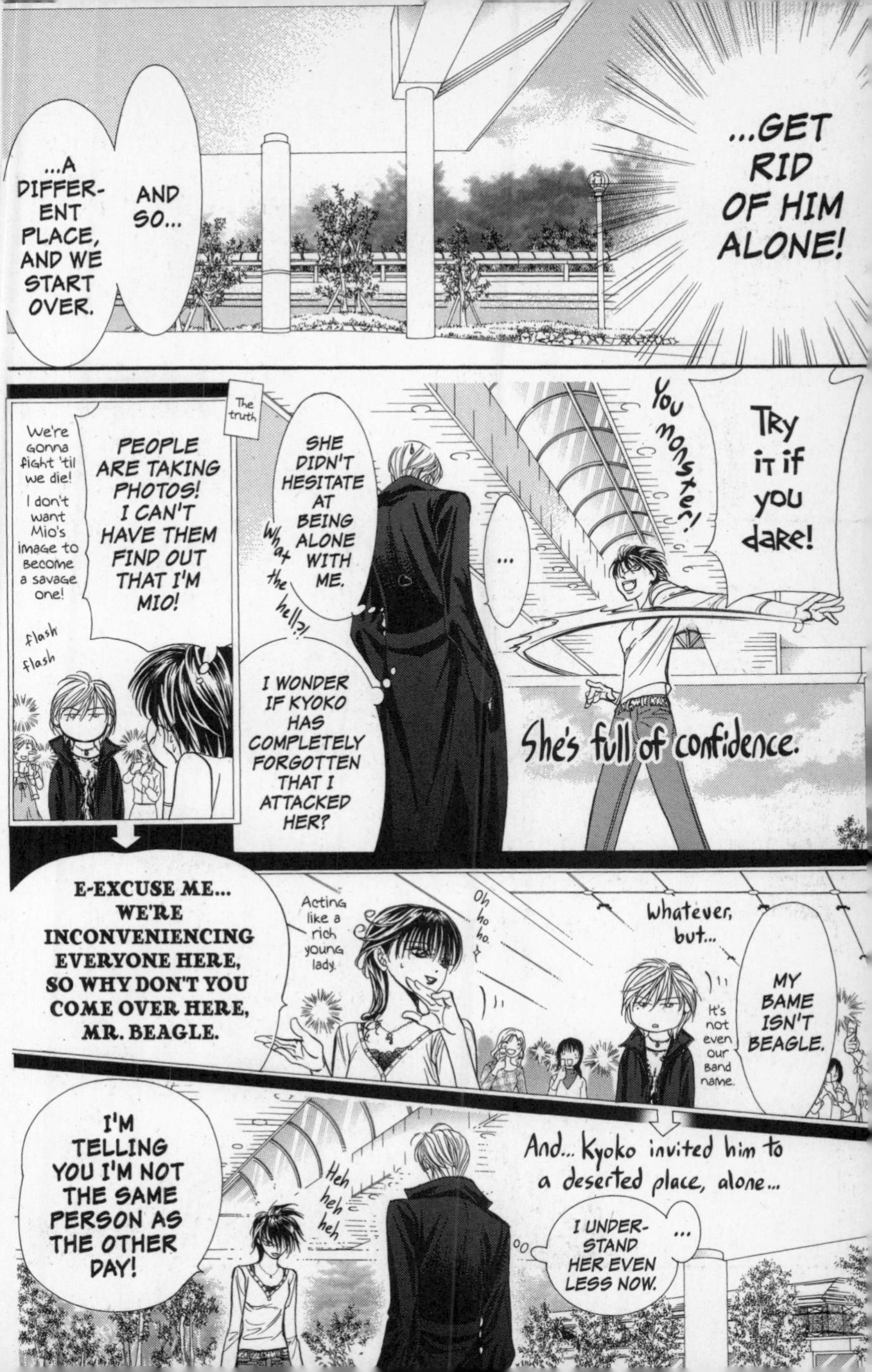
...GET RID OF HIM ALONE!
AND SO...
...A DIFFERENT PLACE, AND WE START OVER.
Try it if you dare!
You monster!
...
She's full of confidence.
SHE DIDN'T HESITATE AT BEING ALONE WITH ME.
What the hell?!
I WONDER IF KYOKO HAS COMPLETELY FORGOTTEN THAT I ATTACKED HER?
The truth
PEOPLE ARE TAKING PHOTOS! I CAN'T HAVE THEM FIND OUT THAT I'M MIO!
We're gonna fight 'til we die!
I don't want Mio's image to become a savage one!
flash
flash
Whatever, but...
MY BAME ISN'T BEAGLE.
It's not even our band name.
Oh ho ho.
Acting like a rich young lady.
E-EXCUSE ME... WE'RE INCONVENIENCING EVERYONE HERE, SO WHY DON'T YOU COME OVER HERE, MR. BEAGLE.
And... Kyoko invited him to a deserted place, alone...
...
I UNDERSTAND HER EVEN LESS NOW.
Heh heh heh
I'M TELLING YOU I'M NOT THE SAME PERSON AS THE OTHER DAY!

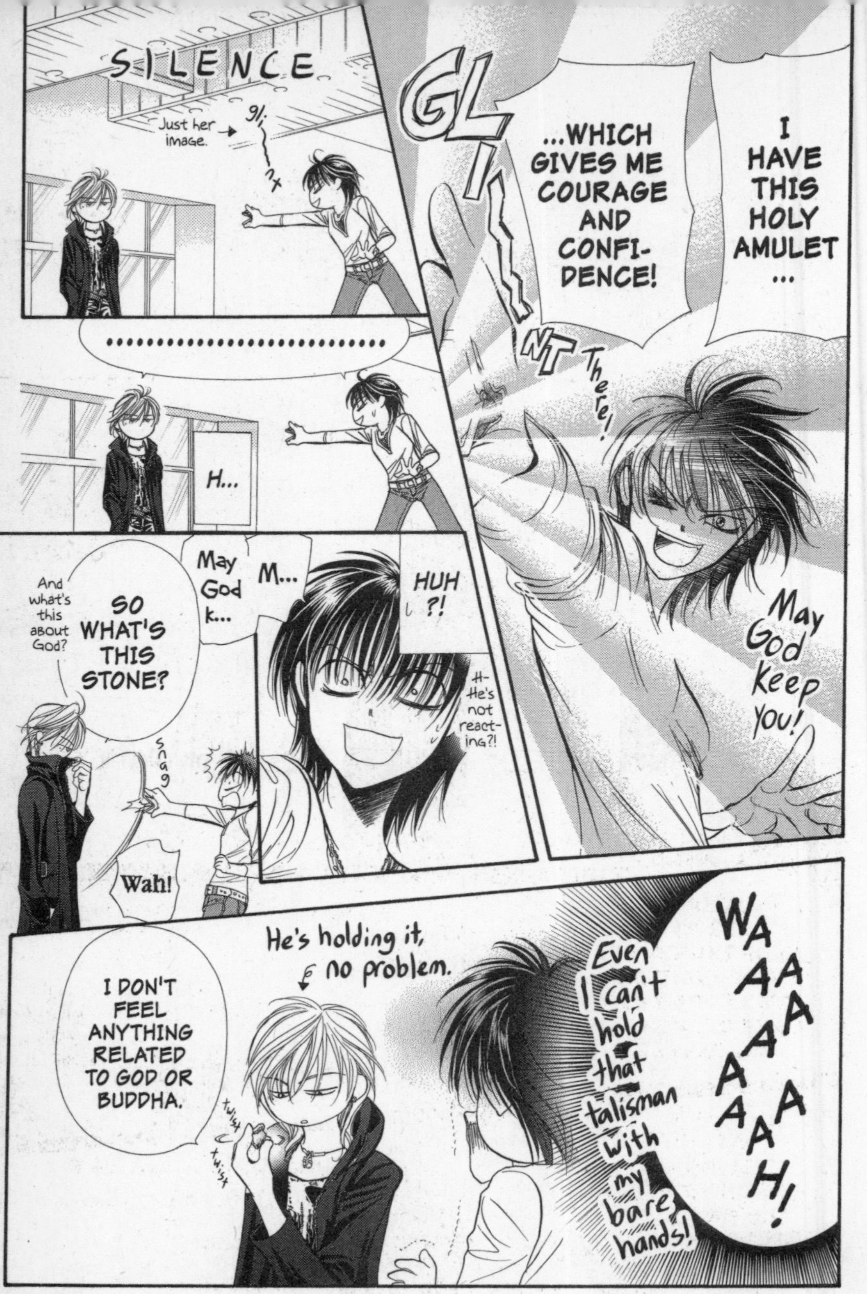
GLINT
I HAVE THIS HOLY AMULET...
...WHICH GIVES ME COURAGE AND CONFIDENCE!
There!
May God keep you!
SILENCE
gli-nt
Just her image.
....
H...
HUH?!
M...
May God k...
H-He's not reacting?!
SO WHAT'S THIS STONE?
And what's this about God?
snag
Wah!
WAAAAAAAAAH!
Even I can't hold that talisman with my bare hands!
He's holding it, no problem.
I DON'T FEEL ANYTHING RELATED TO GOD OR BUDDHA.
twist
twist

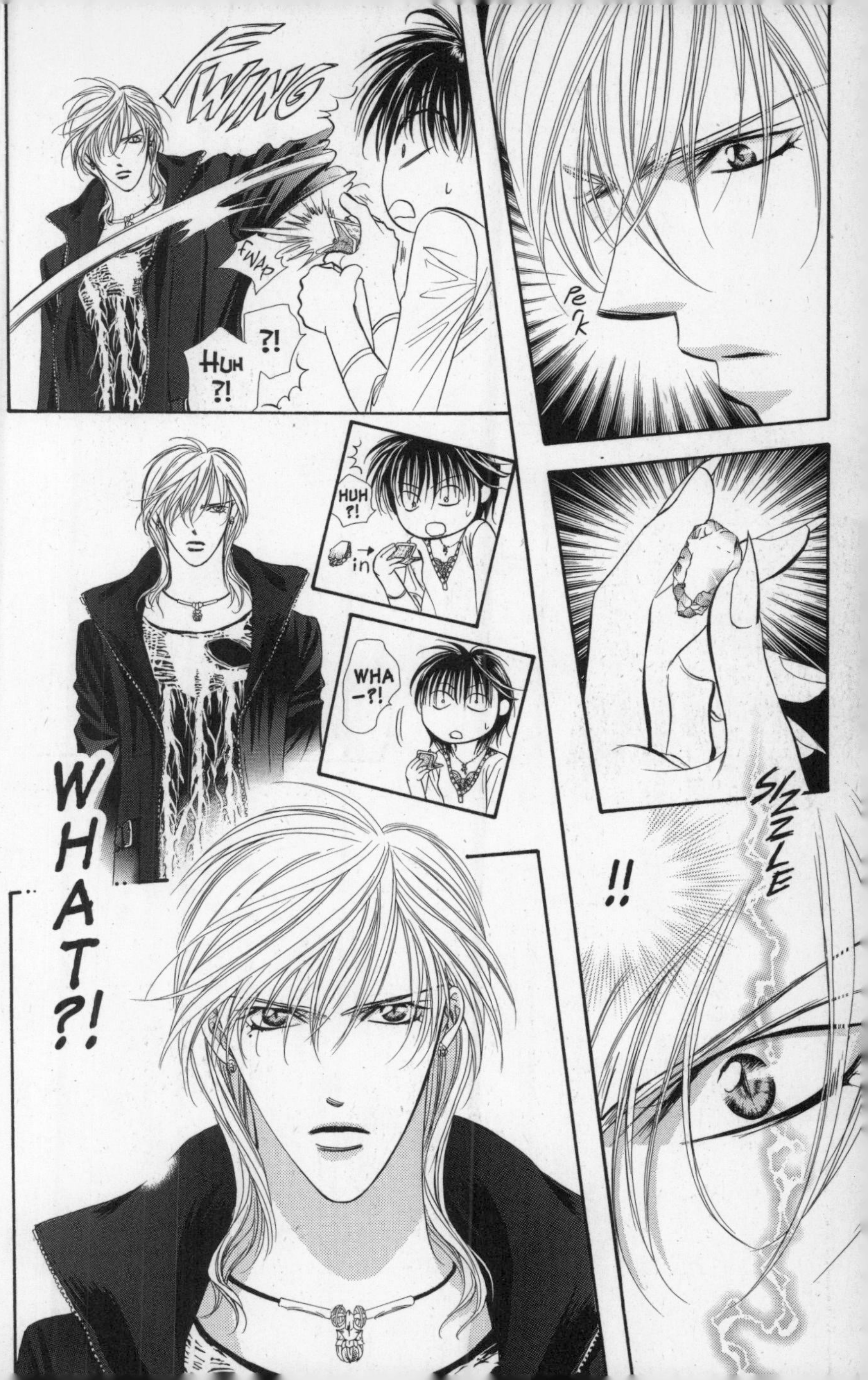
PERK
FWING
FWAP
?!
HUH ?!
HUH ?!
in
WHA —?!
WHAT ?!
SIZZLE
!!

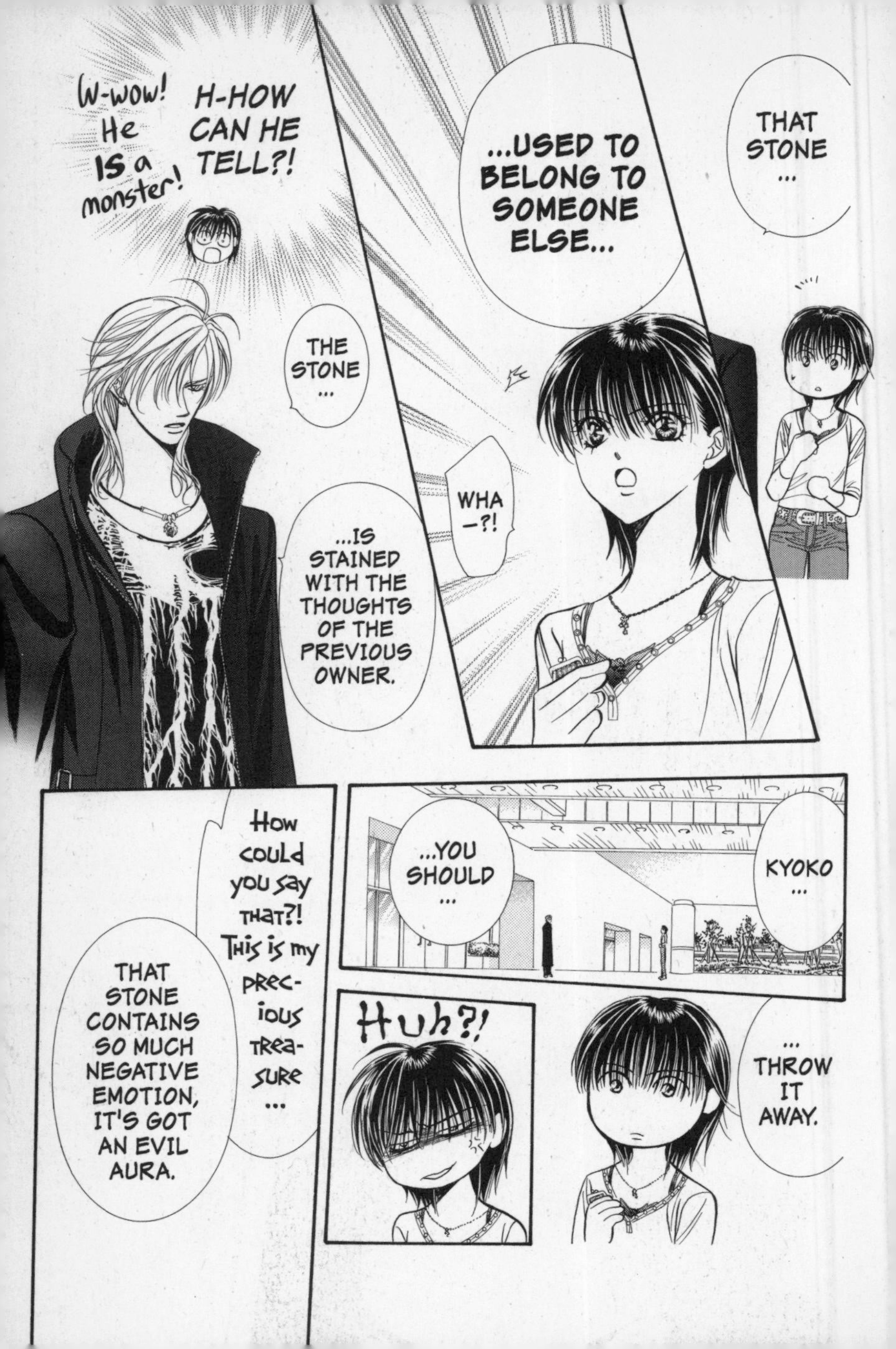

THAT STONE ...
...USED TO BELONG TO SOMEONE ELSE...
WHA—?!
H-HOW CAN HE TELL?!
W-WOW! He IS a monster!
THE STONE ...
...IS STAINED WITH THE THOUGHTS OF THE PREVIOUS OWNER.
KYOKO ...
...YOU SHOULD ...
... THROW IT AWAY.
Huh?!
How could you say THAT?! This is my prec-ious trea-sure ...
THAT STONE CONTAINS SO MUCH NEGATIVE EMOTION, IT'S GOT AN EVIL AURA.

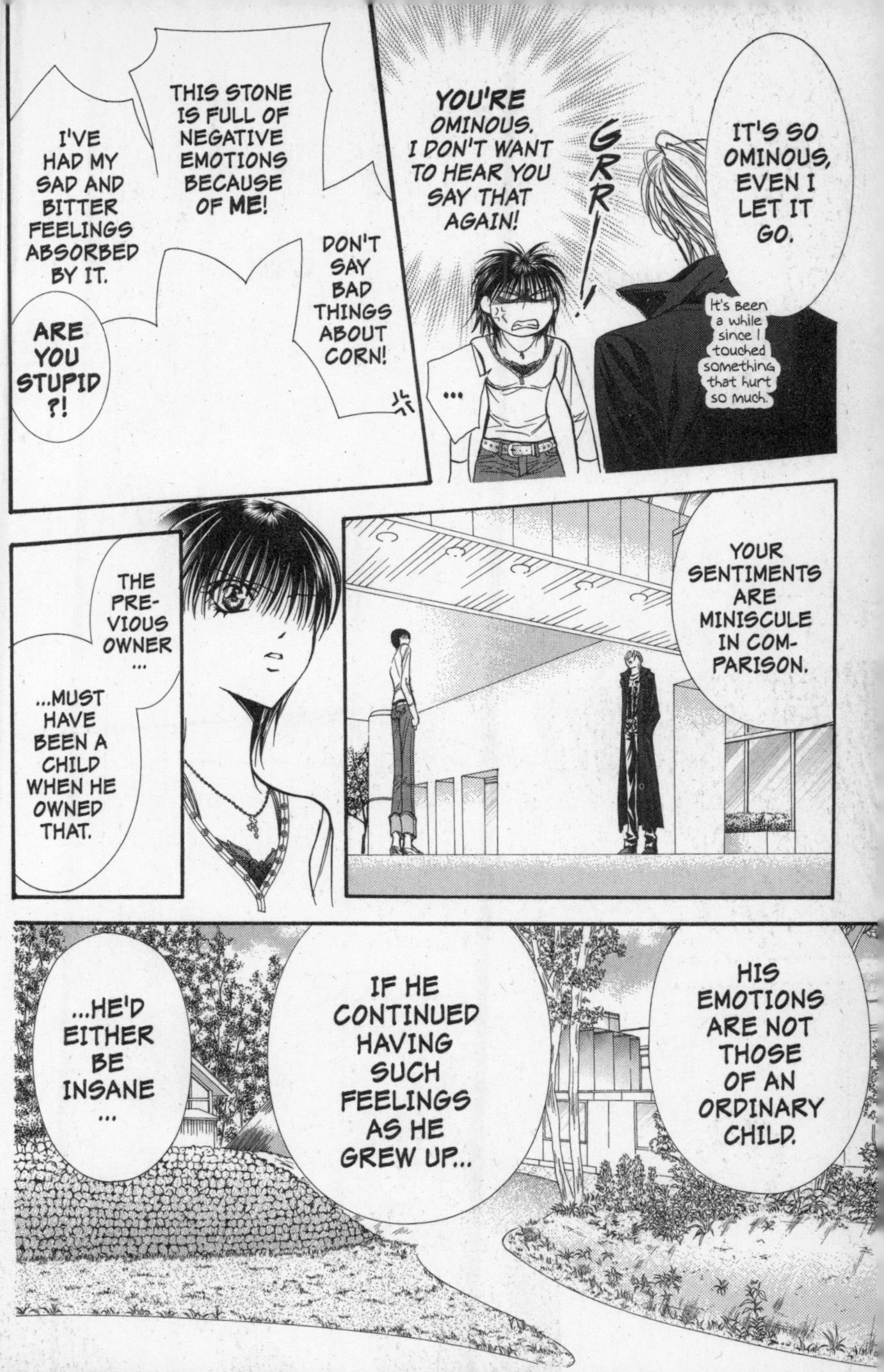
IT'S SO OMINOUS, EVEN I LET IT GO.
It's been a while since I touched something that hurt so much.
GRR!
YOU'RE OMINOUS. I DON'T WANT TO HEAR YOU SAY THAT AGAIN!
...
THIS STONE IS FULL OF NEGATIVE EMOTIONS BECAUSE OF ME!
I'VE HAD MY SAD AND BITTER FEELINGS ABSORBED BY IT.
DON'T SAY BAD THINGS ABOUT CORN!
ARE YOU STUPID?!
YOUR SENTIMENTS ARE MINISCULE IN COMPARISON.
THE PREVIOUS OWNER...
...MUST HAVE BEEN A CHILD WHEN HE OWNED THAT.
HIS EMOTIONS ARE NOT THOSE OF AN ORDINARY CHILD.
IF HE CONTINUED HAVING SUCH FEELINGS AS HE GREW UP...
...HE'D EITHER BE INSANE...

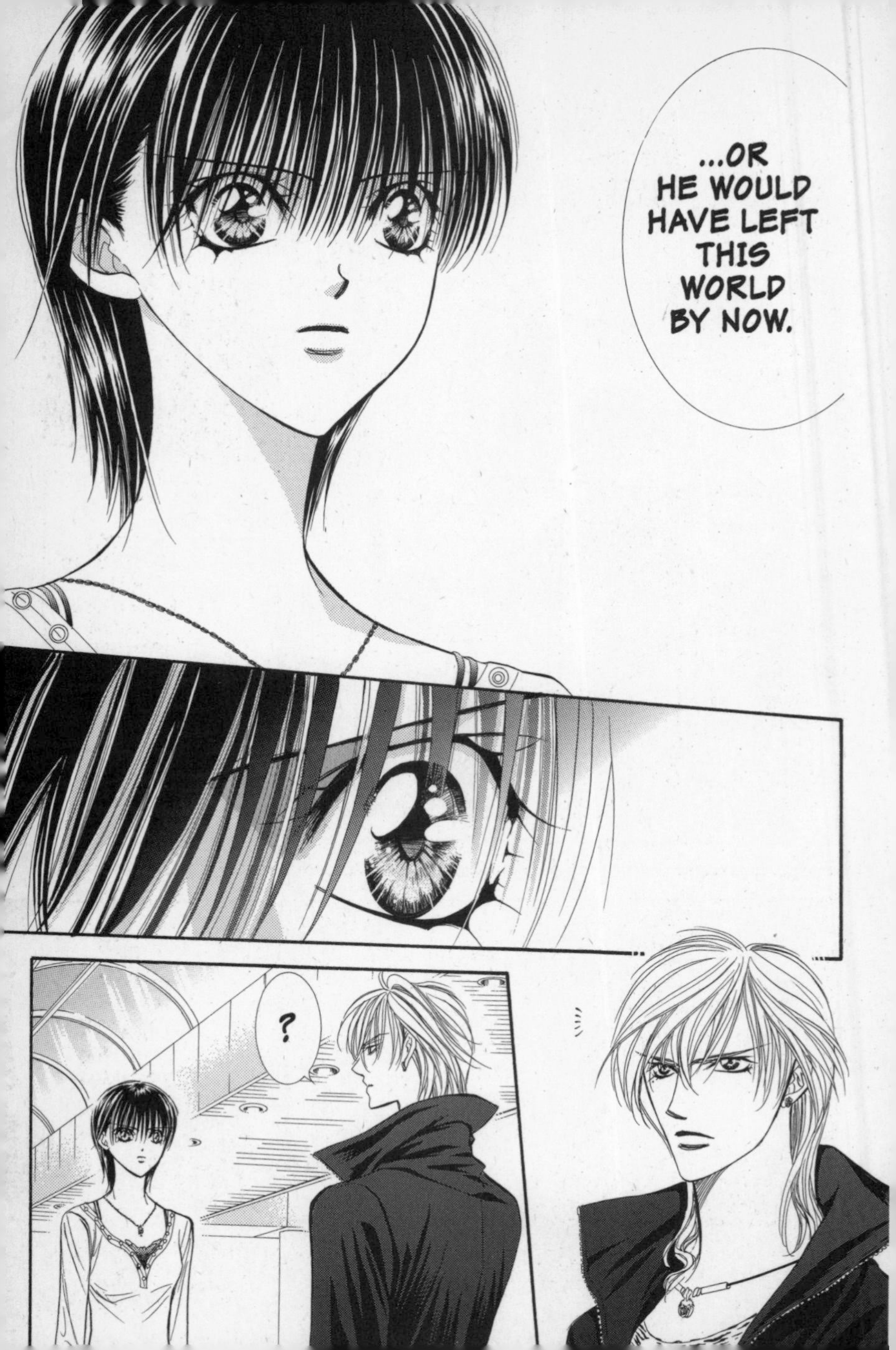
...OR HE WOULD HAVE LEFT THIS WORLD BY NOW.
?

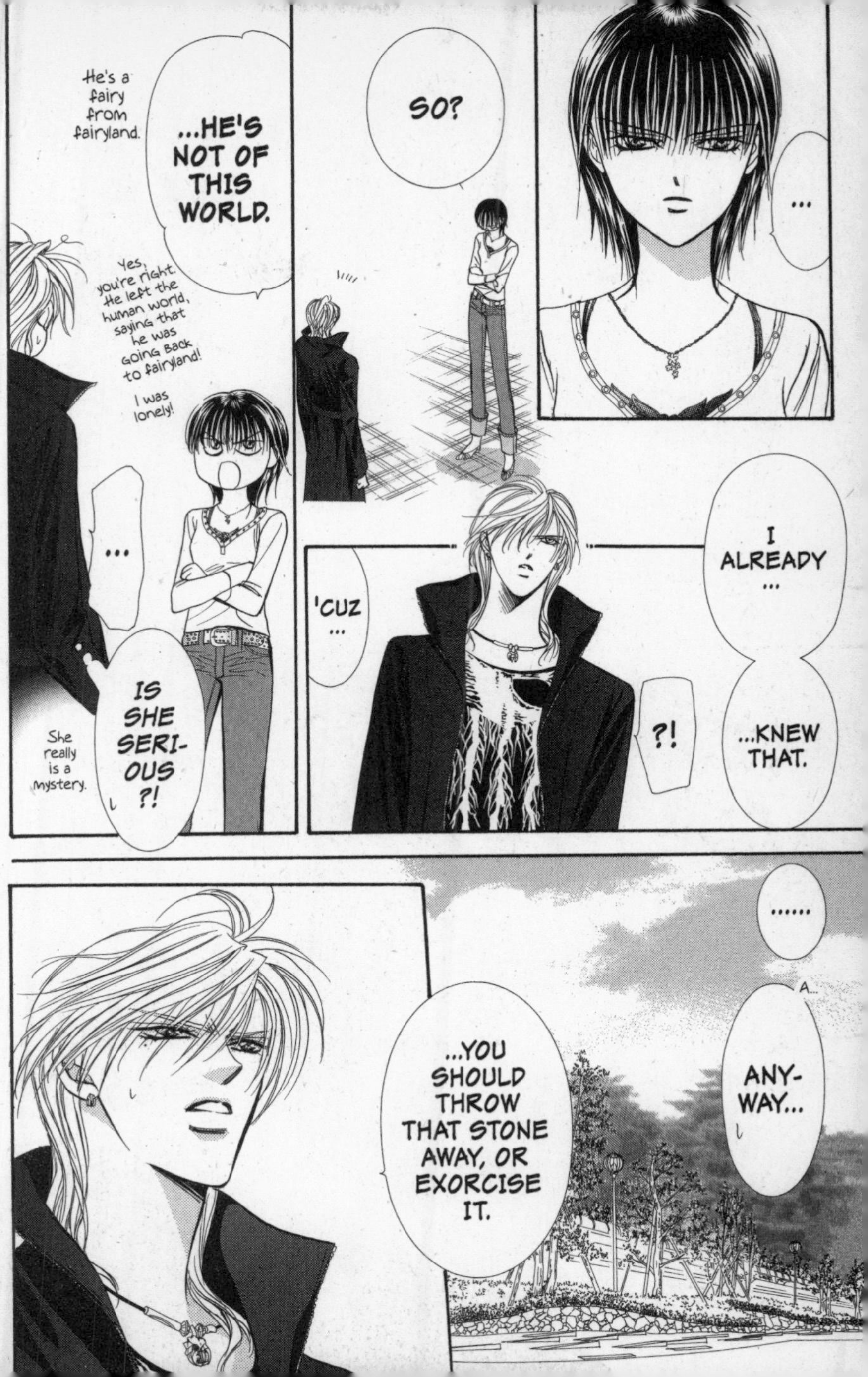
...
SO?
I ALREADY ...
...KNEW THAT.
?!
'CUZ ...
...HE'S NOT OF THIS WORLD.
He's a fairy from fairyland.
Yes, you're right. He left the human world, saying that he was going back to fairyland!
I was lonely!
...
IS SHE SERI-OUS ?!
She really is a mystery.
......
A... ANY-WAY...
...YOU SHOULD THROW THAT STONE AWAY, OR EXORCISE IT.

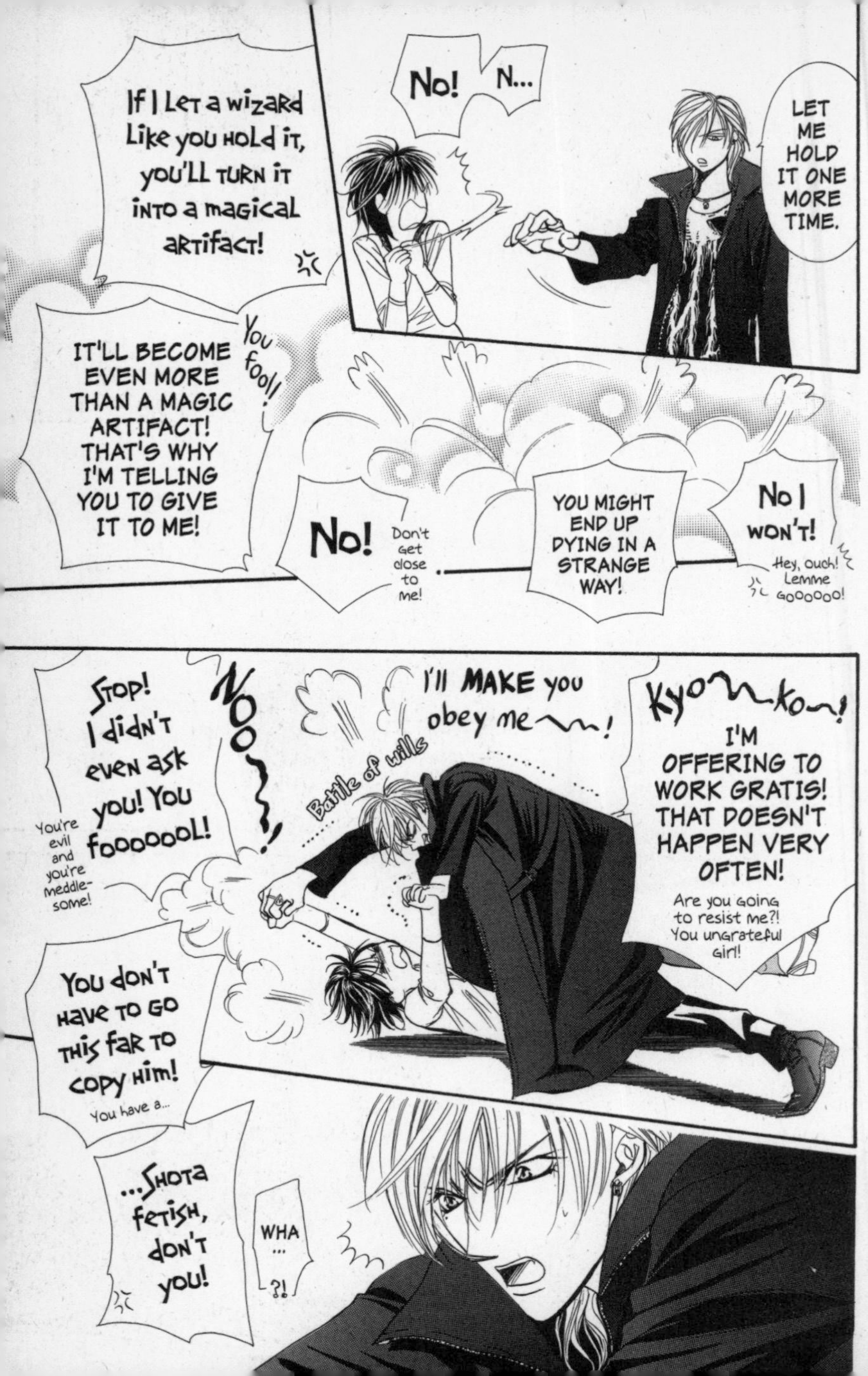
LET ME HOLD IT ONE MORE TIME.
N...
No!
If I let a wizard like you hold it, you'll turn it into a magical artifact!
No I won't!
Hey, ouch! Lemme goooooo!
YOU MIGHT END UP DYING IN A STRANGE WAY!
No!
Don't get close to me!
IT'LL BECOME EVEN MORE THAN A MAGIC ARTIFACT! THAT'S WHY I'M TELLING YOU TO GIVE IT TO ME!
You fool!
Kyo~ko~!
I'M OFFERING TO WORK GRATIS! THAT DOESN'T HAPPEN VERY OFTEN!
Are you going to resist me?! You ungrateful girl!
I'll MAKE you obey me~!
Battle of wills
Noo~!
Stop! I didn't even ask you! You foooooL!
You're evil and you're meddle-some!
You don't have to go this far to copy him!
You have a...
...Shota fetish, don't you!
WHA ... ?!

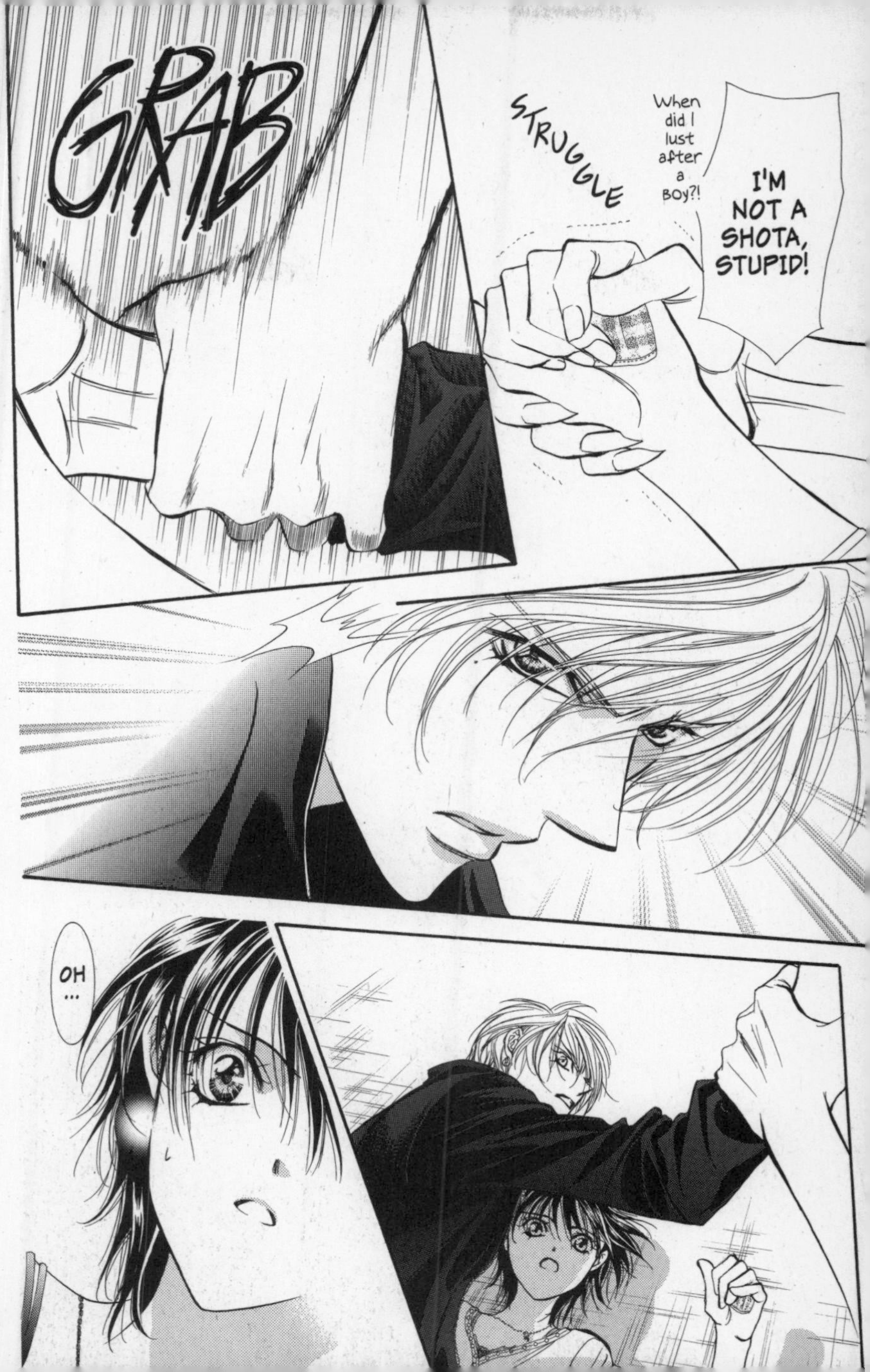
I'M NOT A SHOTA, STUPID!
When did I lust after a Boy?!
STRUGGLE
GRAB
OH ...

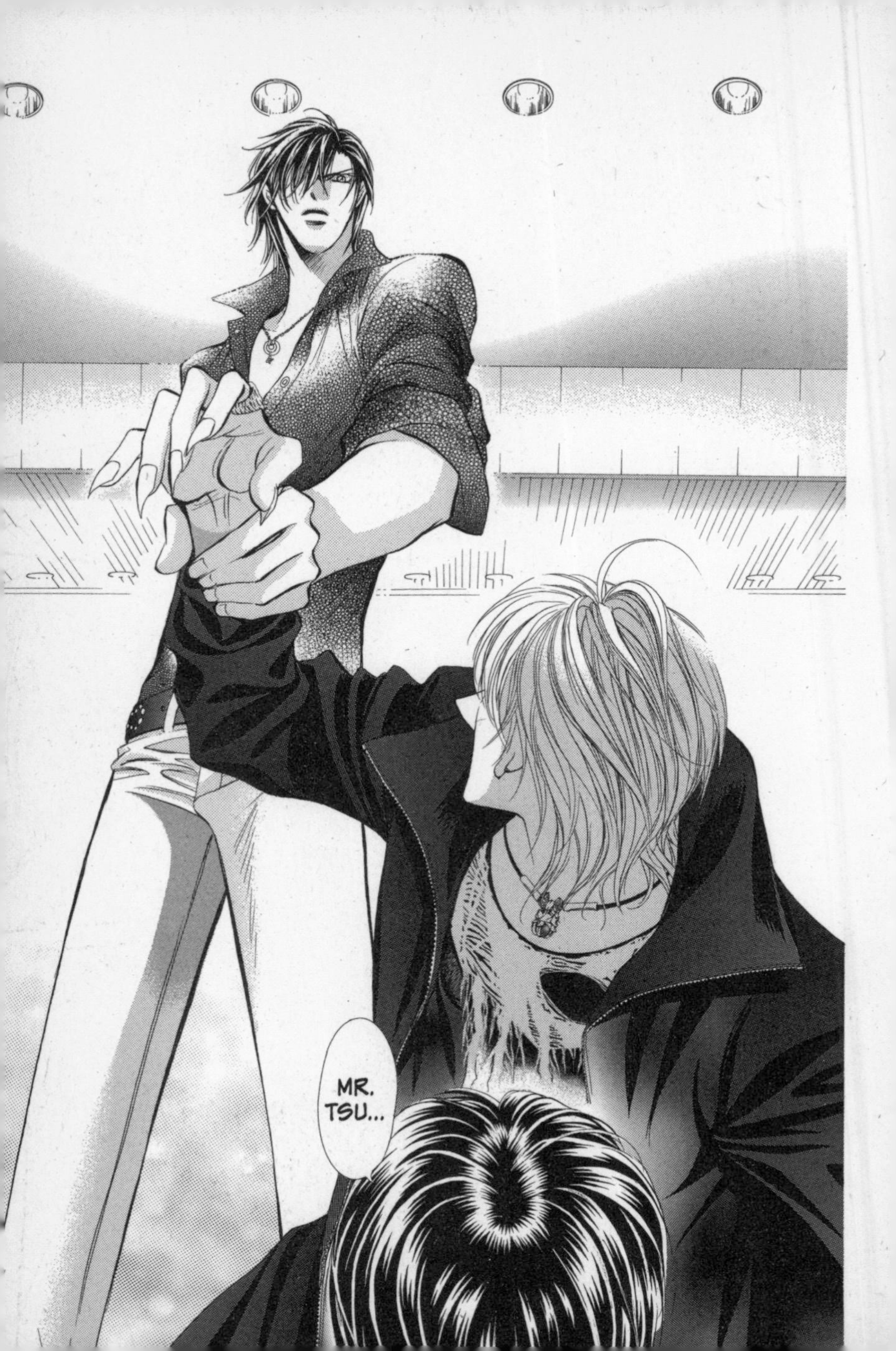
MR. TSU...

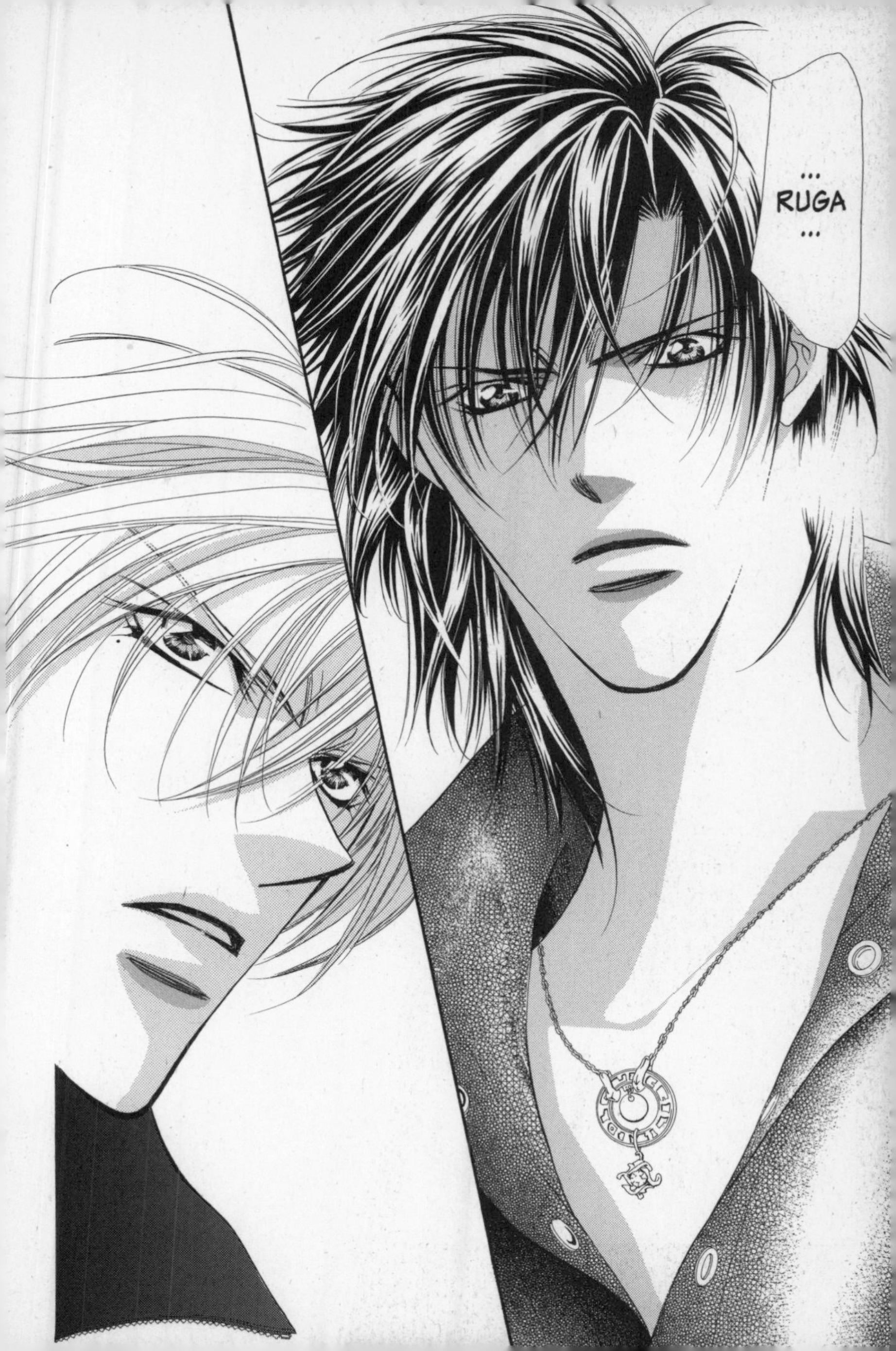
... RUGA ...

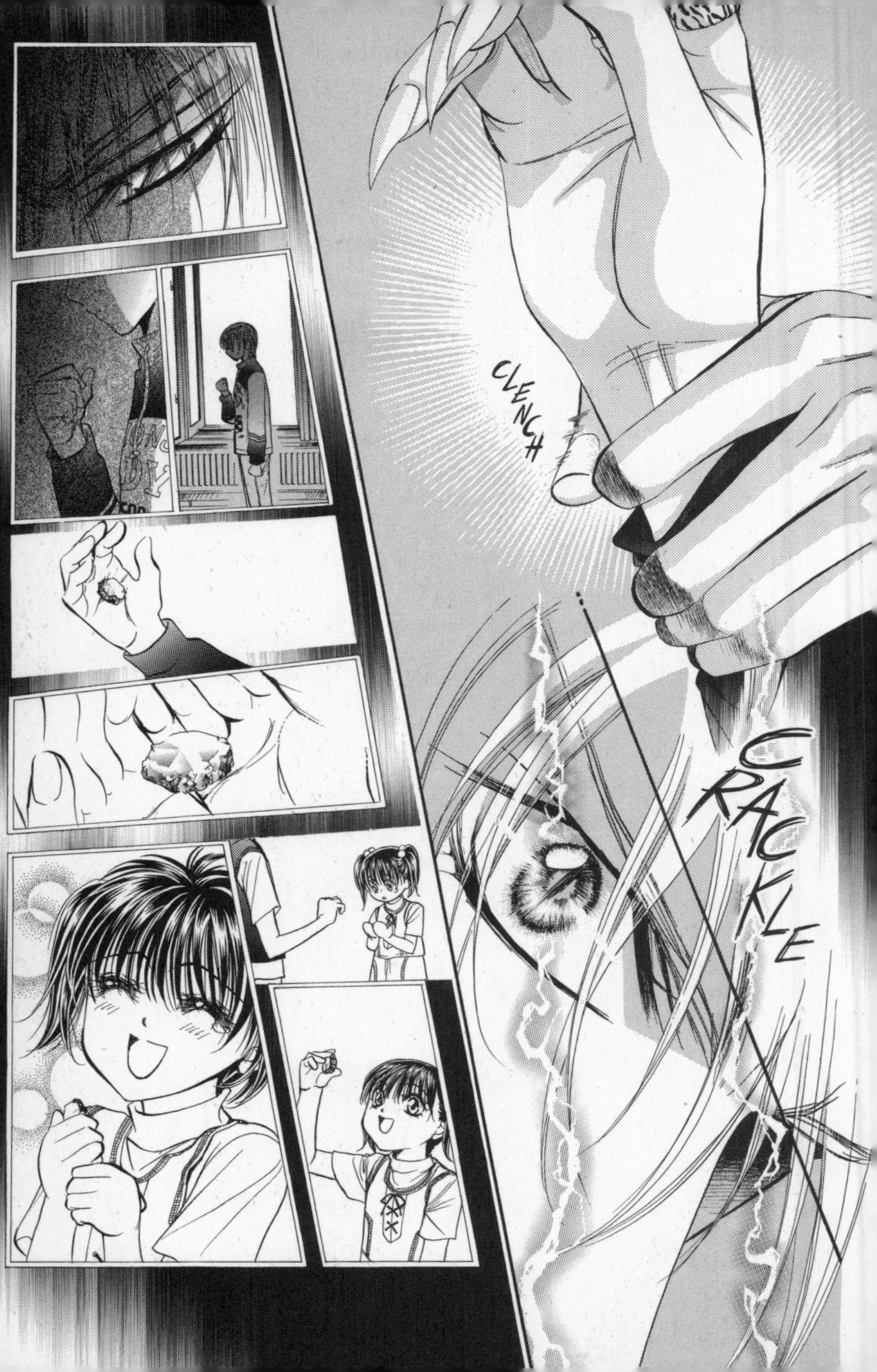
CLENCH
CRACKLE

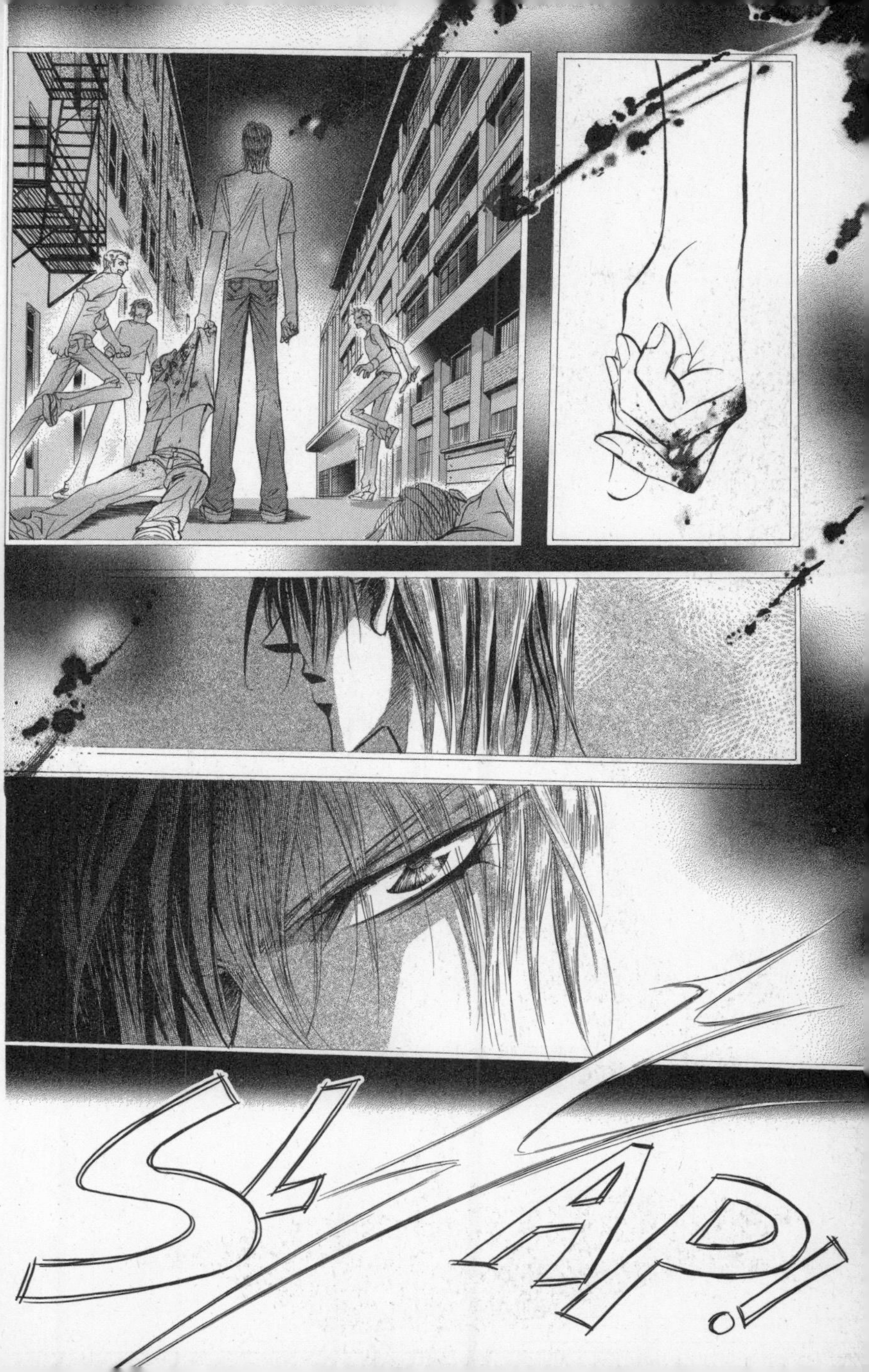
SLAP!

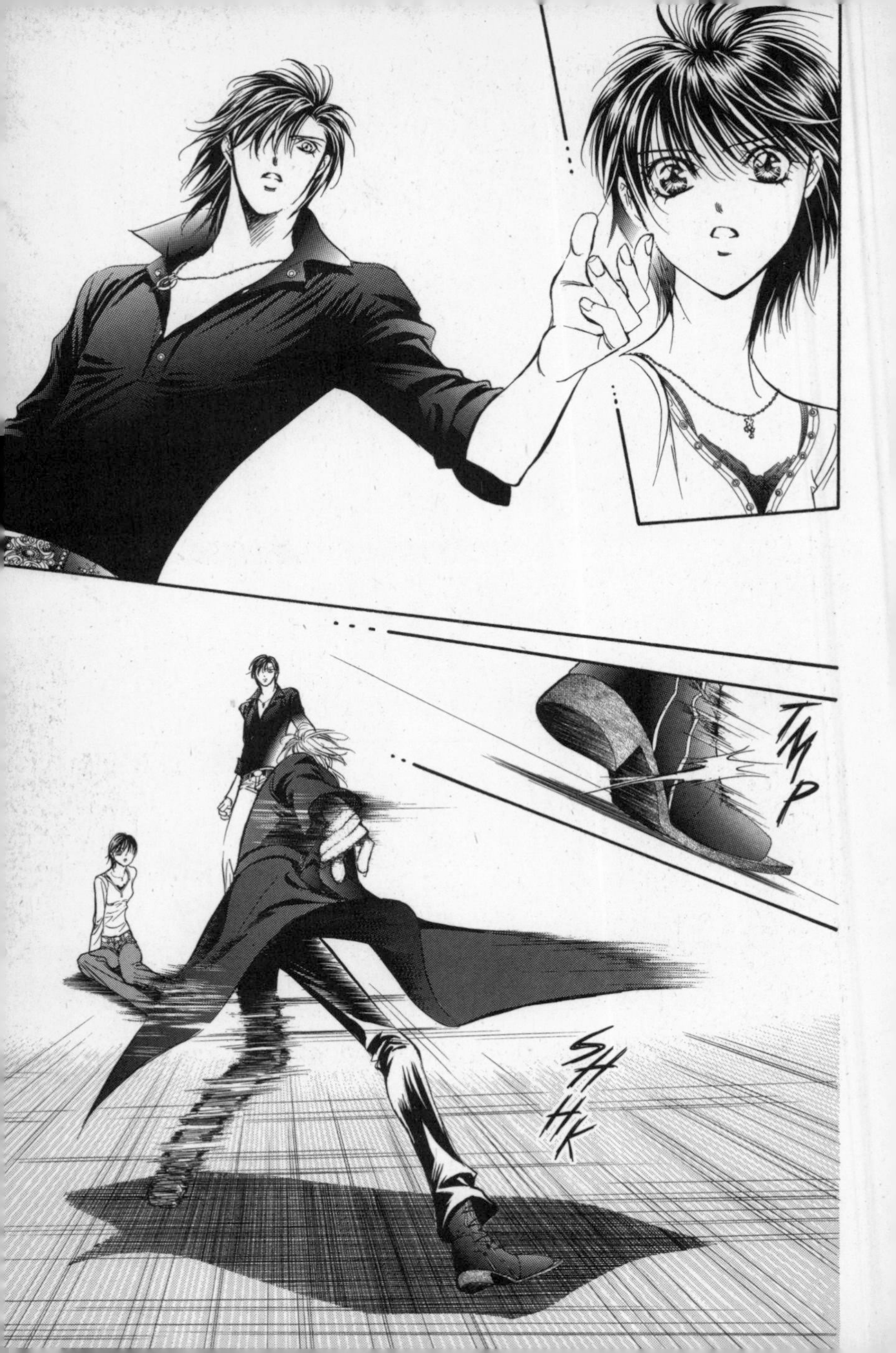
TMP
SHHK

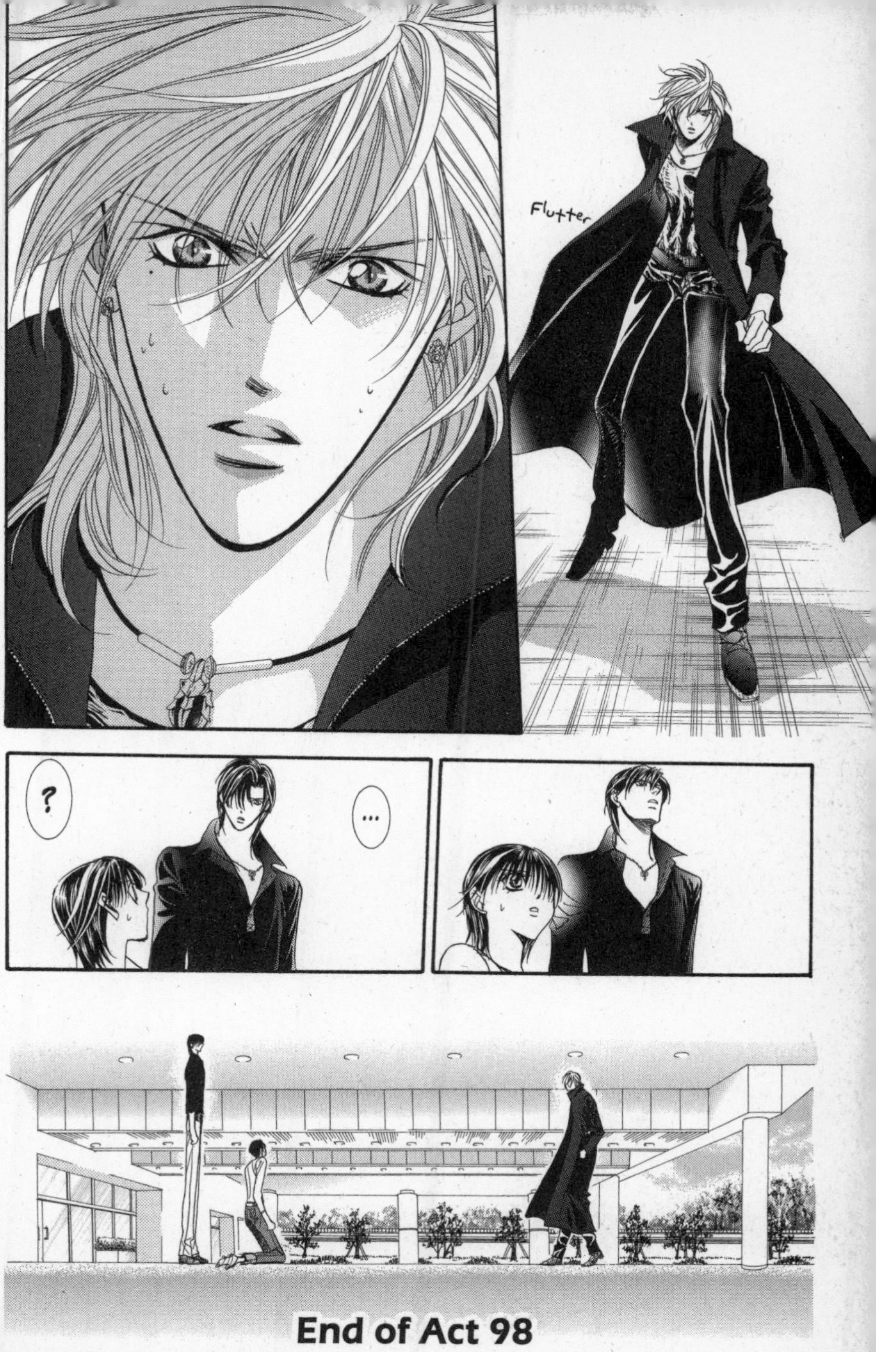
Flutter
...
?
End of Act 98

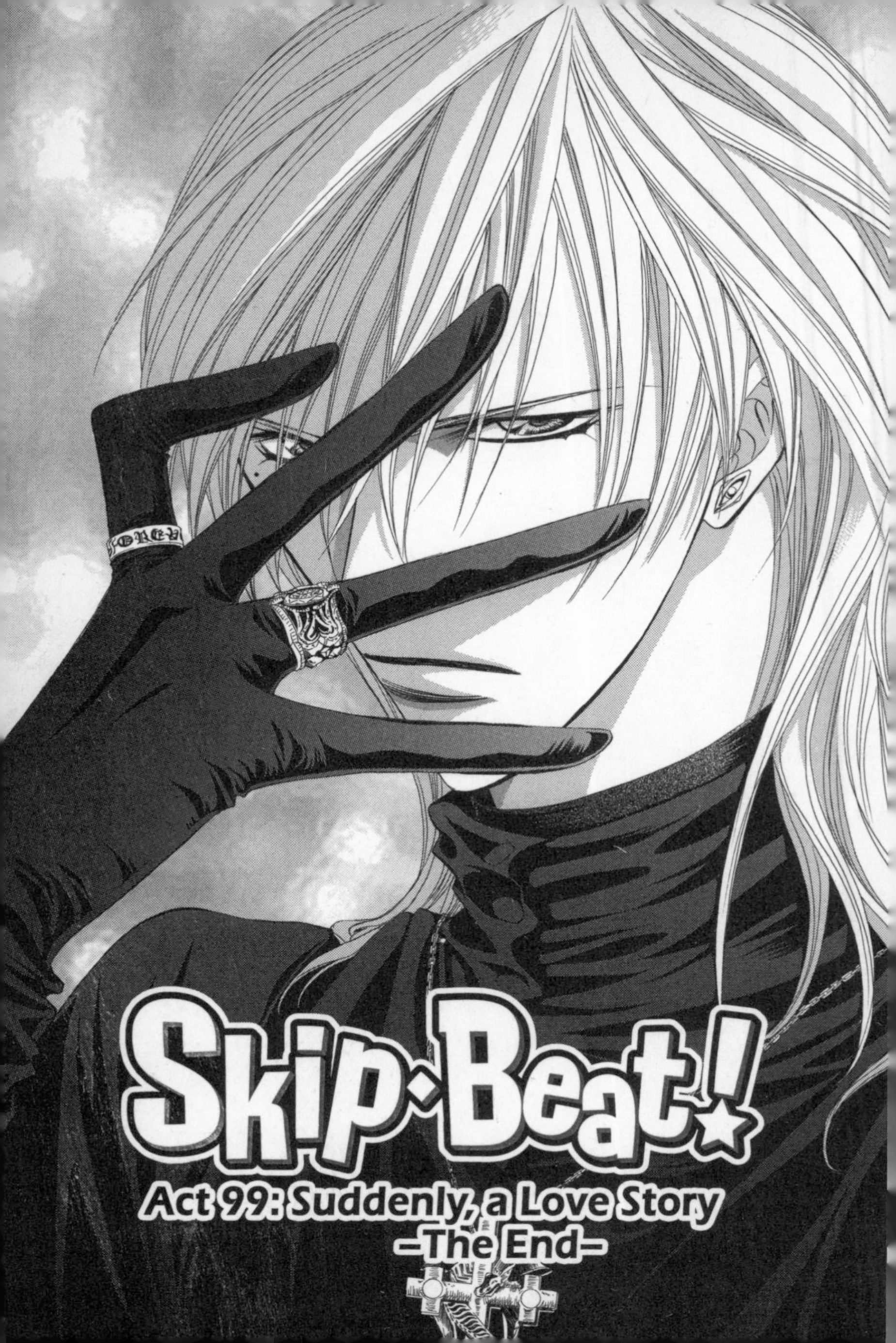
Skip·Beat!
Act 99: Suddenly, a Love Story
-The End-

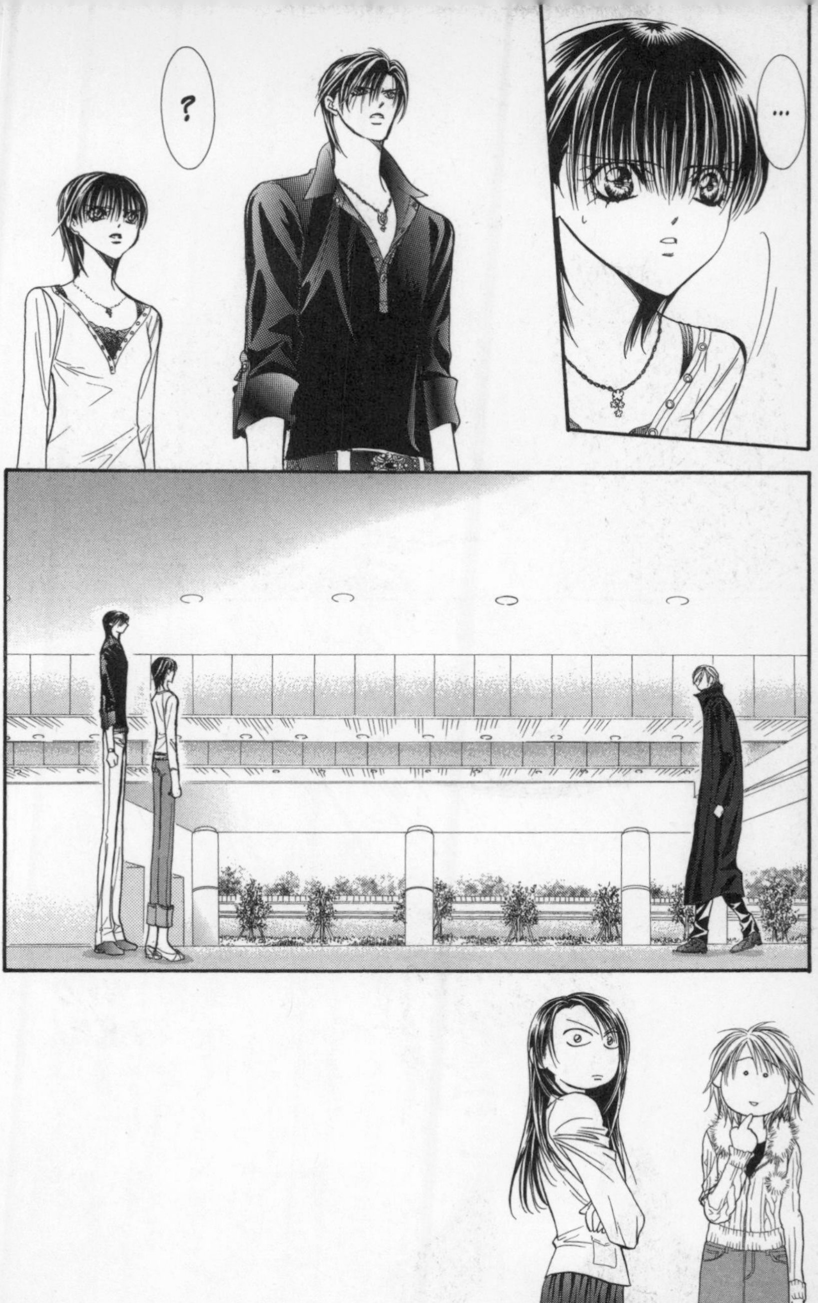
...
?

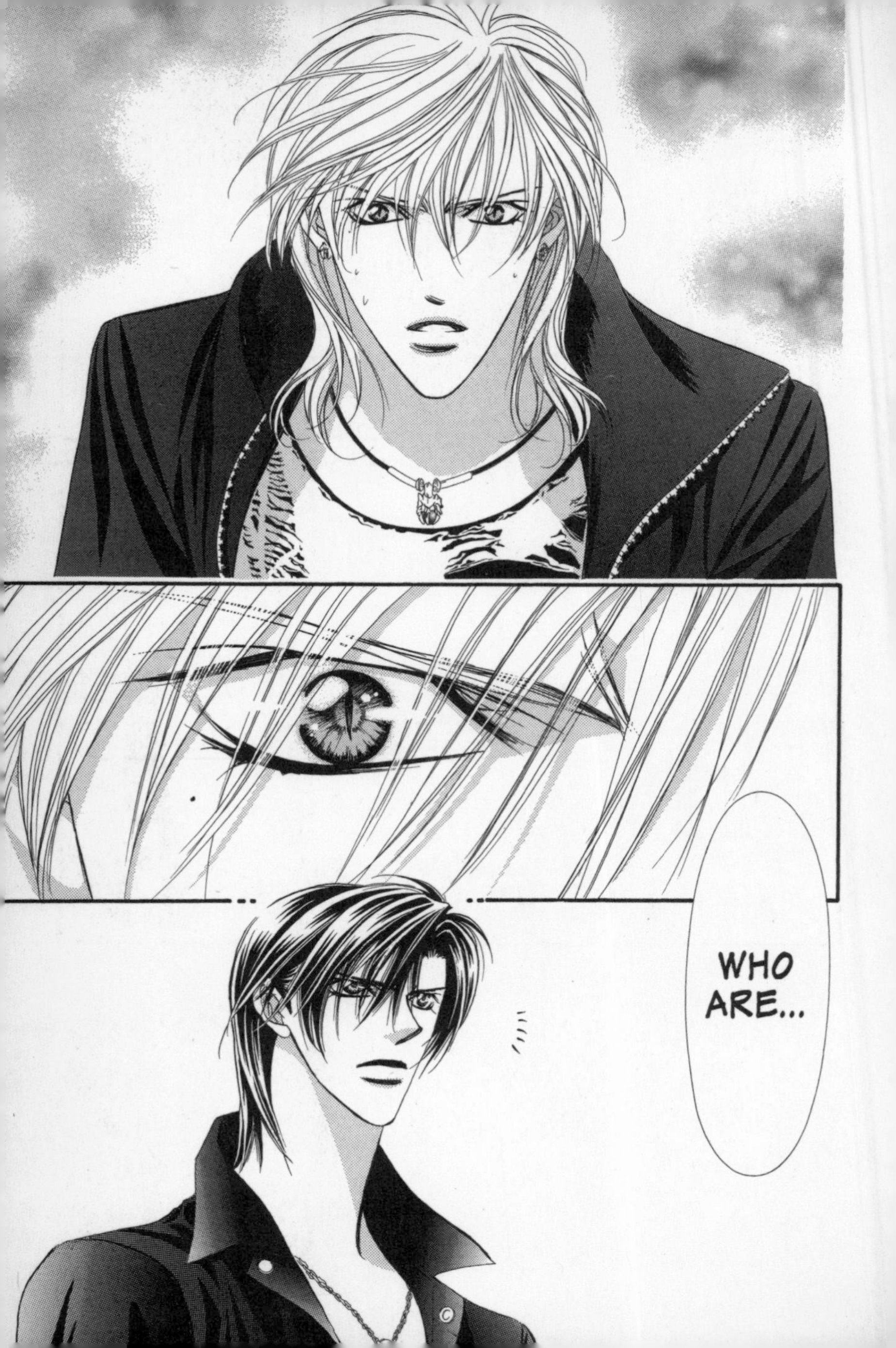
WHO ARE...

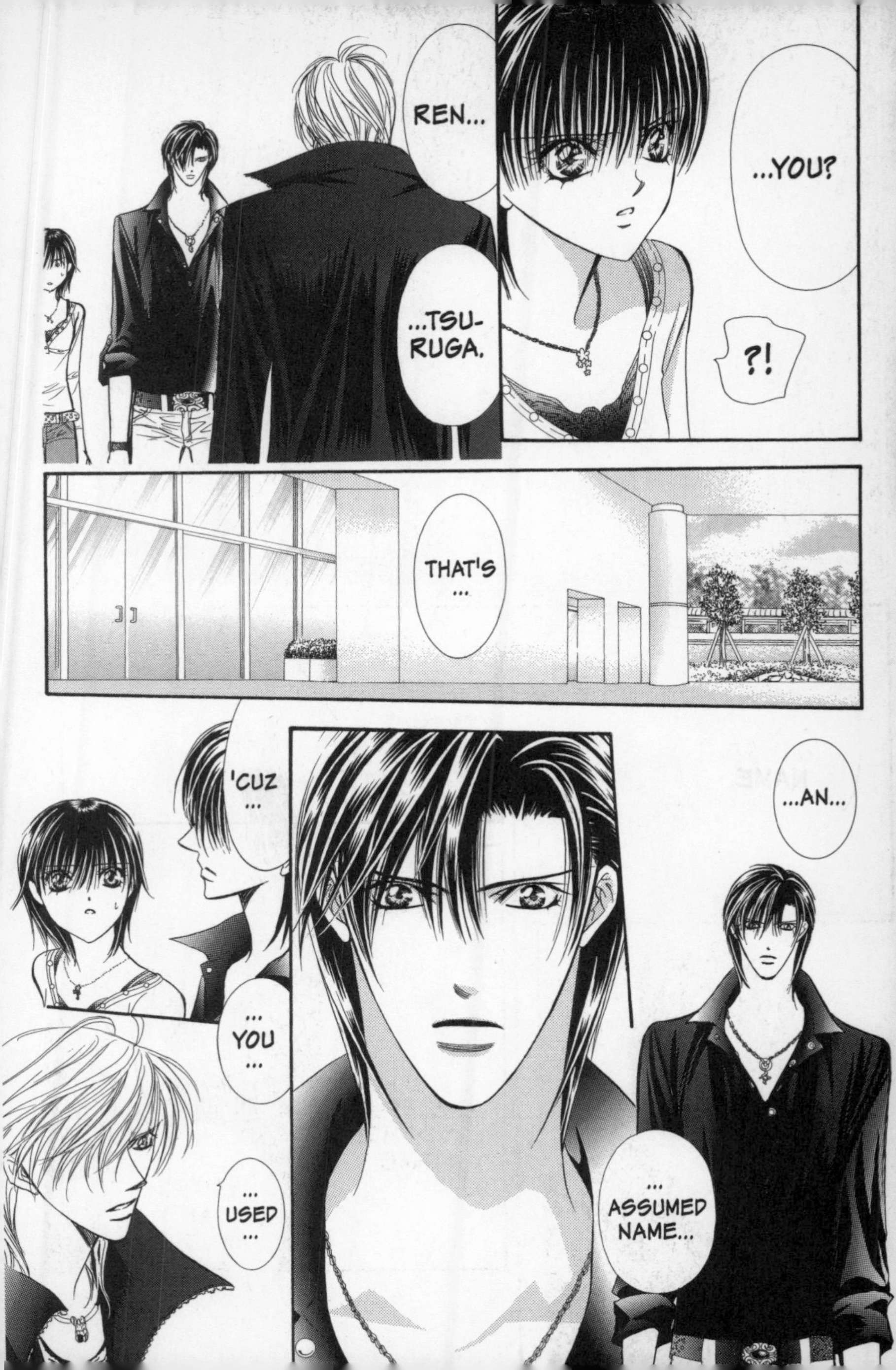
...YOU?
?!
REN...
...TSU-RUGA.
THAT'S ...
...AN...
... ASSUMED NAME...
'CUZ ...
... YOU ...
... USED ...

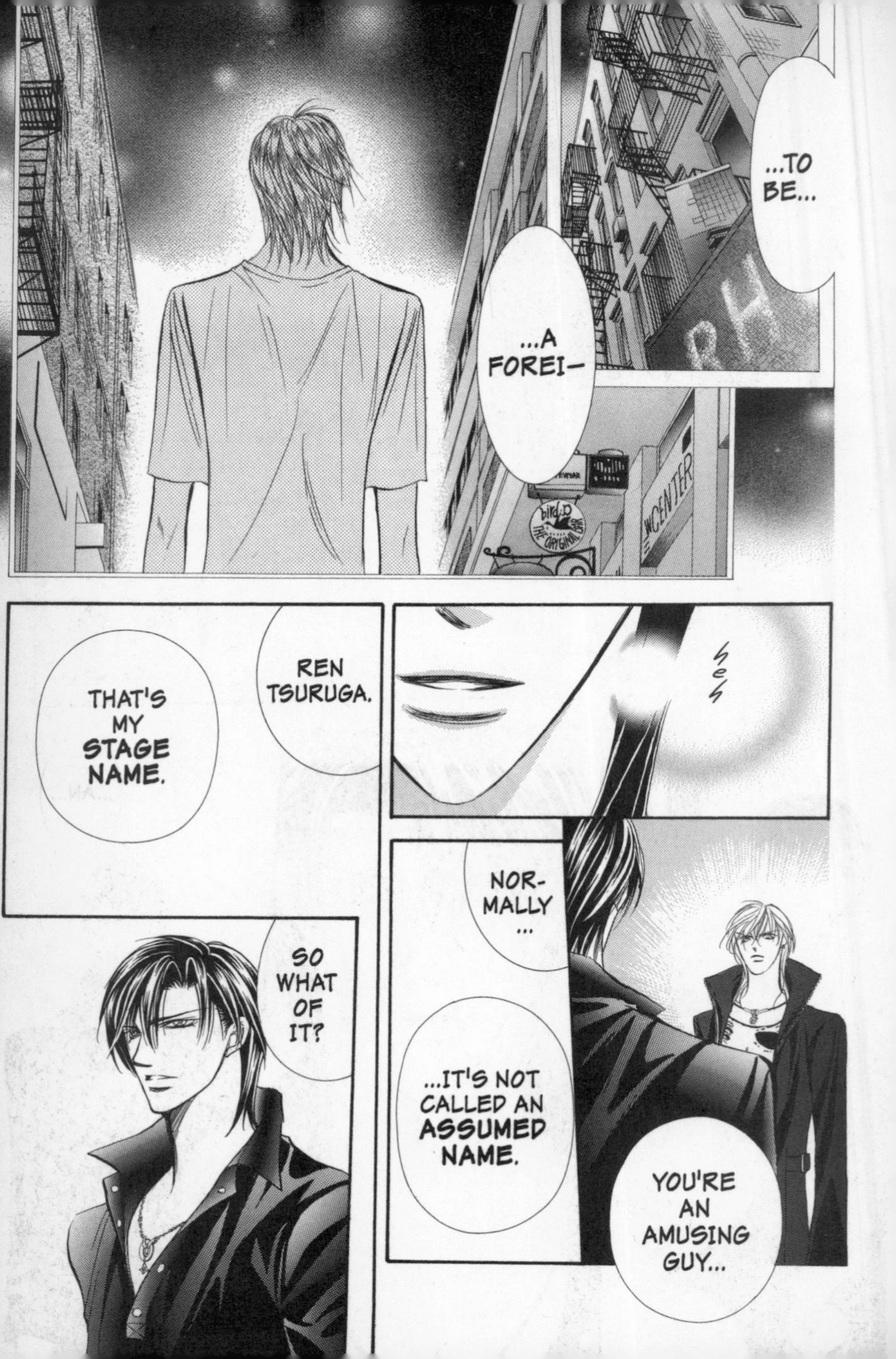
...TO BE...
...A FOREI—
heh
REN TSURUGA.
THAT'S MY STAGE NAME.
NOR-MALLY...
...IT'S NOT CALLED AN ASSUMED NAME.
YOU'RE AN AMUSING GUY...
SO WHAT OF IT?

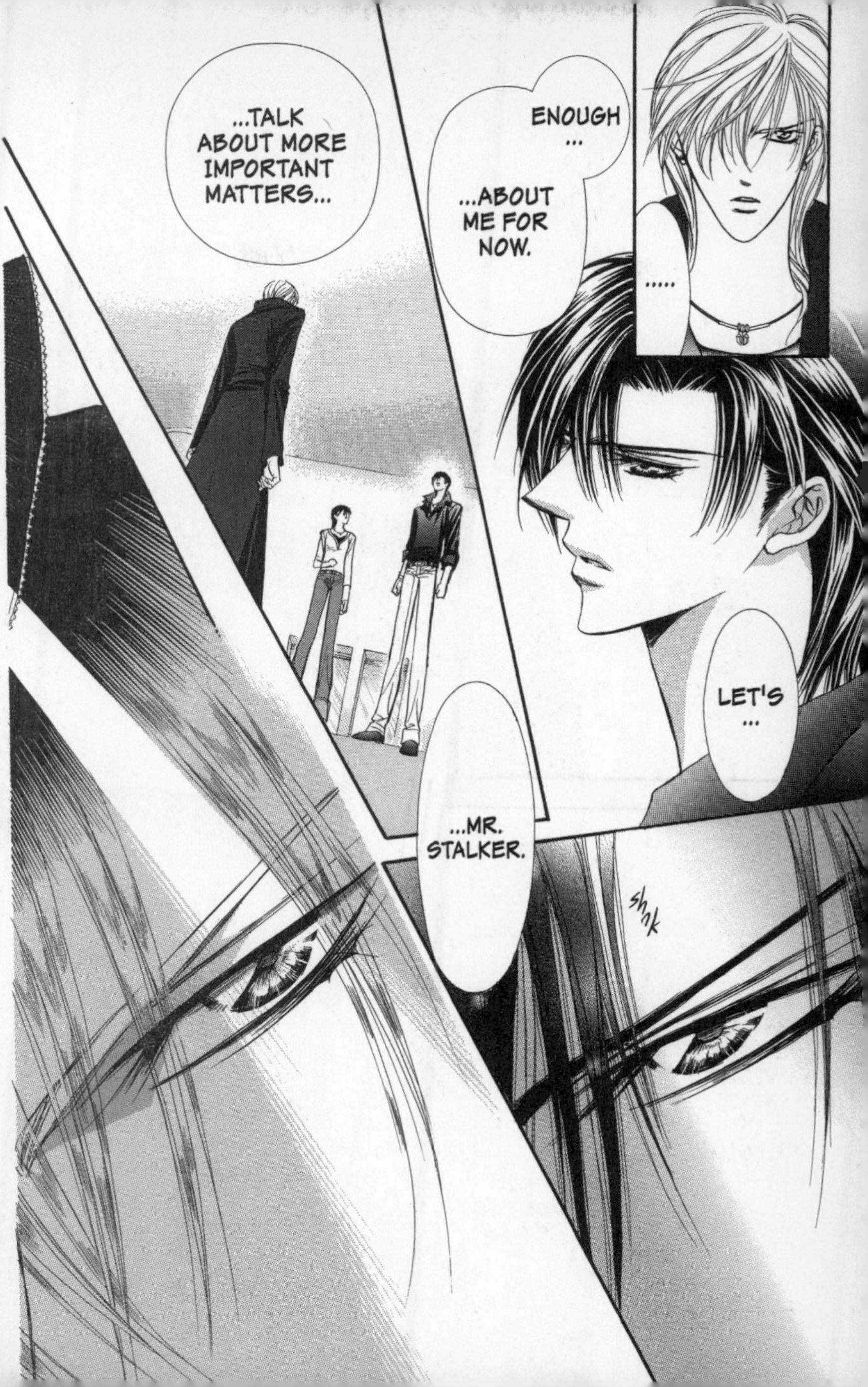
.....
ENOUGH ... ...ABOUT ME FOR NOW.
LET'S ...
...TALK ABOUT MORE IMPORTANT MATTERS...
...MR. STALKER.
shnk

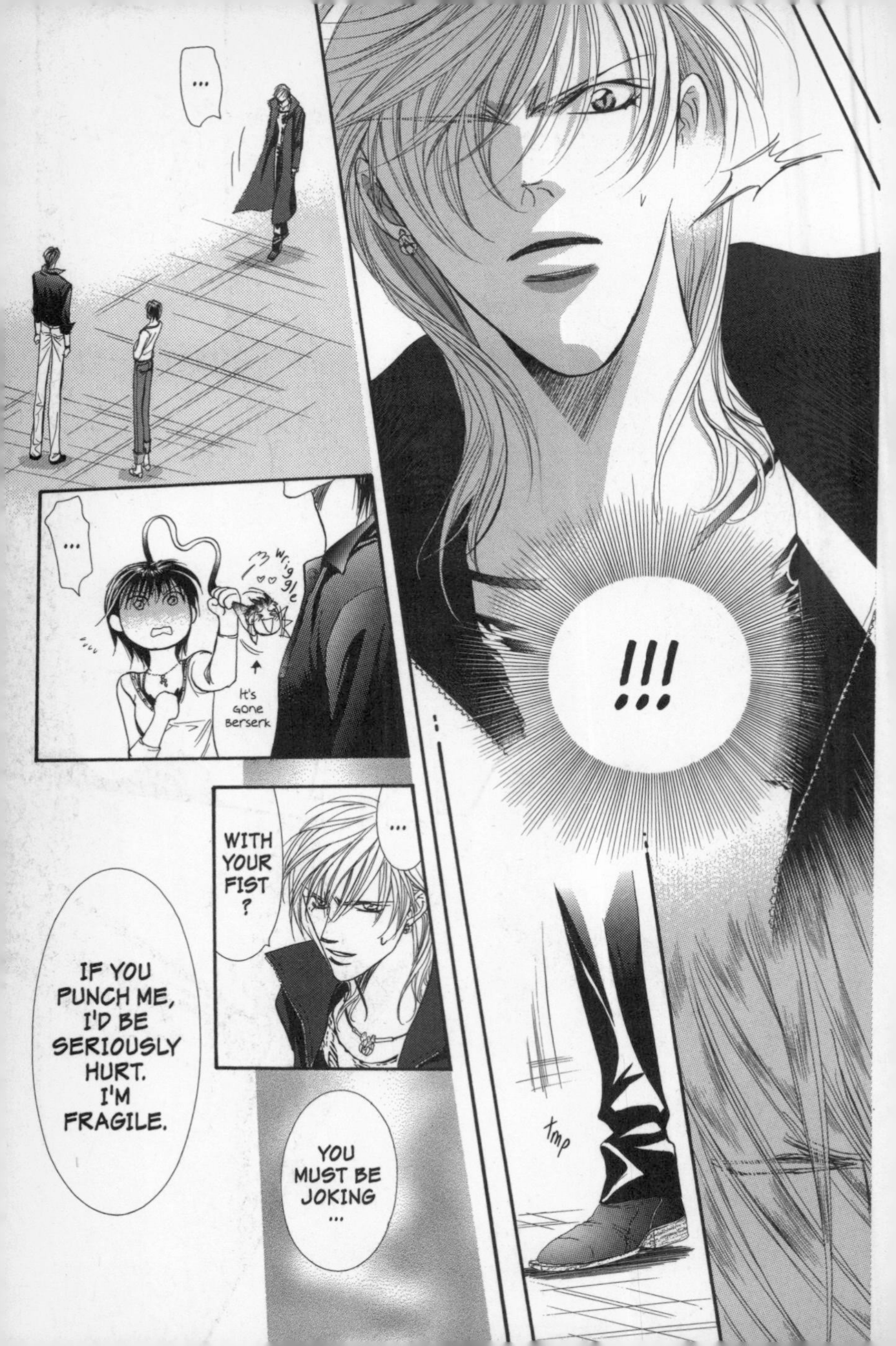
!!!
Xmp
...
...
Wriggle
It's Gone Berserk
...
WITH YOUR FIST?
IF YOU PUNCH ME, I'D BE SERIOUSLY HURT. I'M FRAGILE.
YOU MUST BE JOKING ...

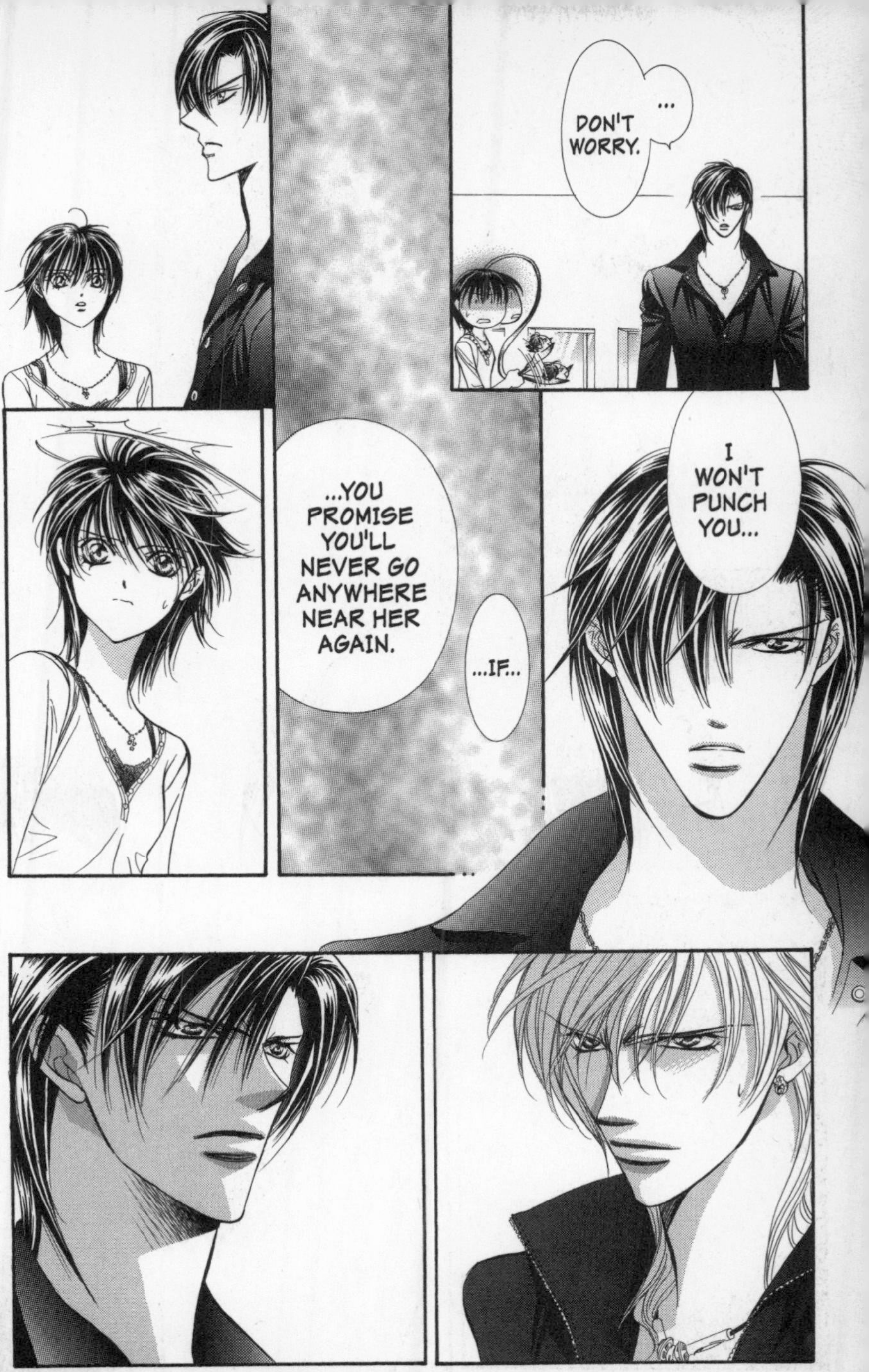
... DON'T WORRY.
I WON'T PUNCH YOU...
...IF...
...YOU PROMISE YOU'LL NEVER GO ANYWHERE NEAR HER AGAIN.

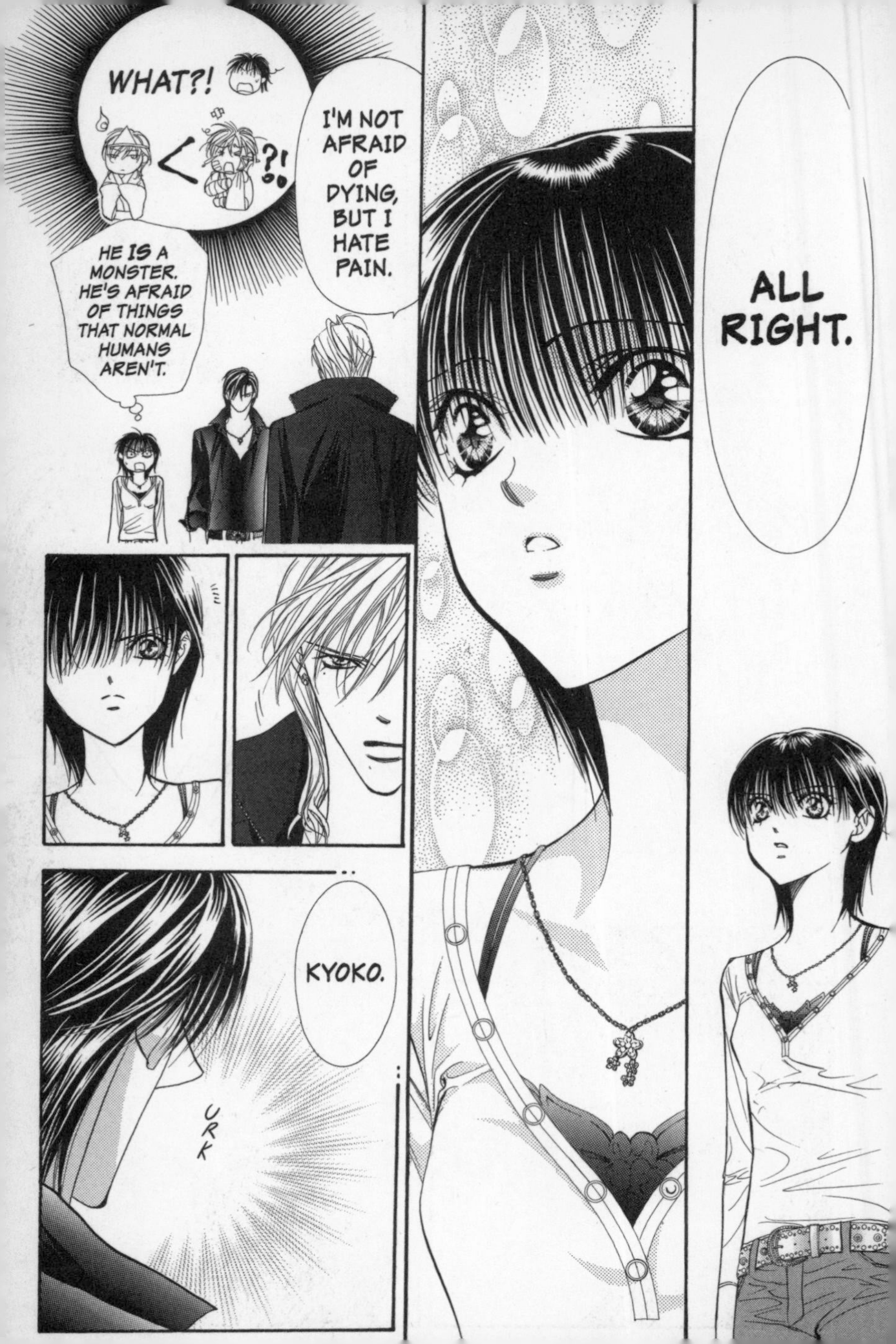
ALL RIGHT.
I'M NOT AFRAID OF DYING, BUT I HATE PAIN.
WHAT?!
?!
HE IS A MONSTER. HE'S AFRAID OF THINGS THAT NORMAL HUMANS AREN'T.
KYOKO.
URK

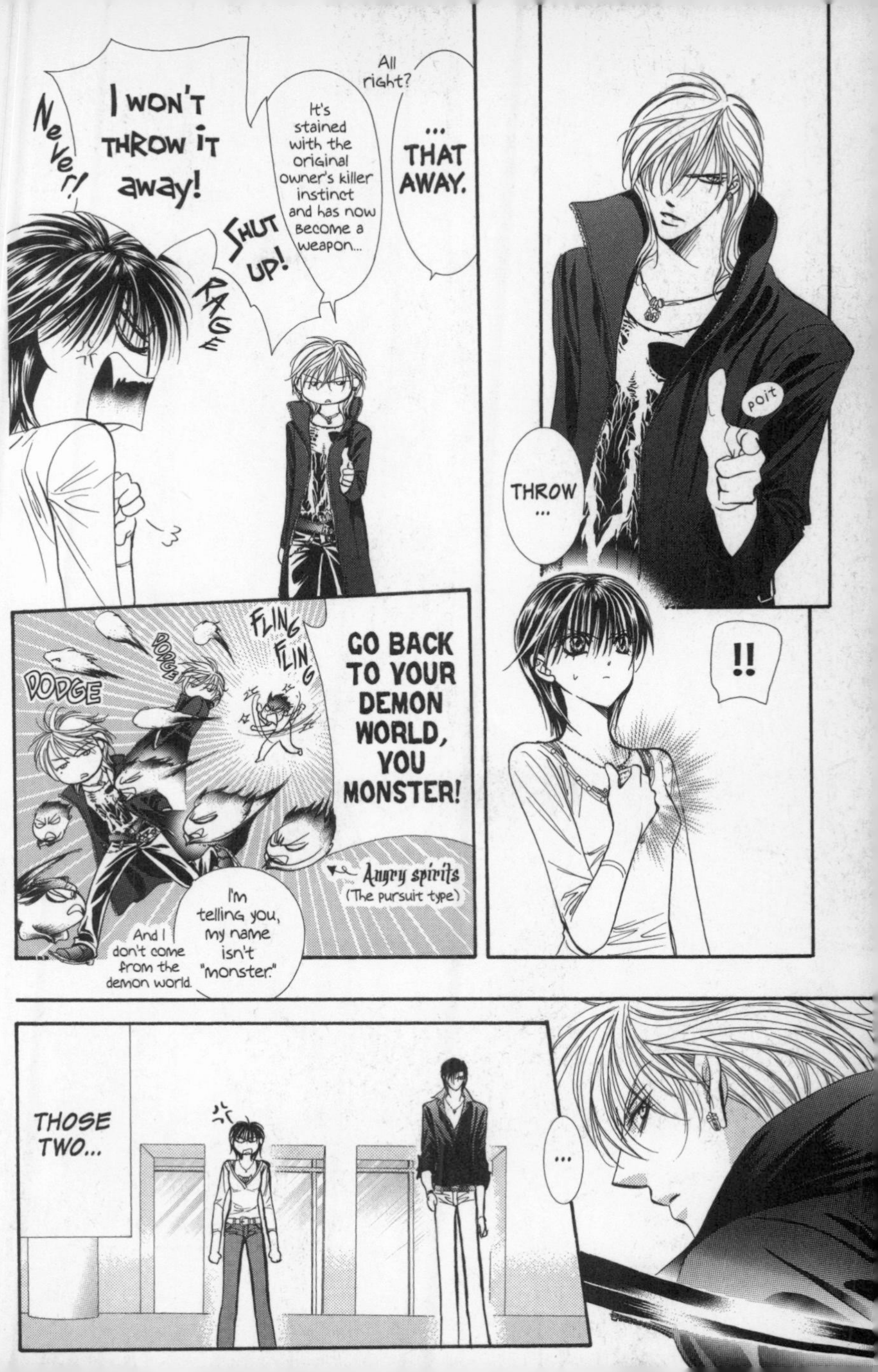
THROW ...
poit
... THAT AWAY.
All right?
It's stained with the original owner's killer instinct and has now become a weapon...
SHUT UP!
I WON'T THROW IT away!
Never!
RAGE
!!
GO BACK TO YOUR DEMON WORLD, YOU MONSTER!
FLING FLING
DODGE
DODGE
Angry spirits (The pursuit type)
I'm telling you, my name isn't "monster."
And I don't come from the demon world.
...
THOSE TWO...

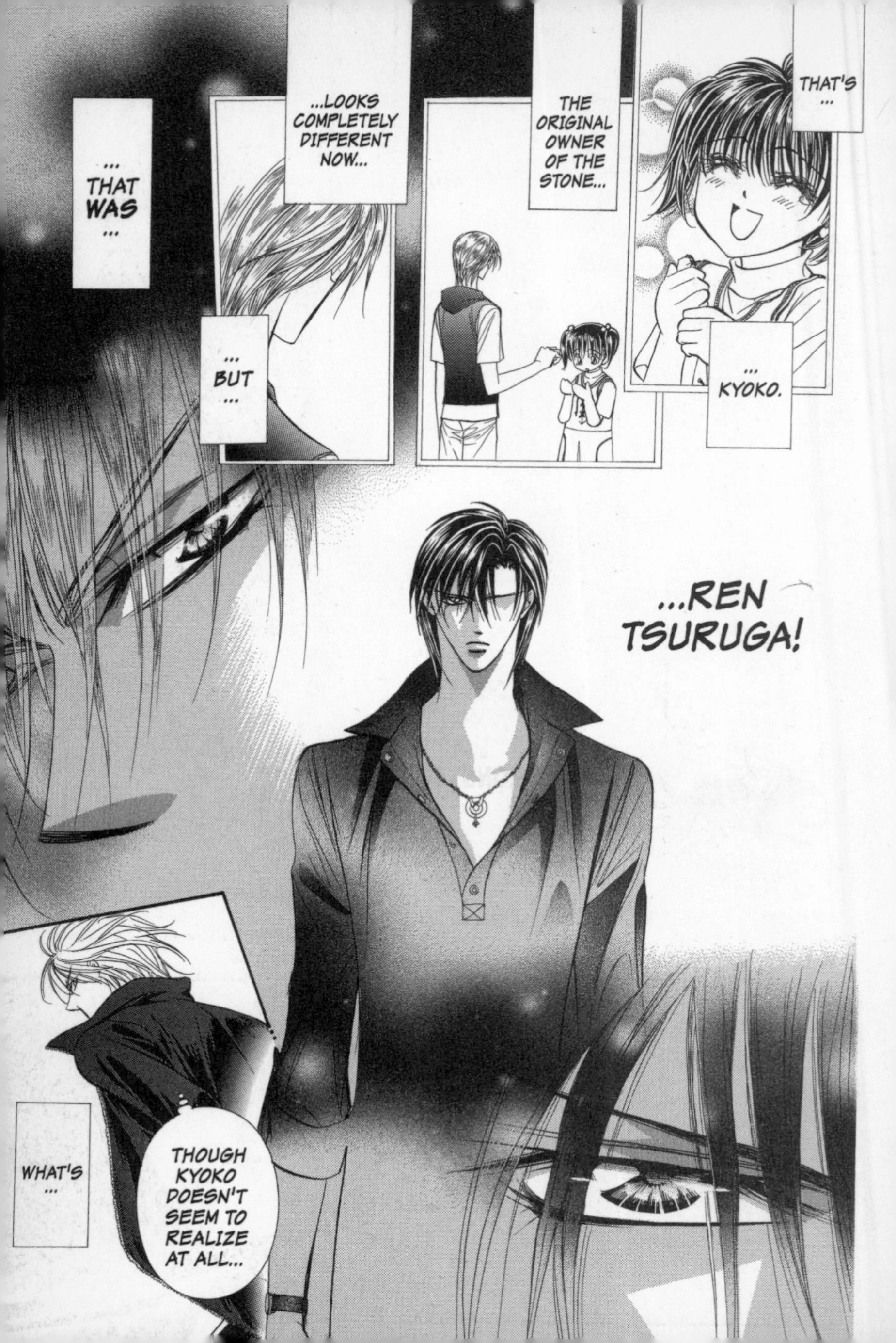
THAT'S ...
... KYOKO.
THE ORIGINAL OWNER OF THE STONE...
...LOOKS COMPLETELY DIFFERENT NOW...
... BUT ...
... THAT WAS ...
...REN TSURUGA!
THOUGH KYOKO DOESN'T SEEM TO REALIZE AT ALL...
WHAT'S ...

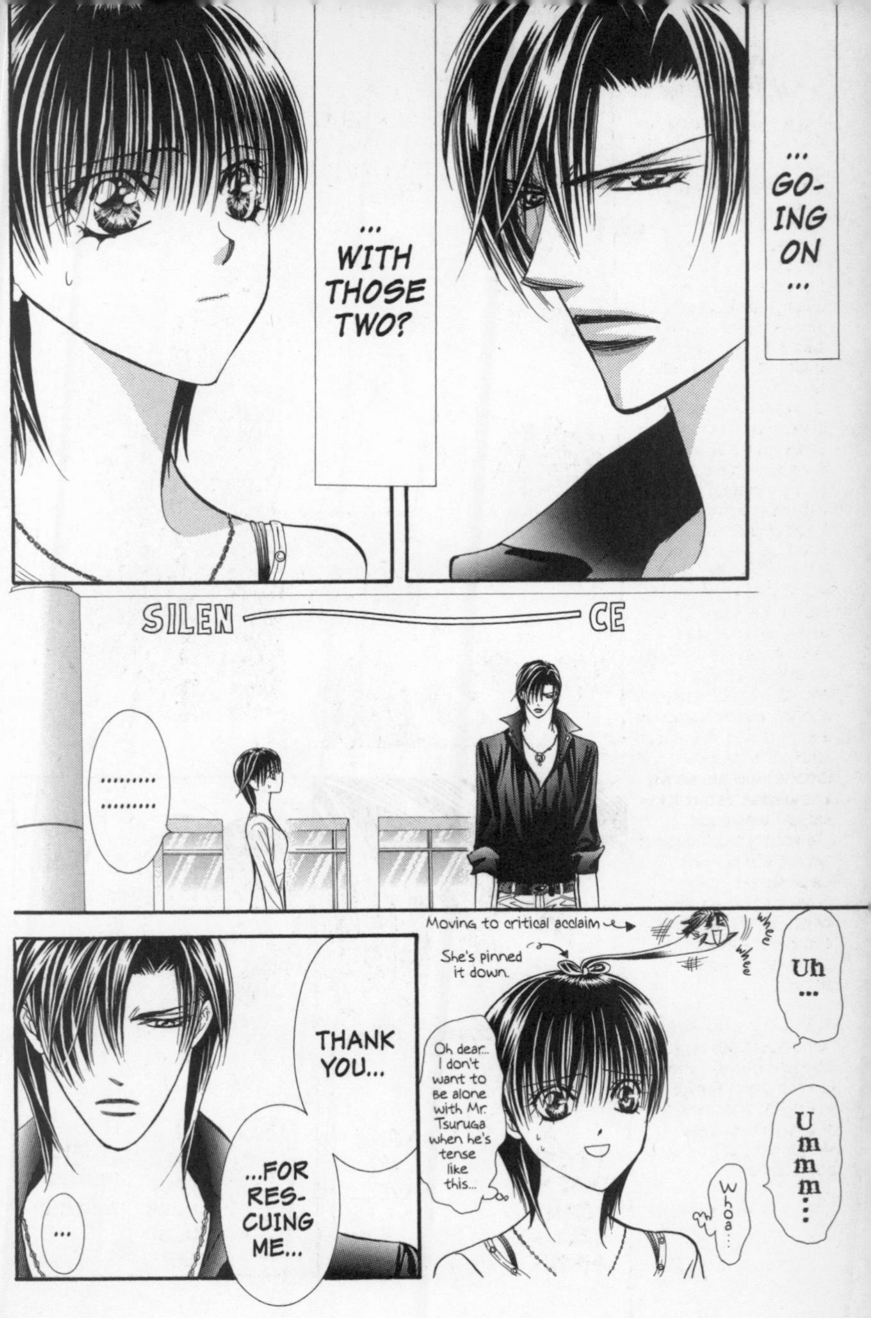
... GO-ING ON ...
... WITH THOSE TWO?
SILEN — CE
....
Uh ...
Ummm...
Moving to critical acclaim
whee whee
She's pinned it down.
Whoa...
Oh dear... I don't want to be alone with Mr. Tsuruga when he's tense like this...
THANK YOU...
...FOR RESCUING ME...
...

Finally, a follow-up

I think what changed the most about me since I started drawing *Skip•Beat* are my interests...until I started, I had no interest at all, but because I drew about it in *Skip•Beat*, I gradually got into it... *Skip•Beat* is about showbiz...but I didn't get into showbiz...no... even now, I basically have no interest in showbiz...when I sometimes hear celebrities talking about stuff that might be useful in my manga, I listen intently...but no...what I got interested in...are stones...natural stones ...the stone that appears in *Skip•Beat* is Corn (Kinseiseki), but when this series started, I wasn't that interested in stones, and I'd just looked at a book about minerals a bit to decide what Kyoko's treasure (stone) will be, so my knowledge about Kinseiseki was poor... ...I'd pretty much decided on Kinseiseki just because the color changes... ...so...the opportunity has finally come to follow up on it, so I'll write about it.

In Vol. 4, I only wrote "Kinseiseki (water sapphire)," but generally, books about power stones, stone shops and jewelry shops that sell mineral accessories...

-To be continued -

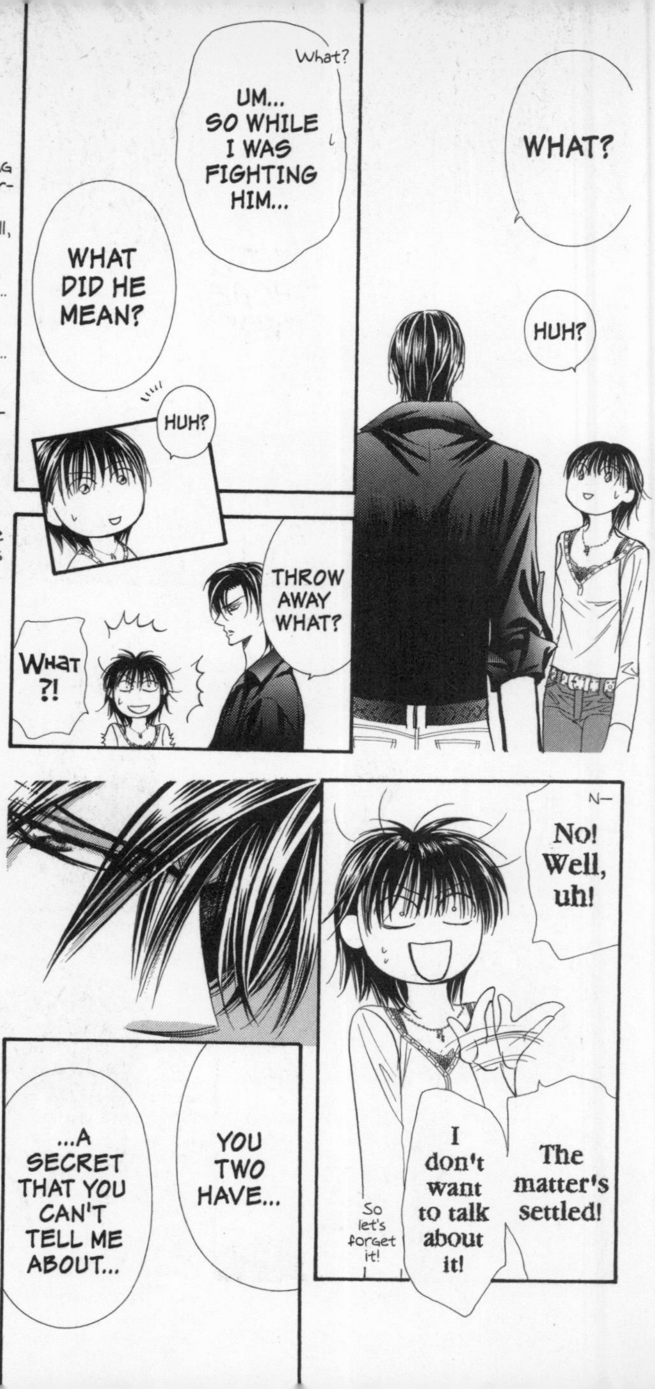
WHAT?
HUH?
What?
UM... SO WHILE I WAS FIGHTING HIM...
WHAT DID HE MEAN?
HUH?
THROW AWAY WHAT?
WHAT ?!
N—
No! Well, uh!
The matter's settled!
I don't want to talk about it!
So let's forget it!
YOU TWO HAVE...
...A SECRET THAT YOU CAN'T TELL ME ABOUT...

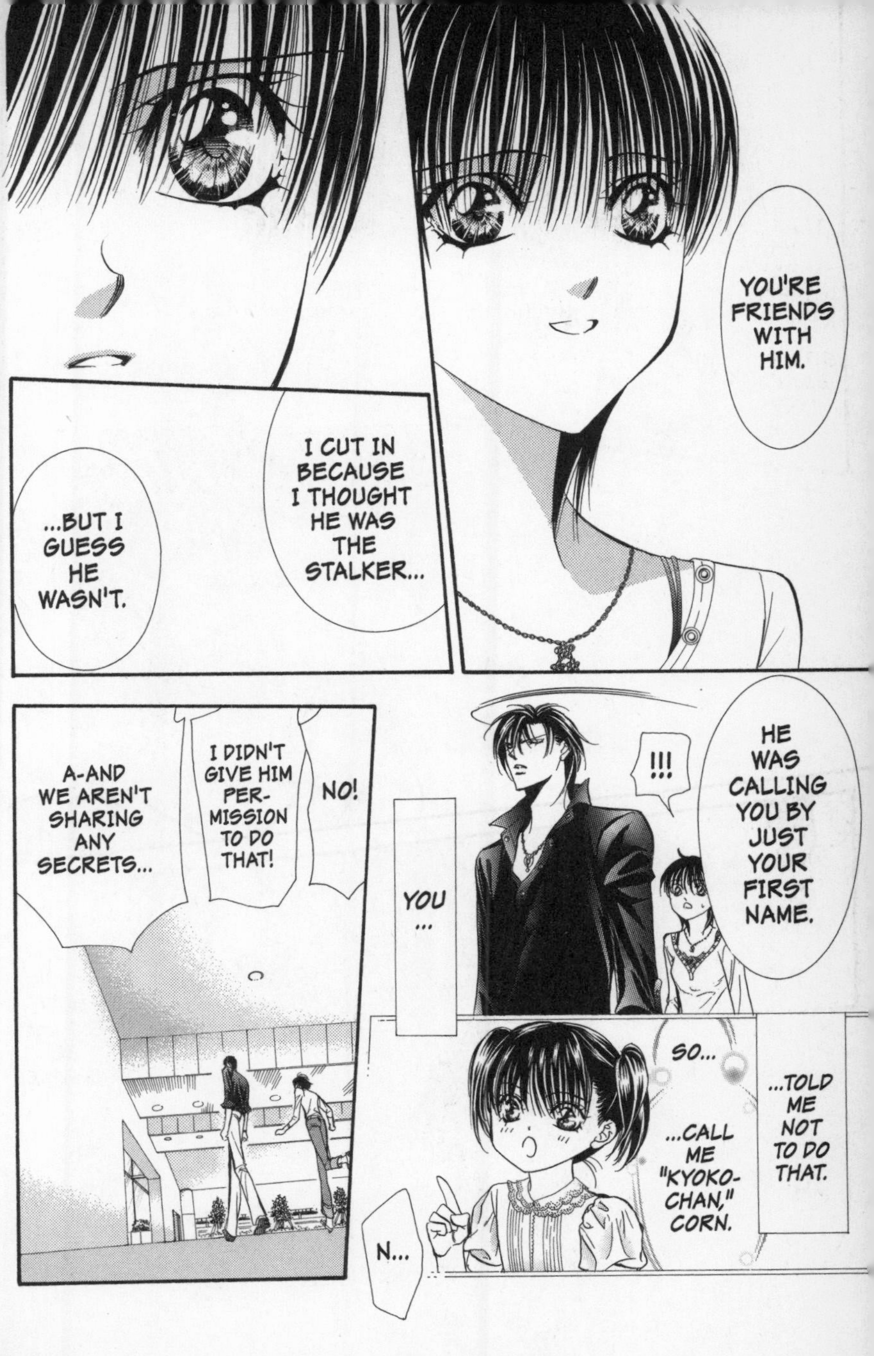
YOU'RE FRIENDS WITH HIM.
I CUT IN BECAUSE I THOUGHT HE WAS THE STALKER...
...BUT I GUESS HE WASN'T.
HE WAS CALLING YOU BY JUST YOUR FIRST NAME.
!!!
YOU ...
...TOLD ME NOT TO DO THAT.
SO...
...CALL ME "KYOKO-CHAN," CORN.
N...
NO!
I DIDN'T GIVE HIM PER-MISSION TO DO THAT!
A-AND WE AREN'T SHARING ANY SECRETS...

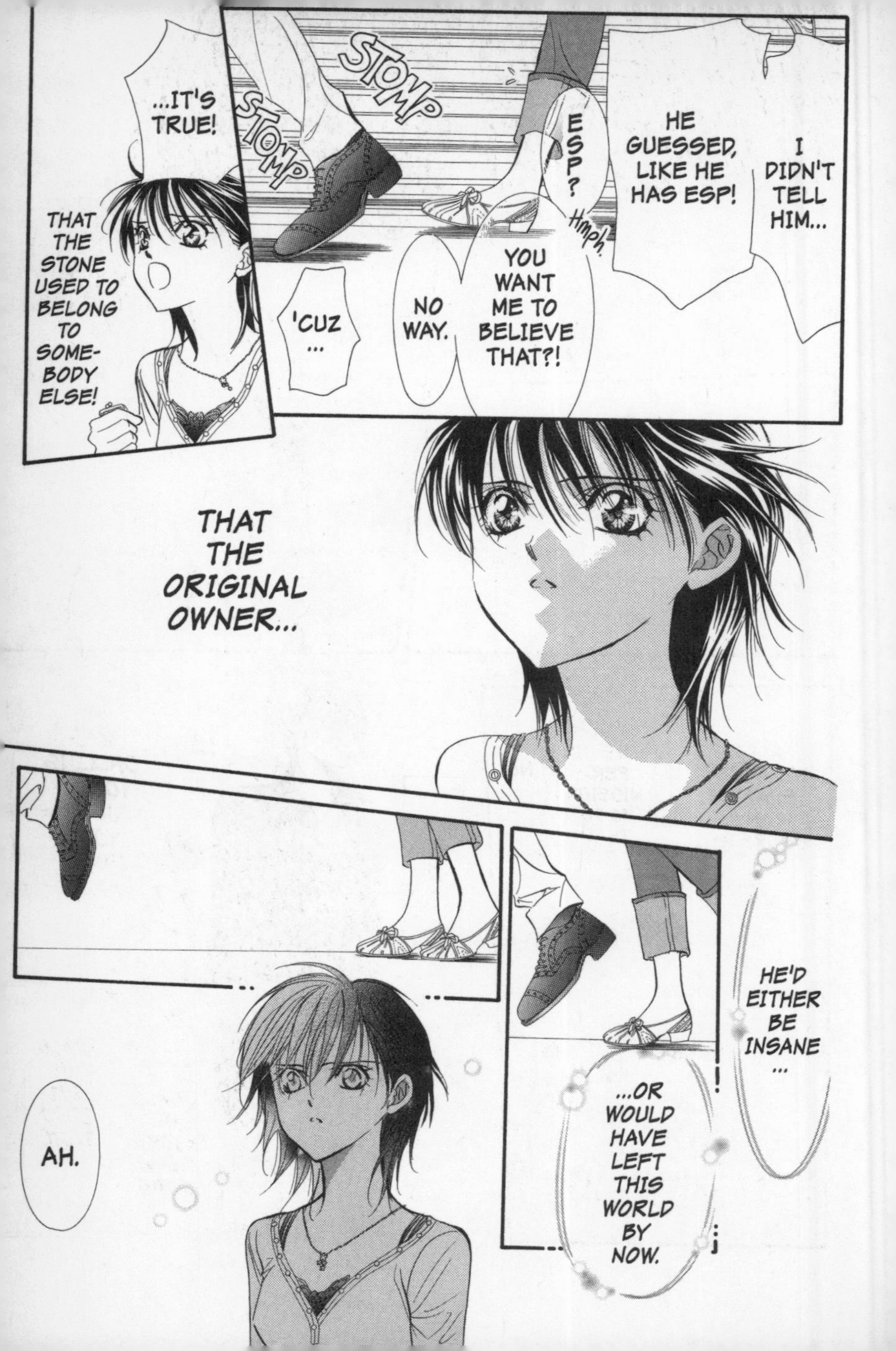
I DIDN'T TELL HIM...
HE GUESSED, LIKE HE HAS ESP!
STOMP
STOMP
ESP?
Hmph.
YOU WANT ME TO BELIEVE THAT?!
NO WAY.
'CUZ...
...IT'S TRUE!
THAT THE STONE USED TO BELONG TO SOMEBODY ELSE!
THAT THE ORIGINAL OWNER...
HE'D EITHER BE INSANE...
...OR WOULD HAVE LEFT THIS WORLD BY NOW.
AH.

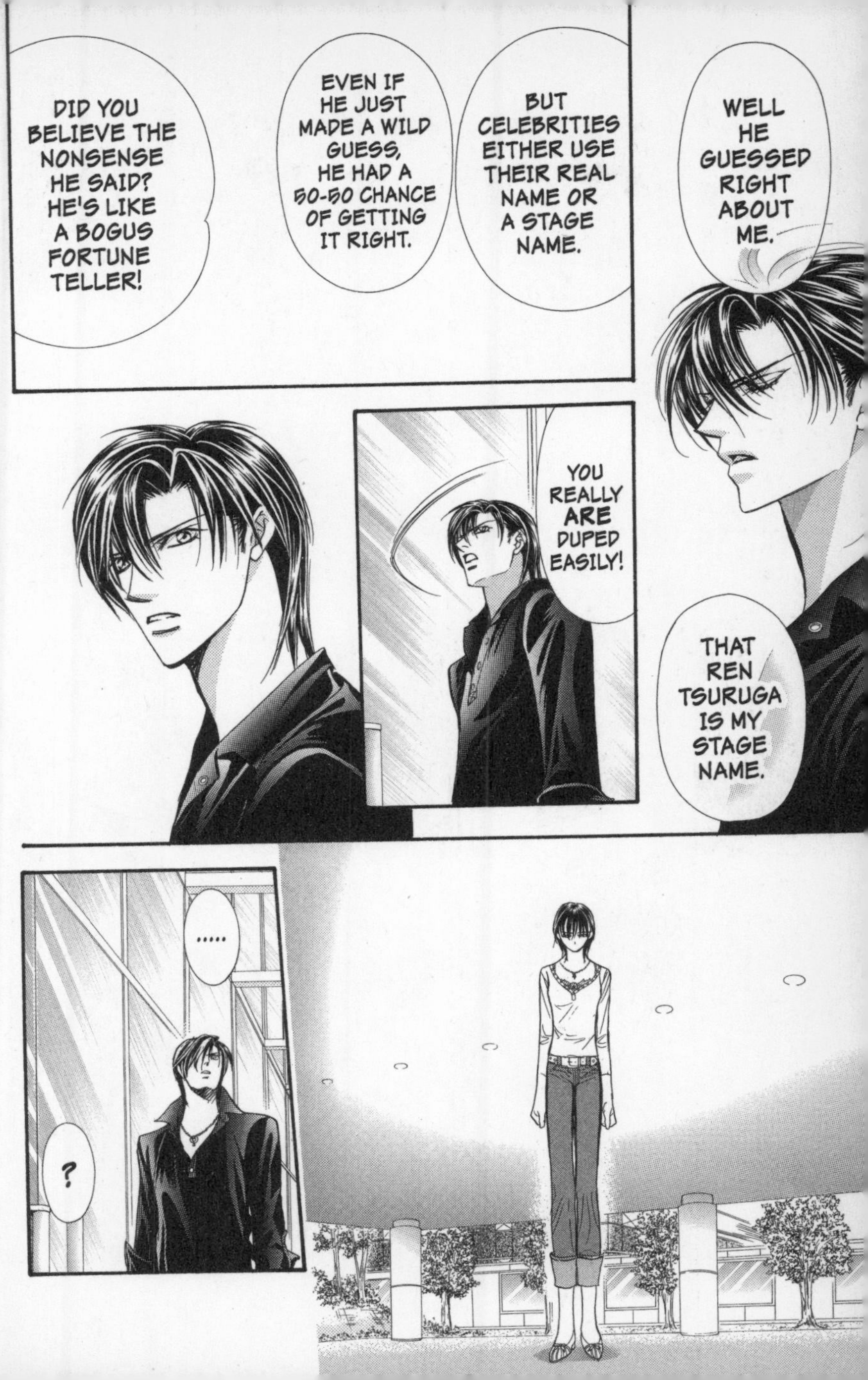
WELL HE GUESSED RIGHT ABOUT ME.
THAT REN TSURUGA IS MY STAGE NAME.
BUT CELEBRITIES EITHER USE THEIR REAL NAME OR A STAGE NAME.
EVEN IF HE JUST MADE A WILD GUESS, HE HAD A 50-50 CHANCE OF GETTING IT RIGHT.
DID YOU BELIEVE THE NONSENSE HE SAID? HE'S LIKE A BOGUS FORTUNE TELLER!
YOU REALLY ARE DUPED EASILY!
......
?

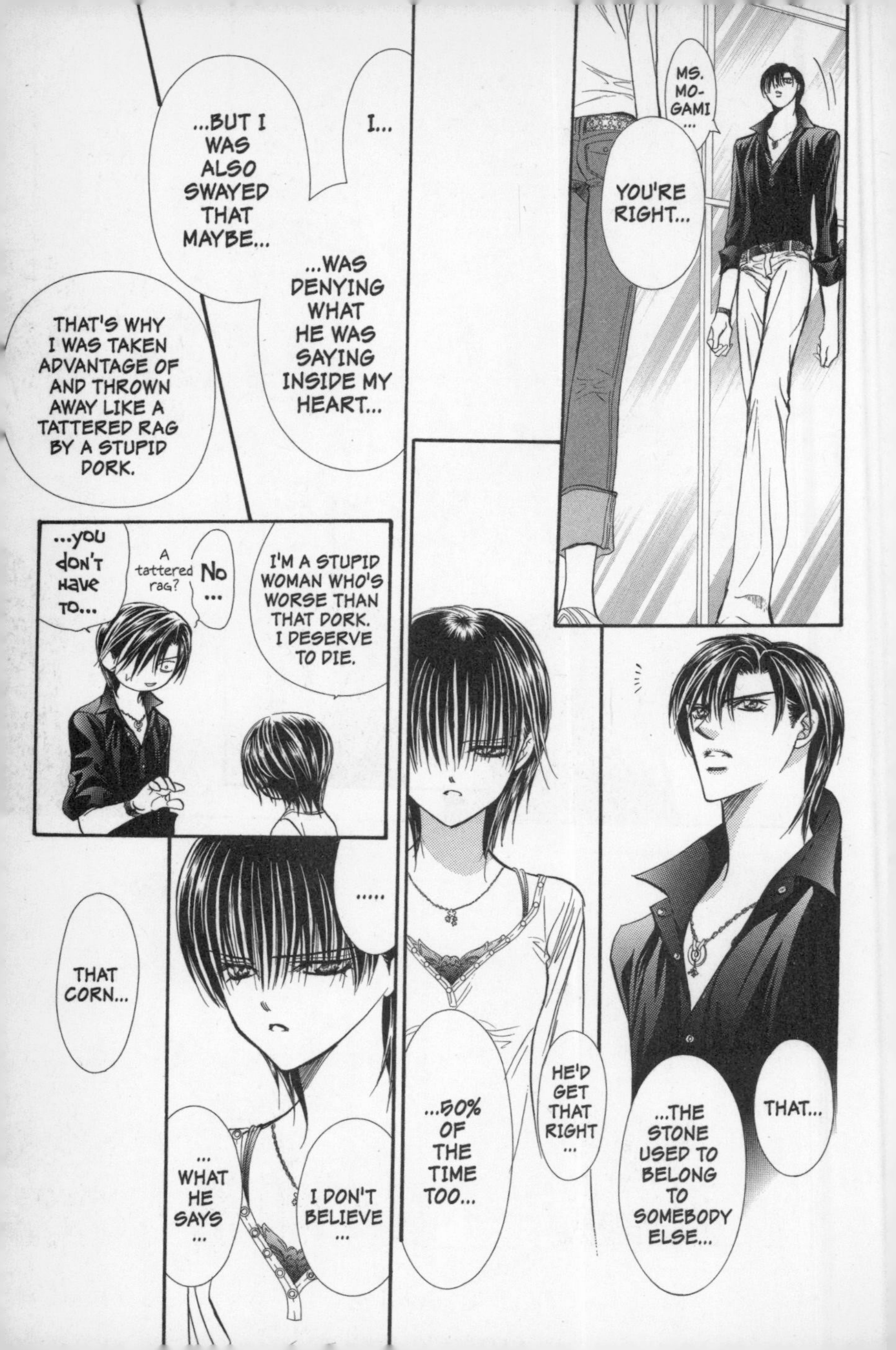
MS. MO-GAMI...
YOU'RE RIGHT...
I...
...BUT I WAS ALSO SWAYED THAT MAYBE...
...WAS DENYING WHAT HE WAS SAYING INSIDE MY HEART...
THAT'S WHY I WAS TAKEN ADVANTAGE OF AND THROWN AWAY LIKE A TATTERED RAG BY A STUPID DORK.
I'M A STUPID WOMAN WHO'S WORSE THAN THAT DORK. I DESERVE TO DIE.
No...
A tattered rag?
...you don't have to...
THAT...
...THE STONE USED TO BELONG TO SOMEBODY ELSE...
HE'D GET THAT RIGHT...
...50% OF THE TIME TOO...
.....
I DON'T BELIEVE...
...WHAT HE SAYS...
THAT CORN...

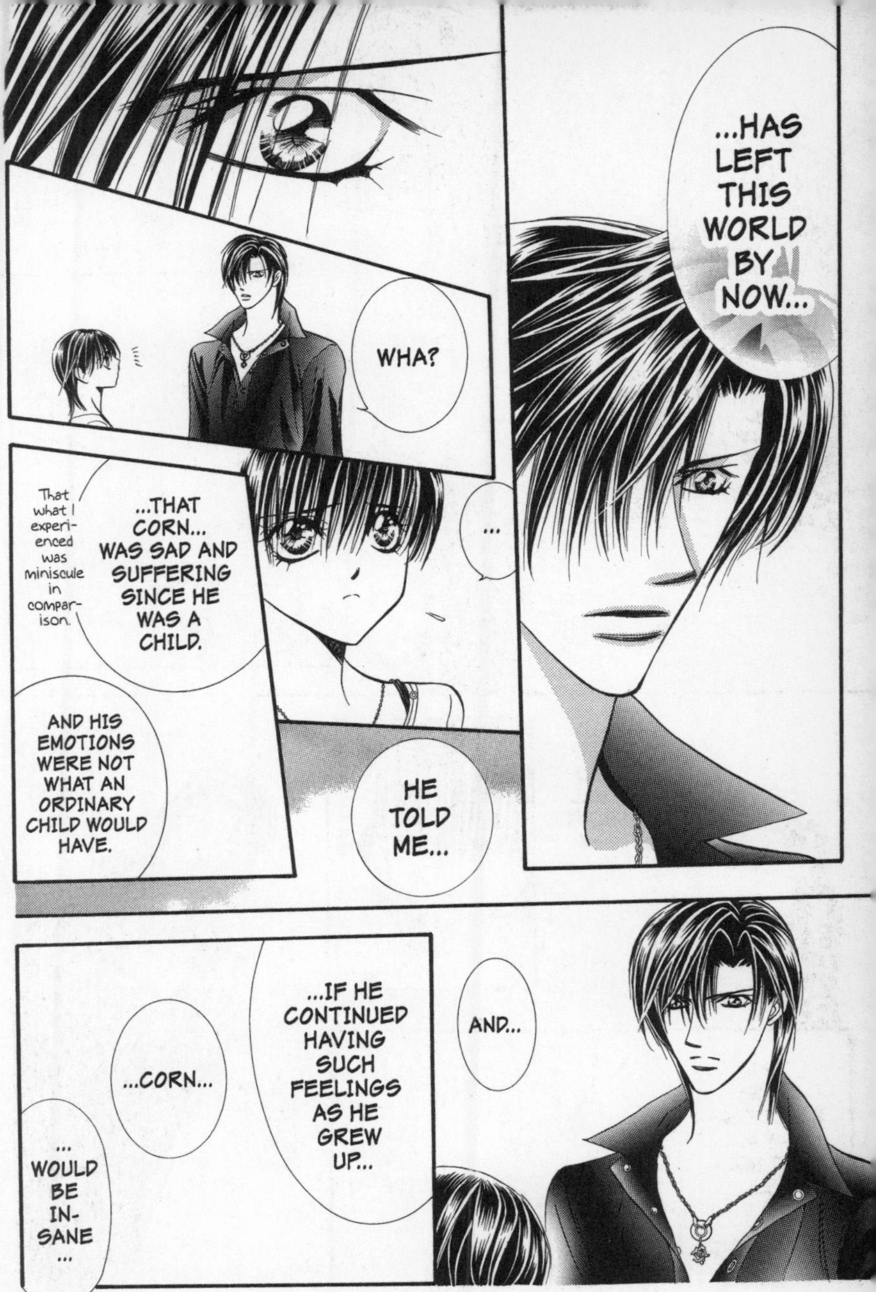
...HAS LEFT THIS WORLD BY NOW...
WHA?
...
...THAT CORN... WAS SAD AND SUFFERING SINCE HE WAS A CHILD.
That what I experienced was miniscule in comparison.
HE TOLD ME...
AND HIS EMOTIONS WERE NOT WHAT AN ORDINARY CHILD WOULD HAVE.
AND...
...IF HE CONTINUED HAVING SUCH FEELINGS AS HE GREW UP...
...CORN...
...WOULD BE IN-SANE...

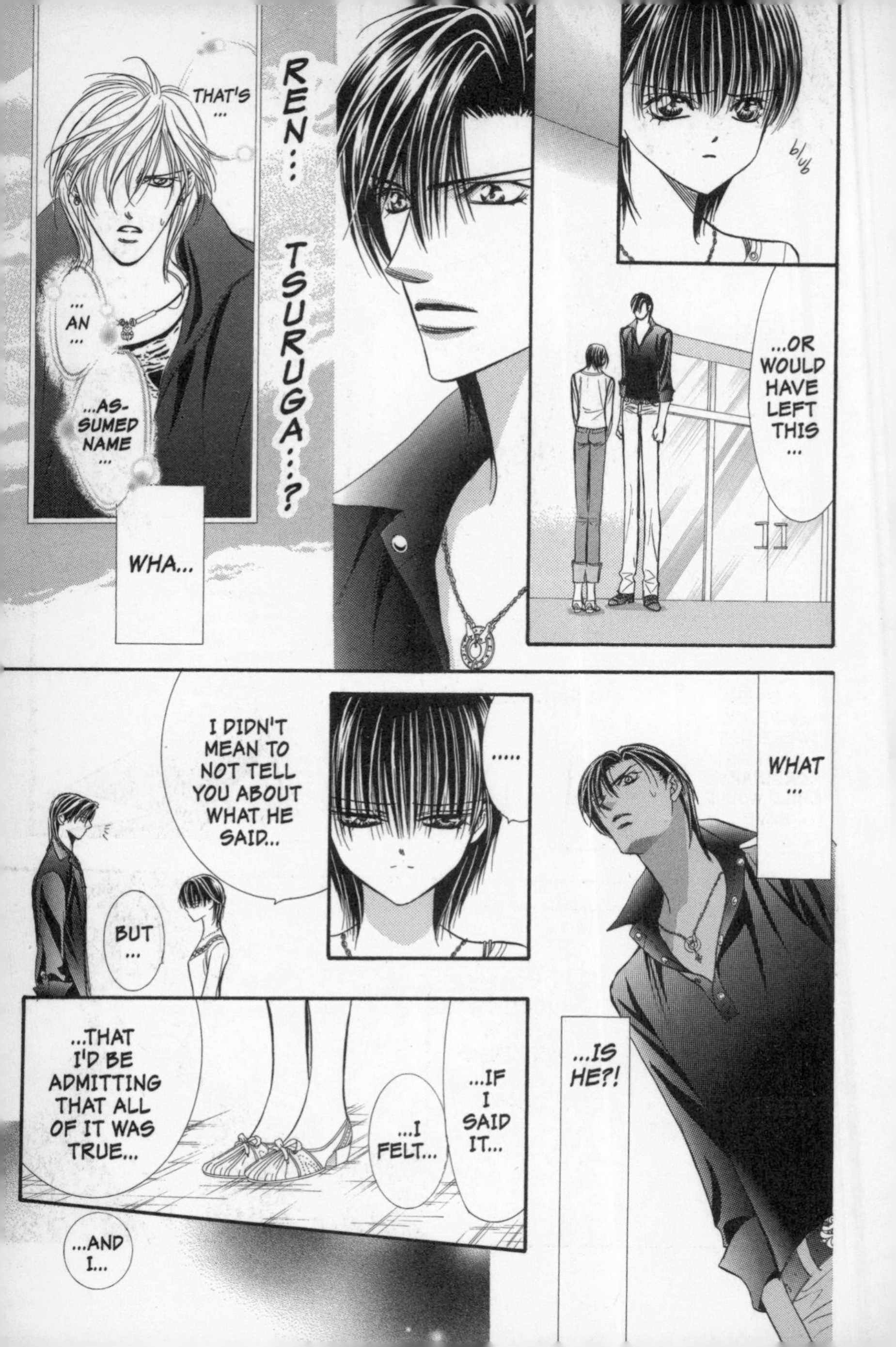
blub
...OR WOULD HAVE LEFT THIS ...
REN... TSURUGA...?
THAT'S ...
... AN ...
...AS-SUMED NAME ...
WHA...
WHAT ...
...IS HE?!
.....
I DIDN'T MEAN TO NOT TELL YOU ABOUT WHAT HE SAID...
BUT ...
...IF I SAID IT...
...I FELT...
...THAT I'D BE ADMITTING THAT ALL OF IT WAS TRUE...
...AND I...

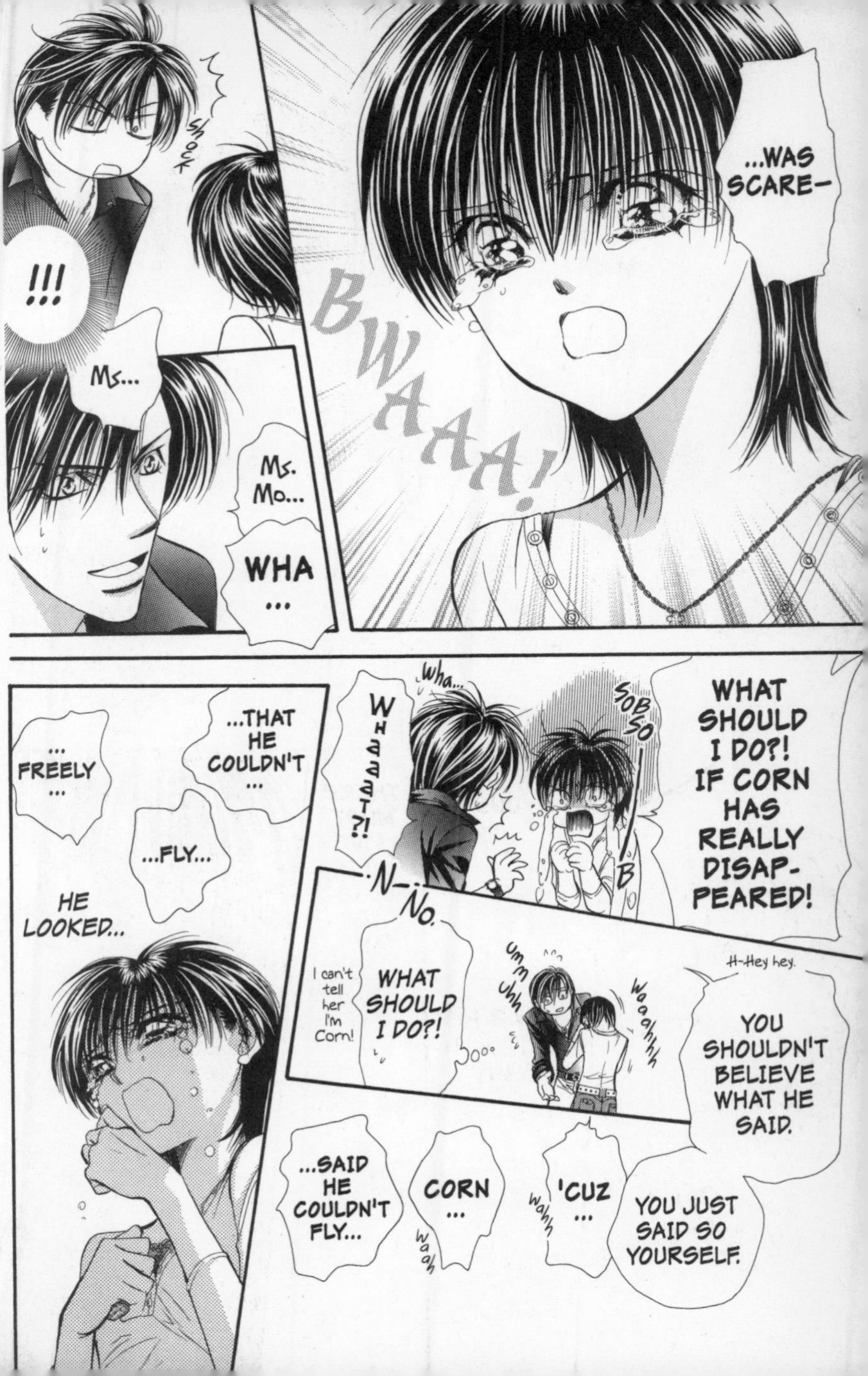
...WAS SCARE—
BWAAA!
SHOCK
!!!
Ms...
Ms. Mo...
WHA ...
WHAT SHOULD I DO?! IF CORN HAS REALLY DISAPPEARED!
SOBSOB
wha...
Whaaaat?!
N-No.
WHAT SHOULD I DO?!
I can't tell her I'm Corn!
Um uhh
Waaahhh
H-Hey hey.
YOU SHOULDN'T BELIEVE WHAT HE SAID.
YOU JUST SAID SO YOURSELF.
'CUZ ...
wahh
CORN ...
Waah
...SAID HE COULDN'T FLY...
...THAT HE COULDN'T ...
... FREELY ...
...FLY...
HE LOOKED...

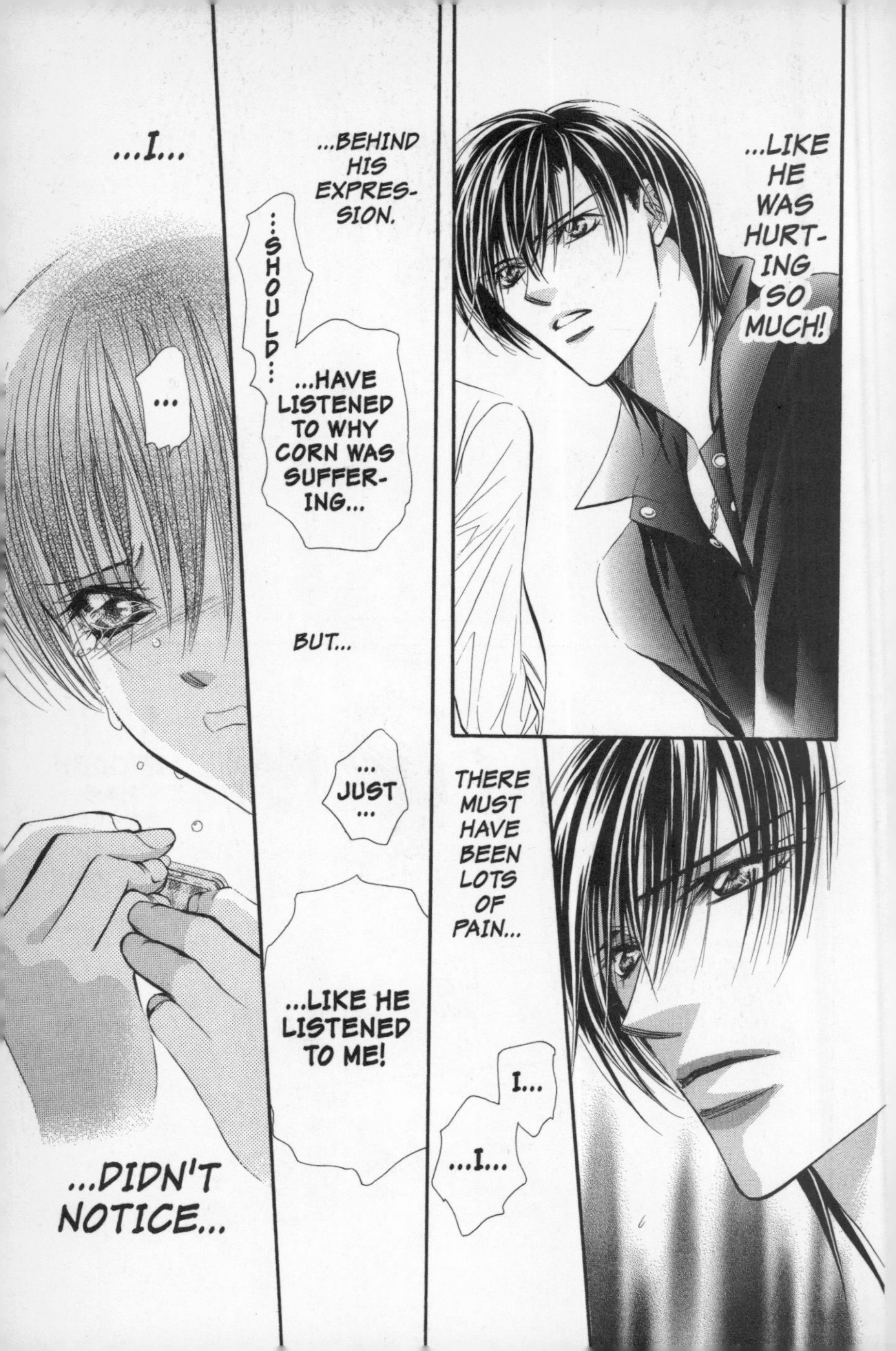
...LIKE HE WAS HURTING SO MUCH!
THERE MUST HAVE BEEN LOTS OF PAIN...
I...
...I...
...BEHIND HIS EXPRES-SION.
...SHOULD...
...HAVE LISTENED TO WHY CORN WAS SUFFER-ING...
BUT...
...JUST...
...LIKE HE LISTENED TO ME!
...I...
...
...DIDN'T NOTICE...

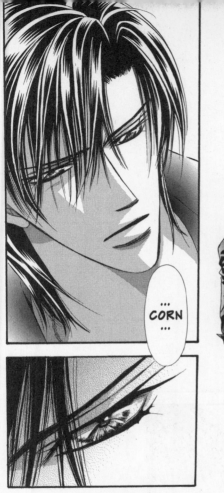

...CORN...

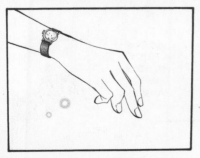

...AT ALL...

I'M SORRY...

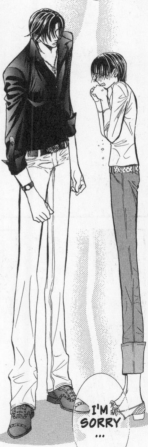

I'M SORRY...

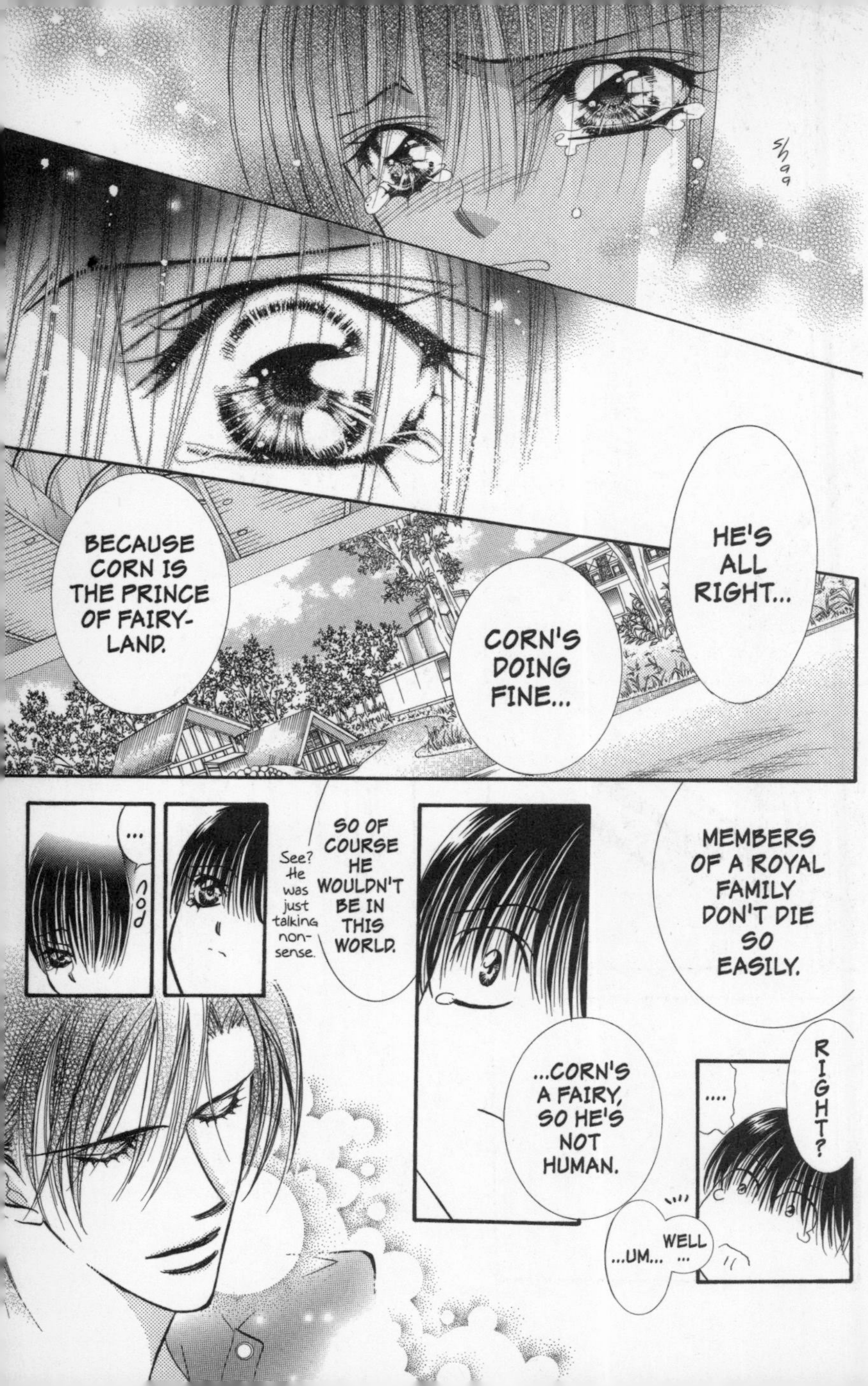
shaa
HE'S ALL RIGHT...
CORN'S DOING FINE...
BECAUSE CORN IS THE PRINCE OF FAIRY-LAND.
MEMBERS OF A ROYAL FAMILY DON'T DIE SO EASILY.
SO OF COURSE HE WOULDN'T BE IN THIS WORLD.
See? He was just talking non-sense.
...
nod
RIGHT?
....
WELL ...
...UM...
...CORN'S A FAIRY, SO HE'S NOT HUMAN.

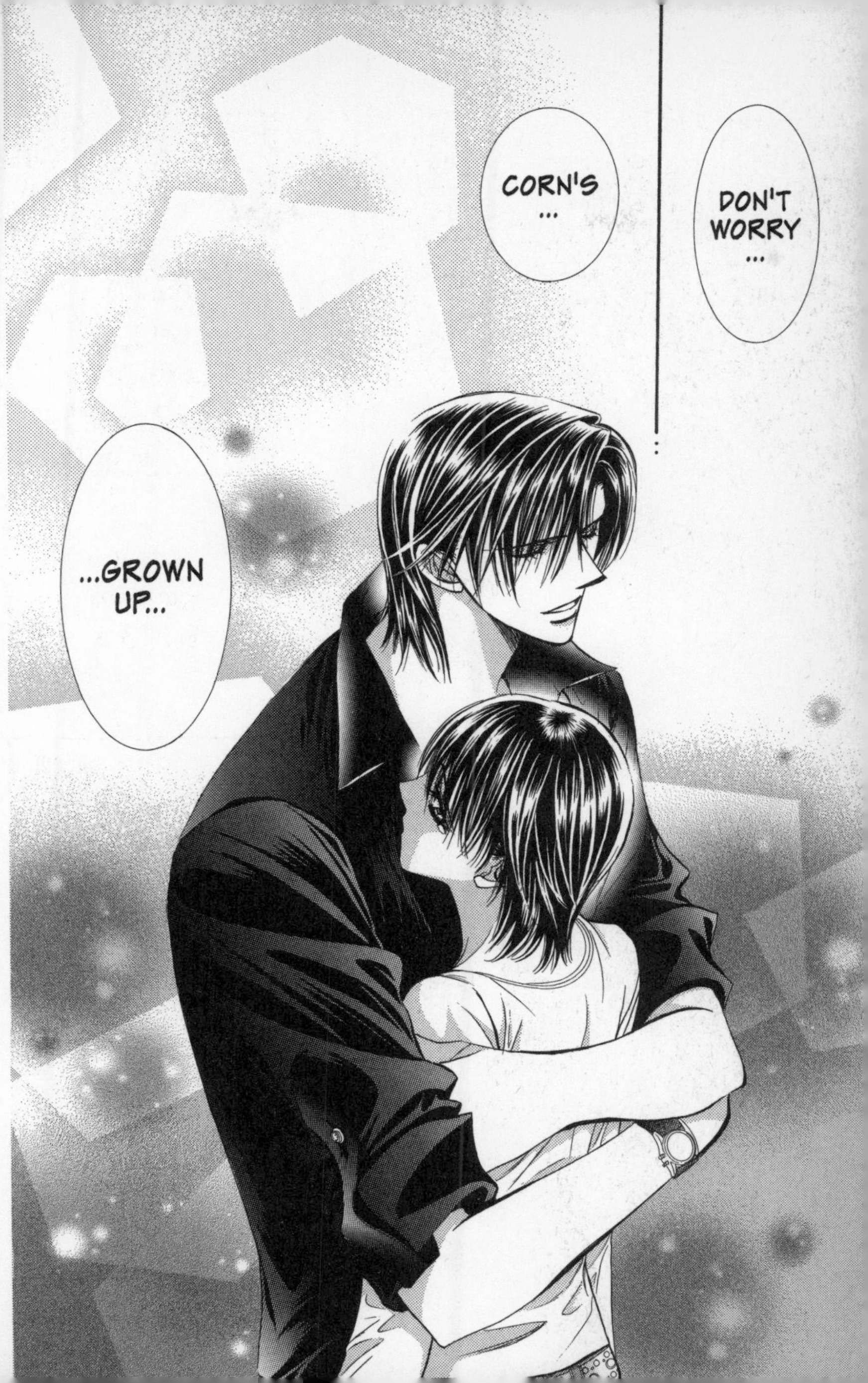
DON'T WORRY ...
CORN'S ...
...GROWN UP...

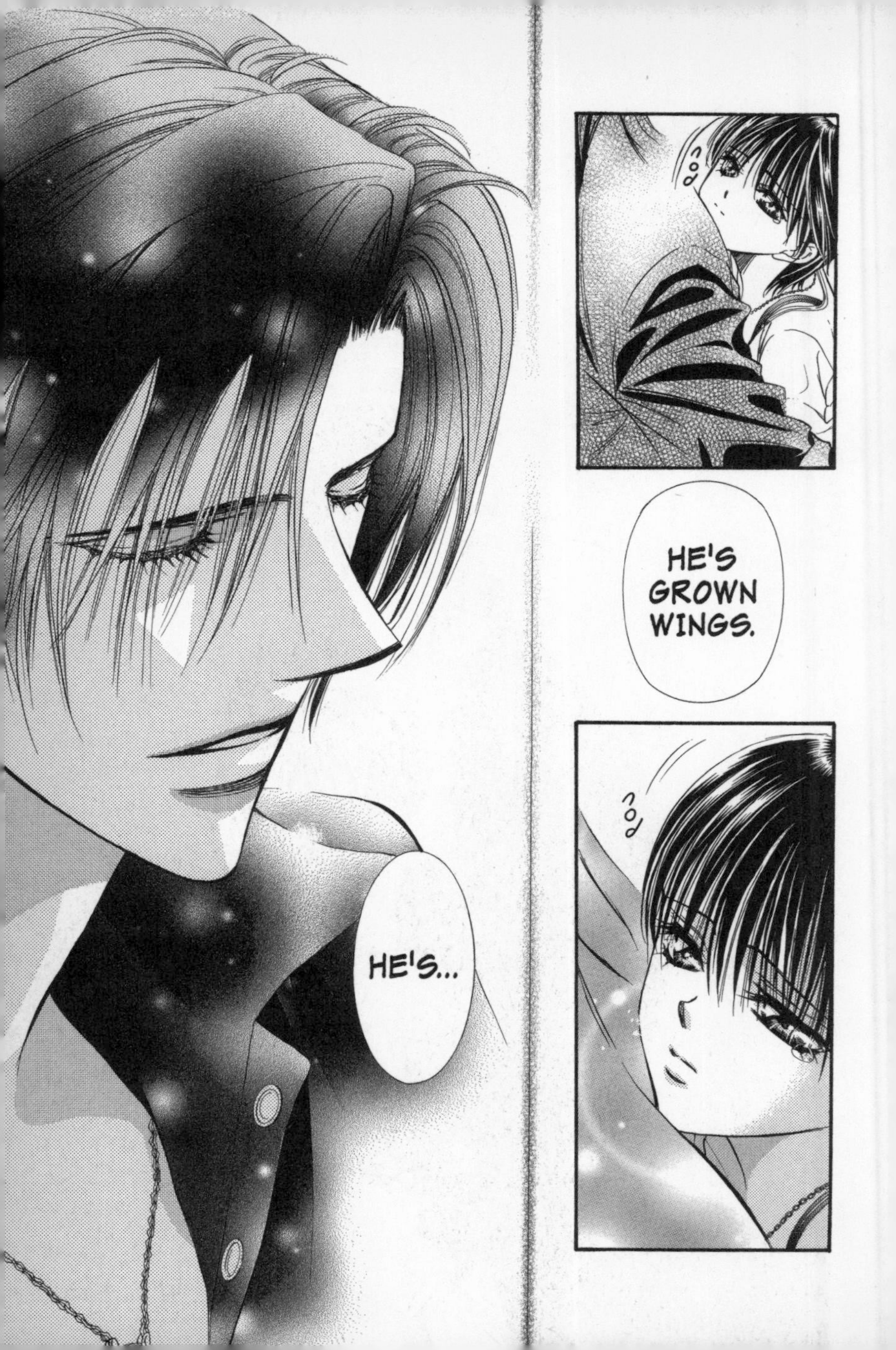
HE'S GROWN WINGS.
HE'S...

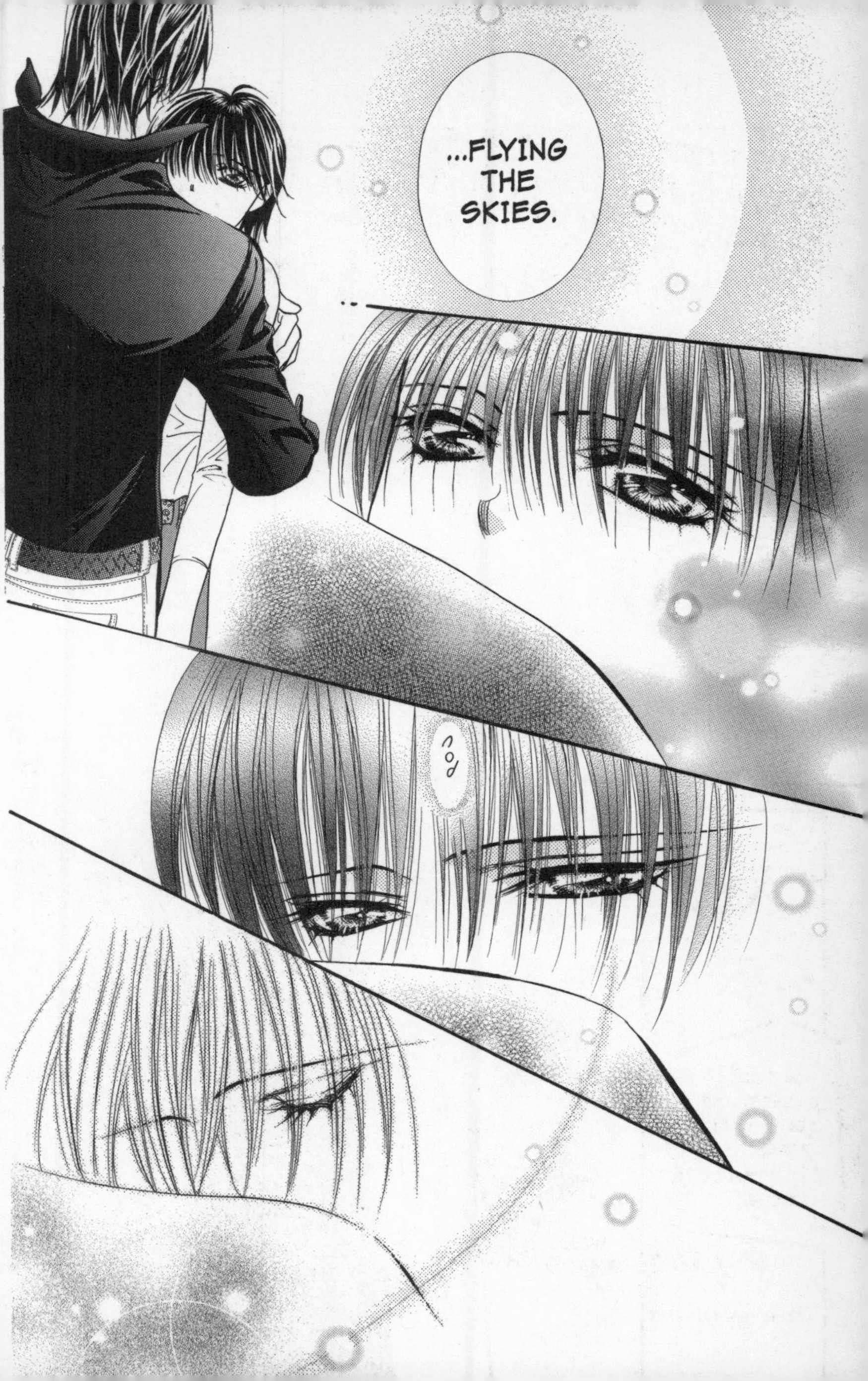
...FLYING THE SKIES.
pon

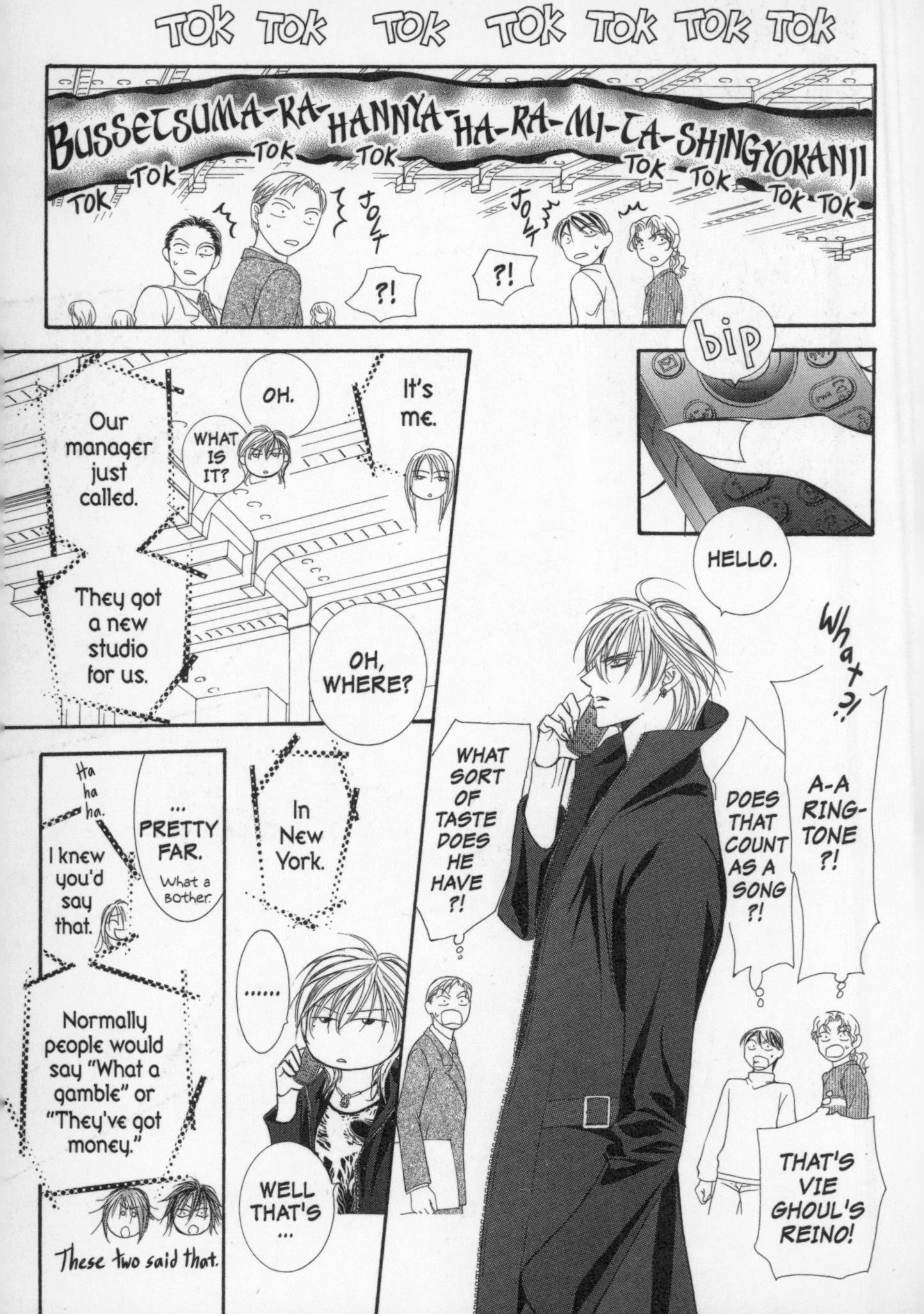
TOK TOK TOK TOK TOK TOK TOK
BUSSETSUMA-KA-HANNYA-HA-RA-MI-TA-SHINGYOKANJI
TOK TOK TOK TOK TOK TOK TOK TOK
JOLT
?!
JOLT
?!
bip
HELLO.
What?!
A-A RINGTONE?!
DOES THAT COUNT AS A SONG?!
WHAT SORT OF TASTE DOES HE HAVE?!
THAT'S VIE GHOUL'S REINO!
It's me.
OH.
WHAT IS IT?
Our manager just called.
They got a new studio for us.
OH, WHERE?
In New York.
... PRETTY FAR.
What a bother.
Ha ha ha.
I knew you'd say that.
Normally people would say "What a gamble" or "They've got money."
These two said that.
......
WELL THAT'S ...

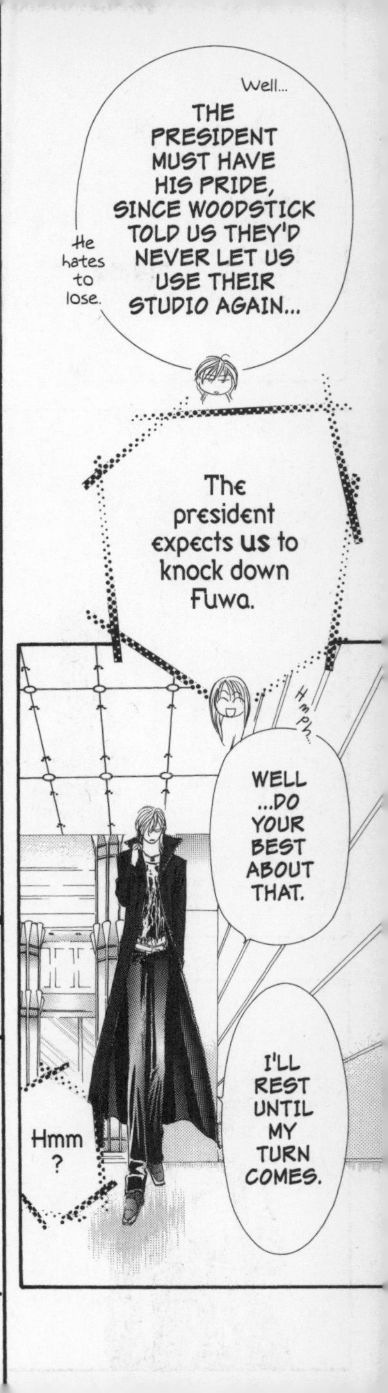
Well...
THE PRESIDENT MUST HAVE HIS PRIDE, SINCE WOODSTICK TOLD US THEY'D NEVER LET US USE THEIR STUDIO AGAIN...
He hates to lose.
The president expects us to knock down Fuwa.
Hmph.
WELL ...DO YOUR BEST ABOUT THAT.
I'LL REST UNTIL MY TURN COMES.
Hmm?

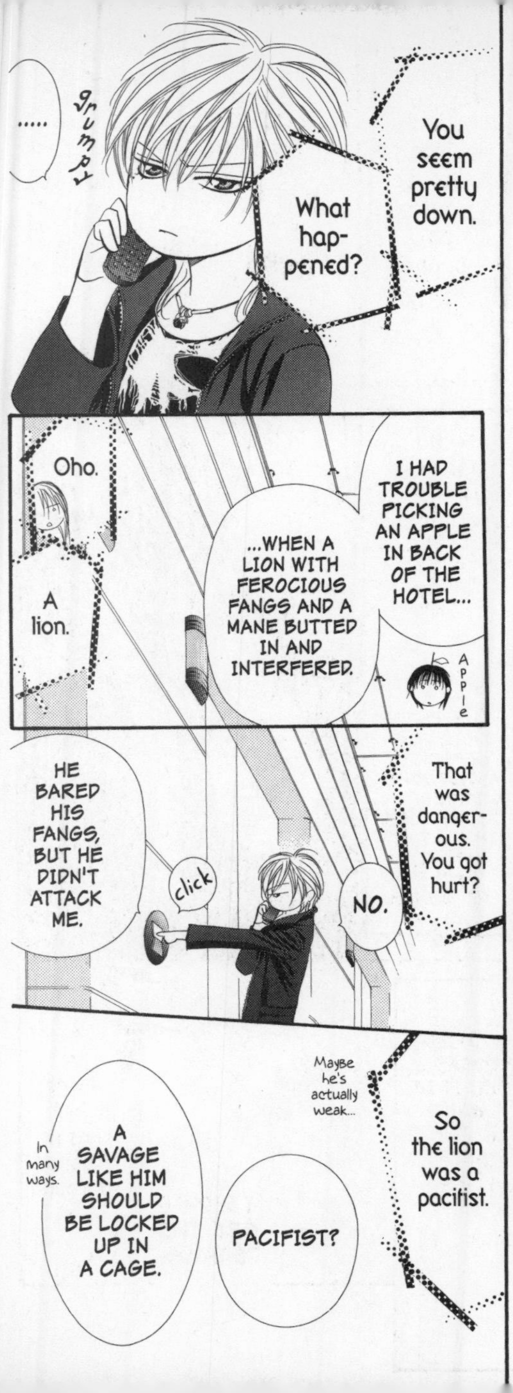
You seem pretty down.
What hap-pened?
grumpy
.....
I HAD TROUBLE PICKING AN APPLE IN BACK OF THE HOTEL...
Apple
...WHEN A LION WITH FEROCIOUS FANGS AND A MANE BUTTED IN AND INTERFERED.
Oho.
A lion.
That was danger-ous. You got hurt?
NO.
click
HE BARED HIS FANGS, BUT HE DIDN'T ATTACK ME.
Maybe he's actually weak...
So the lion was a pacifist.
PACIFIST?
A SAVAGE LIKE HIM SHOULD BE LOCKED UP IN A CAGE.
In many ways.

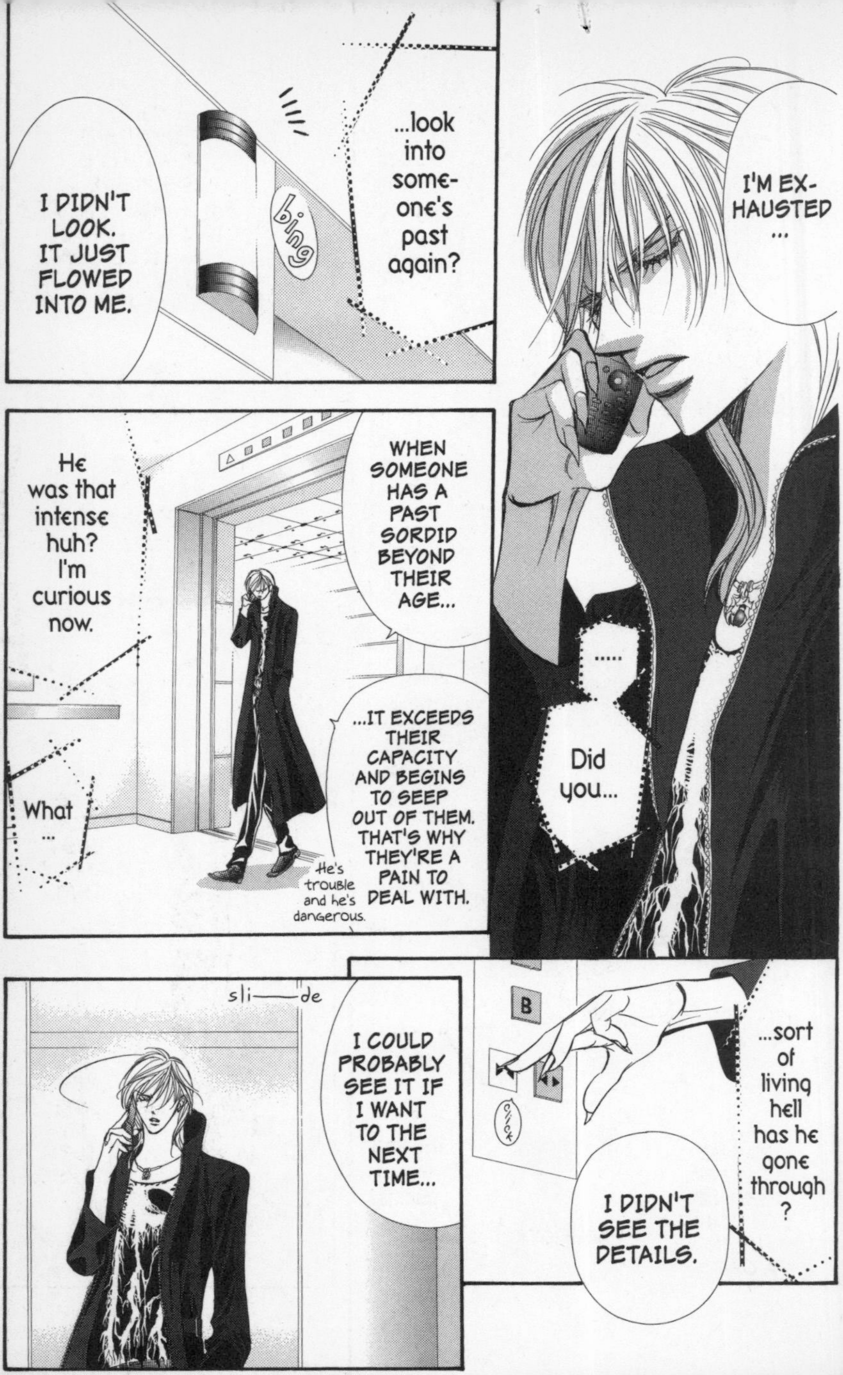

I'M EX-HAUSTED ...
.....
Did you...
...look into someone's past again?
bing
I DIDN'T LOOK. IT JUST FLOWED INTO ME.
WHEN SOMEONE HAS A PAST SORDID BEYOND THEIR AGE...
...IT EXCEEDS THEIR CAPACITY AND BEGINS TO SEEP OUT OF THEM. THAT'S WHY THEY'RE A PAIN TO DEAL WITH.
He's trouble and he's dangerous.
He was that intense huh? I'm curious now.
What ...
...sort of living hell has he gone through?
B
click
I DIDN'T SEE THE DETAILS.
I COULD PROBABLY SEE IT IF I WANT TO THE NEXT TIME...
sli—de

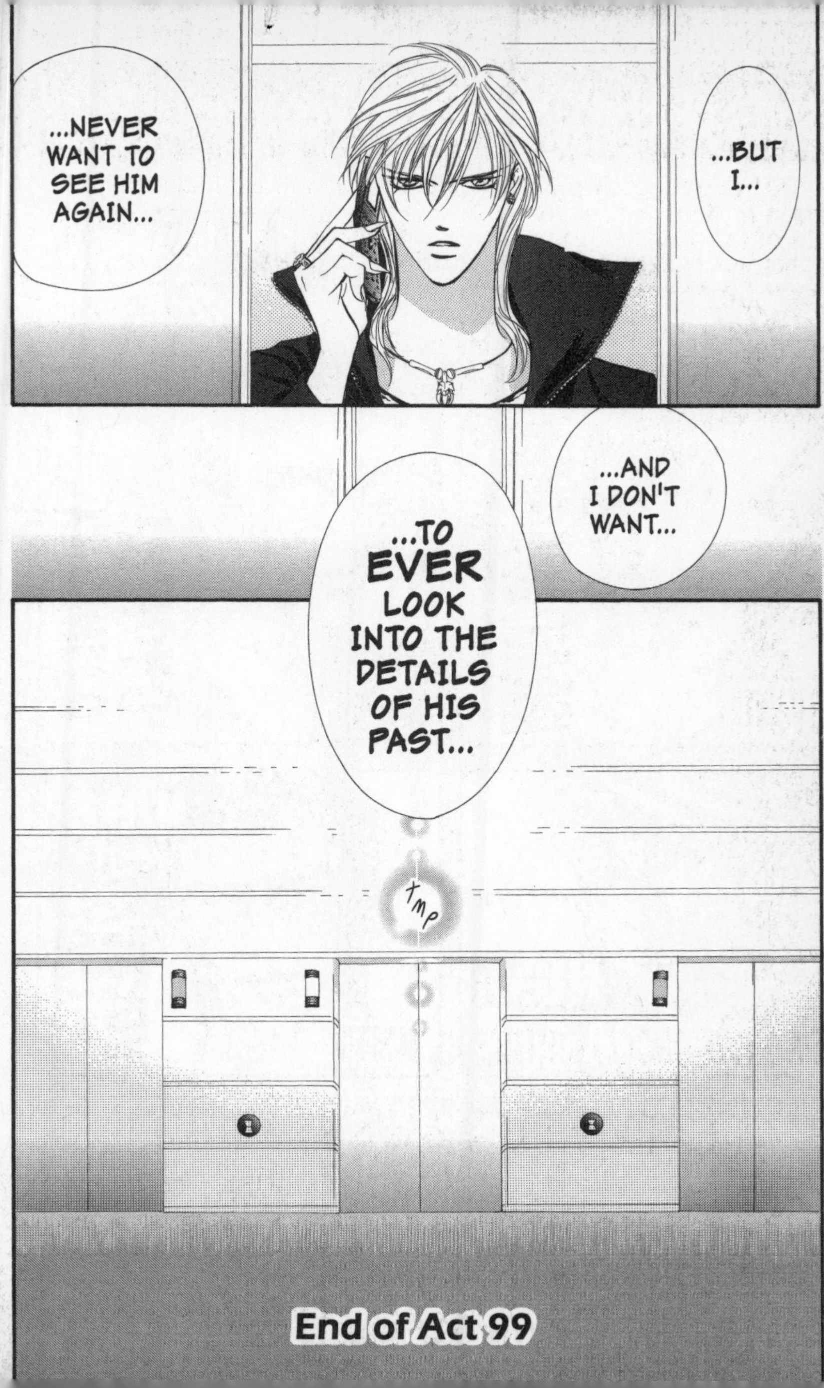
...BUT I...
...NEVER WANT TO SEE HIM AGAIN...
...AND I DON'T WANT...
...TO EVER LOOK INTO THE DETAILS OF HIS PAST...
XMP
End of Act 99

To commemorate the 100th chapter ☆ Skip•Beat! by Yoshiki Nakamura

Results of the Character Popularity Poll!!

The 100th chapter of *Skip•Beat!* was published in Issue 4, 2007 of *Hana to Yume*. Below are the results of the character popularity poll that was held to commemorate it!

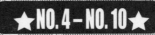

★NO. 4 – NO. 10★

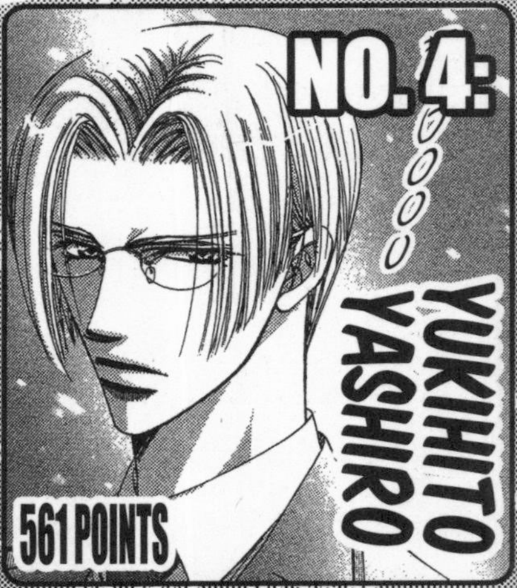
NO. 4:
YUKIHITO YASHIRO
561 POINTS

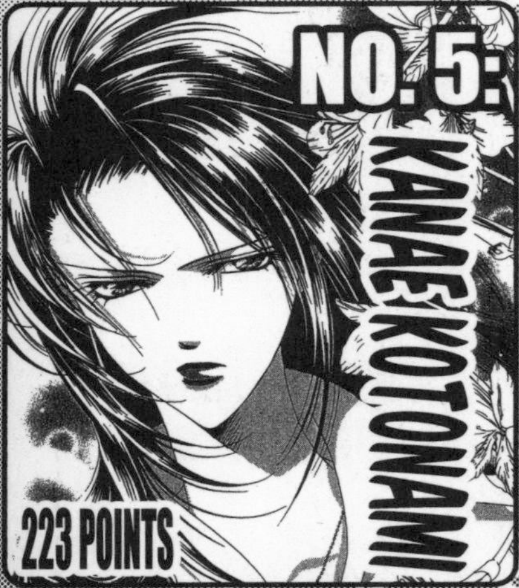
NO. 5:
KANAE KOTONAMI
223 POINTS

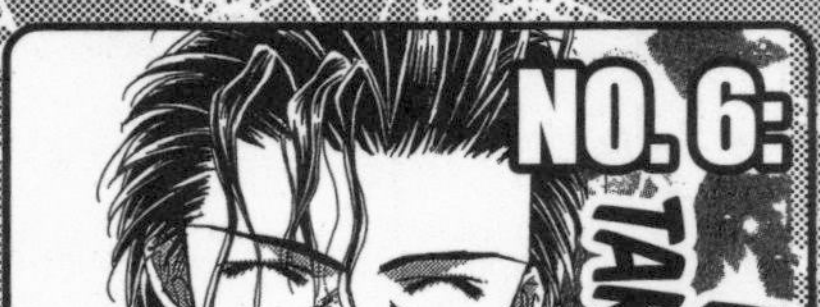
NO. 6:
LORY TAKARADA
184 POINTS

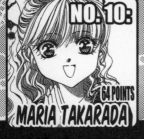

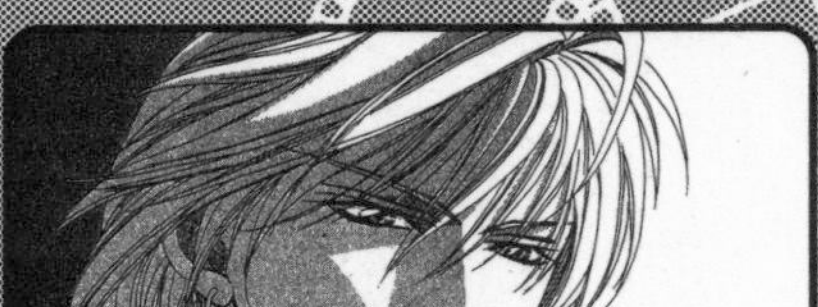
NO. 7:
REINO (VIE GHOUL)
154 POINTS

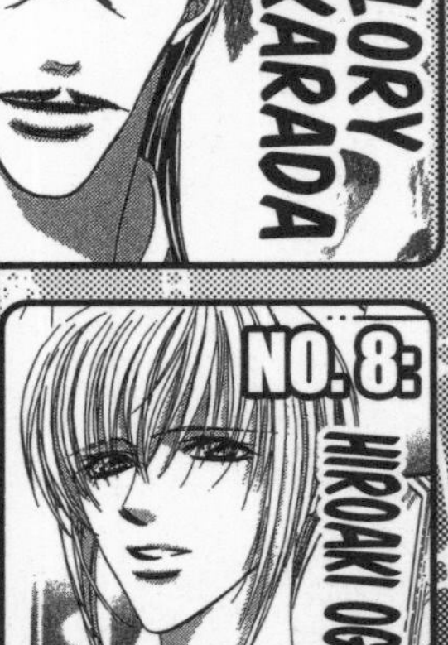
NO. 8:
HIROAKI OGATA
98 POINTS

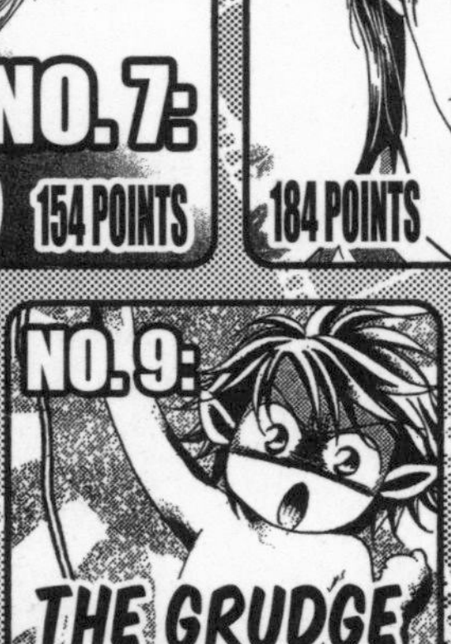
NO. 9:
THE GRUDGE KYOKOS
86 POINTS

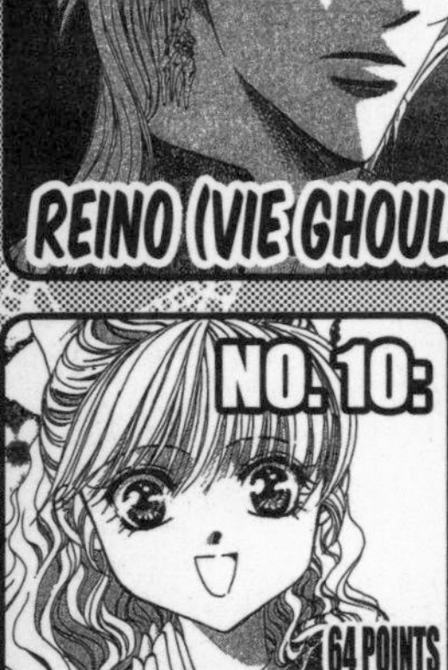
NO. 10:
64 POINTS
MARIA TAKARADA

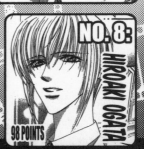

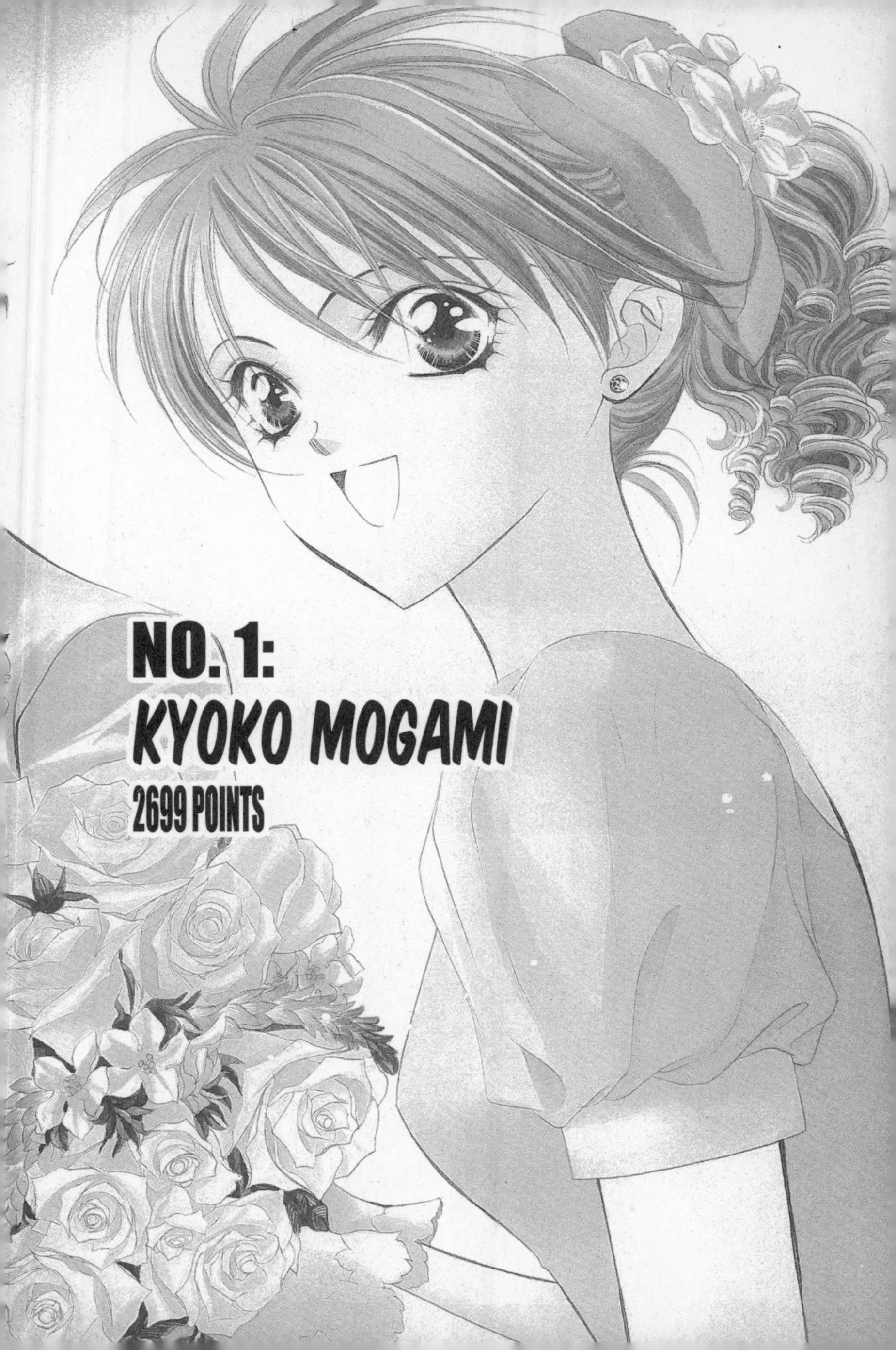
NO. 1:
KYOKO MOGAMI
2699 POINTS

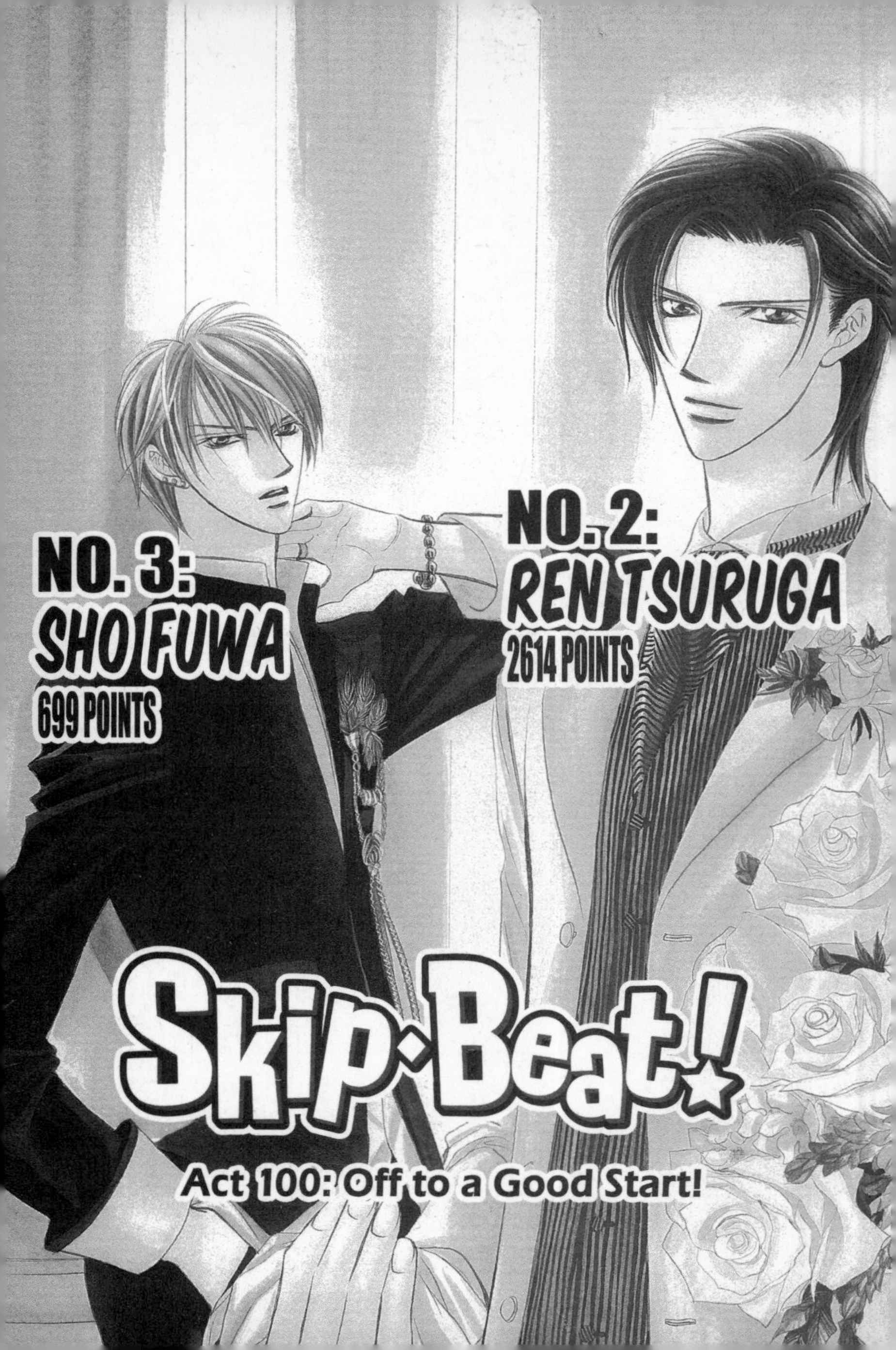
NO. 2:
REN TSURUGA
2614 POINTS
NO. 3:
SHO FUWA
699 POINTS
Skip·Beat!
Act 100: Off to a Good Start!

★ No. 11 and Below ★

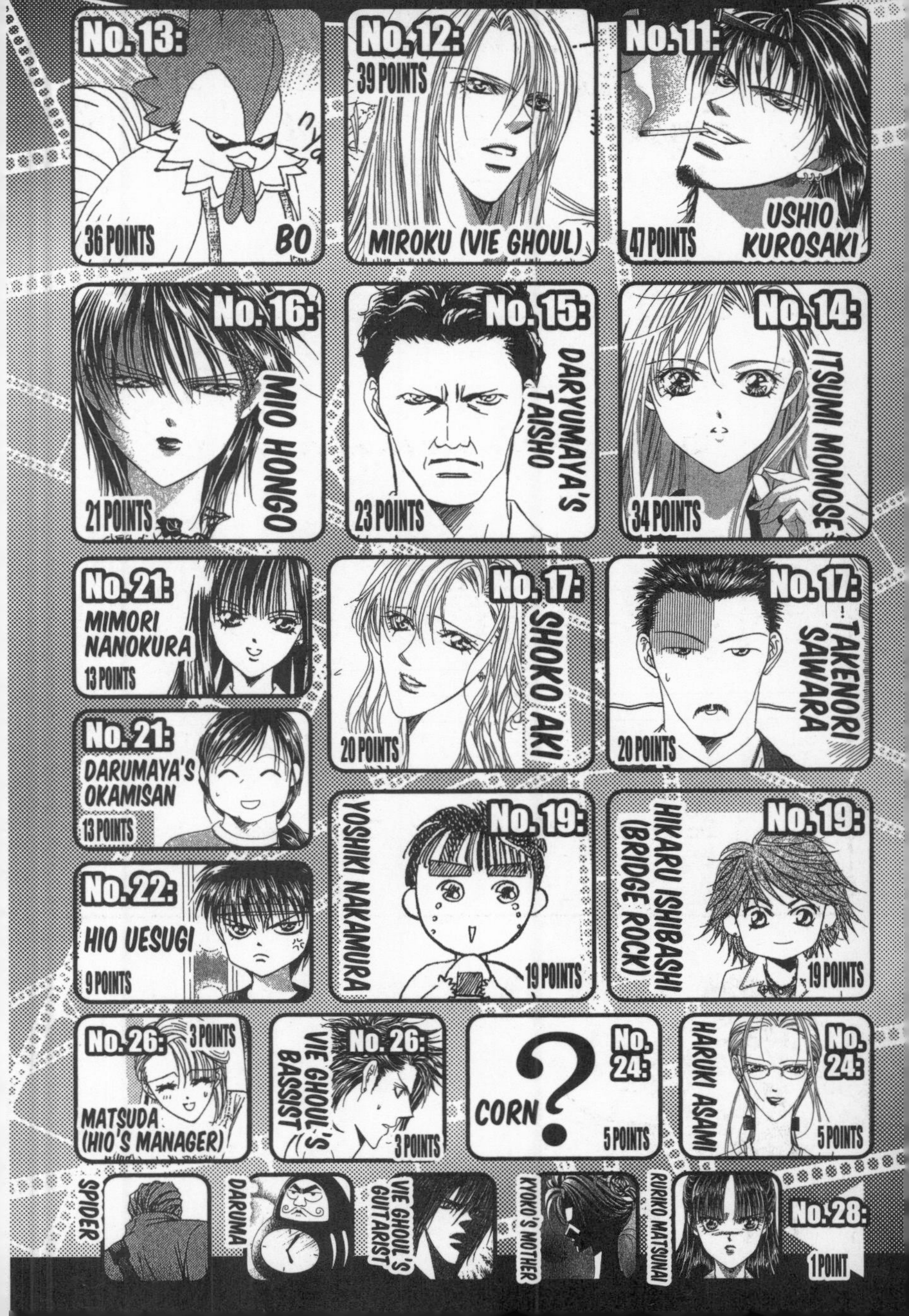

No. 11:
47 POINTS
USHIO KUROSAKI
No. 12:
39 POINTS
MIROKU (VIE GHOUL)
No. 13:
36 POINTS
BO
No. 14:
ITSUMI MOMOSE
34 POINTS
No. 15:
DARYUMAYA'S TAISHO
23 POINTS
No. 16:
MIO HONGO
21 POINTS
No. 17:
TAKENORI SAWARA
20 POINTS
No. 17:
SHOKO AKI
20 POINTS
No. 21:
MIMORI NANOKURA
13 POINTS
No. 21:
DARUMAYA'S OKAMISAN
13 POINTS
No. 22:
HIO UESUGI
9 POINTS
No. 19:
HIKARU ISHIBASHI (BRIDGE ROCK)
19 POINTS
No. 19:
YOSHIKI NAKAMURA
19 POINTS
No. 24:
HARUKI ASAMI
5 POINTS
No. 24:
CORN
5 POINTS
No. 26:
VIE GHOUL'S BASSIST
3 POINTS
No. 26:
3 POINTS
MATSUDA (HIO'S MANAGER)
No. 28:
1 POINT
RURIKO MATSUNAI
KYOKO'S MOTHER
VIE GHOUL'S GUITARIST
DARUMA
SPIDER

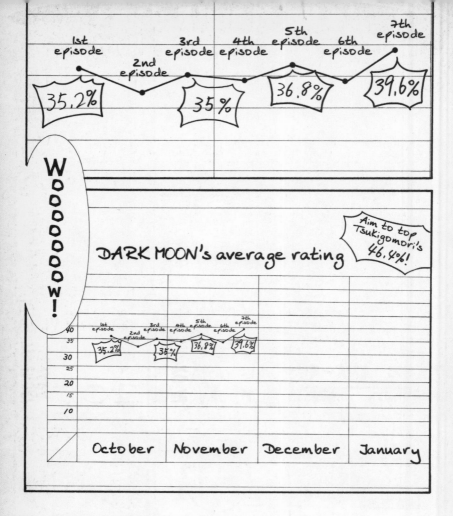

1st episode 35.2%
2nd episode
3rd episode 35%
4th episode
5th episode 36.8%
6th episode
7th episode 39.6%

WOOOOOOW!

DARK MOON's average rating

Aim to top Tsukigomori's 46.4%!

	October	November	December	January
40				
35				
30				
25				
20				
15				
10				

1st episode 35.2%
2nd episode
3rd episode 35%
4th episode
5th episode 36.8%
6th episode
7th episode 39.6%

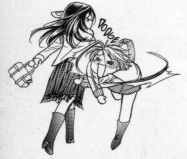

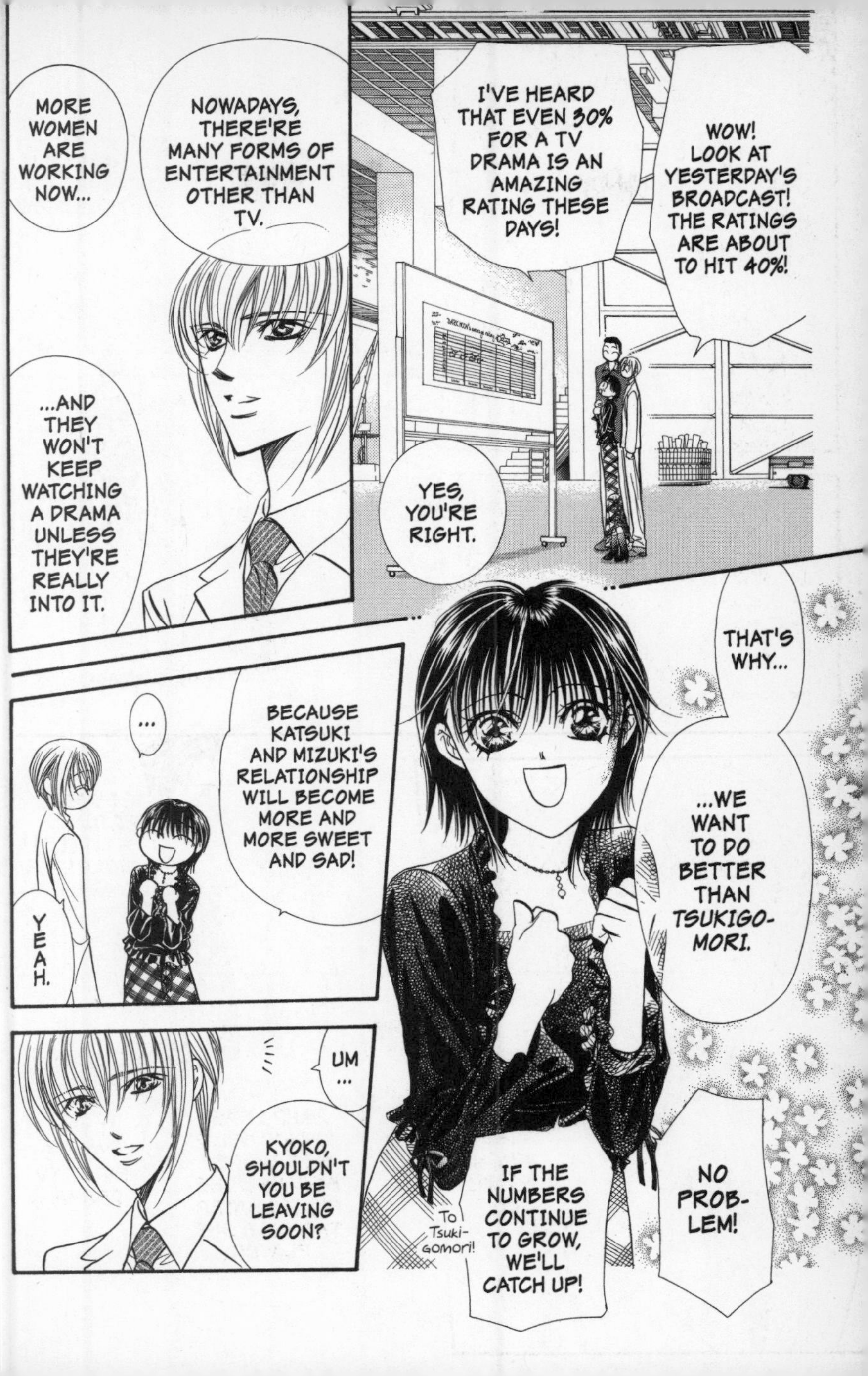
WOW! LOOK AT YESTERDAY'S BROADCAST! THE RATINGS ARE ABOUT TO HIT 40%!
I'VE HEARD THAT EVEN 30% FOR A TV DRAMA IS AN AMAZING RATING THESE DAYS!
YES, YOU'RE RIGHT.
NOWADAYS, THERE'RE MANY FORMS OF ENTERTAINMENT OTHER THAN TV.
MORE WOMEN ARE WORKING NOW...
...AND THEY WON'T KEEP WATCHING A DRAMA UNLESS THEY'RE REALLY INTO IT.
THAT'S WHY...
...WE WANT TO DO BETTER THAN TSUKIGO-MORI.
NO PROB-LEM!
IF THE NUMBERS CONTINUE TO GROW, WE'LL CATCH UP!
To Tsuki-Gomori!
BECAUSE KATSUKI AND MIZUKI'S RELATIONSHIP WILL BECOME MORE AND MORE SWEET AND SAD!
...
YEAH.
UM ...
KYOKO, SHOULDN'T YOU BE LEAVING SOON?

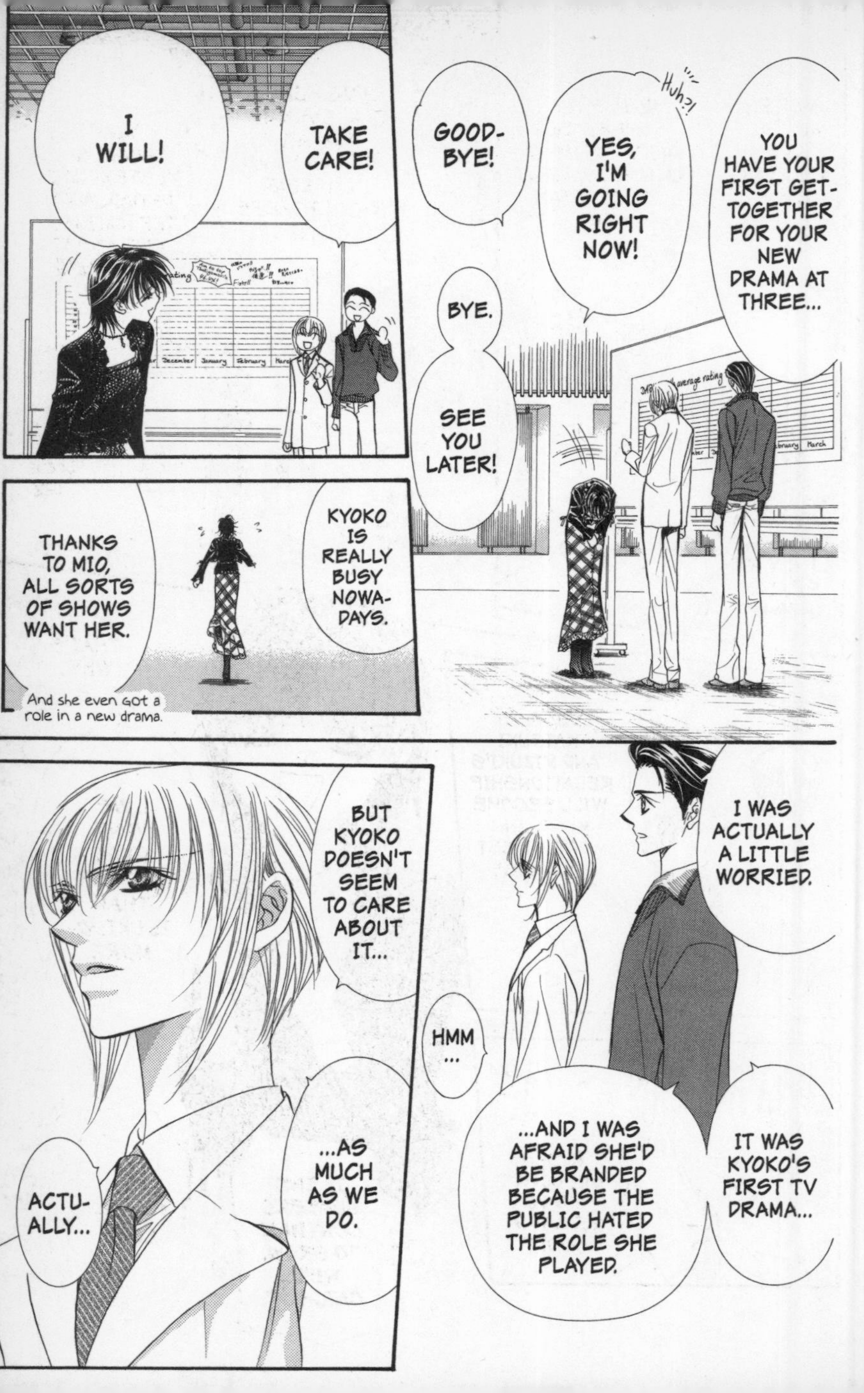
YOU HAVE YOUR FIRST GET-TOGETHER FOR YOUR NEW DRAMA AT THREE...
Huh?!
YES, I'M GOING RIGHT NOW!
GOOD-BYE!
BYE.
SEE YOU LATER!
TAKE CARE!
I WILL!
KYOKO IS REALLY BUSY NOWADAYS.
THANKS TO MIO, ALL SORTS OF SHOWS WANT HER.
And she even got a role in a new drama.
I WAS ACTUALLY A LITTLE WORRIED.
IT WAS KYOKO'S FIRST TV DRAMA...
...AND I WAS AFRAID SHE'D BE BRANDED BECAUSE THE PUBLIC HATED THE ROLE SHE PLAYED.
HMM ...
BUT KYOKO DOESN'T SEEM TO CARE ABOUT IT...
...AS MUCH AS WE DO.
ACTU-ALLY...

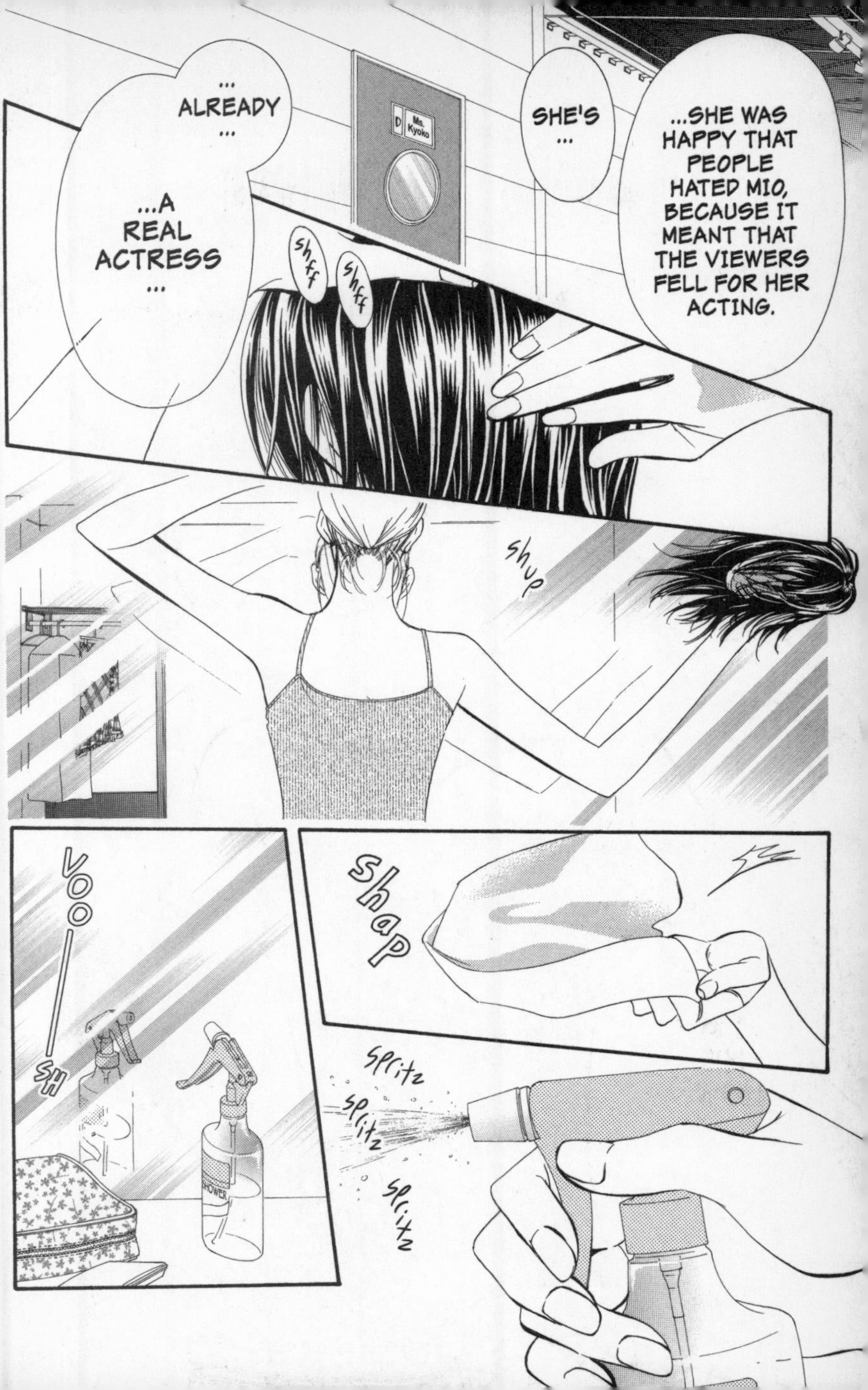

...SHE WAS HAPPY THAT PEOPLE HATED MIO, BECAUSE IT MEANT THAT THE VIEWERS FELL FOR HER ACTING.
SHE'S ...
... ALREADY ...
...A REAL ACTRESS ...
D Ms. Kyoko
shff
shff
shup
Shap
VOO—SH
spritz
spritz
spritz
SHOWER

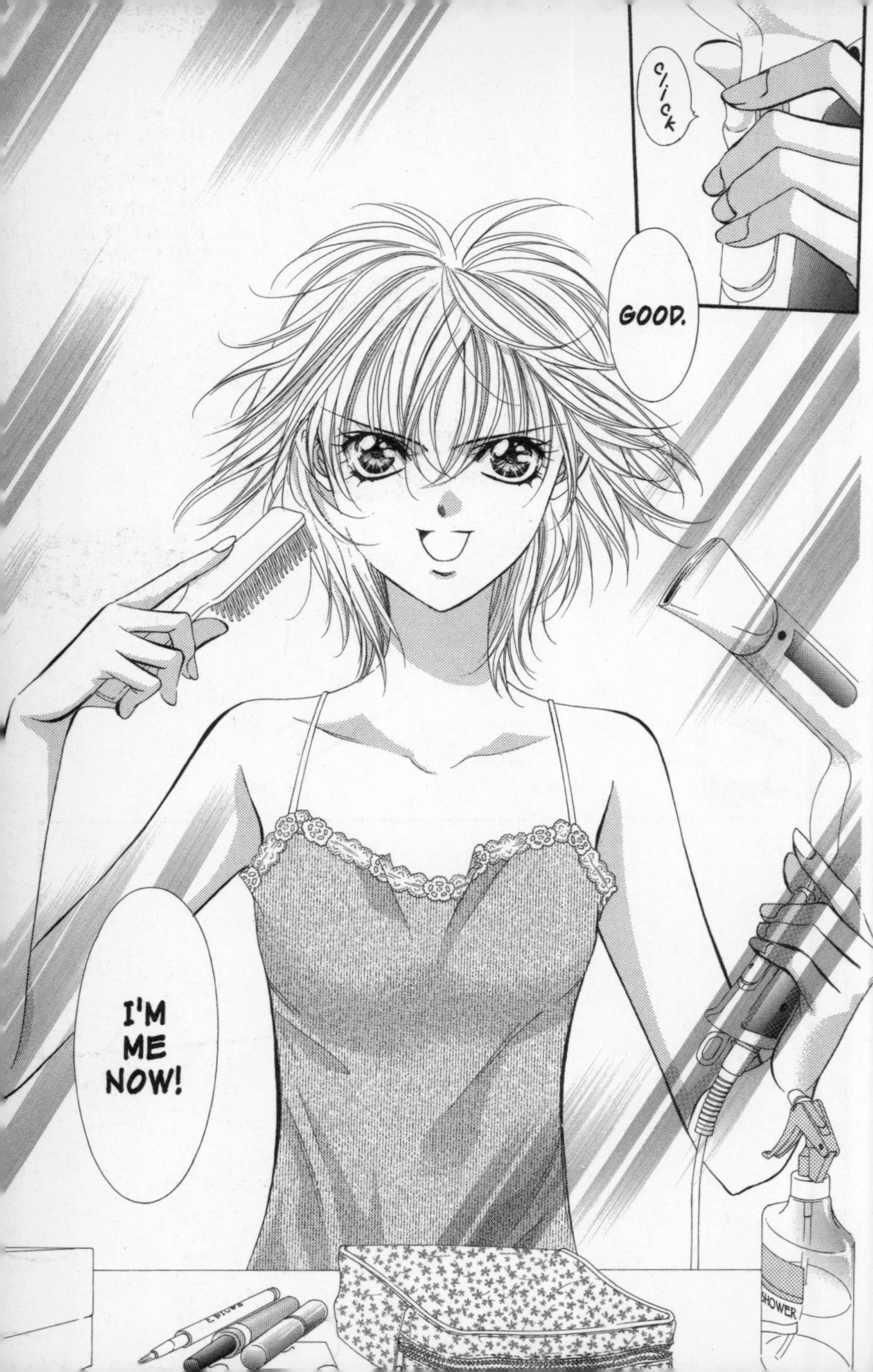
CLICK
GOOD.
I'M ME NOW!
SHOWER

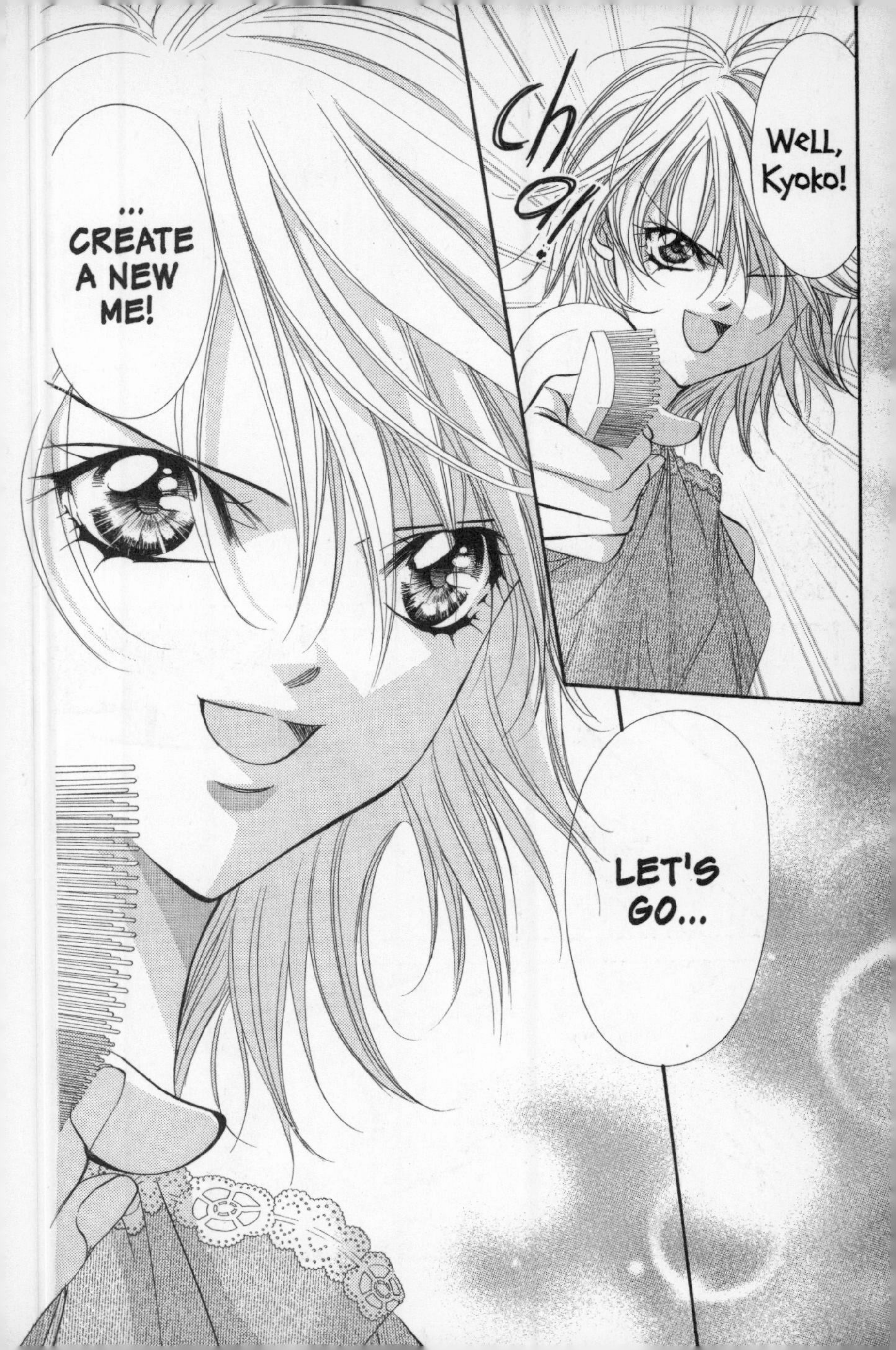
Well, Kyoko!
Let's go...
... create a new me!

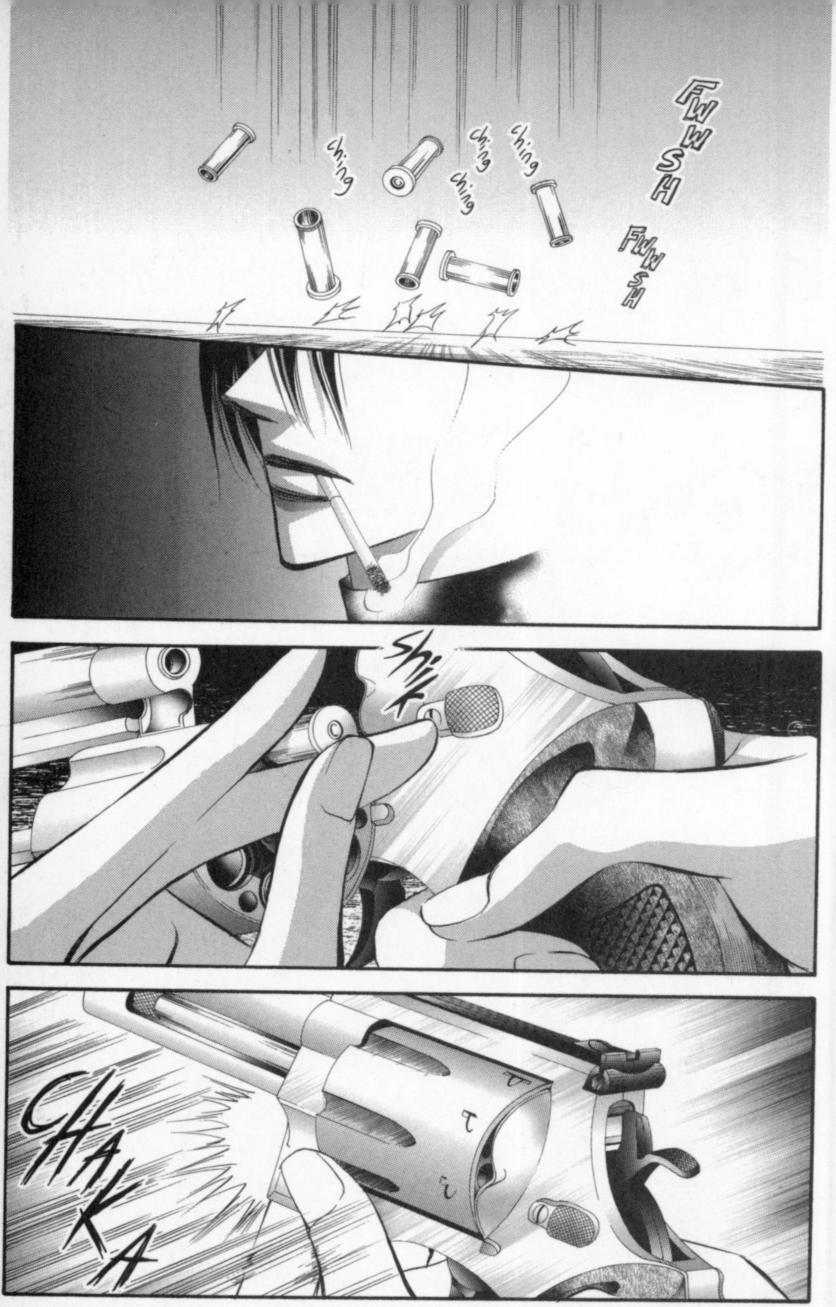

FWWSH
FWWSH
ching
ching
ching
ching
shiik
CHAKA

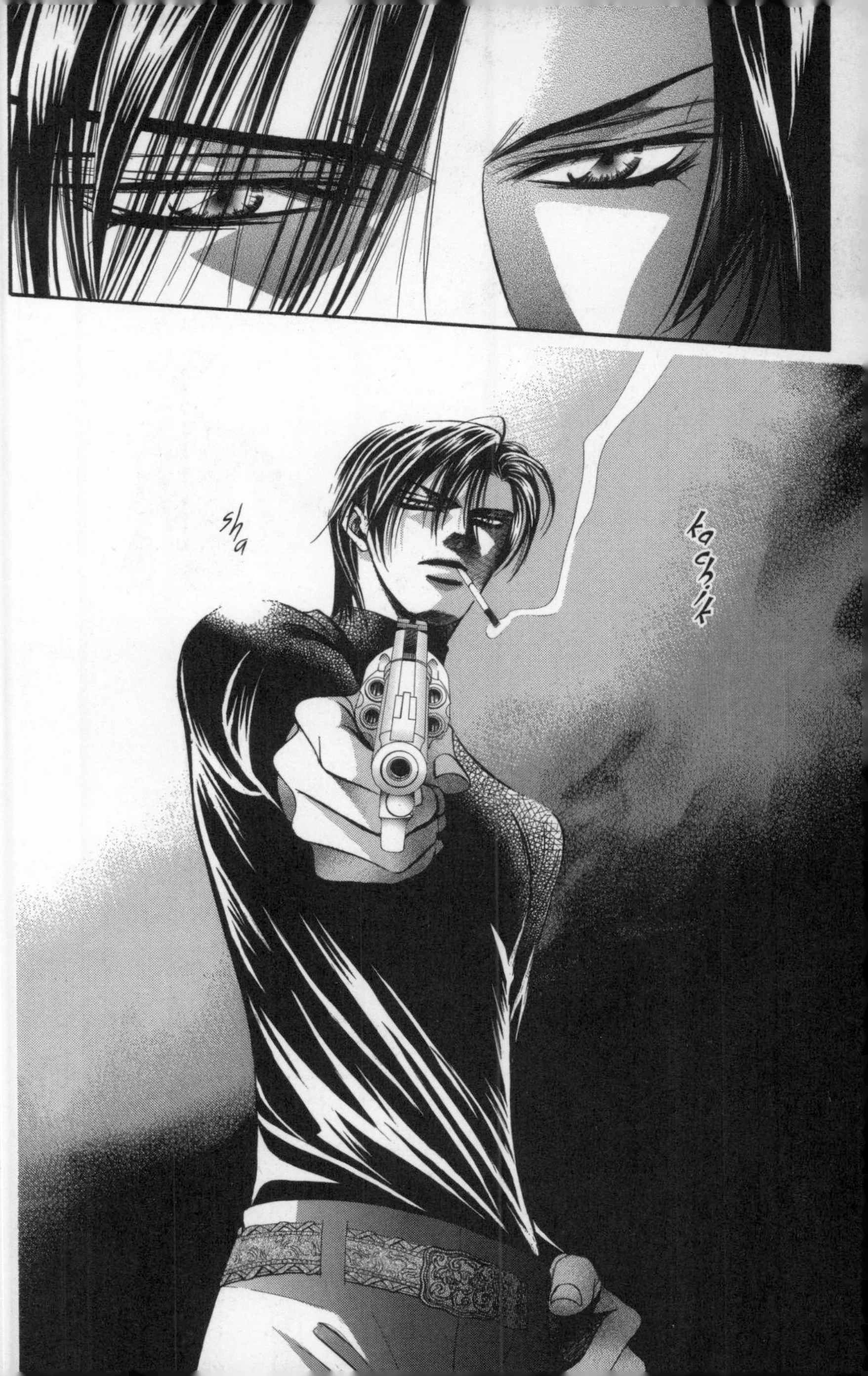
ka chik
sha

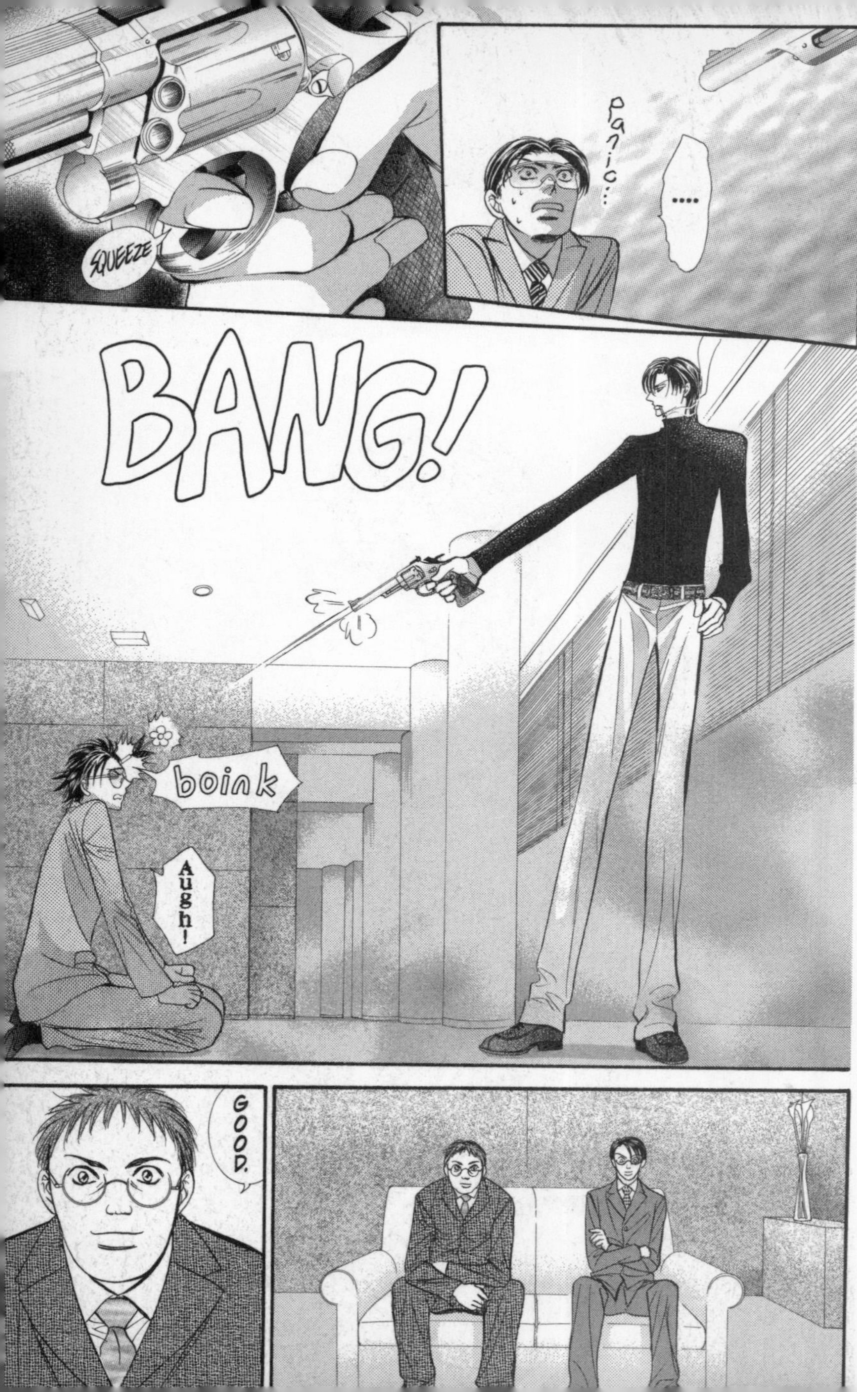

Panic...
....
SQUEEZE
BANG!
boink
Augh!
GOOD.

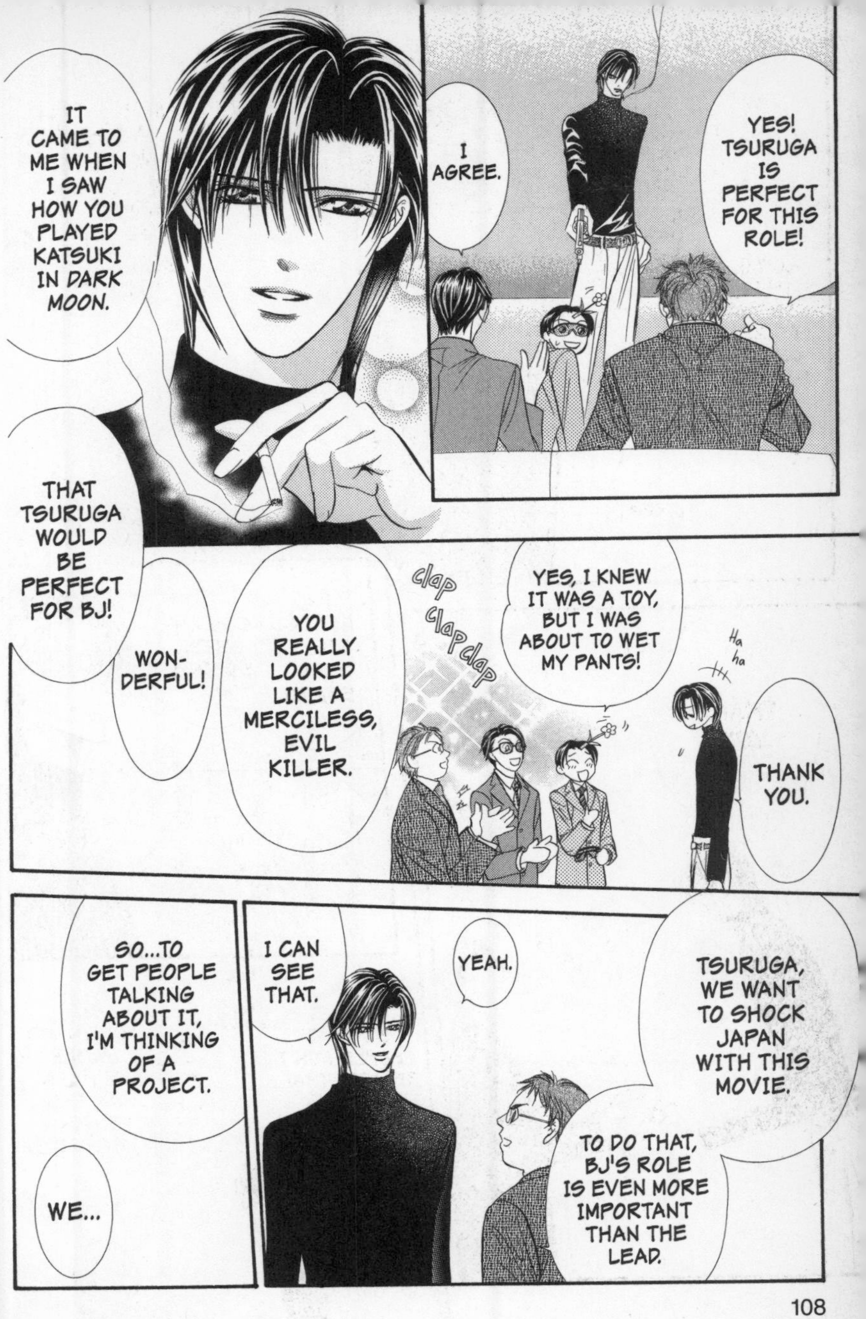
YES! TSURUGA IS PERFECT FOR THIS ROLE!
I AGREE.
IT CAME TO ME WHEN I SAW HOW YOU PLAYED KATSUKI IN DARK MOON.
THAT TSURUGA WOULD BE PERFECT FOR BJ!
THANK YOU.
Ha ha
YES, I KNEW IT WAS A TOY, BUT I WAS ABOUT TO WET MY PANTS!
clap clap clap
YOU REALLY LOOKED LIKE A MERCILESS, EVIL KILLER.
WON-DERFUL!
TSURUGA, WE WANT TO SHOCK JAPAN WITH THIS MOVIE.
TO DO THAT, BJ'S ROLE IS EVEN MORE IMPORTANT THAN THE LEAD.
YEAH.
I CAN SEE THAT.
SO...TO GET PEOPLE TALKING ABOUT IT, I'M THINKING OF A PROJECT.
WE...

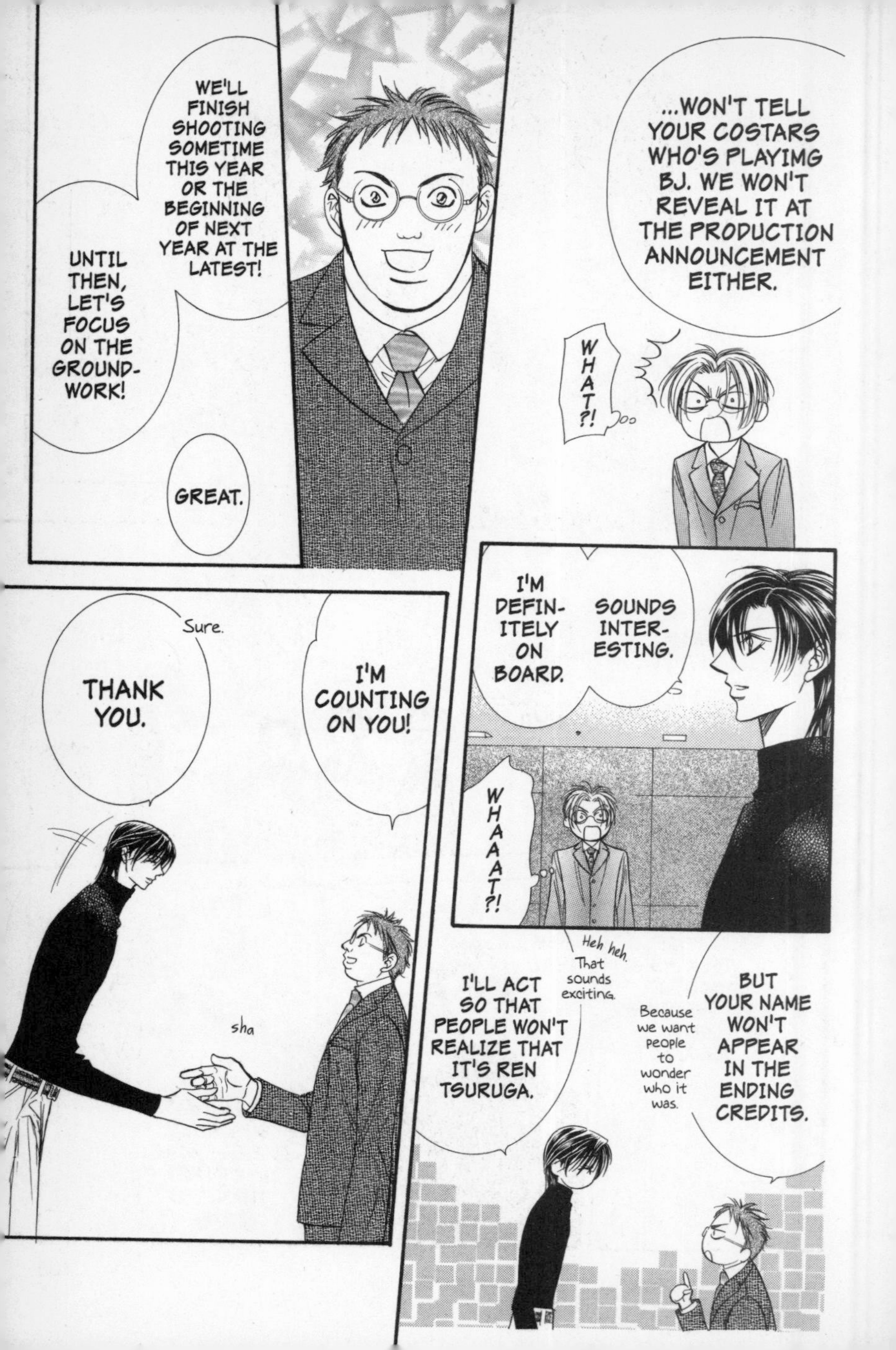
...WON'T TELL YOUR COSTARS WHO'S PLAYIMG BJ. WE WON'T REVEAL IT AT THE PRODUCTION ANNOUNCEMENT EITHER.
WHAT?!
SOUNDS INTER-ESTING.
I'M DEFIN-ITELY ON BOARD.
WHAAAAT?!
BUT YOUR NAME WON'T APPEAR IN THE ENDING CREDITS.
Because we want people to wonder who it was.
Heh heh. That sounds exciting.
I'LL ACT SO THAT PEOPLE WON'T REALIZE THAT IT'S REN TSURUGA.
WE'LL FINISH SHOOTING SOMETIME THIS YEAR OR THE BEGINNING OF NEXT YEAR AT THE LATEST!
UNTIL THEN, LET'S FOCUS ON THE GROUND-WORK!
GREAT.
I'M COUNTING ON YOU!
Sure.
THANK YOU.
sha

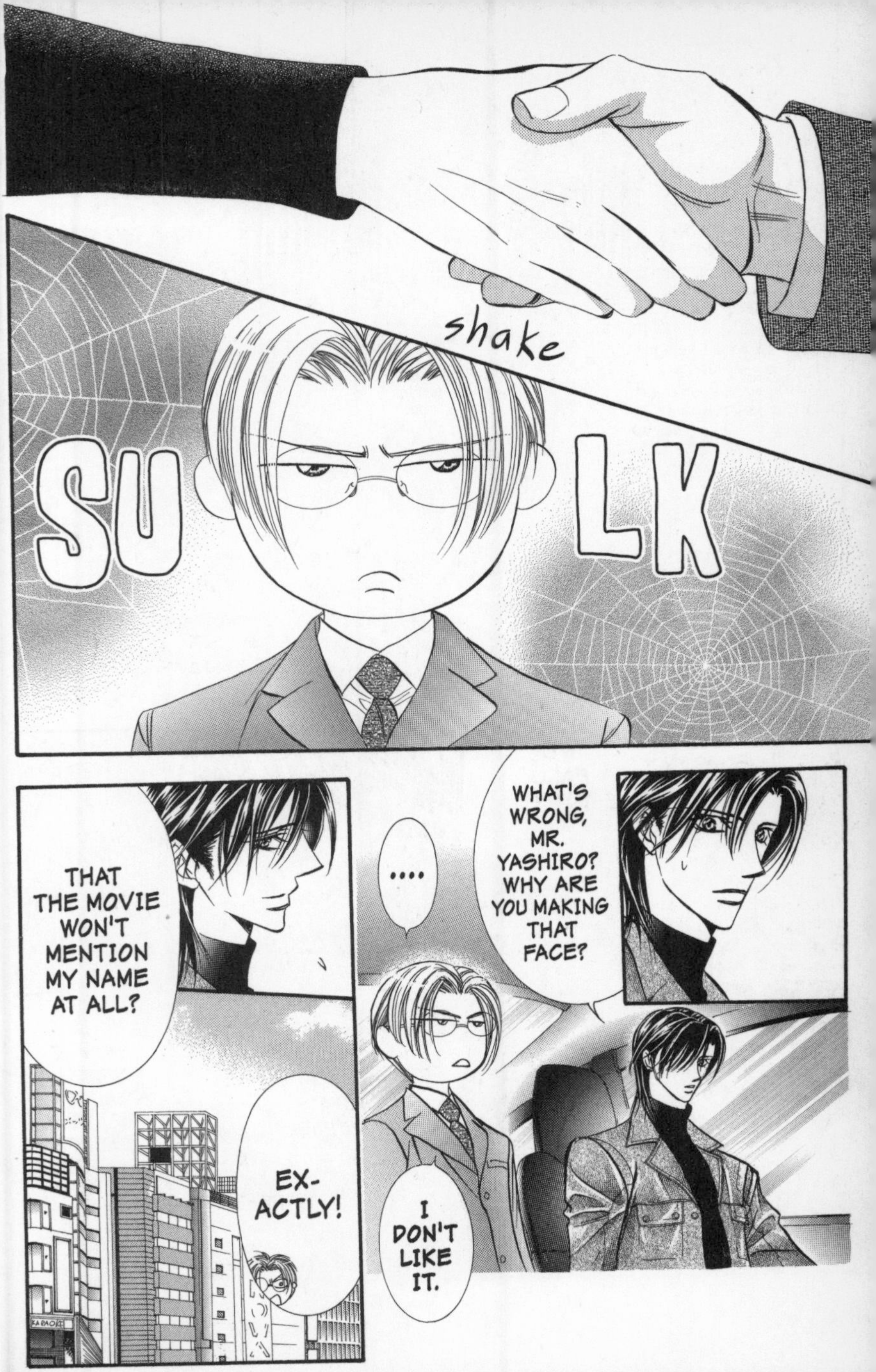
shake
SULK
WHAT'S WRONG, MR. YASHIRO? WHY ARE YOU MAKING THAT FACE?
....
I DON'T LIKE IT.
THAT THE MOVIE WON'T MENTION MY NAME AT ALL?
EX-ACTLY!

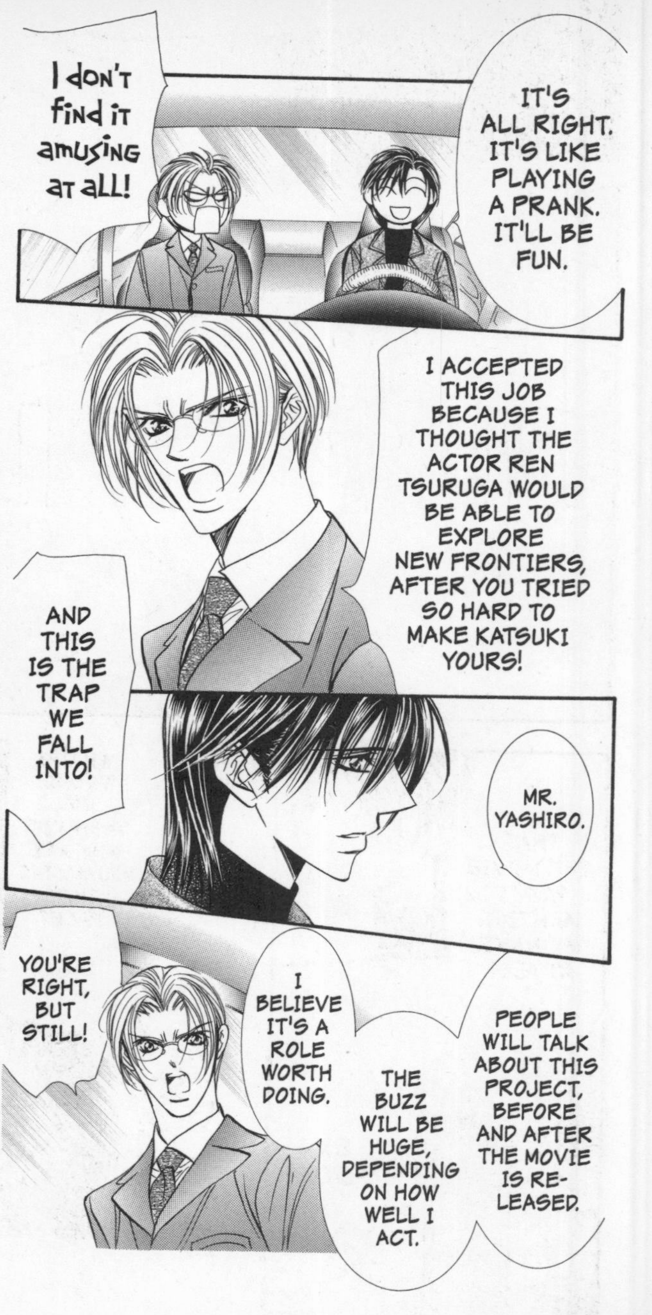
IT'S ALL RIGHT. IT'S LIKE PLAYING A PRANK. IT'LL BE FUN.
I don't find it amusing at all!
I ACCEPTED THIS JOB BECAUSE I THOUGHT THE ACTOR REN TSURUGA WOULD BE ABLE TO EXPLORE NEW FRONTIERS, AFTER YOU TRIED SO HARD TO MAKE KATSUKI YOURS!
AND THIS IS THE TRAP WE FALL INTO!
MR. YASHIRO.
PEOPLE WILL TALK ABOUT THIS PROJECT, BEFORE AND AFTER THE MOVIE IS RE-LEASED.
THE BUZZ WILL BE HUGE, DEPENDING ON HOW WELL I ACT.
I BELIEVE IT'S A ROLE WORTH DOING.
YOU'RE RIGHT, BUT STILL!

***Kinseiseki* = Cordierite in English**

Jewelry shops call it "iolite." "Water sapphire" is a popular name too, But...the name "iolite" is probably used more often...I didn't know this Back then, But it must have Been common knowledge for people who like stones...

Now I know a little Bit about the names of stones, so it's an even more embarrassing episode...

...So anyway, after I got into natural stones, I've Been Buying various stones I've fallen in love with, But I haven't Bought the crucial iolite yet...I've seen them a couple times at stone shops, But I haven't en-countered one where I felt "Th-This is the one!!"...I'd Be happy if someday, I can find one like Corn, where the color changes so much that I can say "It's magic"...

...By the way...

The handmade iolite cellphone charms and Bracelets that readers have given me...I have Been using them with gratitude. People who aren't interested in stones at all will think "You're paying that much for just a stone?! Are you stupid?!"

- Continued -

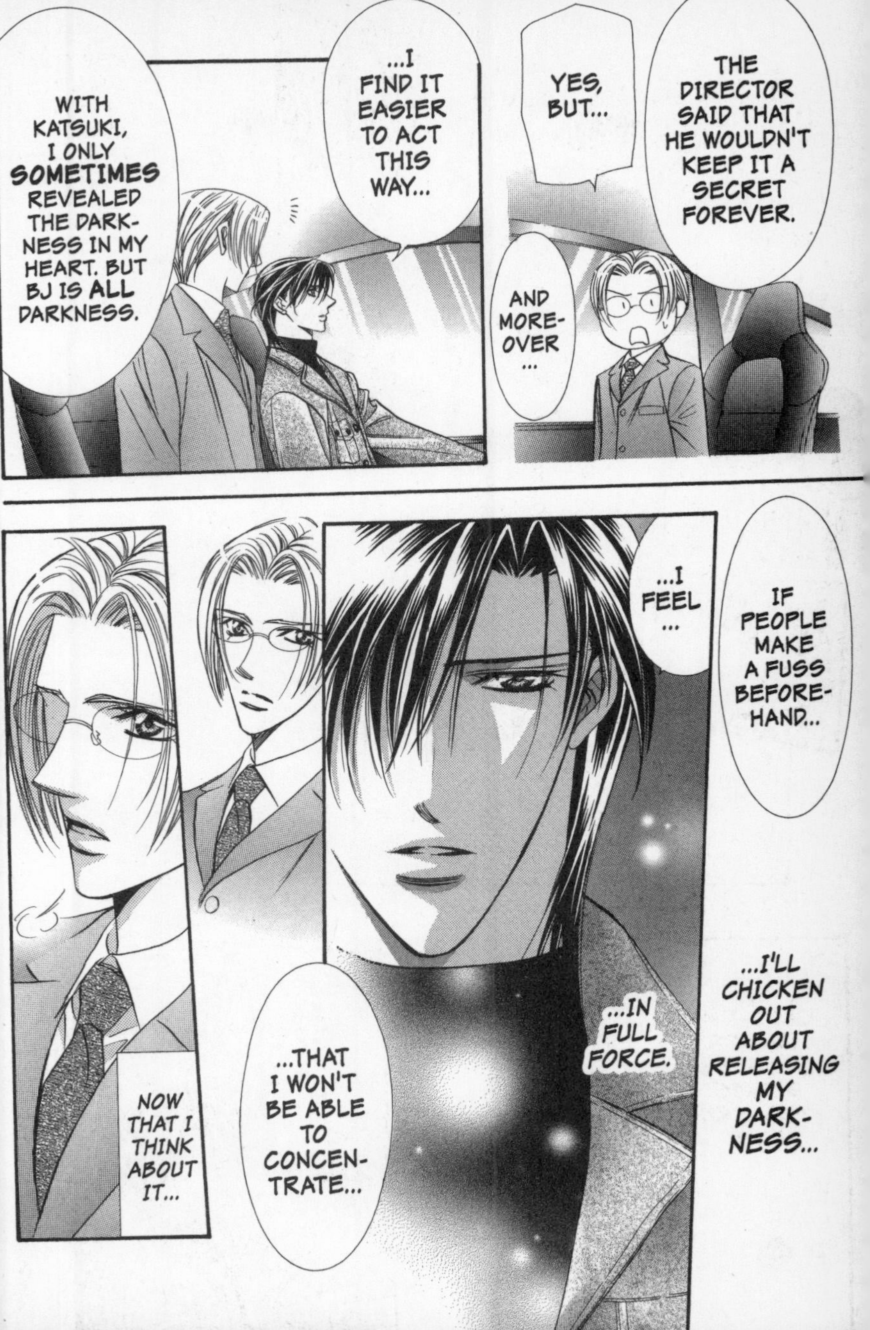
THE DIRECTOR SAID THAT HE WOULDN'T KEEP IT A SECRET FOREVER.
YES, BUT...
AND MOREOVER...
...I FIND IT EASIER TO ACT THIS WAY...
WITH KATSUKI, I ONLY SOMETIMES REVEALED THE DARKNESS IN MY HEART. BUT BJ IS ALL DARKNESS.
IF PEOPLE MAKE A FUSS BEFOREHAND...
...I FEEL...
...I'LL CHICKEN OUT ABOUT RELEASING MY DARKNESS...
...IN FULL FORCE.
...THAT I WON'T BE ABLE TO CONCENTRATE...
NOW THAT I THINK ABOUT IT...

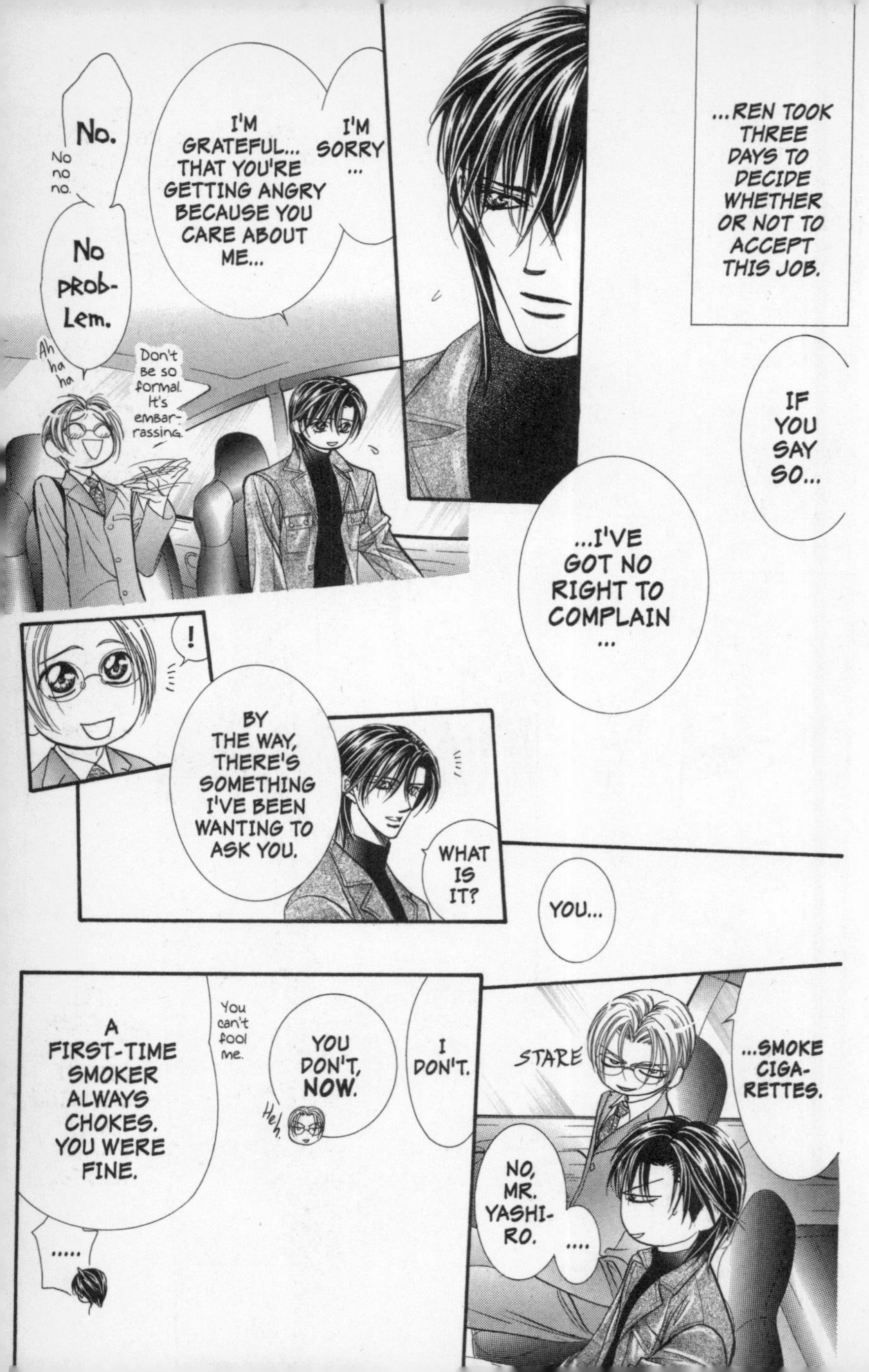
...REN TOOK THREE DAYS TO DECIDE WHETHER OR NOT TO ACCEPT THIS JOB.
IF YOU SAY SO...
...I'VE GOT NO RIGHT TO COMPLAIN ...
I'M SORRY ...
I'M GRATEFUL... THAT YOU'RE GETTING ANGRY BECAUSE YOU CARE ABOUT ME...
No.
No no no.
No prob-lem.
Ah ha ha
Don't be so formal. It's embar-rassing.
!
BY THE WAY, THERE'S SOMETHING I'VE BEEN WANTING TO ASK YOU.
WHAT IS IT?
YOU...
...SMOKE CIGA-RETTES.
STARE
NO, MR. YASHI-RO.
....
I DON'T.
YOU DON'T, NOW.
You can't fool me.
Heh
A FIRST-TIME SMOKER ALWAYS CHOKES. YOU WERE FINE.
.....

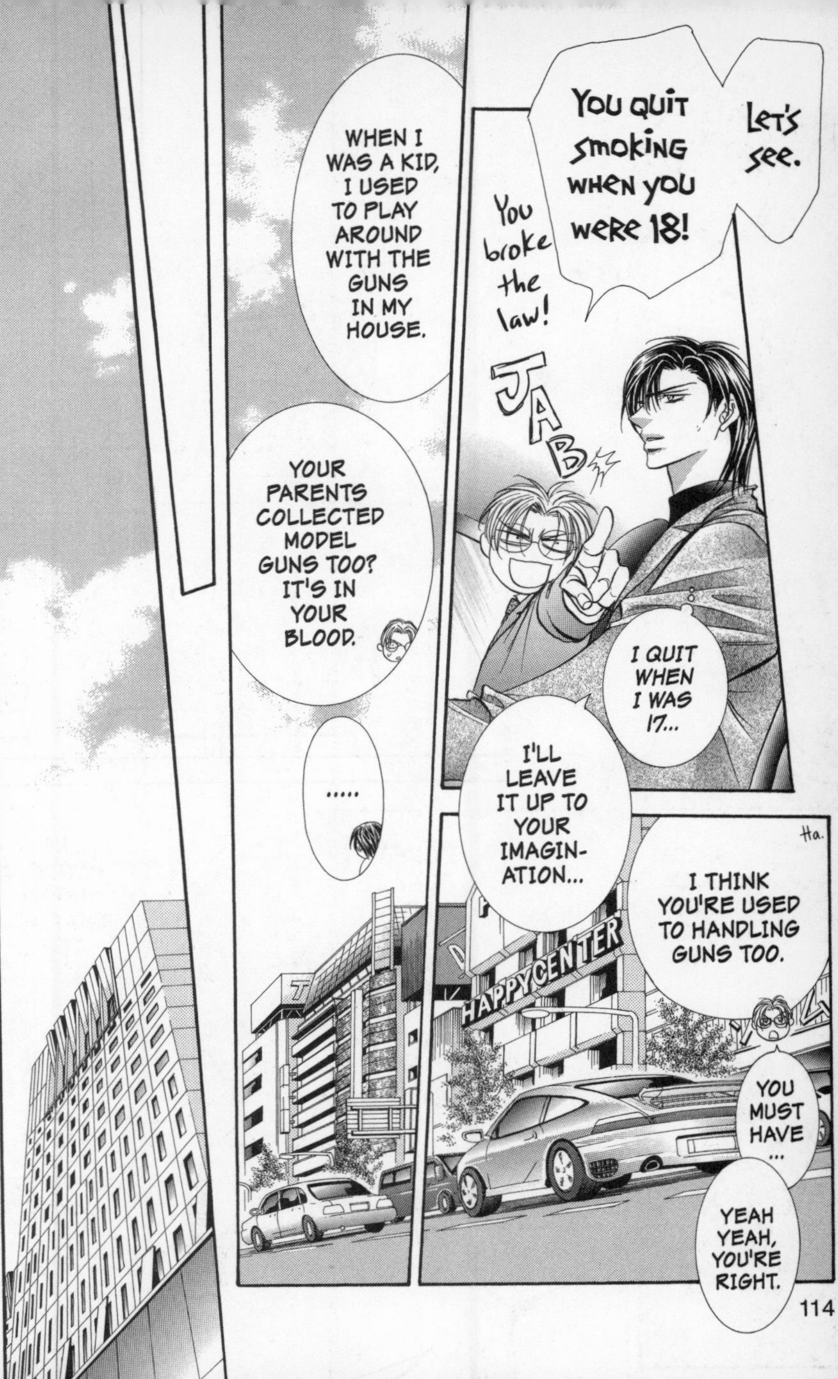
Let's see.
You quit smoking when you were 18!
You broke the law!
JAB
I QUIT WHEN I WAS 17...
I'LL LEAVE IT UP TO YOUR IMAGINATION...
Ha.
I THINK YOU'RE USED TO HANDLING GUNS TOO.
YOU MUST HAVE ...
YEAH YEAH, YOU'RE RIGHT.
HAPPYCENTER
WHEN I WAS A KID, I USED TO PLAY AROUND WITH THE GUNS IN MY HOUSE.
YOUR PARENTS COLLECTED MODEL GUNS TOO? IT'S IN YOUR BLOOD.
.....

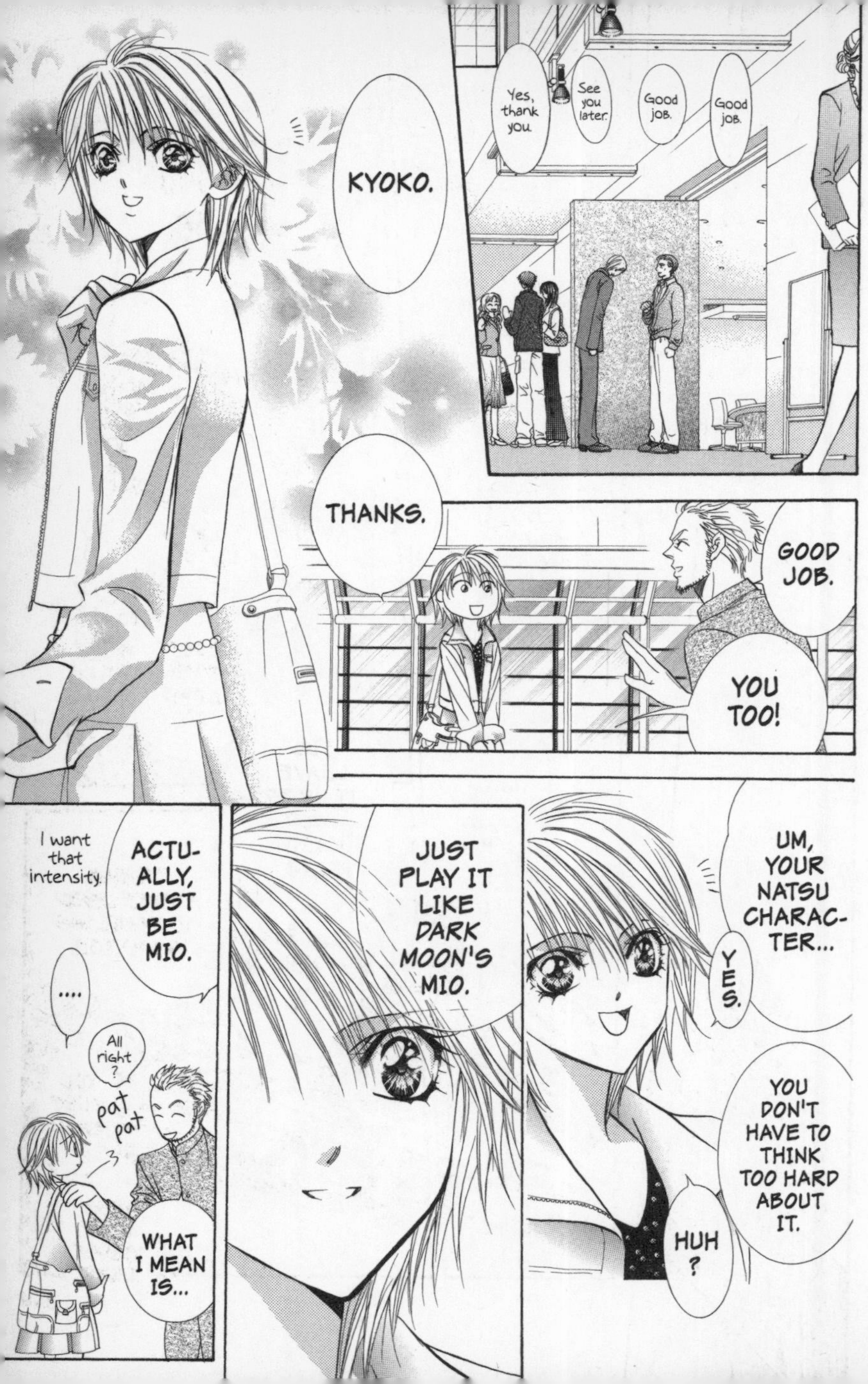
Good job.
Good job.
See you later.
Yes, thank you.
GOOD JOB.
YOU TOO!
THANKS.
KYOKO.
UM, YOUR NATSU CHARAC-TER...
YES.
YOU DON'T HAVE TO THINK TOO HARD ABOUT IT.
HUH?
JUST PLAY IT LIKE DARK MOON'S MIO.
ACTU-ALLY, JUST BE MIO.
I want that intensity.
....
All right?
pat pat
WHAT I MEAN IS...

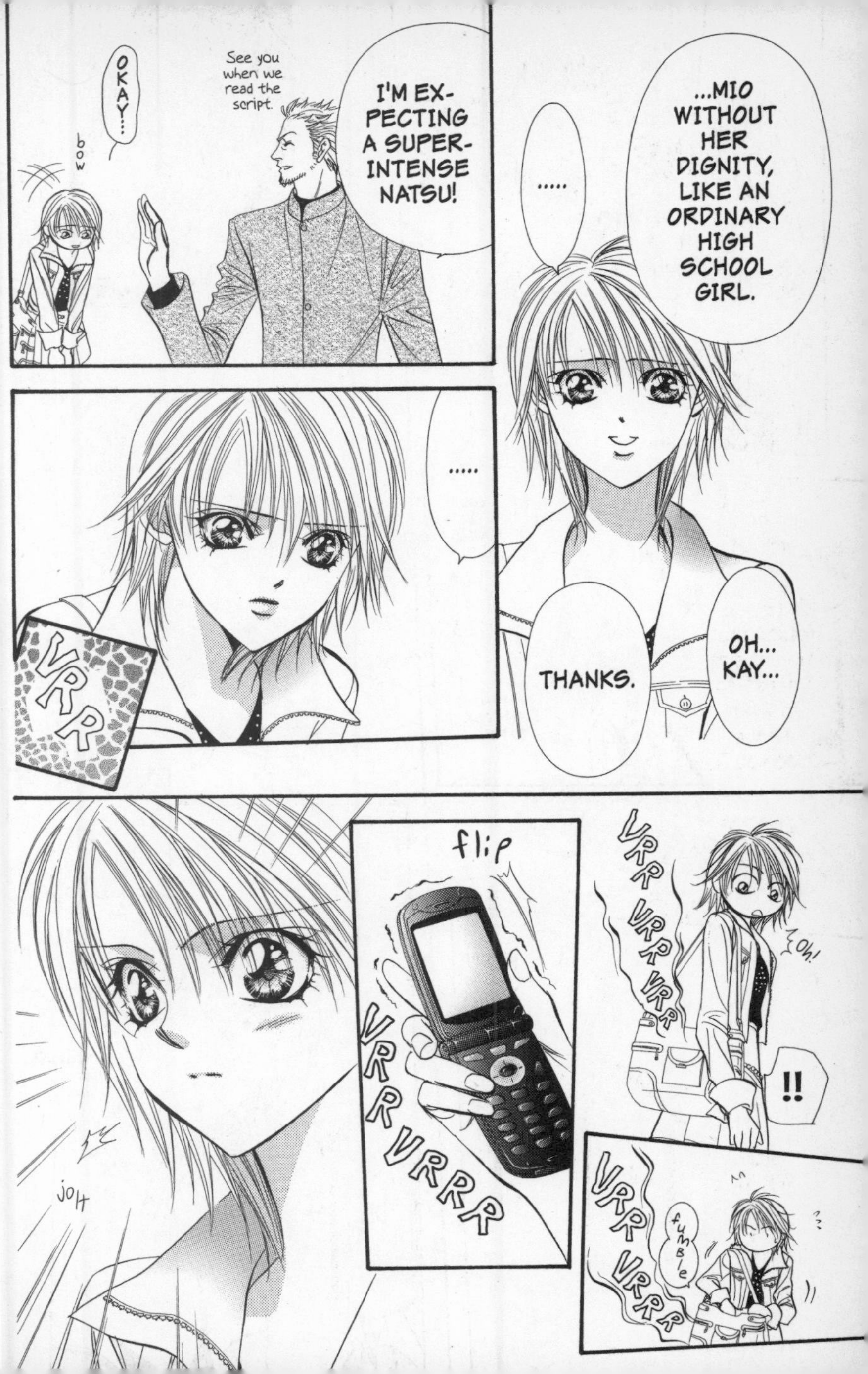
...MIO WITHOUT HER DIGNITY, LIKE AN ORDINARY HIGH SCHOOL GIRL.
.....
OH... KAY...
THANKS.
I'M EX-PECTING A SUPER-INTENSE NATSU!
See you when we read the script.
OKAY...
bow
.....
VRR
VRR VRR VRR
Oh!
!!
VRR VRRR
fumble
flip
VRR VRRR
jolt

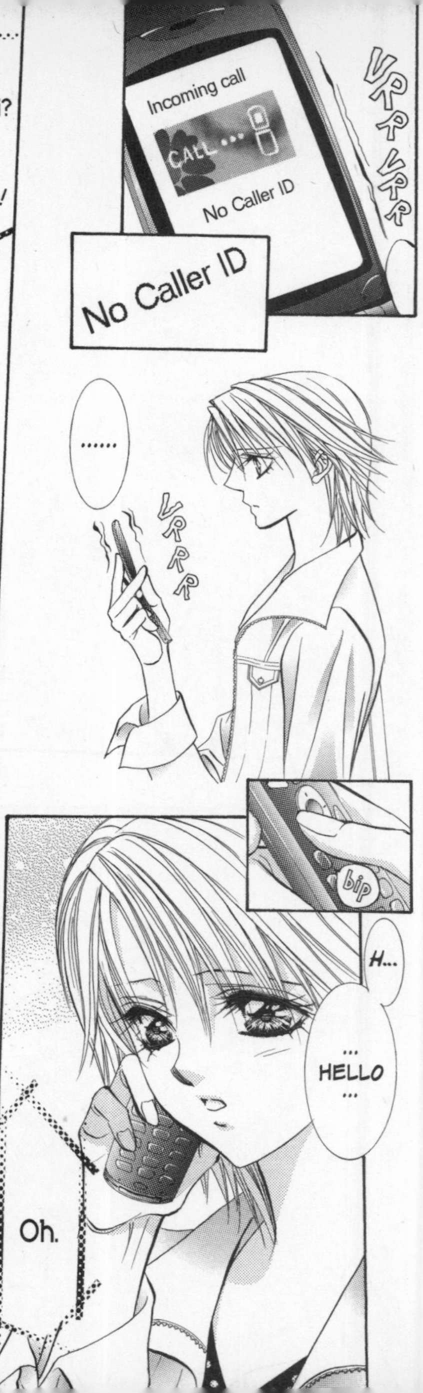
Incoming call
CALL ...
No Caller ID
VRR VRR VRR
No Caller ID
......
VRRR
bip
H...
...HELLO...
Oh.

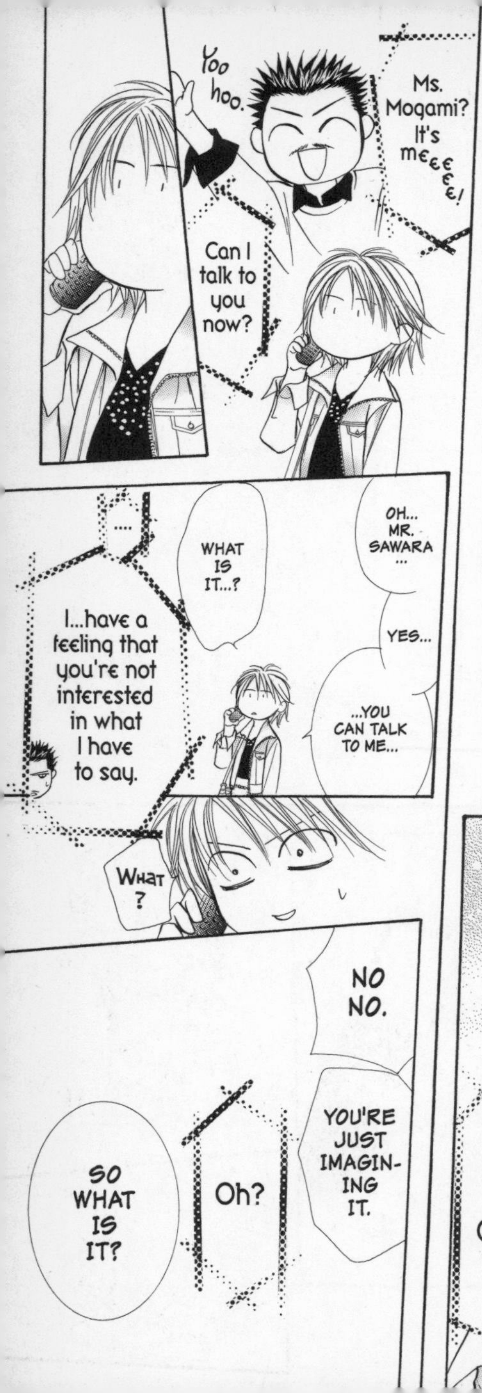
Yoo hoo.
Ms. Mogami? It's meeeee!
Can I talk to you now?
OH... MR. SAWARA...
YES...
...YOU CAN TALK TO ME...
WHAT IS IT...?
....
I...have a feeling that you're not interested in what I have to say.
WHAT?
NO NO.
YOU'RE JUST IMAGINING IT.
Oh?
SO WHAT IS IT?

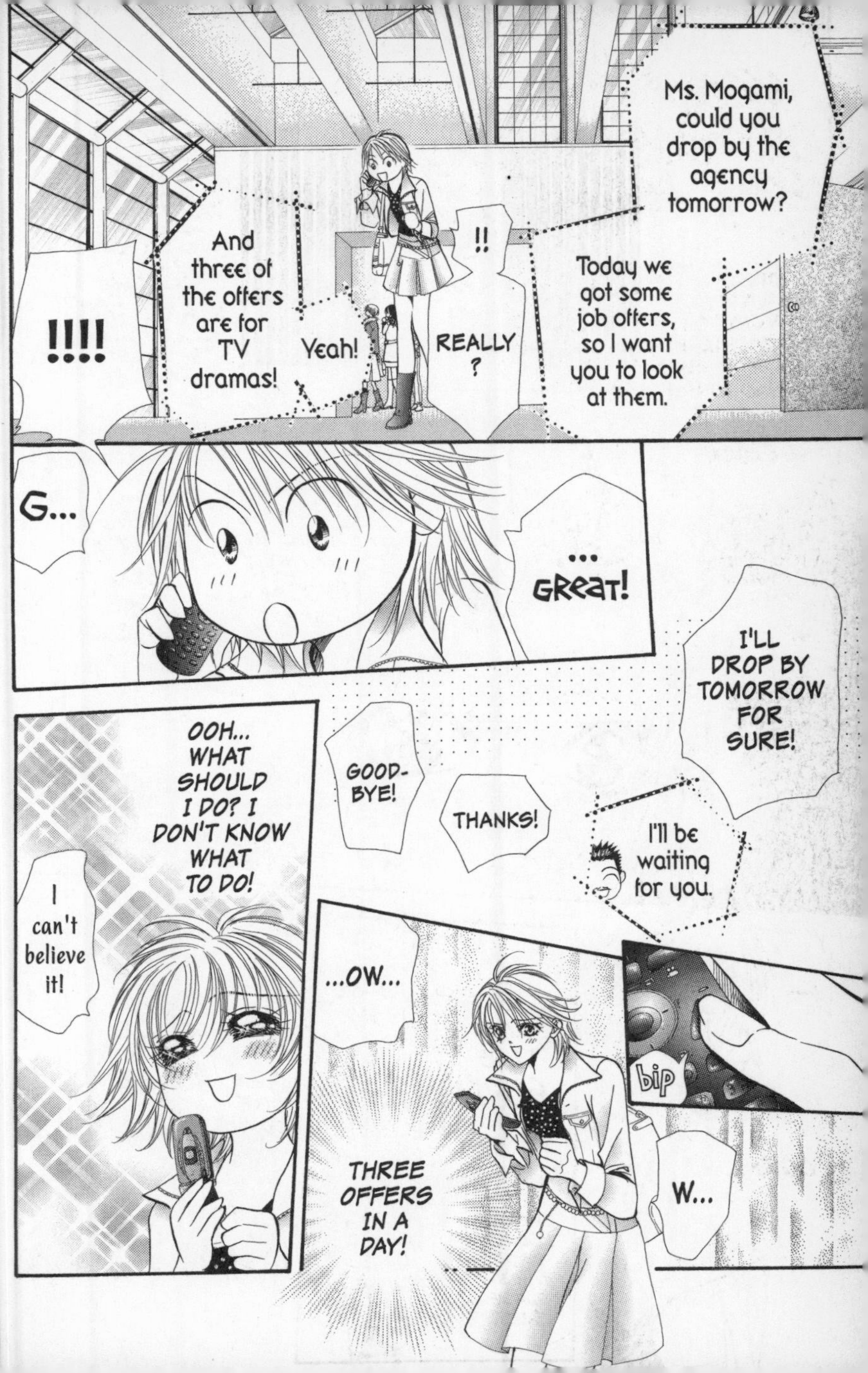

Ms. Mogami, could you drop by the agency tomorrow?
Today we got some job offers, so I want you to look at them.
!!
REALLY?
Yeah!
And three of the offers are for TV dramas!
!!!!
G...
...GREAT!
I'LL DROP BY TOMORROW FOR SURE!
I'll be waiting for you.
THANKS!
GOOD-BYE!
bip
W...
THREE OFFERS IN A DAY!
...OW...
OOH... WHAT SHOULD I DO? I DON'T KNOW WHAT TO DO!
I can't believe it!

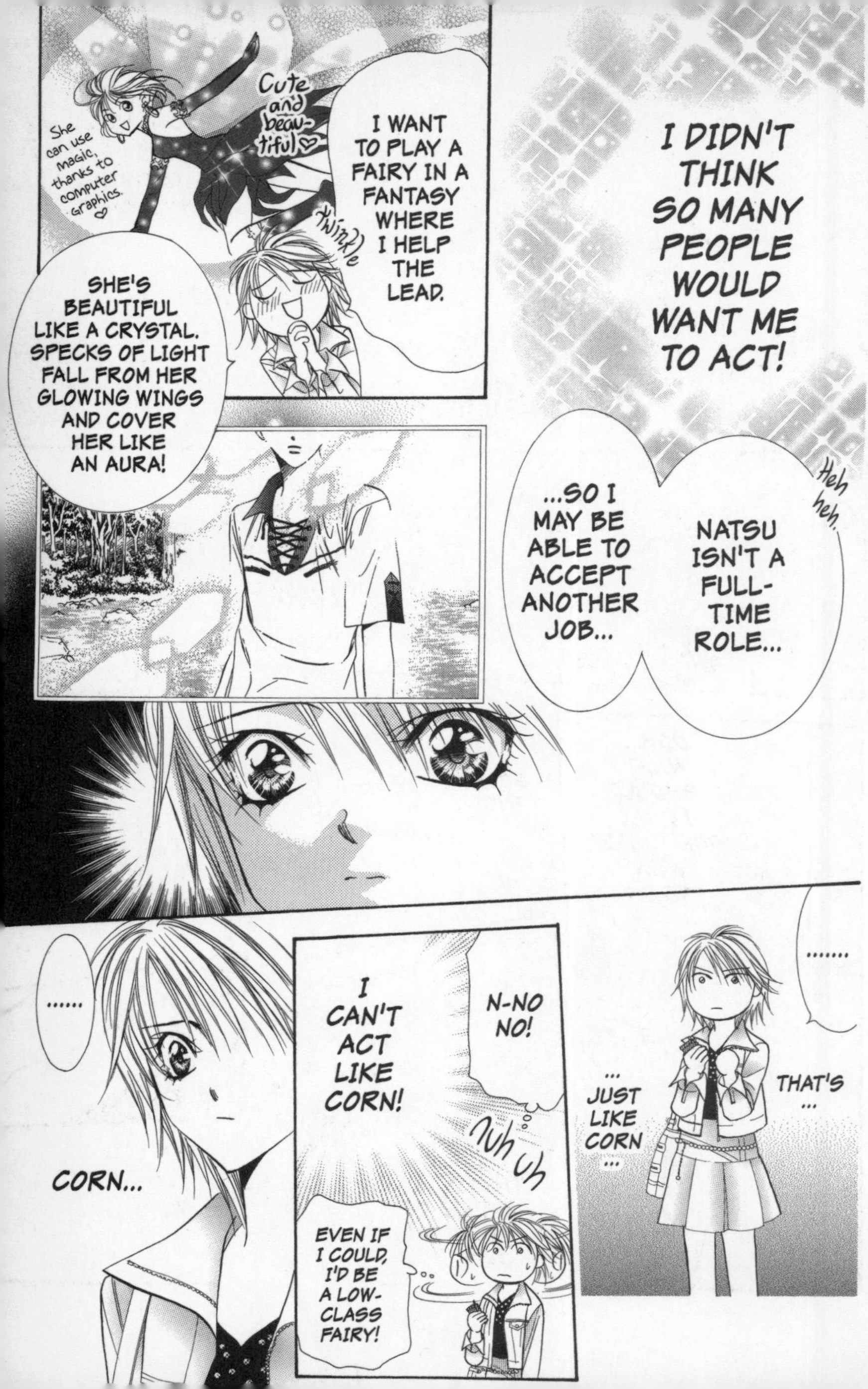
I DIDN'T THINK SO MANY PEOPLE WOULD WANT ME TO ACT!
I WANT TO PLAY A FAIRY IN A FANTASY WHERE I HELP THE LEAD.
Cute and beau-tiful♡
She can use magic, thanks to computer graphics.♡
Twinkle
SHE'S BEAUTIFUL LIKE A CRYSTAL. SPECKS OF LIGHT FALL FROM HER GLOWING WINGS AND COVER HER LIKE AN AURA!
Heh heh.
NATSU ISN'T A FULL-TIME ROLE...
...SO I MAY BE ABLE TO ACCEPT ANOTHER JOB...
......
THAT'S...
...JUST LIKE CORN...
N-NO NO!
I CAN'T ACT LIKE CORN!
uh uh
EVEN IF I COULD, I'D BE A LOW-CLASS FAIRY!
......
CORN...

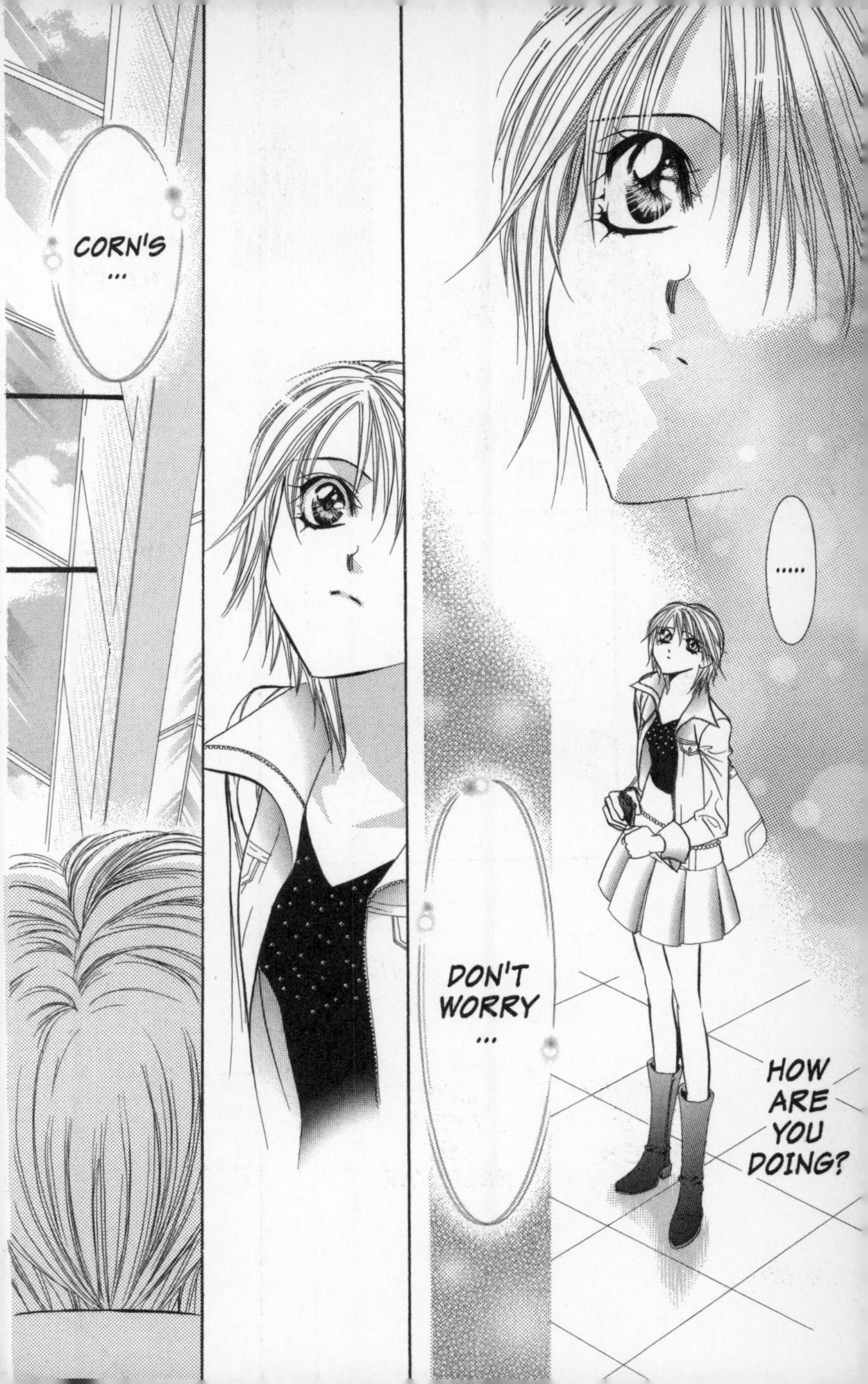
.....
HOW ARE YOU DOING?
DON'T WORRY ...
CORN'S ...

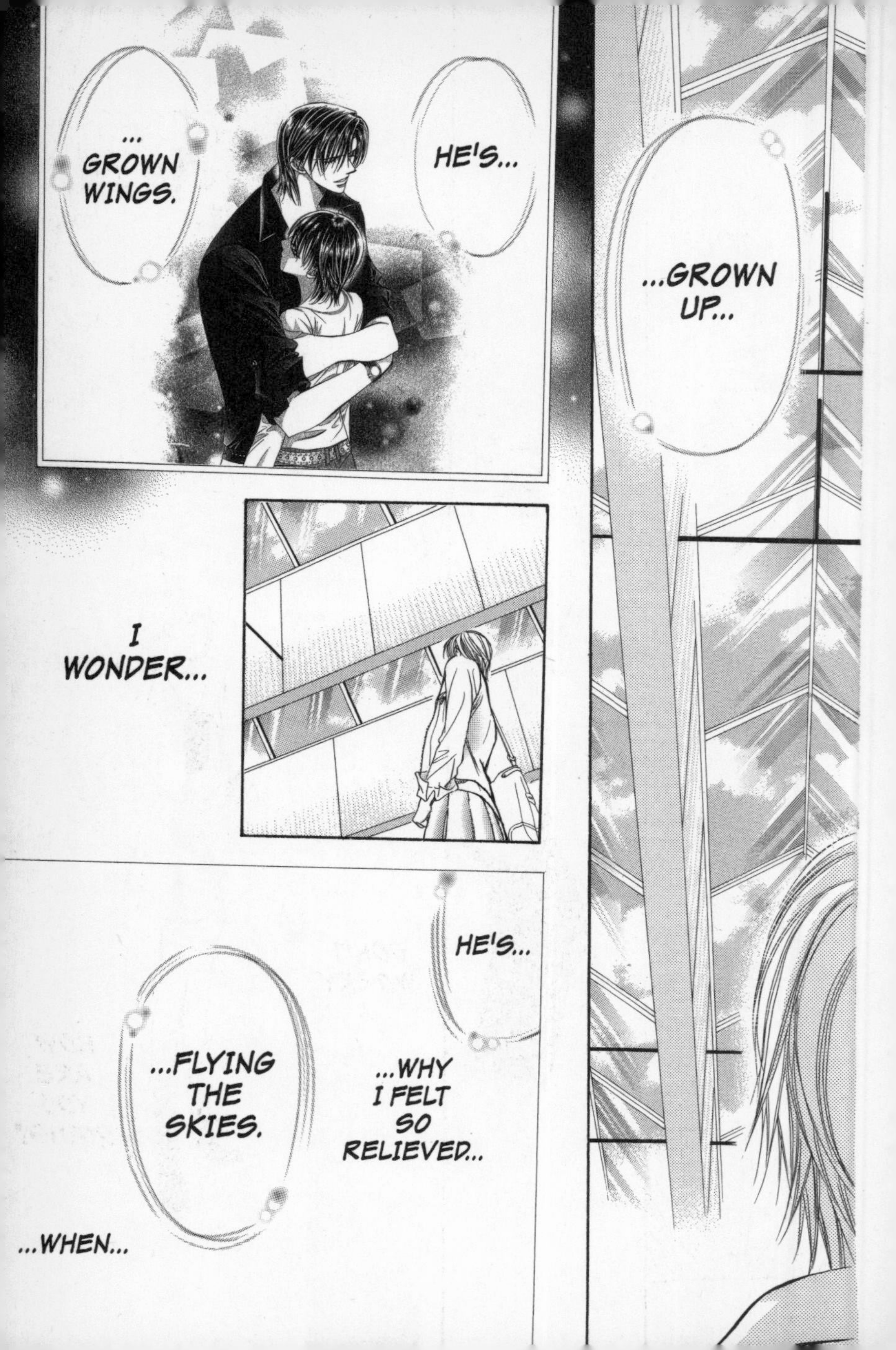
...GROWN UP...
HE'S...
... GROWN WINGS.
I WONDER...
HE'S...
...WHY I FELT SO RELIEVED...
...FLYING THE SKIES.
...WHEN...

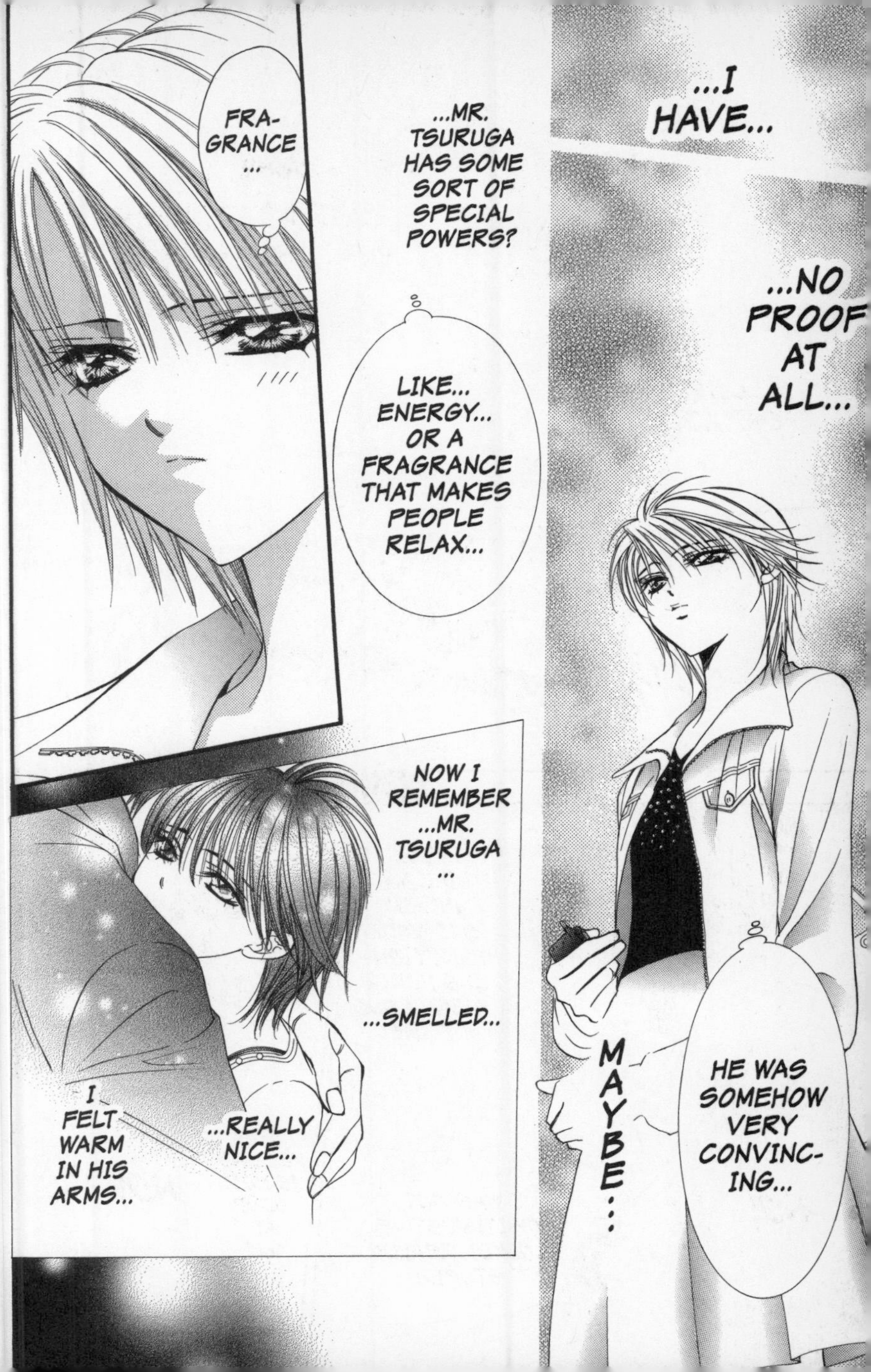
...I HAVE...
...NO PROOF AT ALL...
HE WAS SOMEHOW VERY CONVINCING...
MAYBE...
FRA-GRANCE...
...MR. TSURUGA HAS SOME SORT OF SPECIAL POWERS?
LIKE... ENERGY... OR A FRAGRANCE THAT MAKES PEOPLE RELAX...
NOW I REMEMBER ...MR. TSURUGA ...
...SMELLED...
...REALLY NICE...
I FELT WARM IN HIS ARMS...

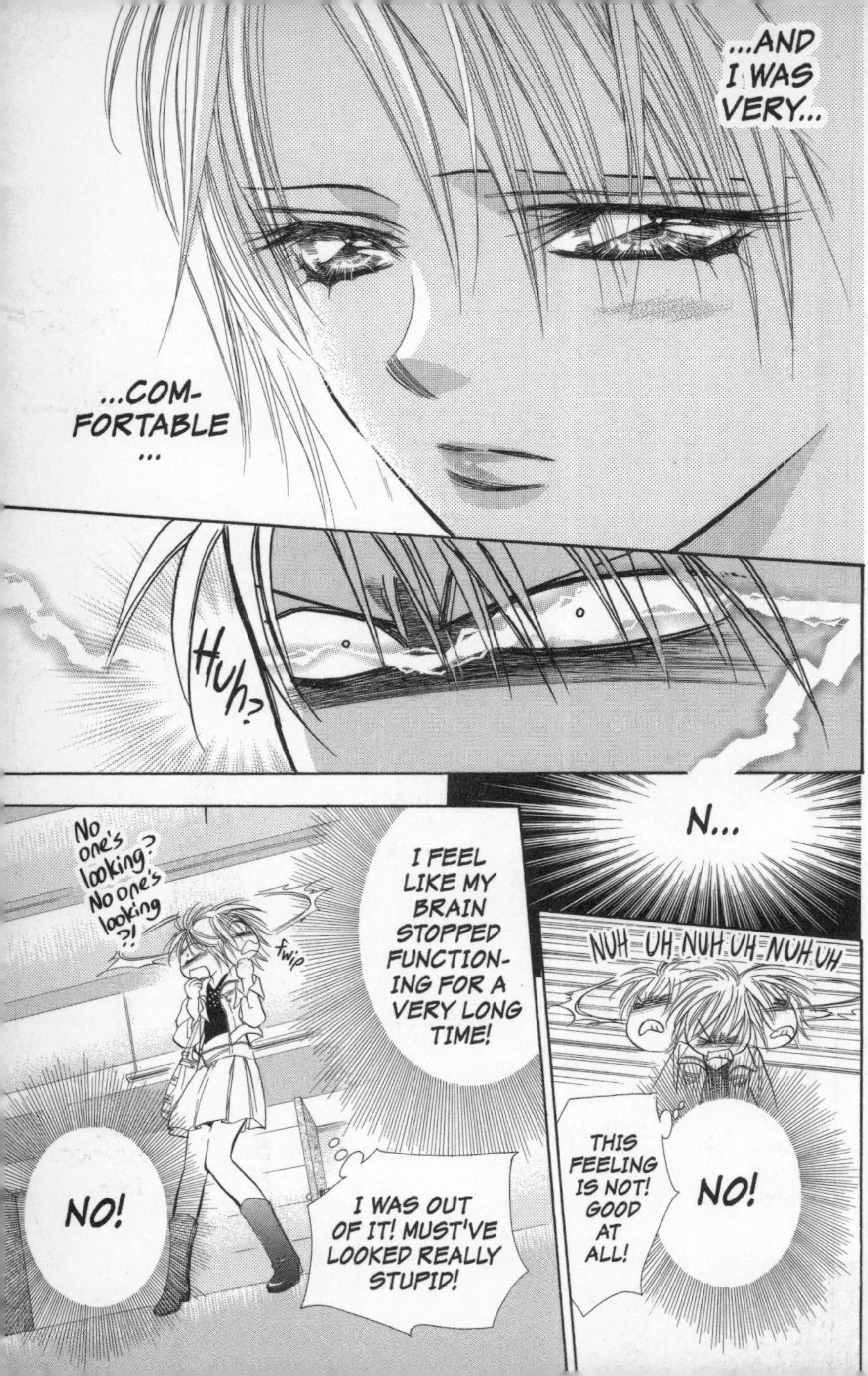
...AND I WAS VERY...
...COM-FORTABLE...
Huh?
N...
NUH UH NUH UH NUH UH
NO!
THIS FEELING IS NOT! GOOD AT ALL!
I FEEL LIKE MY BRAIN STOPPED FUNCTION-ING FOR A VERY LONG TIME!
No one's looking? No one's looking?!
fwip
I WAS OUT OF IT! MUST'VE LOOKED REALLY STUPID!
NO!

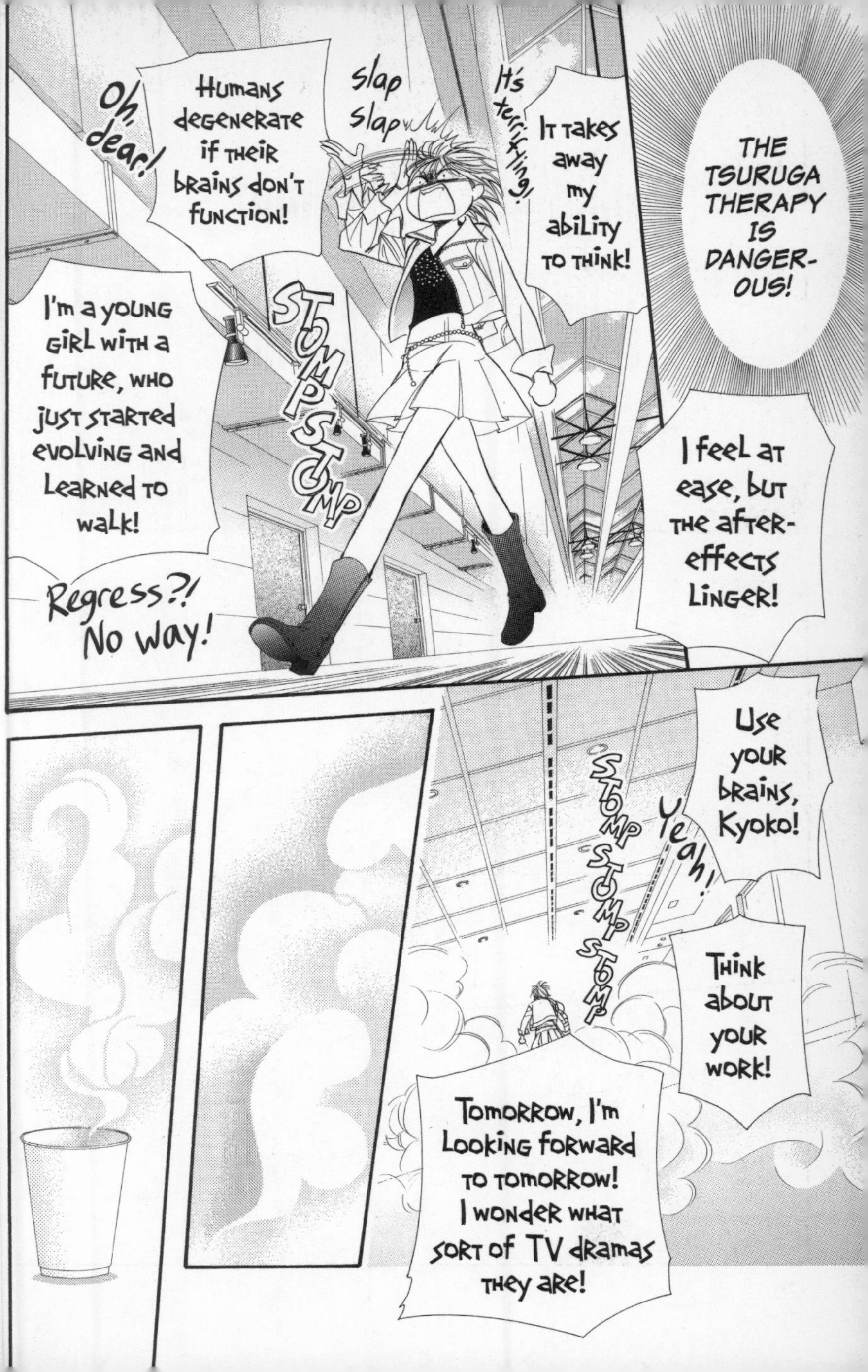
THE TSURUGA THERAPY IS DANGER-OUS!
It takes away my ability to think!
It's terrifying!
slap slap
Humans degenerate if their brains don't function!
Oh dear!
I feel at ease, but the after-effects linger!
STOMP STOMP
I'm a young girl with a future, who just started evolving and learned to walk!
Regress?! No way!
Use your brains, Kyoko!
Yeah!
STOMP STOMP STOMP STOMP
Think about your work!
Tomorrow, I'm looking forward to tomorrow! I wonder what sort of TV dramas they are!

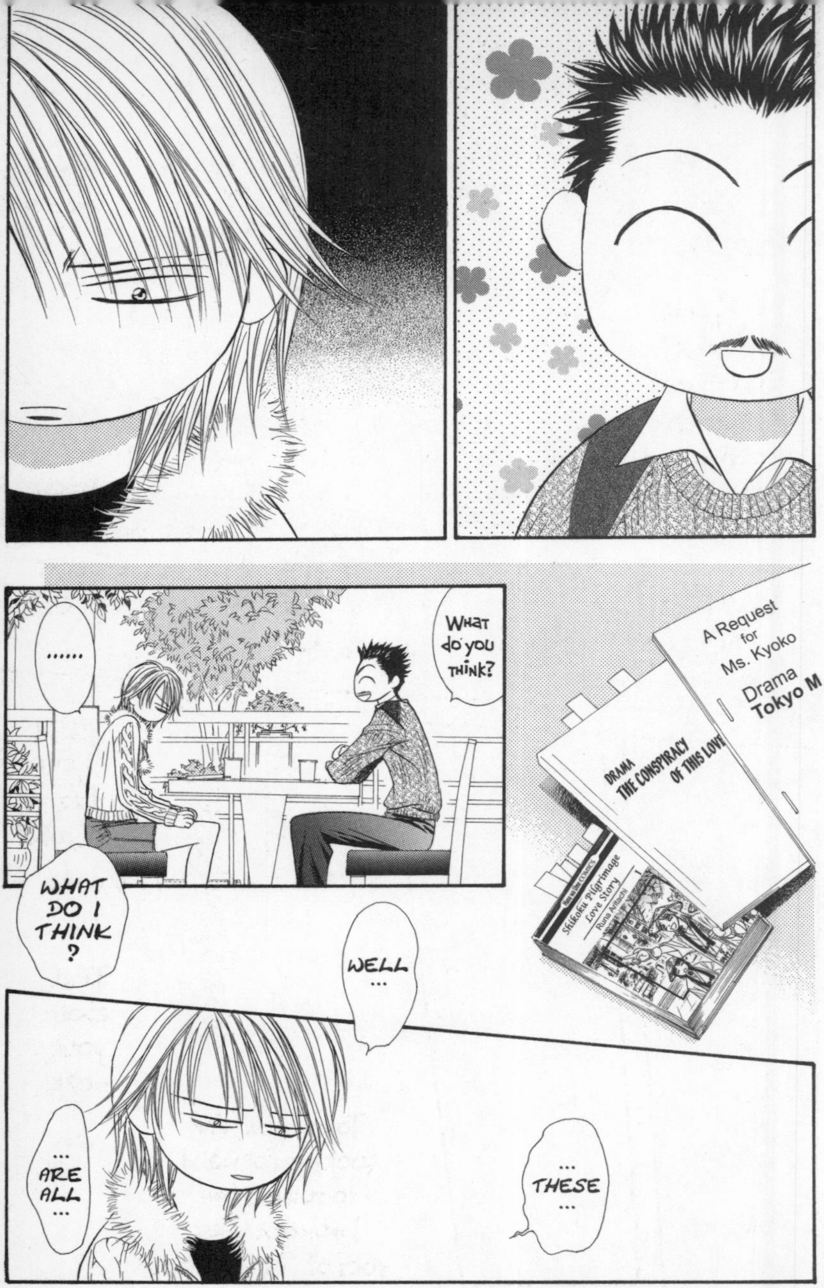
A Request for Ms. Kyoko
Drama Tokyo M
DRAMA THE CONSPIRACY OF THIS LOVE
Shikoku Pilgrimage Love Story
Runa Amachi
What do you think?
......
WHAT DO I THINK?
WELL...
...THESE...
...ARE ALL...

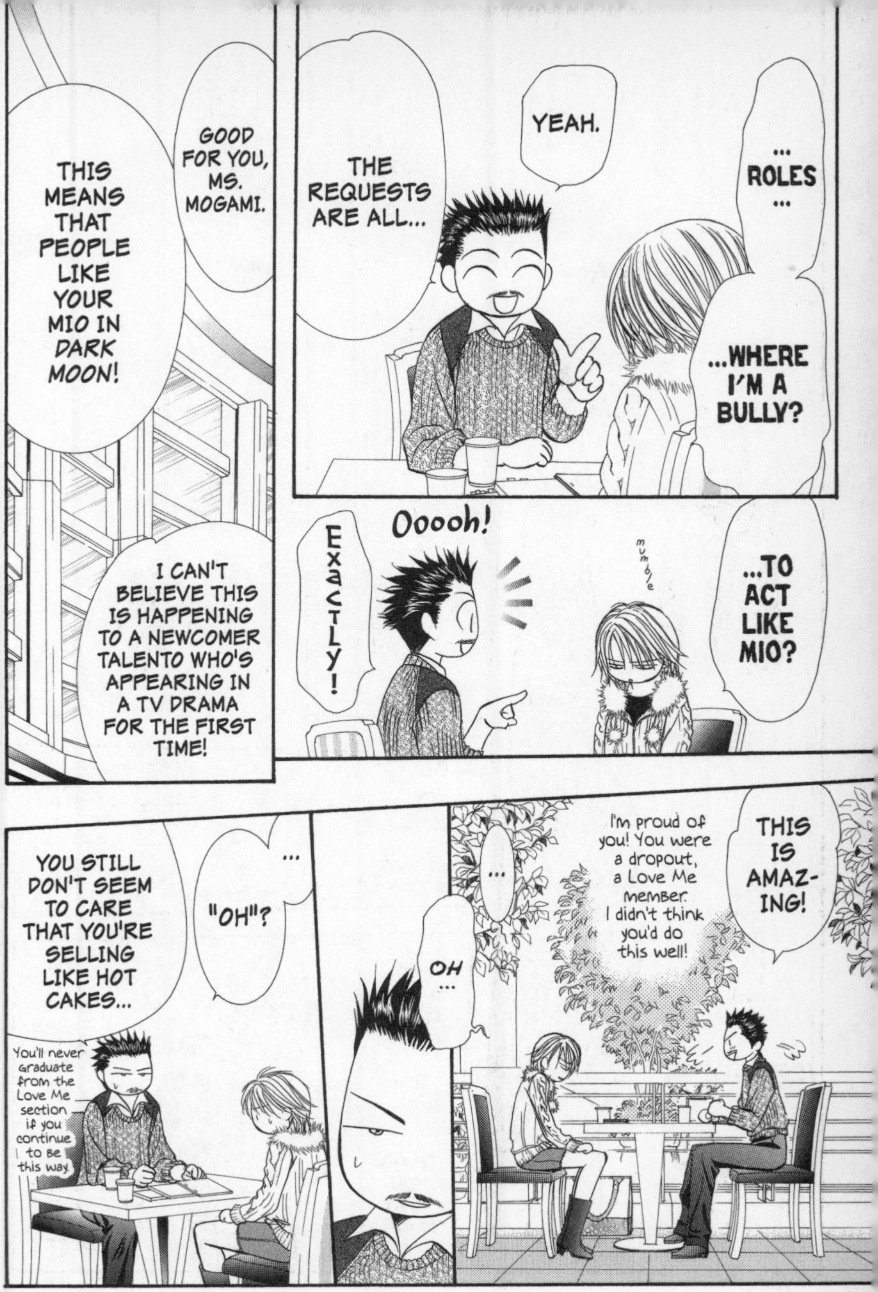
... ROLES ...
YEAH.
THE REQUESTS ARE ALL...
...WHERE I'M A BULLY?
...TO ACT LIKE MIO?
mumble
Ooooh!
Exactly!
GOOD FOR YOU, MS. MOGAMI.
THIS MEANS THAT PEOPLE LIKE YOUR MIO IN DARK MOON!
I CAN'T BELIEVE THIS IS HAPPENING TO A NEWCOMER TALENTO WHO'S APPEARING IN A TV DRAMA FOR THE FIRST TIME!
THIS IS AMAZ-ING!
I'm proud of you! You were a dropout, a Love Me member. I didn't think you'd do this well!
...
OH ...
...
"OH"?
YOU STILL DON'T SEEM TO CARE THAT YOU'RE SELLING LIKE HOT CAKES...
You'll never Graduate from the Love Me section if you continue to Be this way.

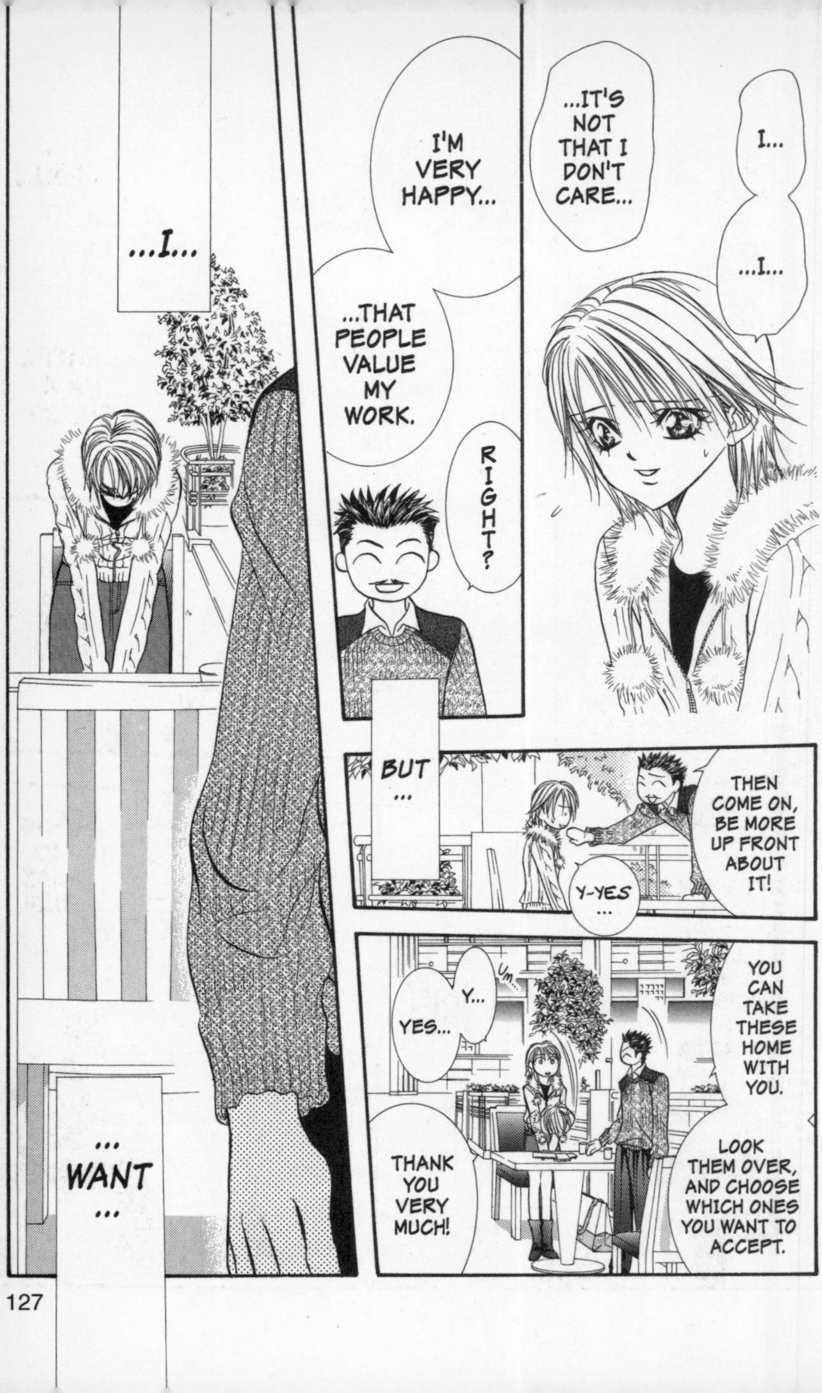
I...
...I...
...IT'S NOT THAT I DON'T CARE...
I'M VERY HAPPY...
...THAT PEOPLE VALUE MY WORK.
RIGHT?
BUT ...
THEN COME ON, BE MORE UP FRONT ABOUT IT!
Y-YES ...
YOU CAN TAKE THESE HOME WITH YOU.
LOOK THEM OVER, AND CHOOSE WHICH ONES YOU WANT TO ACCEPT.
Um...
Y... YES...
THANK YOU VERY MUCH!
...I...
... WANT ...

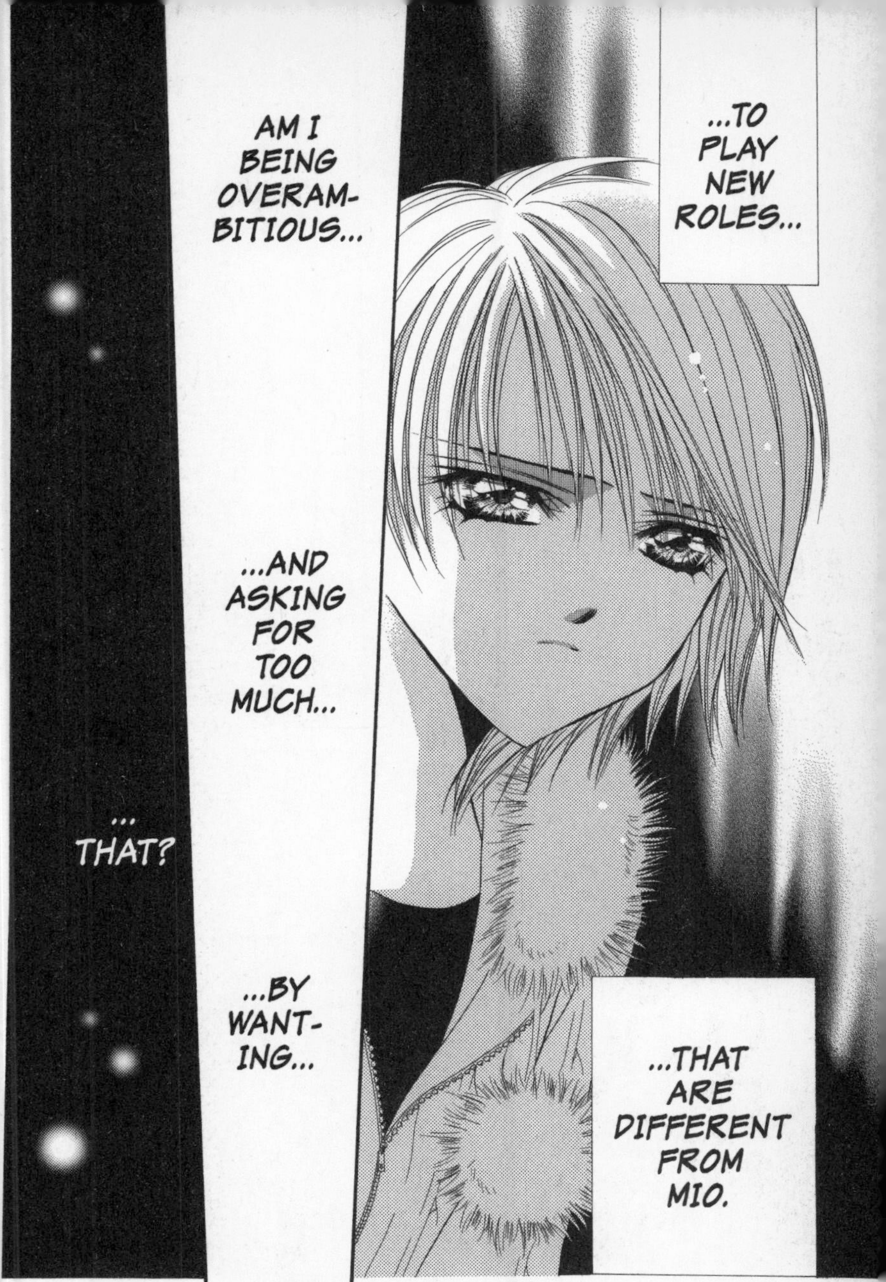
...TO PLAY NEW ROLES...
...THAT ARE DIFFERENT FROM MIO.
AM I BEING OVERAMBITIOUS...
...AND ASKING FOR TOO MUCH...
...BY WANTING...
...THAT?

End of Act 100

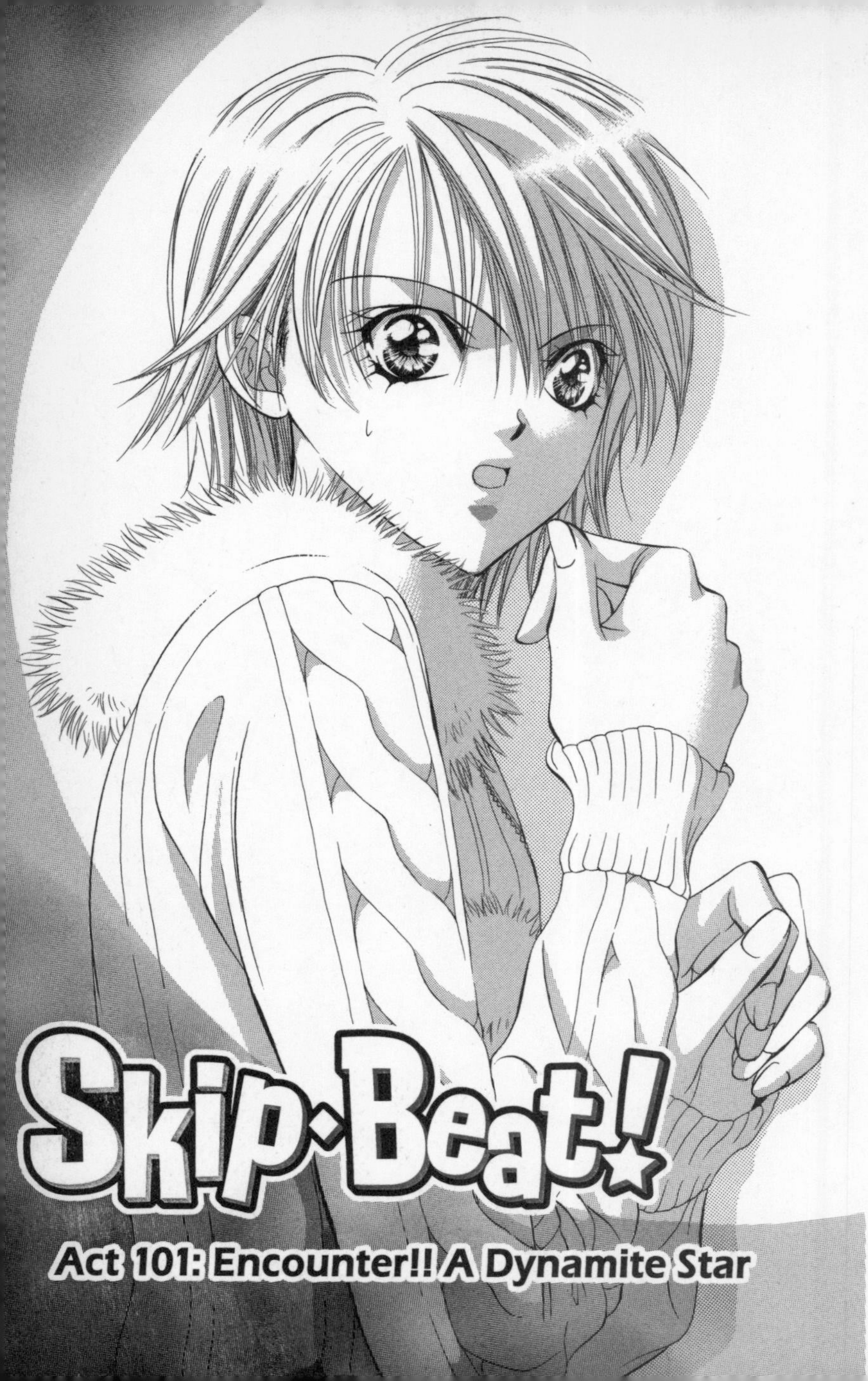
Skip·Beat!
Act 101: Encounter!! A Dynamite Star

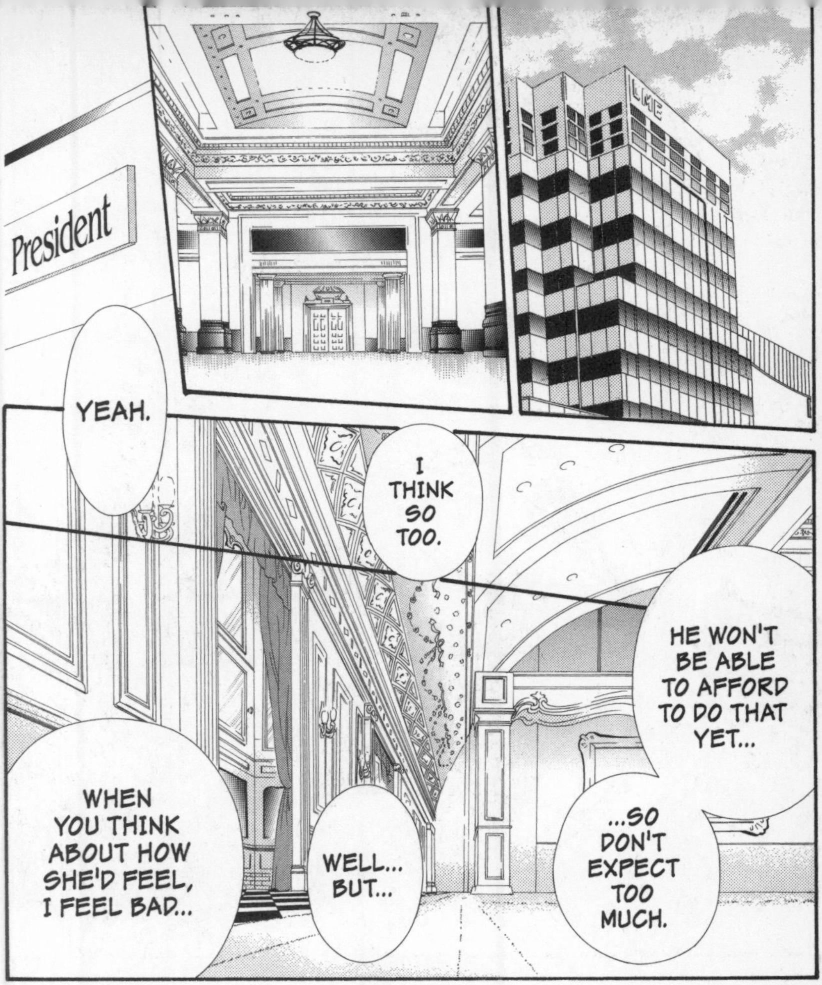
LME
President
I THINK SO TOO.
YEAH.
HE WON'T BE ABLE TO AFFORD TO DO THAT YET...
...SO DON'T EXPECT TOO MUCH.
WELL... BUT...
WHEN YOU THINK ABOUT HOW SHE'D FEEL, I FEEL BAD...

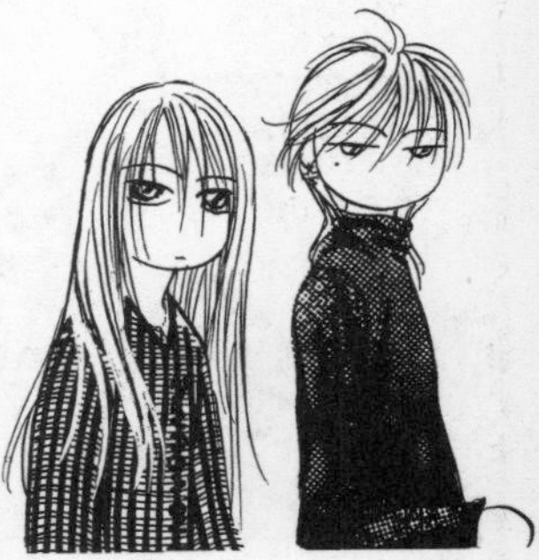

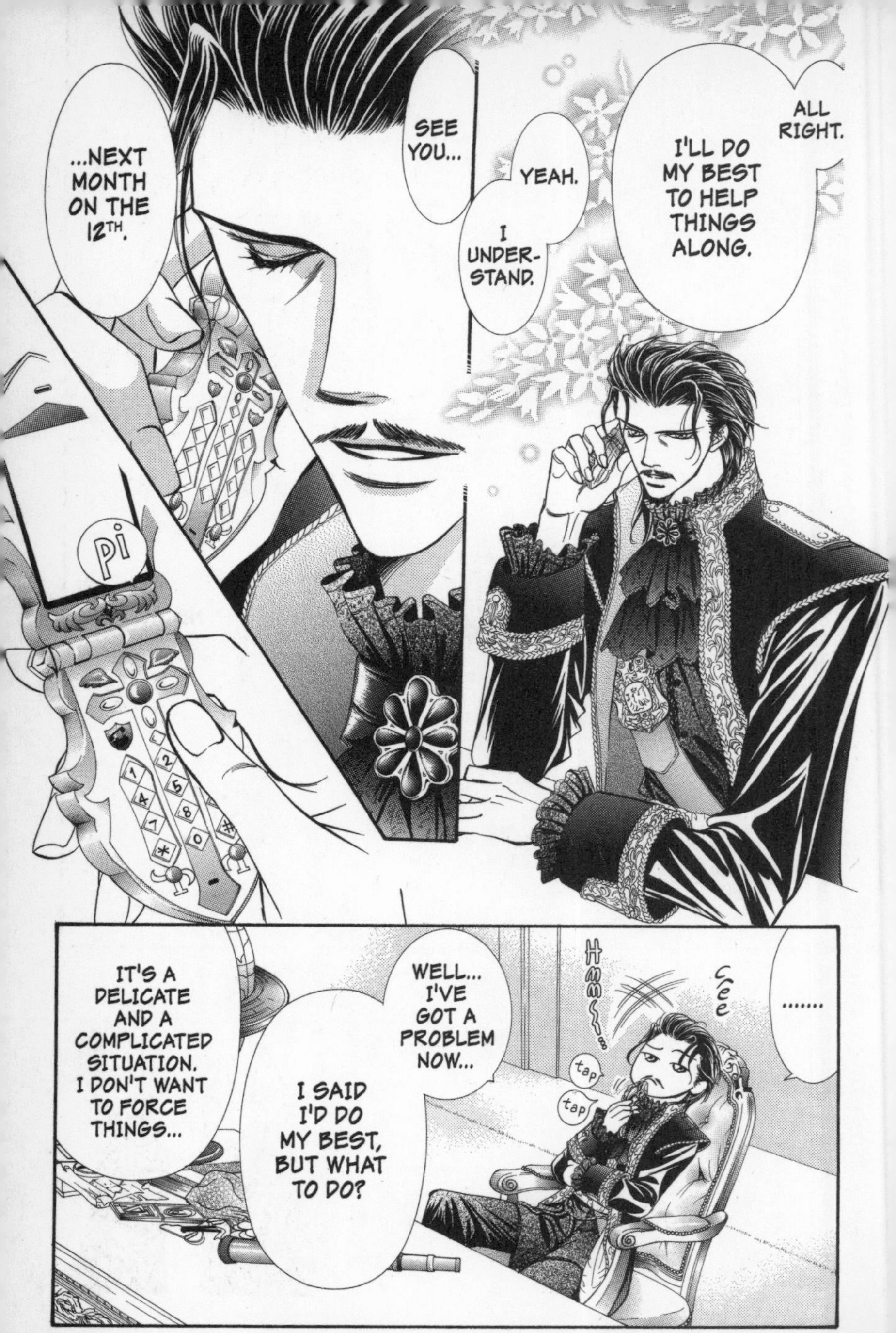
ALL RIGHT.
I'LL DO MY BEST TO HELP THINGS ALONG.
YEAH.
I UNDERSTAND.
SEE YOU...
...NEXT MONTH ON THE 12TH.
pi
....
Hmm~...
tap
tap
WELL... I'VE GOT A PROBLEM NOW...
I SAID I'D DO MY BEST, BUT WHAT TO DO?
IT'S A DELICATE AND A COMPLICATED SITUATION. I DON'T WANT TO FORCE THINGS...

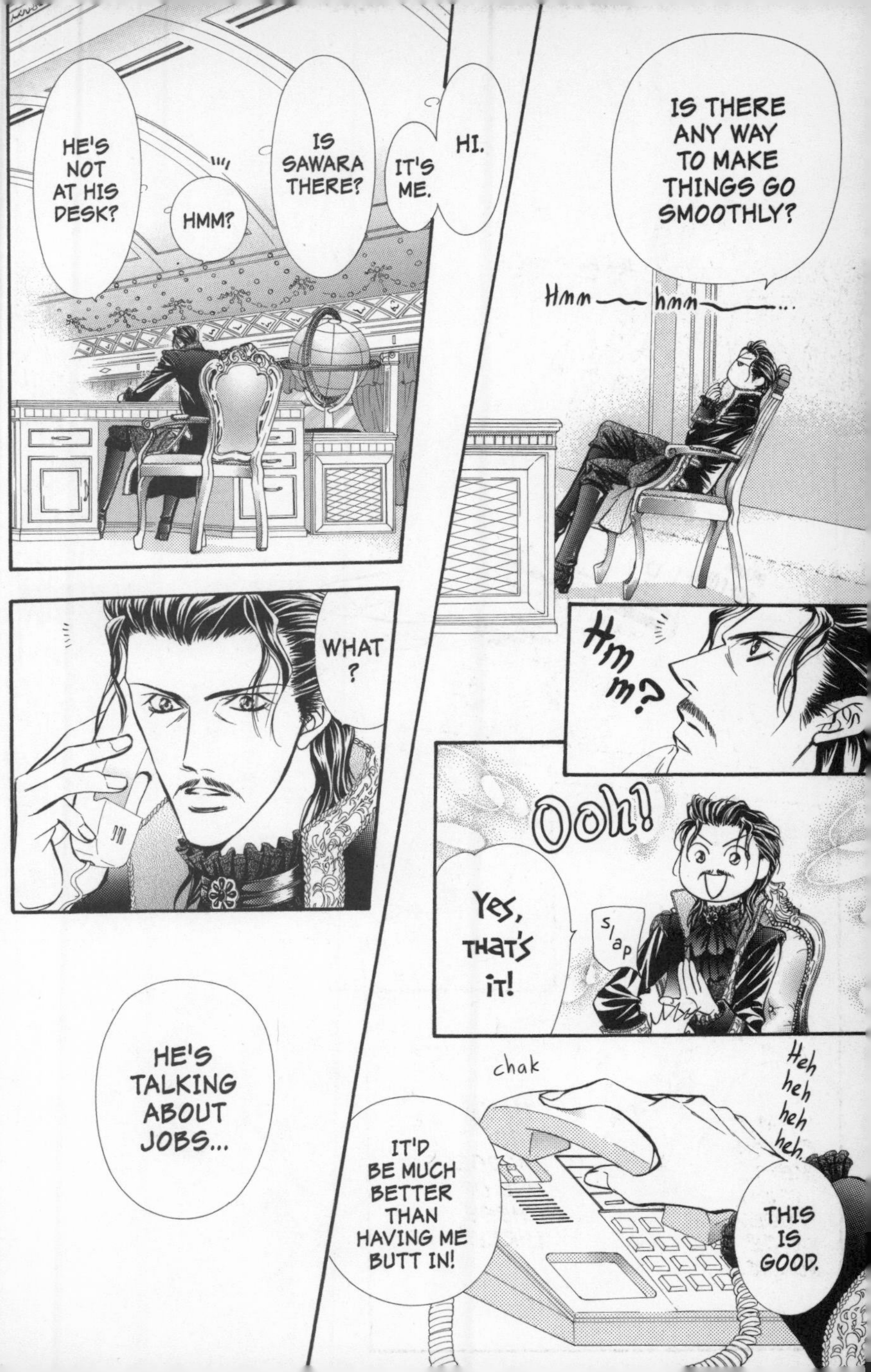

IS THERE ANY WAY TO MAKE THINGS GO SMOOTHLY?
Hmm—hmm—...
Hmm?
Ooh!
Yes, that's it!
slap
chak
Heh heh heh heh.
THIS IS GOOD.
IT'D BE MUCH BETTER THAN HAVING ME BUTT IN!
HI.
IT'S ME.
IS SAWARA THERE?
HMM?
HE'S NOT AT HIS DESK?
WHAT?
HE'S TALKING ABOUT JOBS...

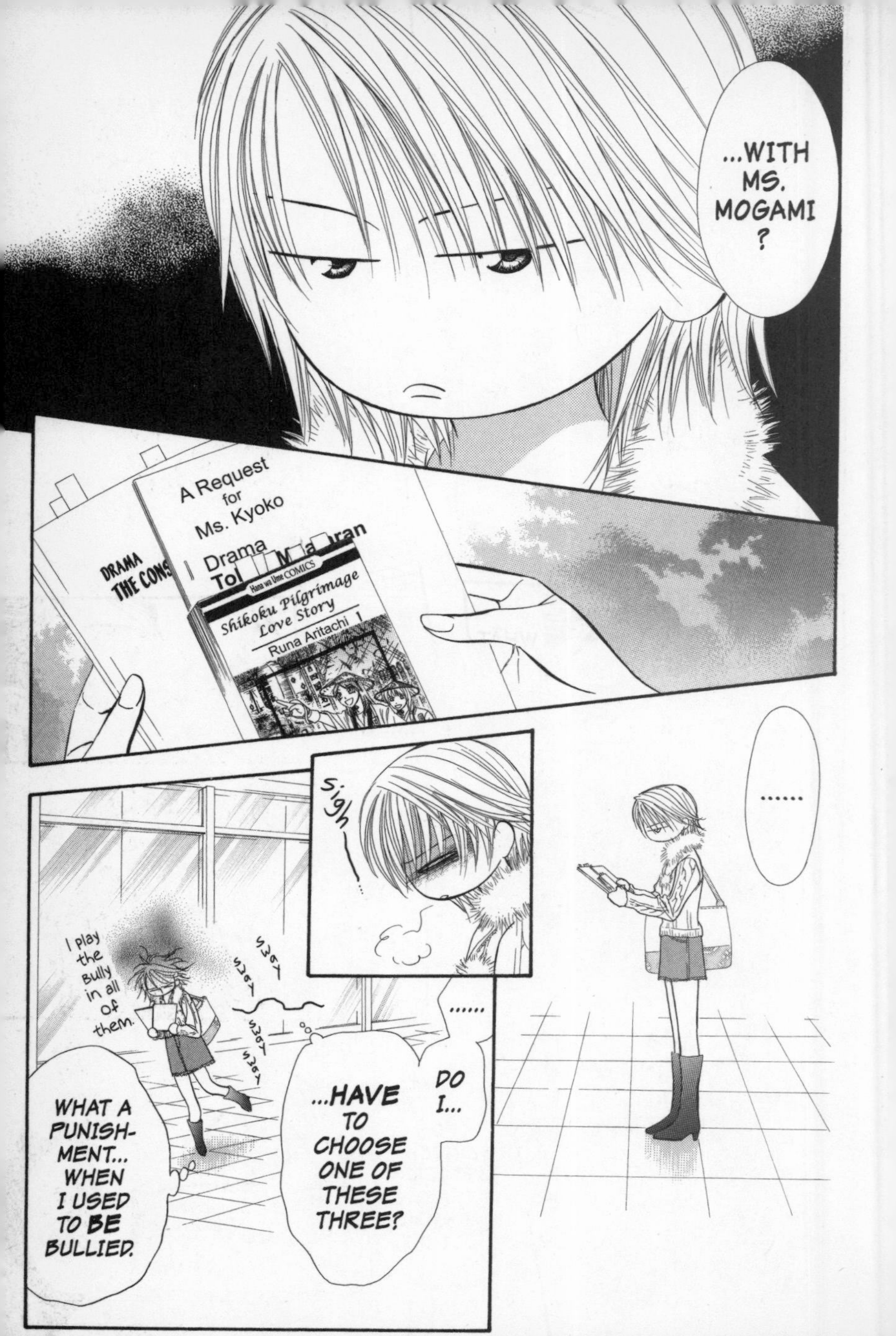
...WITH MS. MOGAMI?
A Request for Ms. Kyoko
Drama
DRAMA THE CONS
Hana wa Ume COMICS
Shikoku Pilgrimage Love Story
Runa Aritachi 1
......
Sigh...
......
DO I...
...HAVE TO CHOOSE ONE OF THESE THREE?
SWAY SWAY SWAY SWAY
I play the bully in all of them.
WHAT A PUNISHMENT... WHEN I USED TO BE BULLIED.

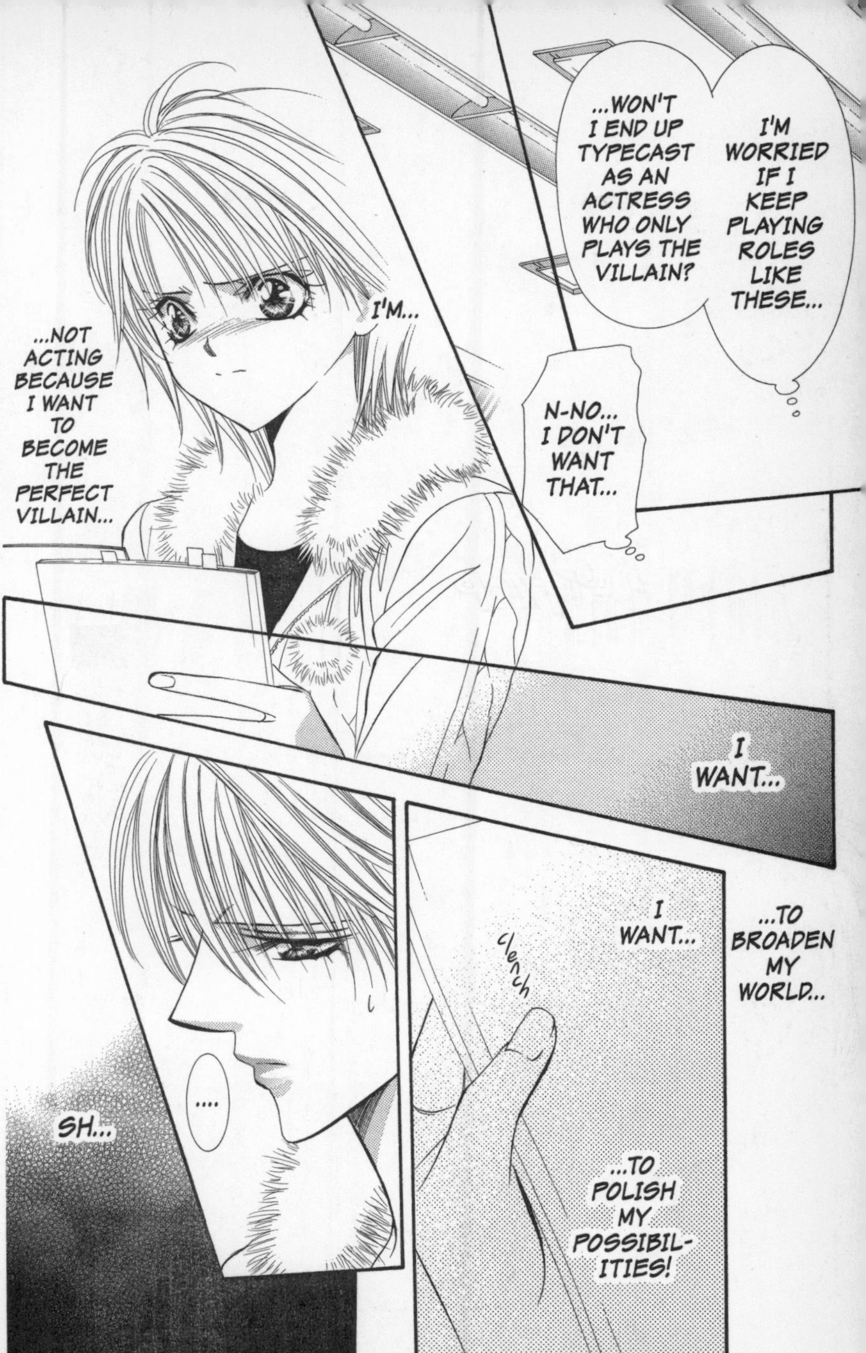
I'M WORRIED IF I KEEP PLAYING ROLES LIKE THESE...
...WON'T I END UP TYPECAST AS AN ACTRESS WHO ONLY PLAYS THE VILLAIN?
N-NO... I DON'T WANT THAT...
I'M...
...NOT ACTING BECAUSE I WANT TO BECOME THE PERFECT VILLAIN...
I WANT...
...TO BROADEN MY WORLD...
I WANT...
clench
...TO POLISH MY POSSIBIL-ITIES!
....
SH...

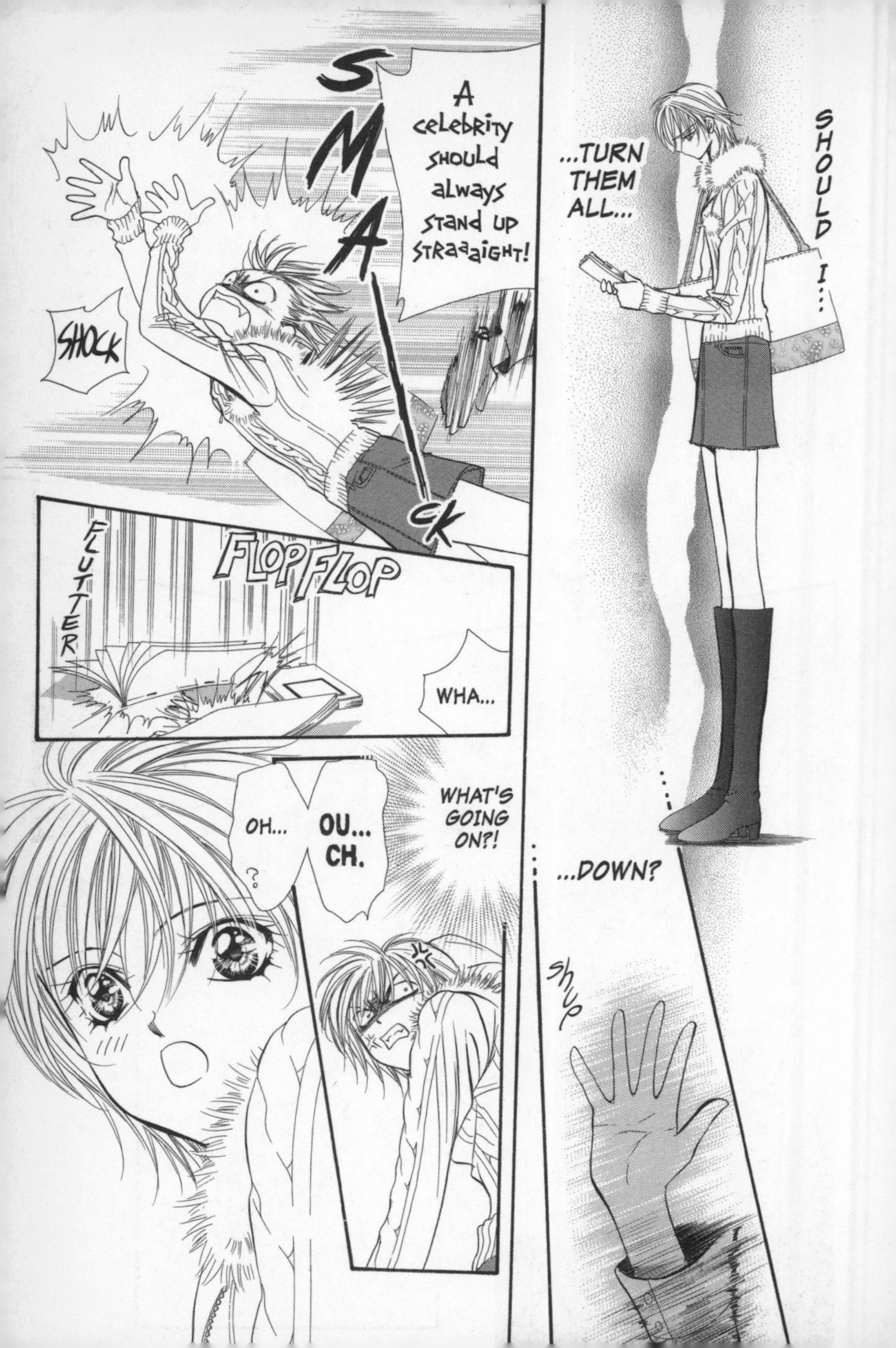
SHOULD I...
...TURN THEM ALL...
...DOWN?
SHUP
SMACK
A celebrity should always stand up straaaight!
SHOCK
WHA...
FLOPFLOP
FLUTTER
WHAT'S GOING ON?!
OU... CH.
OH... ?

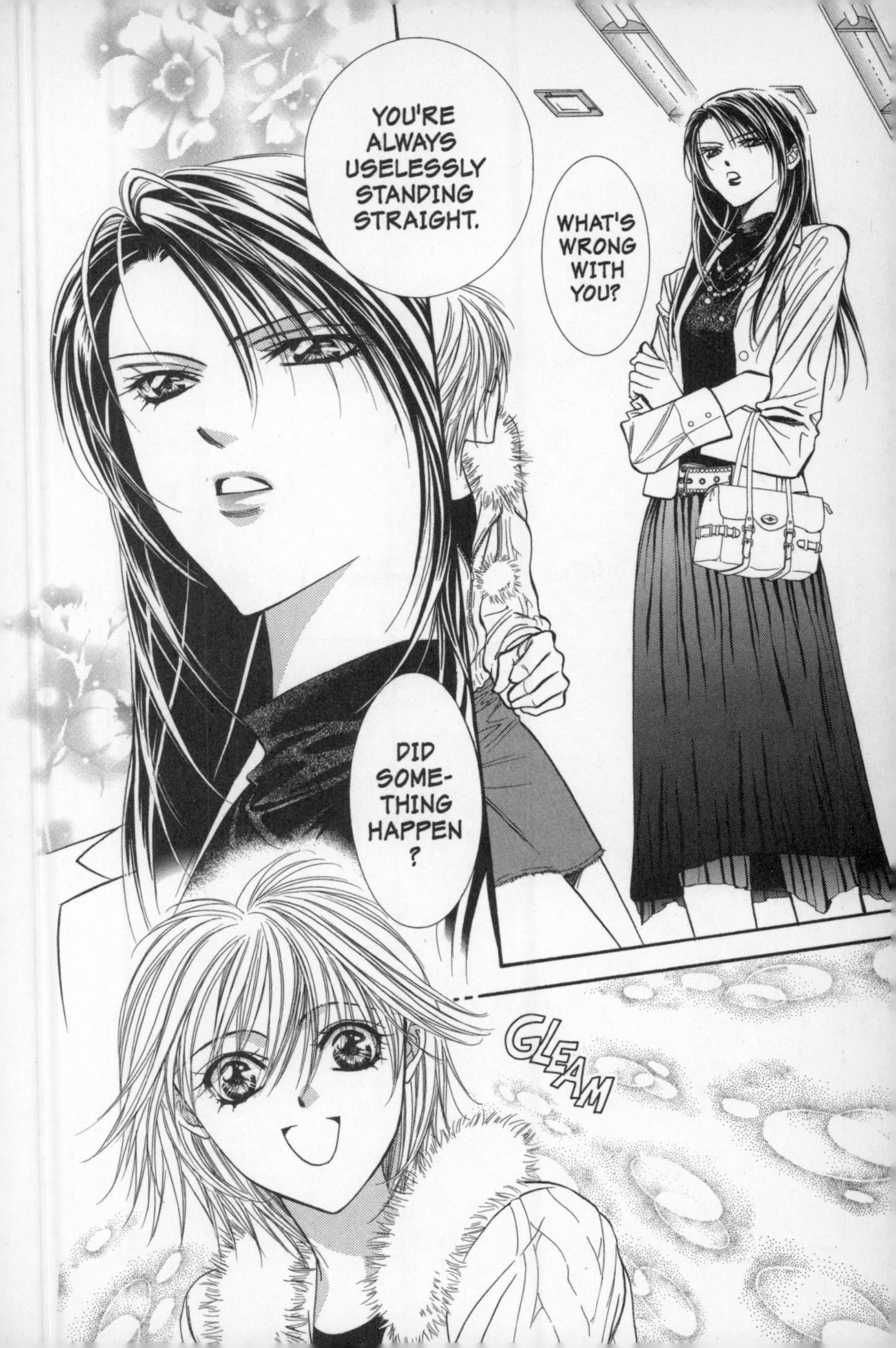
WHAT'S WRONG WITH YOU?
YOU'RE ALWAYS USELESSLY STANDING STRAIGHT.
DID SOME-THING HAPPEN ?
GLEAM

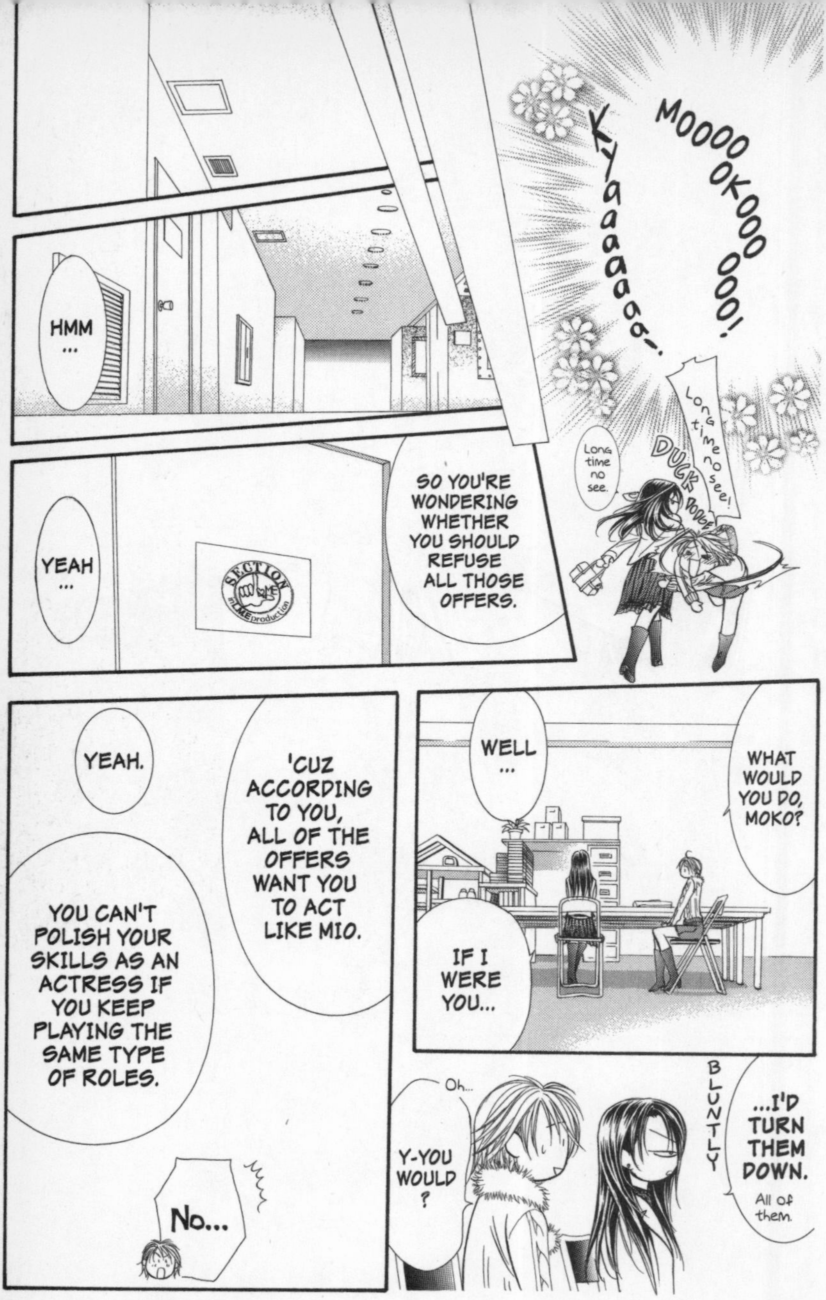
MOOOOOKOOOOOOO!
Kyaaaaaaa!
Long time no see!
Long time no see.
DUCK
DODGE
SO YOU'RE WONDERING WHETHER YOU SHOULD REFUSE ALL THOSE OFFERS.
YEAH...
HMM...
WHAT WOULD YOU DO, MOKO?
WELL...
IF I WERE YOU...
...I'D TURN THEM DOWN.
All of them.
BLUNTLY
Oh...
Y-YOU WOULD?
'CUZ ACCORDING TO YOU, ALL OF THE OFFERS WANT YOU TO ACT LIKE MIO.
YEAH.
YOU CAN'T POLISH YOUR SKILLS AS AN ACTRESS IF YOU KEEP PLAYING THE SAME TYPE OF ROLES.
No...

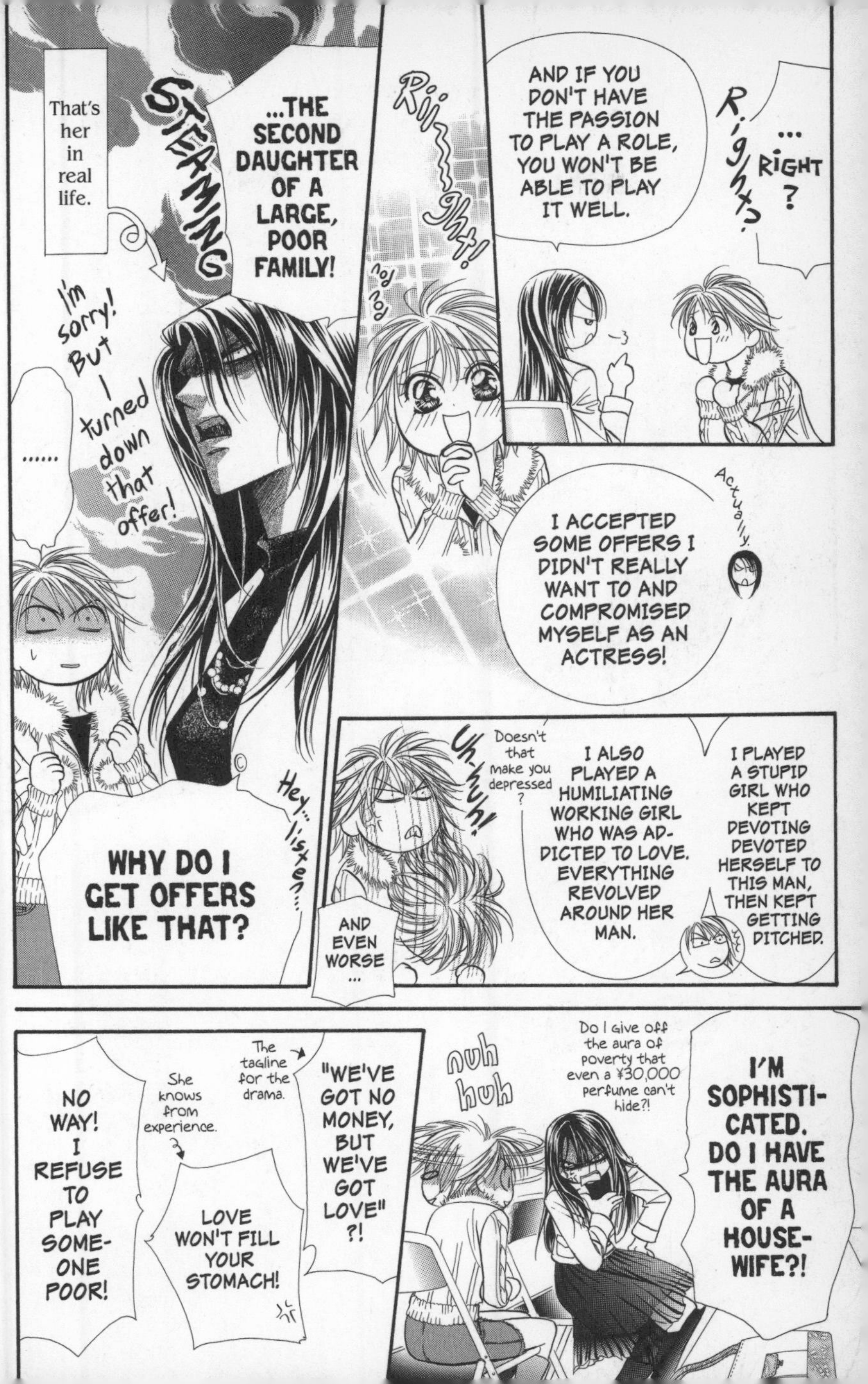
Right?
...RIGHT?
AND IF YOU DON'T HAVE THE PASSION TO PLAY A ROLE, YOU WON'T BE ABLE TO PLAY IT WELL.
Riiiight!
Actually.
I ACCEPTED SOME OFFERS I DIDN'T REALLY WANT TO AND COMPROMISED MYSELF AS AN ACTRESS!
I PLAYED A STUPID GIRL WHO KEPT DEVOTING DEVOTED HERSELF TO THIS MAN, THEN KEPT GETTING DITCHED.
I ALSO PLAYED A HUMILIATING WORKING GIRL WHO WAS ADDICTED TO LOVE. EVERYTHING REVOLVED AROUND HER MAN.
Doesn't that make you depressed?
Uh-huh!
AND EVEN WORSE ...
...THE SECOND DAUGHTER OF A LARGE, POOR FAMILY!
STEAMING
That's her in real life.
I'm sorry! But I turned down that offer!
......
Hey... listen...
WHY DO I GET OFFERS LIKE THAT?
I'M SOPHISTICATED. DO I HAVE THE AURA OF A HOUSEWIFE?!
Do I give off the aura of poverty that even a ¥30,000 perfume can't hide?!
nuh huh
"WE'VE GOT NO MONEY, BUT WE'VE GOT LOVE"?!
The tagline for the drama.
NO WAY! I REFUSE TO PLAY SOMEONE POOR!
She knows from experience.
LOVE WON'T FILL YOUR STOMACH!

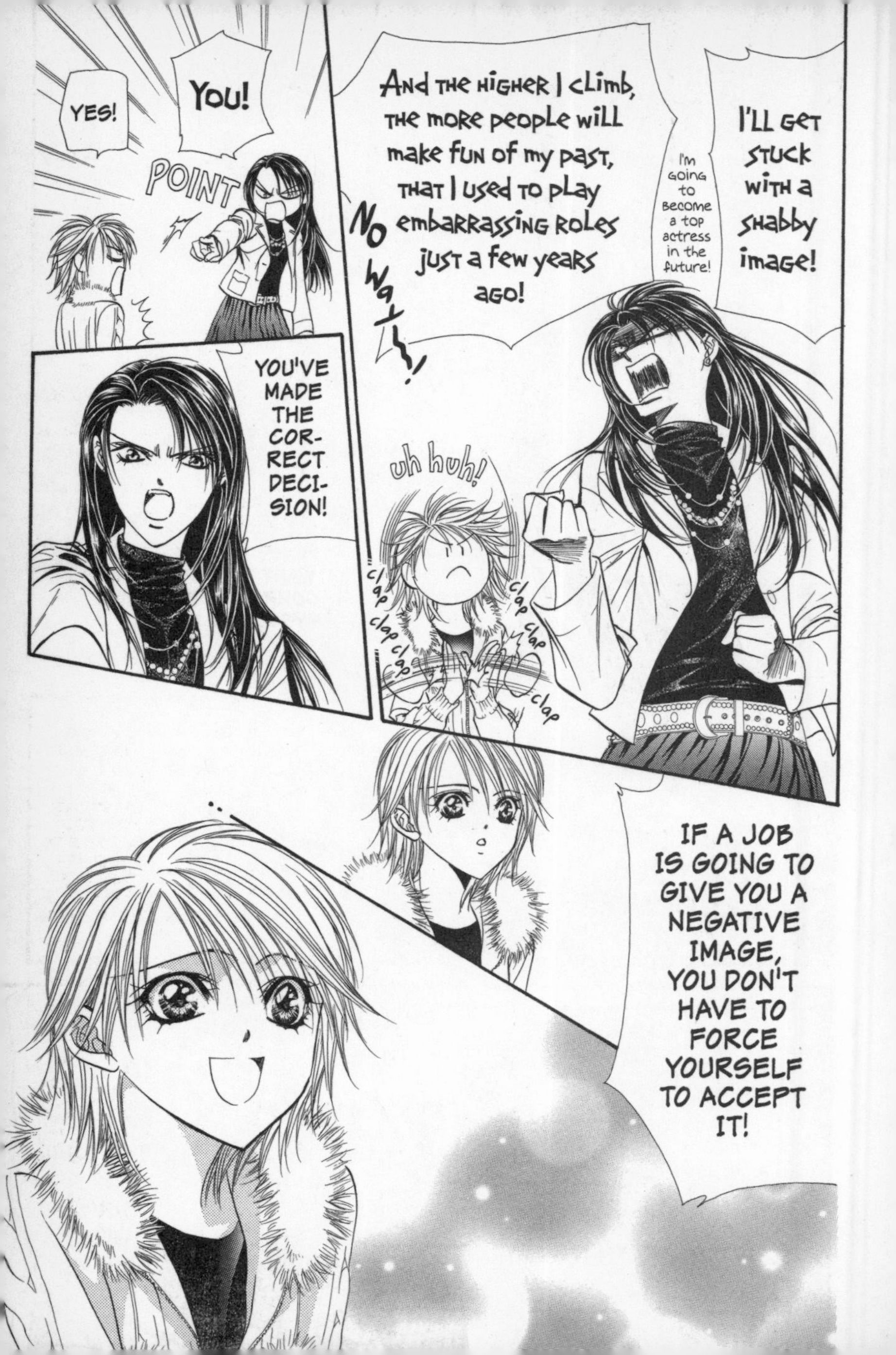
I'LL GET STUCK WITH A SHABBY IMAGE!
I'm going to become a top actress in the future!
And the higher I climb, the more people will make fun of my past, that I used to play embarrassing roles just a few years ago!
No way~!
uh huh!
clap clap clap clap clap clap clap
YOU!
YES!
POINT
YOU'VE MADE THE COR-RECT DECI-SION!
IF A JOB IS GOING TO GIVE YOU A NEGATIVE IMAGE, YOU DON'T HAVE TO FORCE YOURSELF TO ACCEPT IT!
...

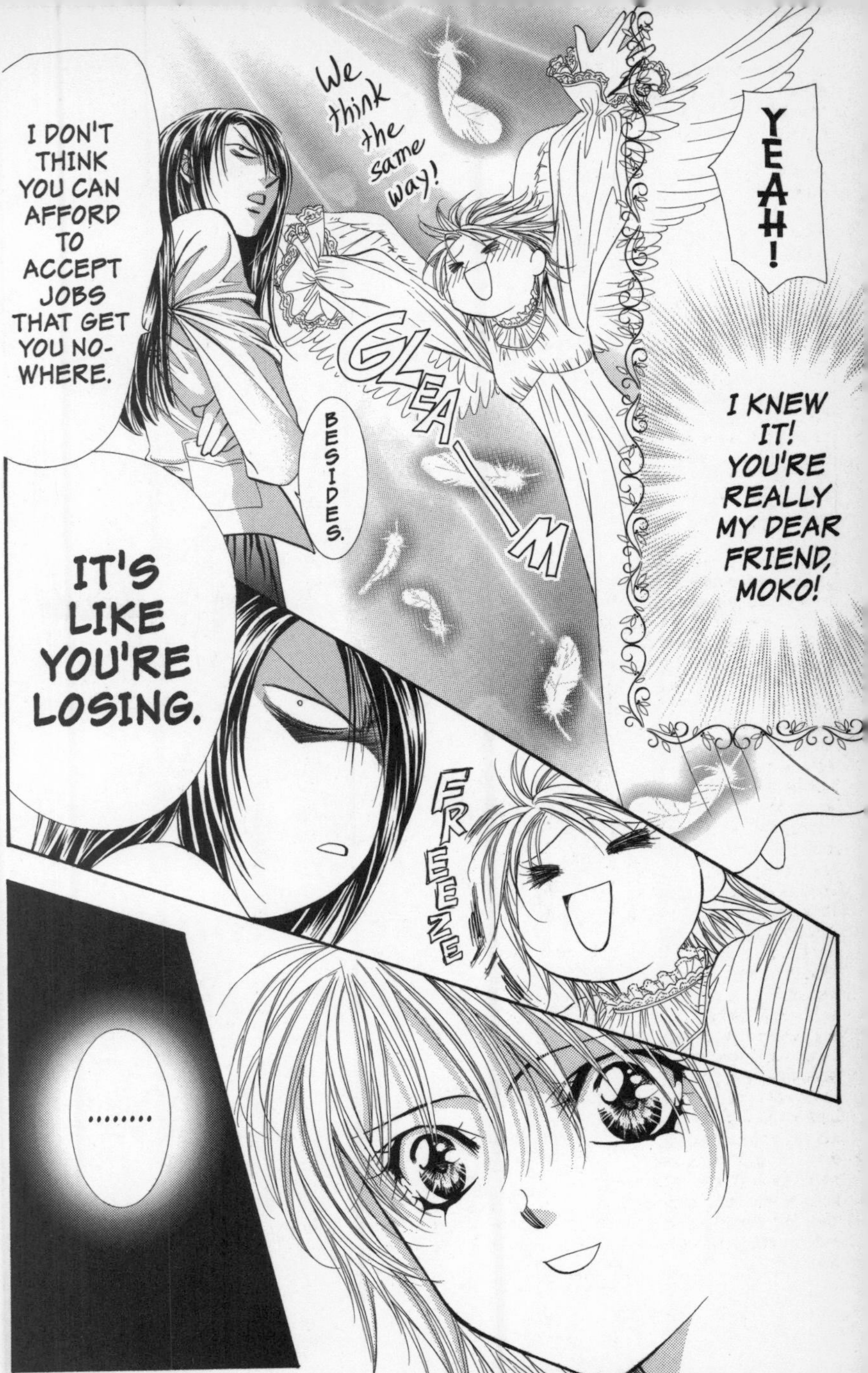
I KNEW IT! YOU'RE REALLY MY DEAR FRIEND, MOKO!
We think the same way!
YEAH!
GLEA-M
I DON'T THINK YOU CAN AFFORD TO ACCEPT JOBS THAT GET YOU NO-WHERE.
BESIDES.
IT'S LIKE YOU'RE LOSING.
FREEZE
....

...Because they cost quite a bit...I'm really thankful and happy... (tears of gratitude)

And for someone like me!!

Thank you so much!! (Wild wailing)

And finally back to normal (3)

What's back to normal?... Kyoko!!...Kyoko's hair color!! Finally!! It's finally back from black to white (brown in the color pages)!! (The Mio wig from Act 100 on is the original long Mio wig).

...It...took a long time... ...I had a hard time... ... in my case, a character with black hair is a little more trouble drawing than a character with white hair, so it takes twice as much time... ... so, now that I don't have to draw Kyoko's black hair all the time, I'm honestly relieved... ... in my previous work (Kurepara)...no...MVP too... ...was I having a hard time then...actually, it wasn't that bad...what I'm doing hasn't changed, but I probably wasn't particular about my drawing or strokes in those days as much as with *Skip Beat*...so with my two previous manga, I was working at an unbelievably fast rate... ...But with the second half of Kurepara, I began to pay attention to both my drawings and strokes...But with Kurepara characters, even if they had black hair, I'd abbreviated the hairlines a lot...

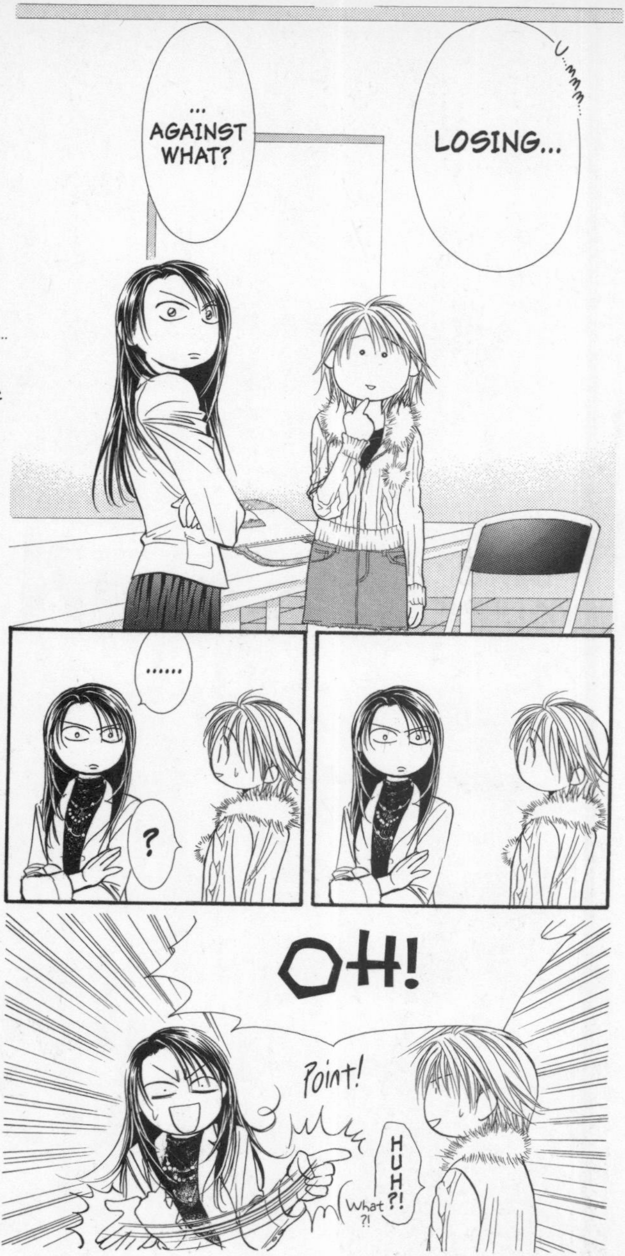
U...mmm...
LOSING...
...AGAINST WHAT?
......
?
OH!
Point!
HUH?!
What?!

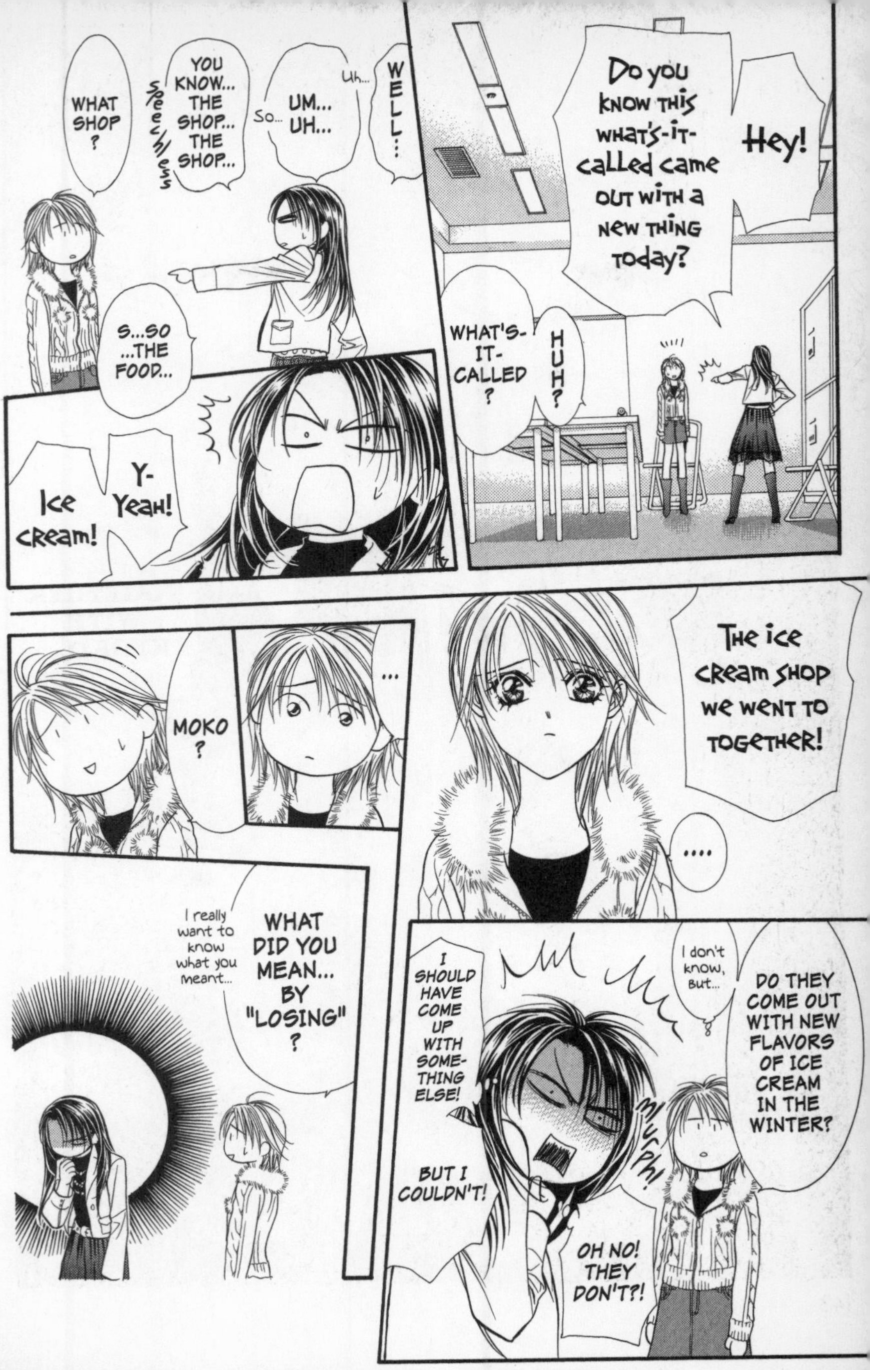

Hey!
Do you know this what's-it-called came out with a new thing today?
HUH?
WHAT'S-IT-CALLED?
WELL...
Uh...
UM... UH...
So...
YOU KNOW... THE SHOP... THE SHOP...
speechless
WHAT SHOP?
S...SO ...THE FOOD...
Y-Yeah!
Ice cream!
The ice cream shop we went to together!
....
...
MOKO?
DO THEY COME OUT WITH NEW FLAVORS OF ICE CREAM IN THE WINTER?
I don't know, but...
OH NO! THEY DON'T?!
MURPH!
I SHOULD HAVE COME UP WITH SOMETHING ELSE!
BUT I COULDN'T!
WHAT DID YOU MEAN... BY "LOSING"?
I really want to know what you meant...

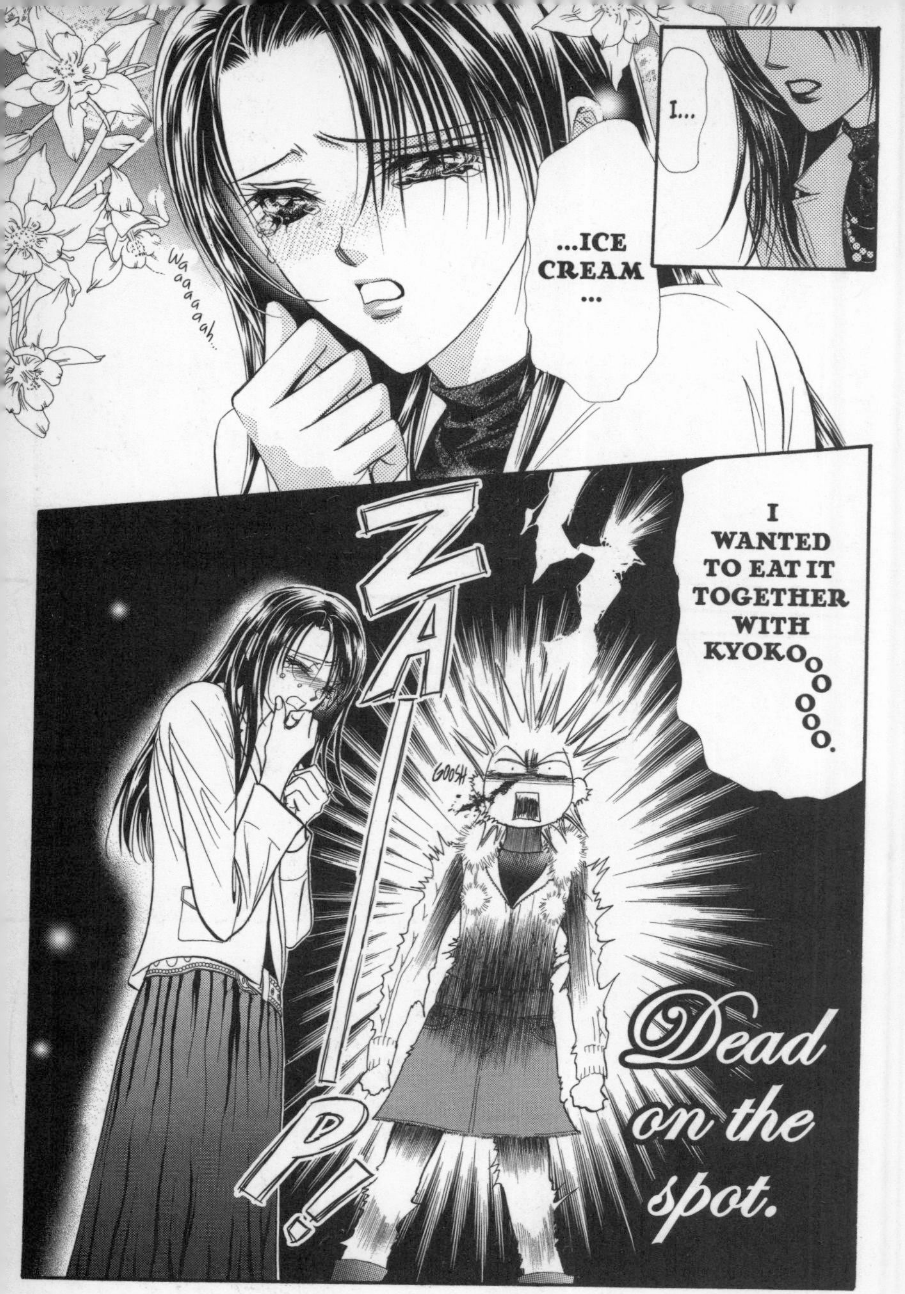
I...
...ICE CREAM ...
Waaaaaah...
I WANTED TO EAT IT TOGETHER WITH KYOKOOOOOOO.
ZAP!!
GOOSH
Dead on the spot.

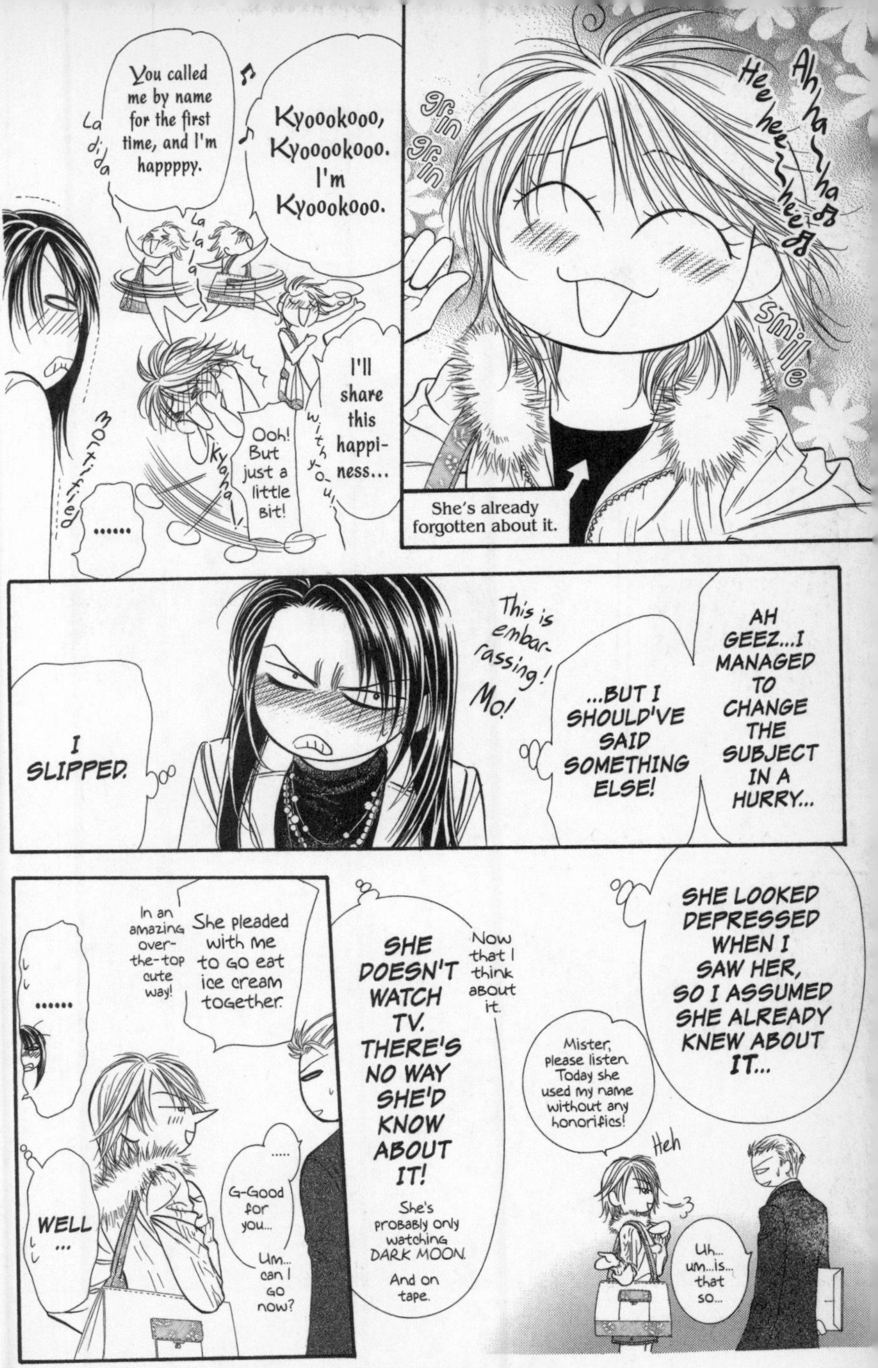
Ah ha~ha♫
Hee hee~hee♫
grin grin
smile
She's already forgotten about it.
Kyoookooo, Kyoooookooo. I'm Kyoookooo.
You called me by name for the first time, and I'm happpppy.
La di da
La la la
I'll share this happiness...
with you!
Ooh! But just a little bit!
Kyaha!
mortified
......
AH GEEZ...I MANAGED TO CHANGE THE SUBJECT IN A HURRY...
...BUT I SHOULD'VE SAID SOMETHING ELSE!
This is embarrassing!
Mo!
I SLIPPED.
SHE LOOKED DEPRESSED WHEN I SAW HER, SO I ASSUMED SHE ALREADY KNEW ABOUT IT...
Mister, please listen. Today she used my name without any honorifics!
Heh
Uh... um...is... that so...
SHE DOESN'T WATCH TV. THERE'S NO WAY SHE'D KNOW ABOUT IT!
Now that I think about it.
She's probably only watching DARK MOON.
And on tape.
She pleaded with me to go eat ice cream together.
In an amazing over-the-top cute way!
......
.....
G-Good for you...
Um... can I go now?
WELL...

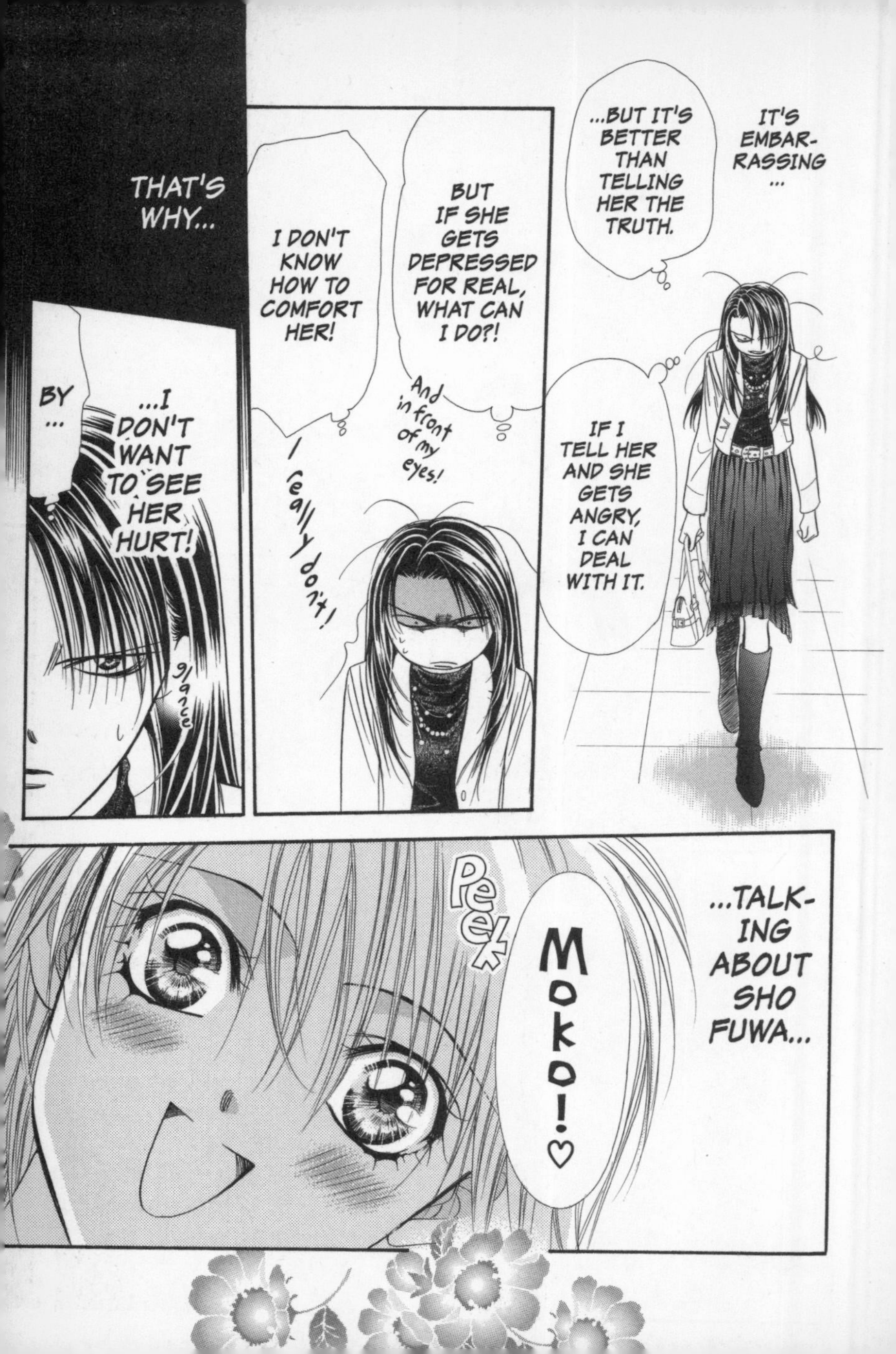

IT'S EMBARRASSING...
...BUT IT'S BETTER THAN TELLING HER THE TRUTH.
IF I TELL HER AND SHE GETS ANGRY, I CAN DEAL WITH IT.
BUT IF SHE GETS DEPRESSED FOR REAL, WHAT CAN I DO?!
And in front of my eyes!
I DON'T KNOW HOW TO COMFORT HER!
I really don't!
THAT'S WHY...
...I DON'T WANT TO SEE HER HURT!
glance
BY ...
...TALKING ABOUT SHO FUWA...
Peek
MOKO!♡

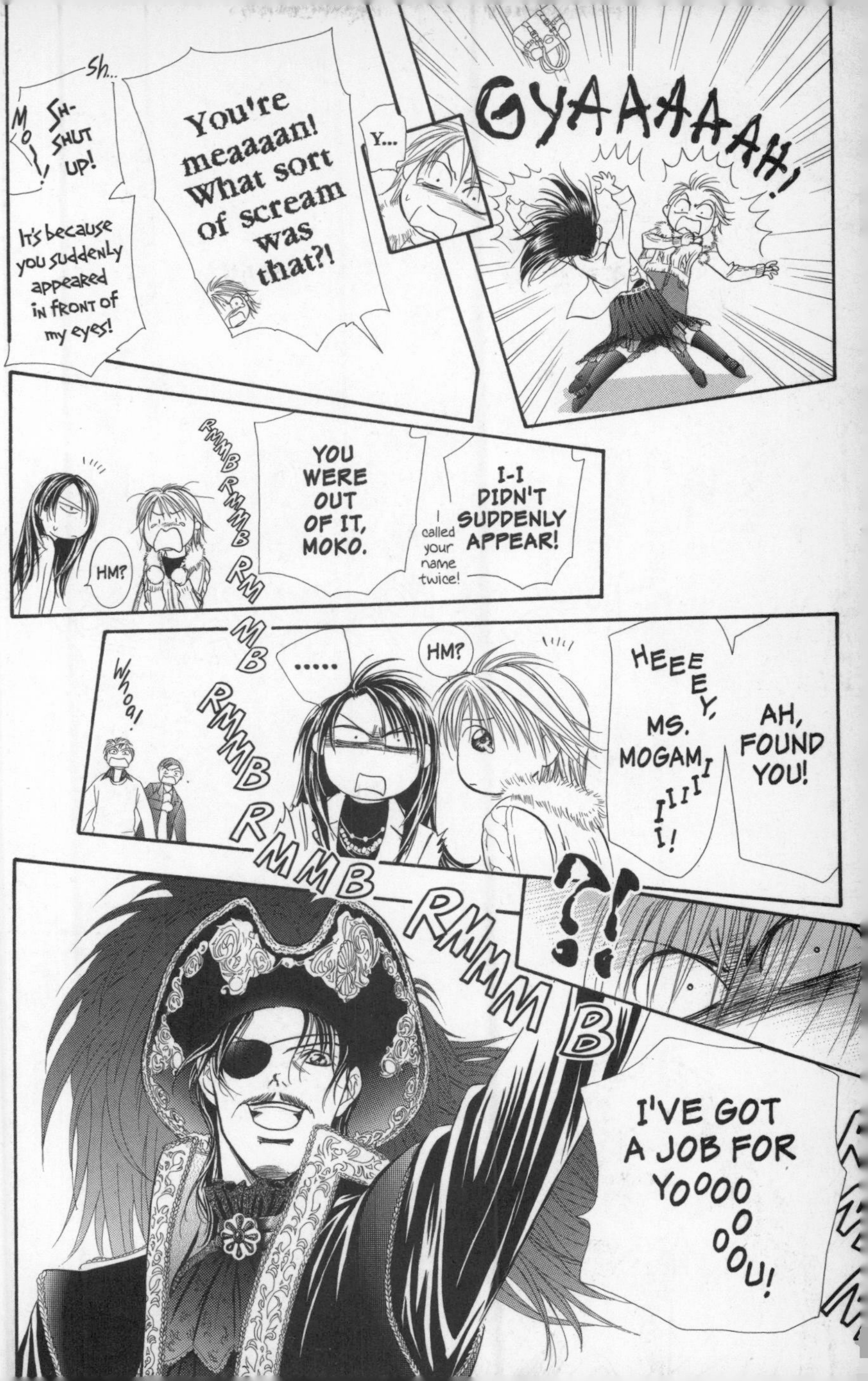
GYAAAAAAH!
Y...
You're meaaaaan! What sort of scream was that?!
Sh...
Sh-shut up!
Mo...!
It's because you suddenly appeared in front of my eyes!
I-I DIDN'T SUDDENLY APPEAR!
I called your name twice!
YOU WERE OUT OF IT, MOKO.
HM?
RMMBRMMBRM
MB
AH, FOUND YOU!
HEEEEY, MS. MOGAMIIIIIII!
HM?
.....
Whoa!
RMMB
R
RMMB-
?!
RMMMMB
I'VE GOT A JOB FOR YOOOOOOOU!

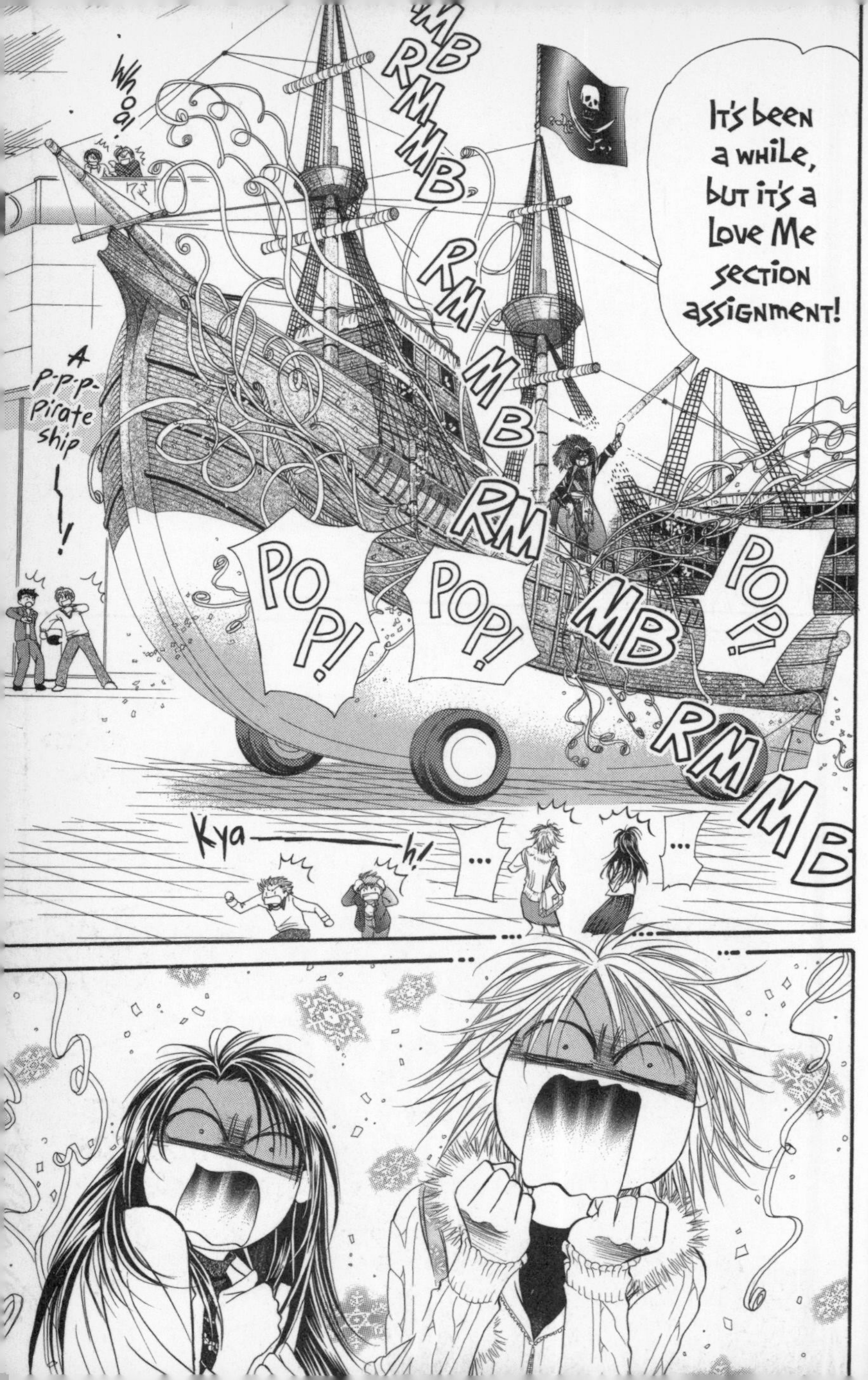
It's been a while, but it's a Love Me section assignment!
MBRMMMB
RMMMB
RMMMB
RMMMB
Whoa!
A p-p-p-pirate ship
!
POP!
POP!
POP!
Kya——————h!
...
...

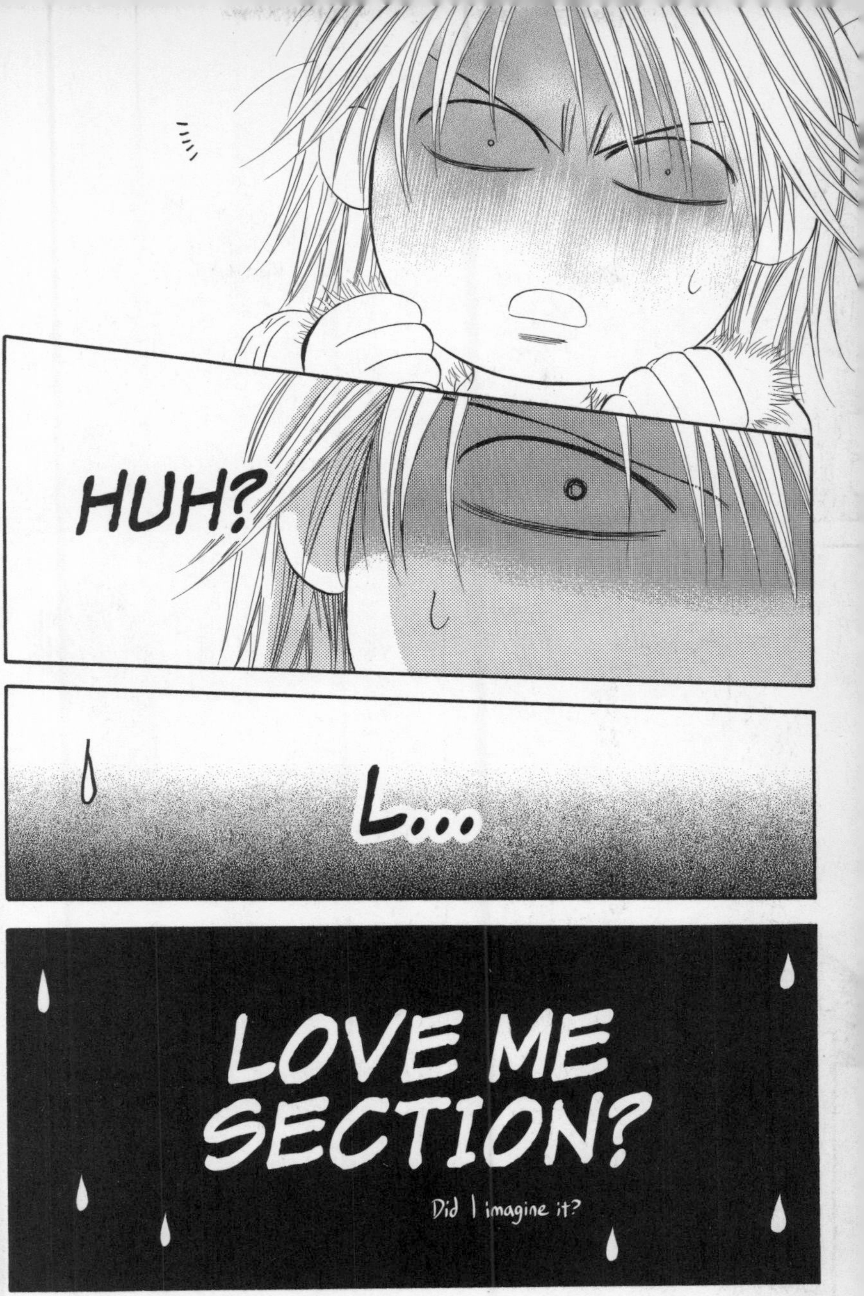
HUH?
L...
LOVE ME SECTION?
Did I imagine it?

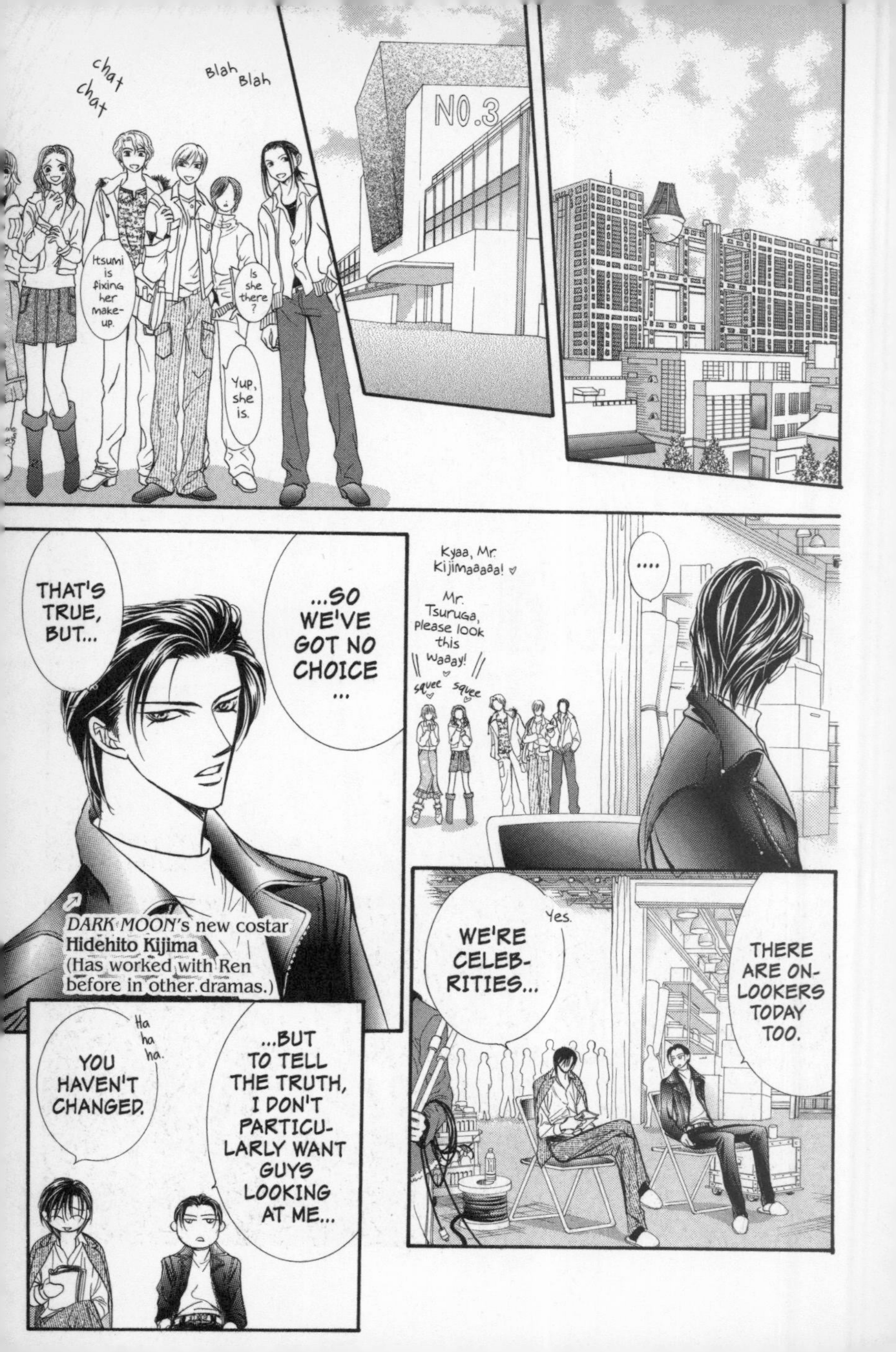
Blah Blah
chat chat
Is she there?
Yup, she is.
Itsumi is fixing her make-up.
....
Kyaa, Mr. Kijimaaaaa!
Mr. Tsuruga, please look this waaay!
squee squee
THERE ARE ON-LOOKERS TODAY TOO.
Yes.
WE'RE CELEB-RITIES...
...SO WE'VE GOT NO CHOICE...
THAT'S TRUE, BUT...
DARK MOON's new costar Hidehito Kijima (Has worked with Ren before in other dramas.)
...BUT TO TELL THE TRUTH, I DON'T PARTICU-LARLY WANT GUYS LOOKING AT ME...
Ha ha ha.
YOU HAVEN'T CHANGED.

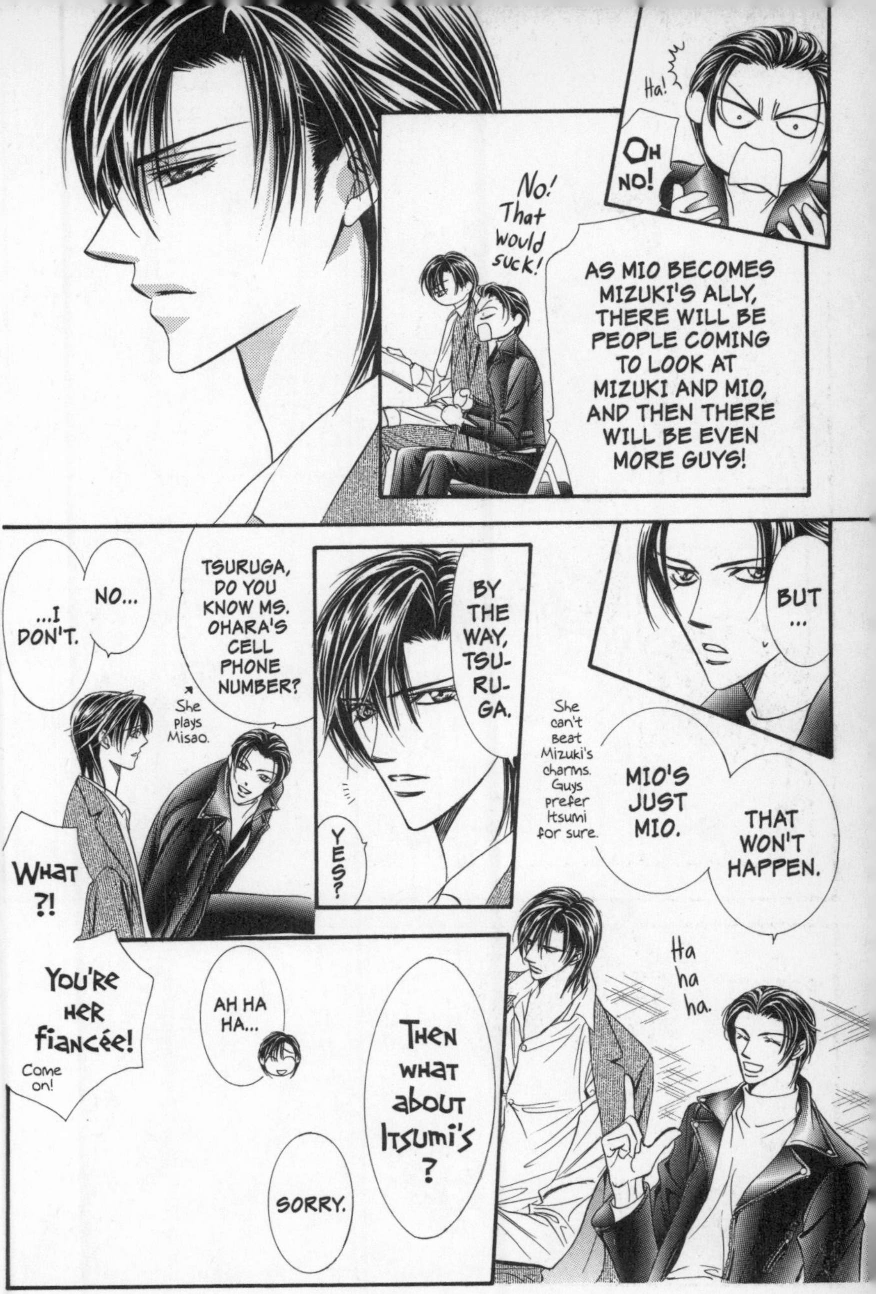
Ha!
OH NO!
AS MIO BECOMES MIZUKI'S ALLY, THERE WILL BE PEOPLE COMING TO LOOK AT MIZUKI AND MIO, AND THEN THERE WILL BE EVEN MORE GUYS!
No! That would suck!
BUT...
THAT WON'T HAPPEN.
MIO'S JUST MIO.
She can't beat Mizuki's charms. Guys prefer Itsumi for sure.
Ha ha ha.
BY THE WAY, TSURUGA.
YES?
TSURUGA, DO YOU KNOW MS. OHARA'S CELL PHONE NUMBER?
She plays Misao.
NO...
...I DON'T.
WHAT?!
Then what about Itsumi's?
AH HA HA...
SORRY.
You're her fiancée!
Come on!

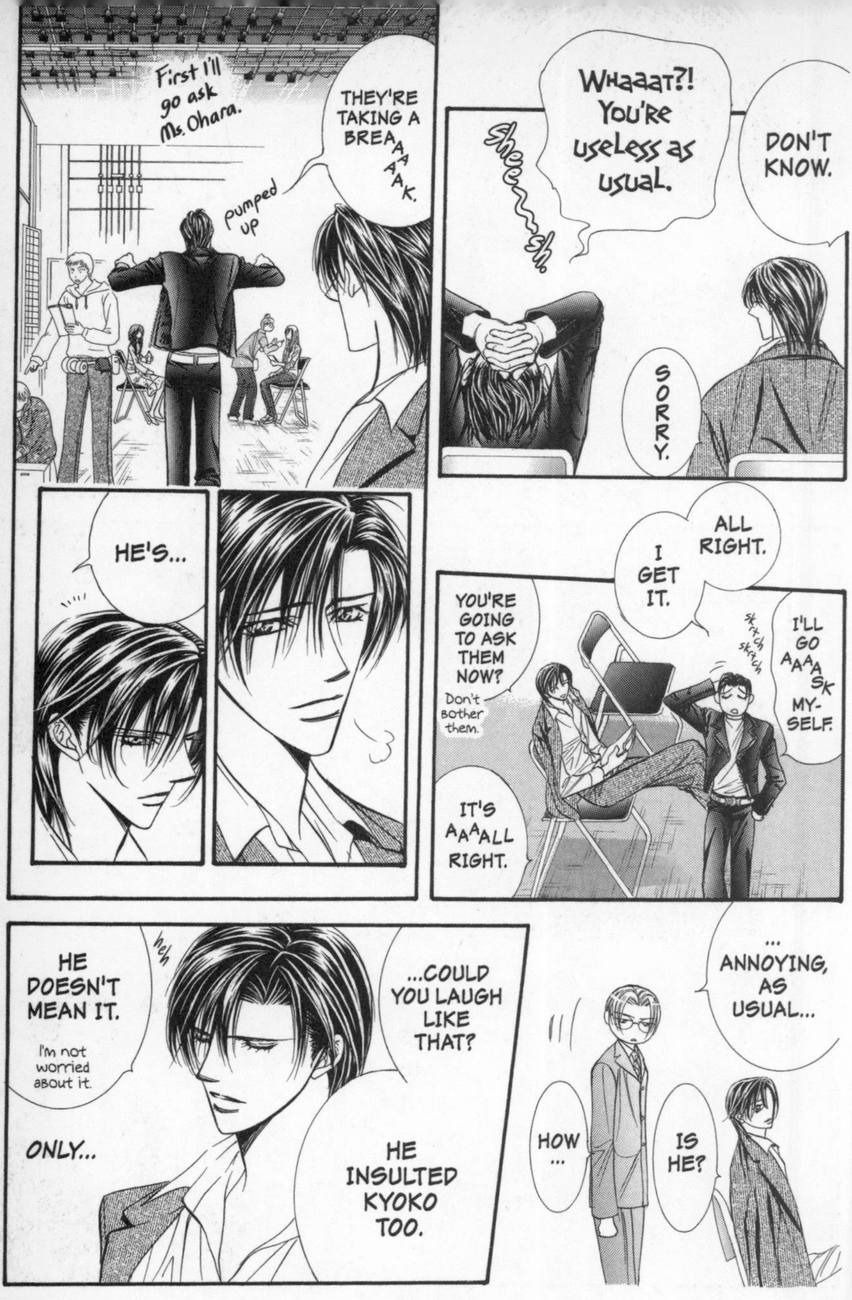

DON'T KNOW.
WHAAAT?! YOU'RE USELESS AS USUAL.
Sheeesh.
SORRY.
THEY'RE TAKING A BREAAAAAK.
First I'll go ask Ms. Ohara.
pumped up
ALL RIGHT.
I GET IT.
I'LL GO AAAASK MYSELF.
skrtch skrtch
YOU'RE GOING TO ASK THEM NOW?
Don't bother them.
IT'S AAAALL RIGHT.
HE'S...
... ANNOYING, AS USUAL...
IS HE?
HOW ...
...COULD YOU LAUGH LIKE THAT?
heh
HE DOESN'T MEAN IT.
I'm not worried about it.
ONLY...
HE INSULTED KYOKO TOO.

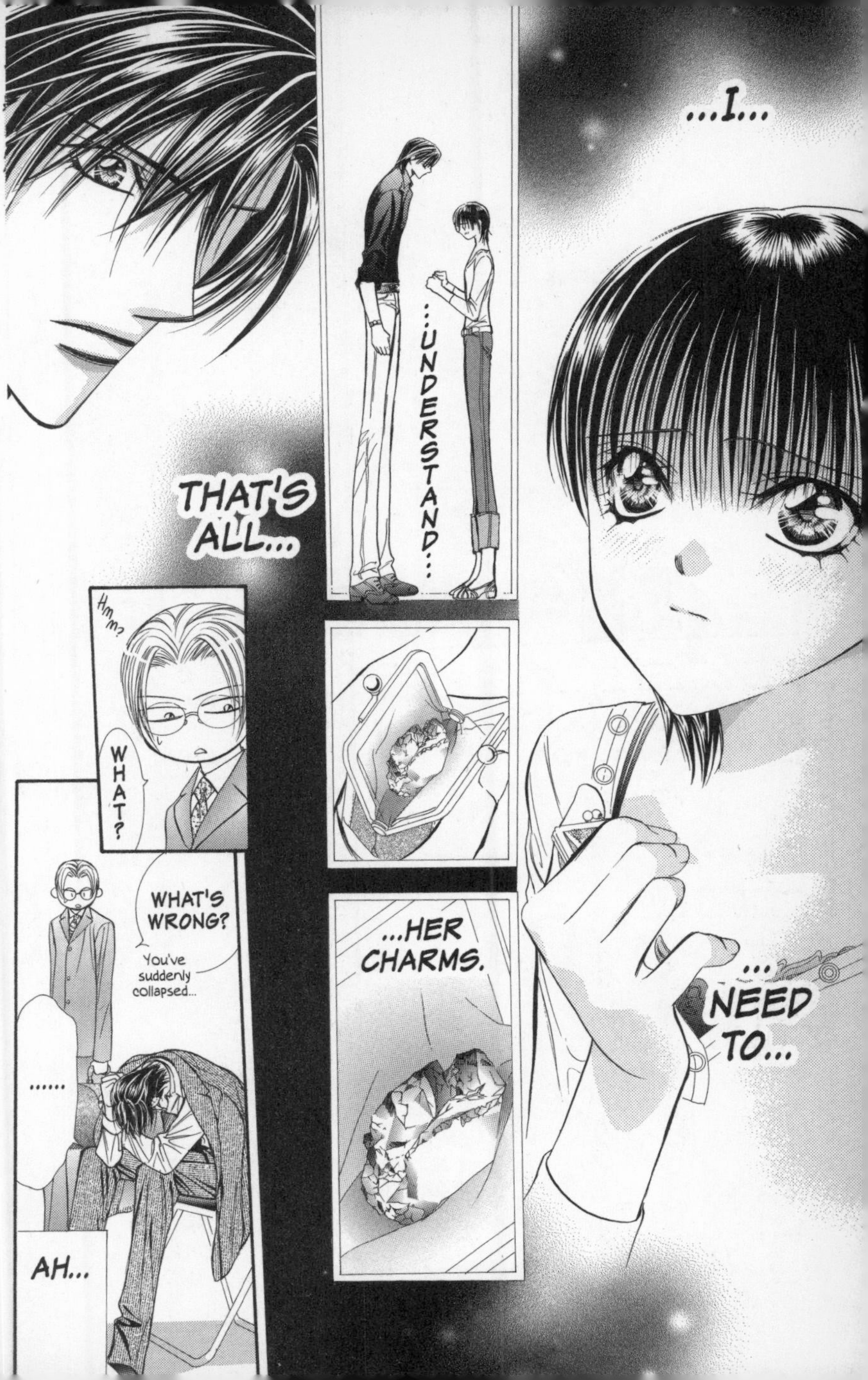
...I...
...NEED TO...
...UNDERSTAND...
...HER CHARMS.
THAT'S ALL...
Hmm?
WHAT?
WHAT'S WRONG?
You've suddenly collapsed...
......
AH...

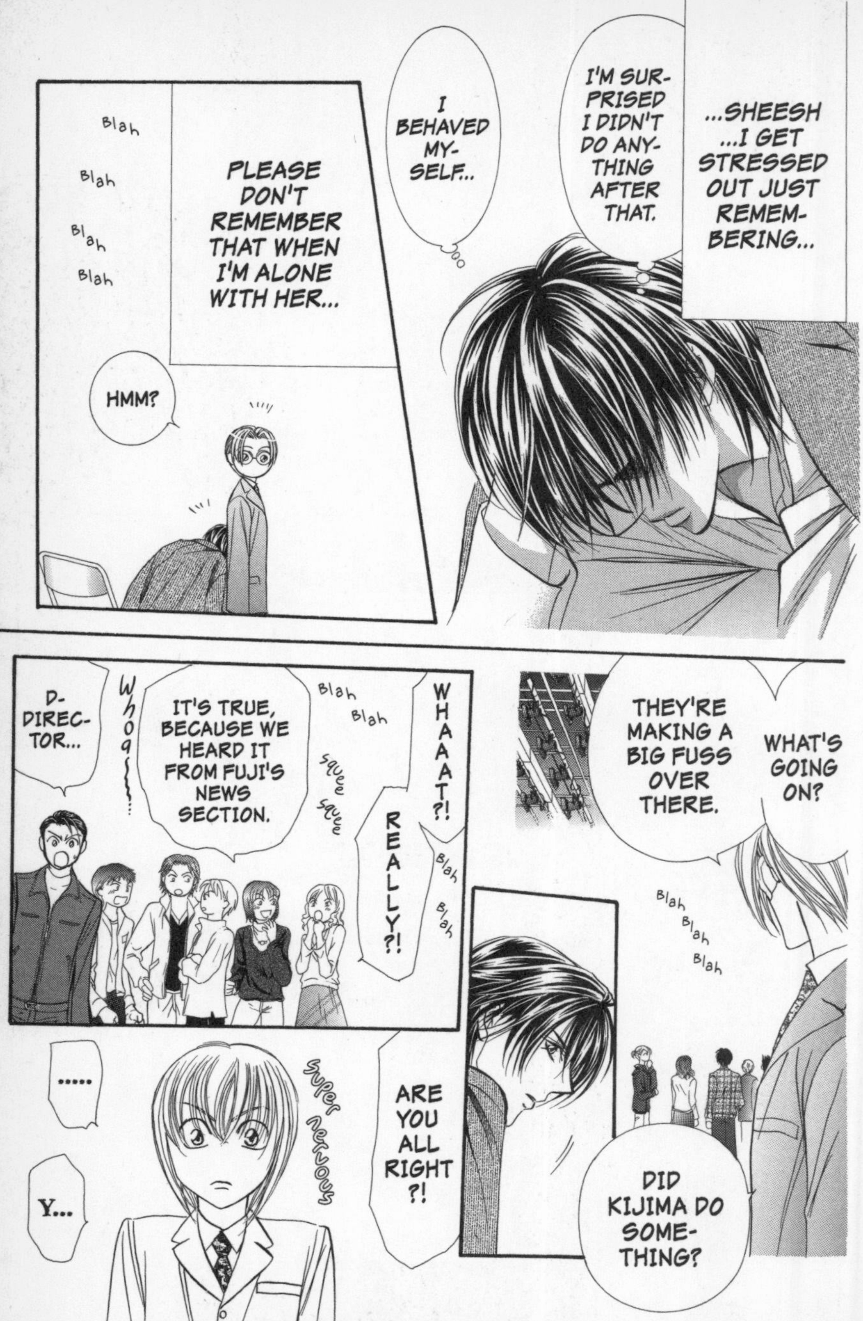
...SHEESH ...I GET STRESSED OUT JUST REMEMBERING...
I'M SURPRISED I DIDN'T DO ANYTHING AFTER THAT.
I BEHAVED MYSELF...
PLEASE DON'T REMEMBER THAT WHEN I'M ALONE WITH HER...
Blah
Blah
Blah
Blah
HMM?
WHAT'S GOING ON?
THEY'RE MAKING A BIG FUSS OVER THERE.
Blah
Blah
Blah
DID KIJIMA DO SOMETHING?
WHAAAT?!
REALLY?!
Blah
Blah
Blah
Blah
squee
squee
IT'S TRUE, BECAUSE WE HEARD IT FROM FUJI'S NEWS SECTION.
Whoa~~
D-DIRECTOR...
ARE YOU ALL RIGHT?!
Super nervous
......
Y...

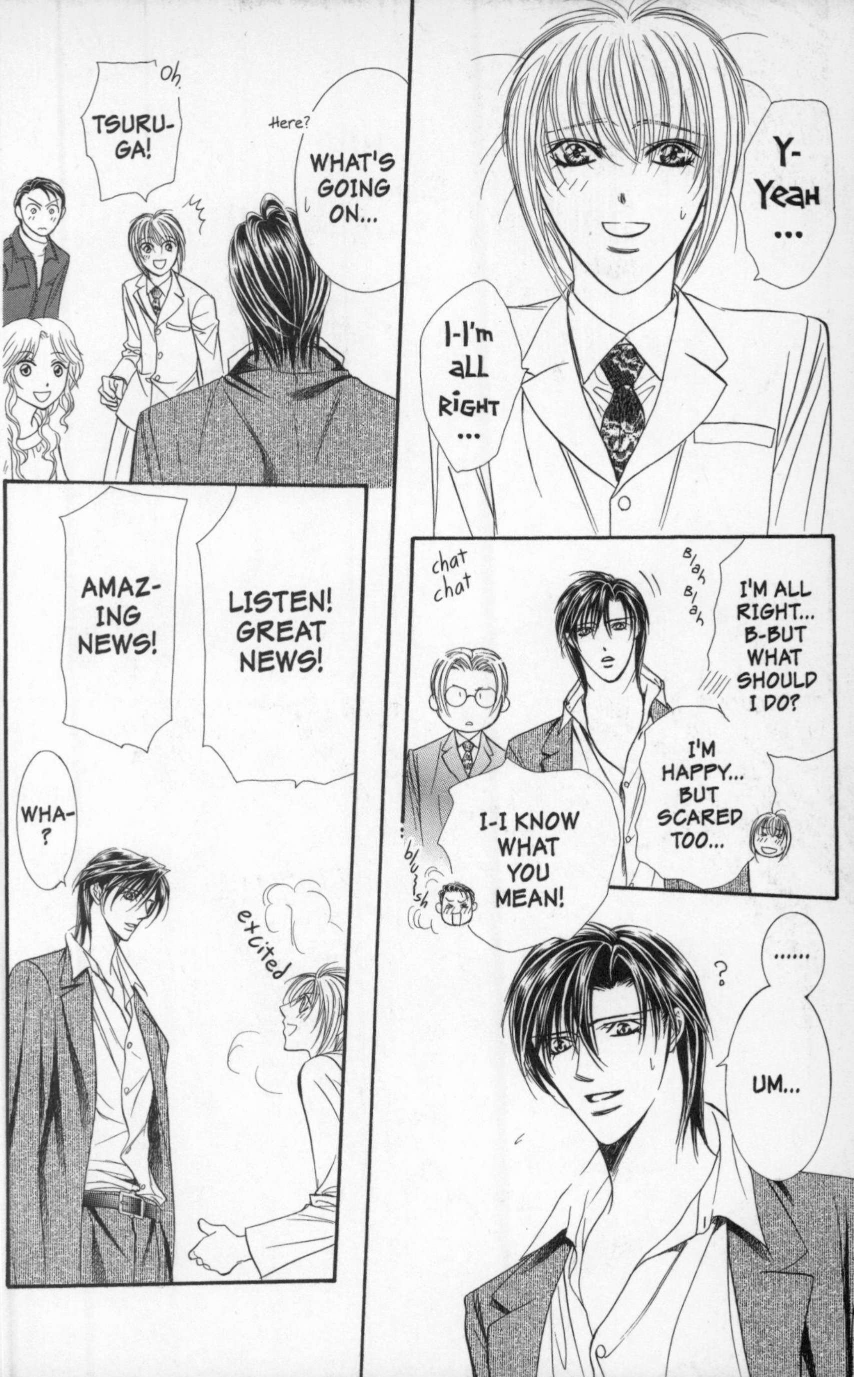
Y-Yeah...
I-I'm all right...
I'M ALL RIGHT... B-BUT WHAT SHOULD I DO?
Blah Blah
chat chat
I'M HAPPY... BUT SCARED TOO...
I-I KNOW WHAT YOU MEAN!
blush
......
?
UM...
WHAT'S GOING ON...
Here?
Oh,
TSURU-GA!
LISTEN! GREAT NEWS!
AMAZ-ING NEWS!
WHA-?
excited

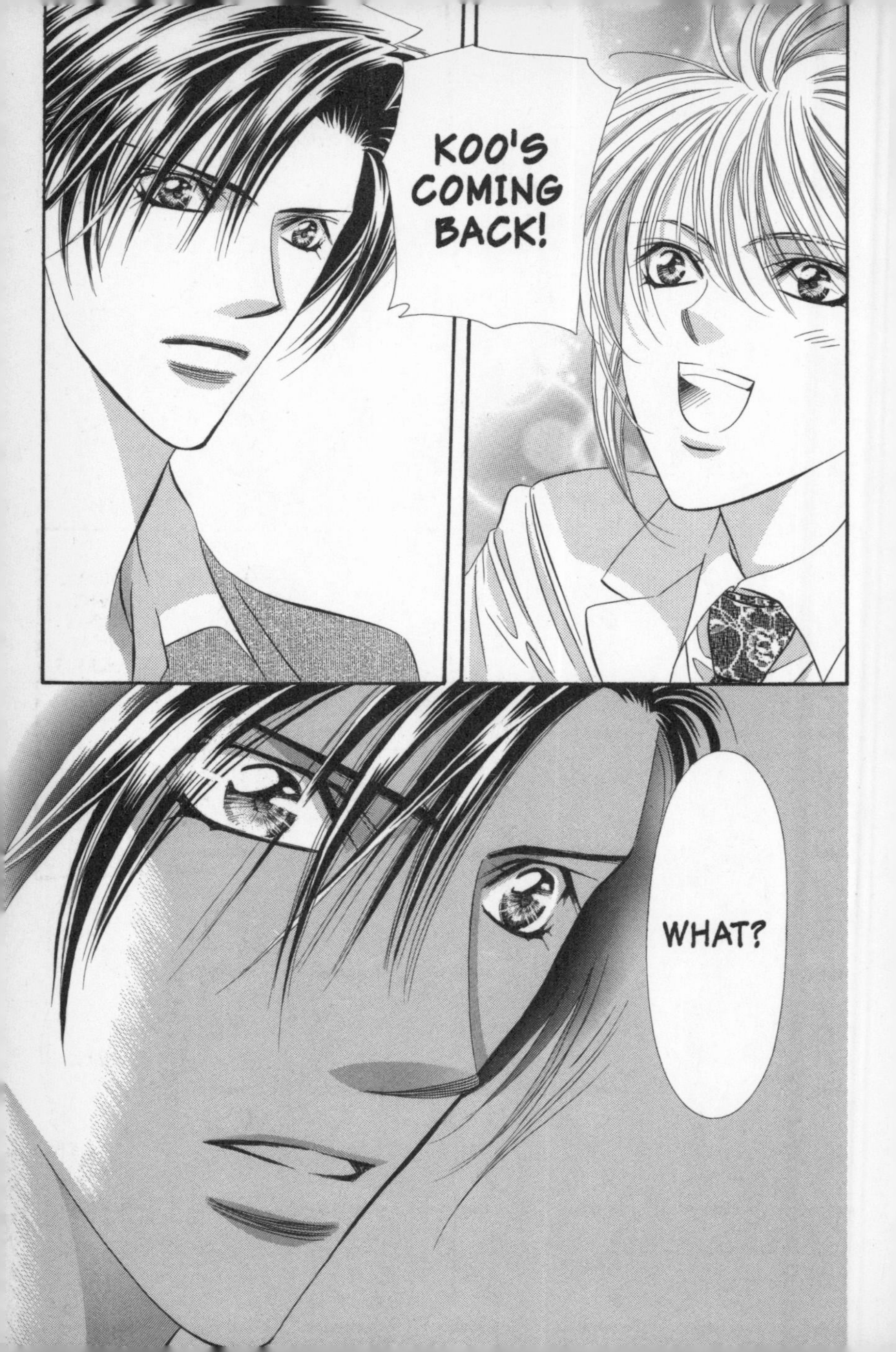
KOO'S COMING BACK!
WHAT?

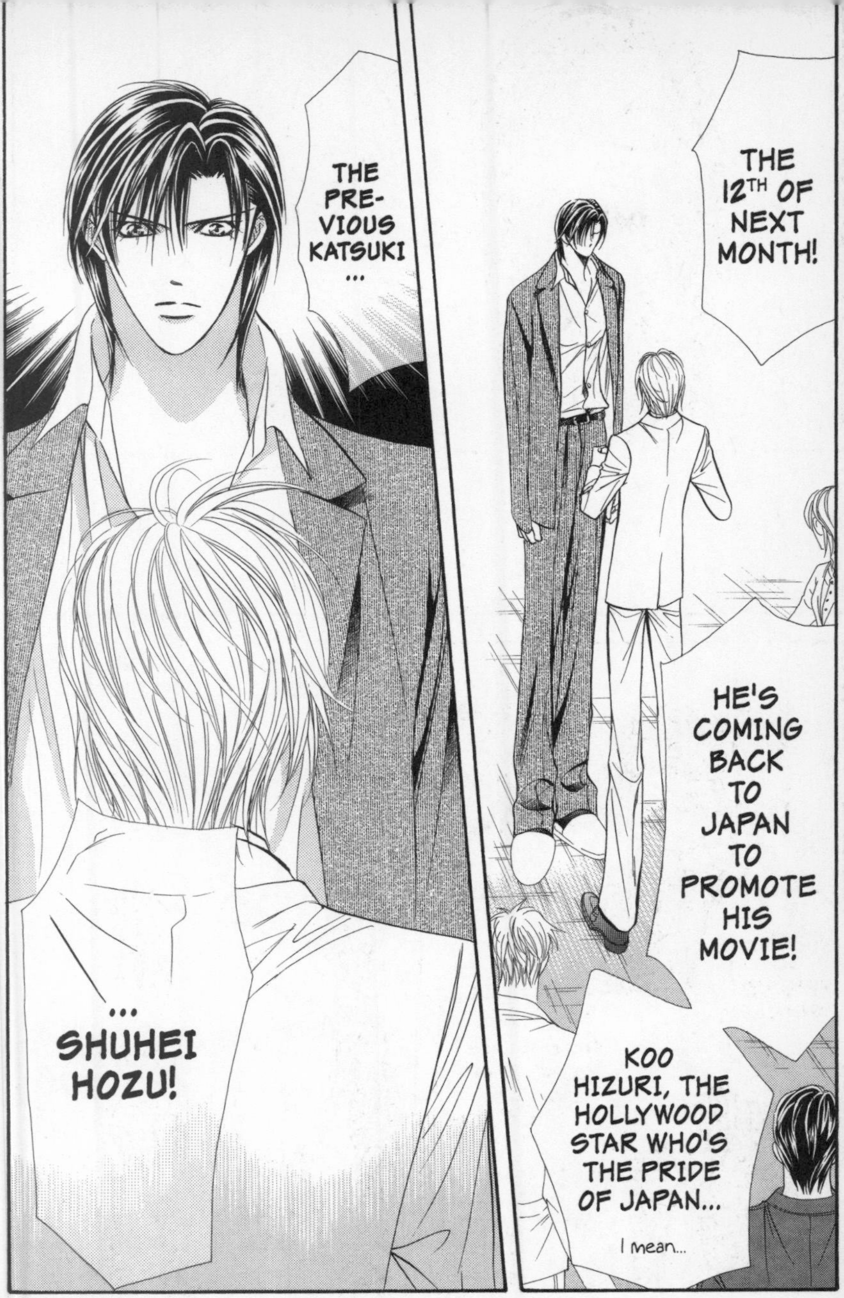
THE 12TH OF NEXT MONTH!
HE'S COMING BACK TO JAPAN TO PROMOTE HIS MOVIE!
KOO HIZURI, THE HOLLYWOOD STAR WHO'S THE PRIDE OF JAPAN...
I mean...
THE PRE-VIOUS KATSUKI ...
... SHUHEI HOZU!

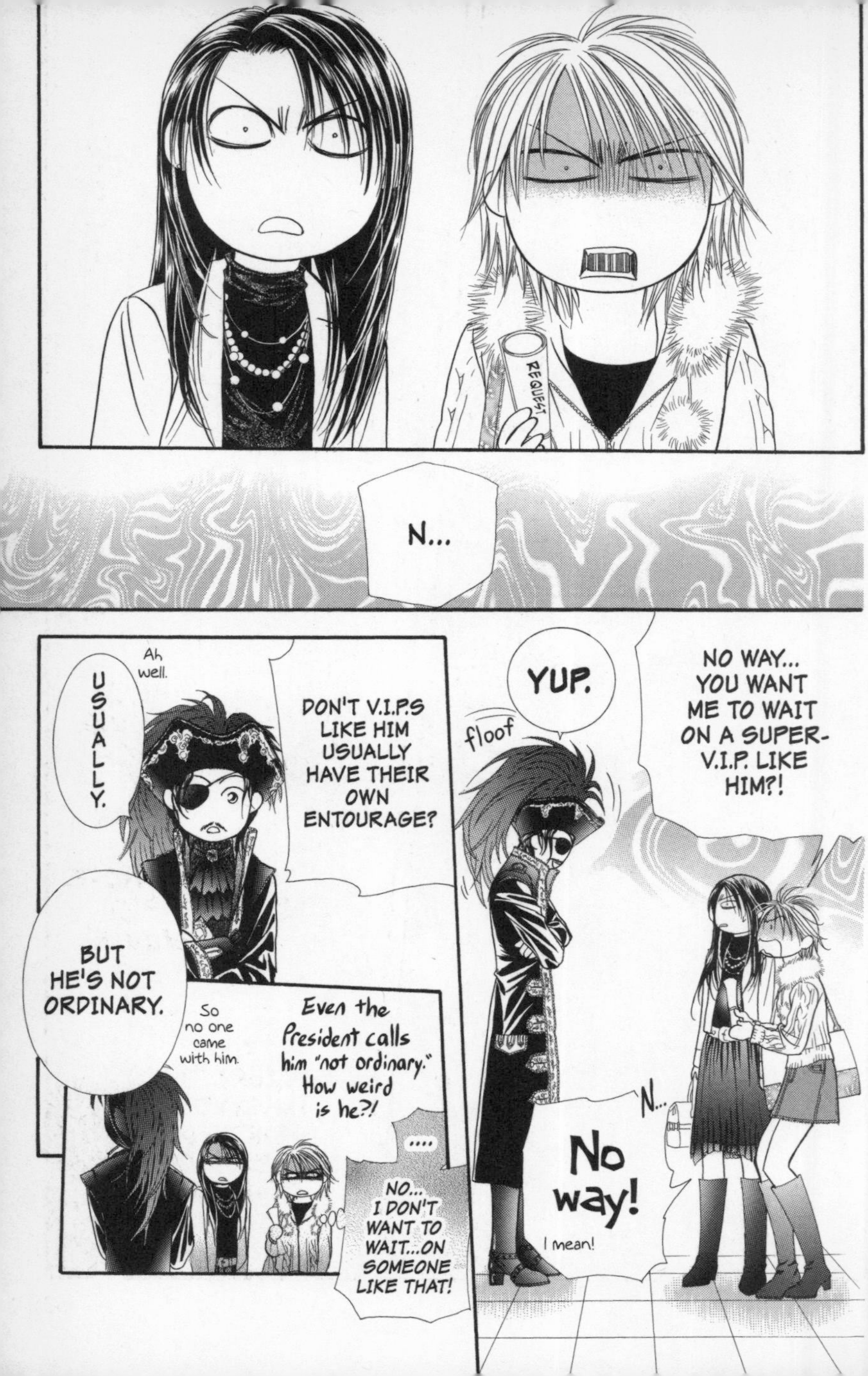
REQUEST
N...
NO WAY... YOU WANT ME TO WAIT ON A SUPER-V.I.P. LIKE HIM?!
YUP.
floof
N...
No way!
I mean!
DON'T V.I.P.S LIKE HIM USUALLY HAVE THEIR OWN ENTOURAGE?
USUALLY.
Ah well.
BUT HE'S NOT ORDINARY.
Even the President calls him "not ordinary." How weird is he?!
So no one came with him.
....
NO... I DON'T WANT TO WAIT...ON SOMEONE LIKE THAT!

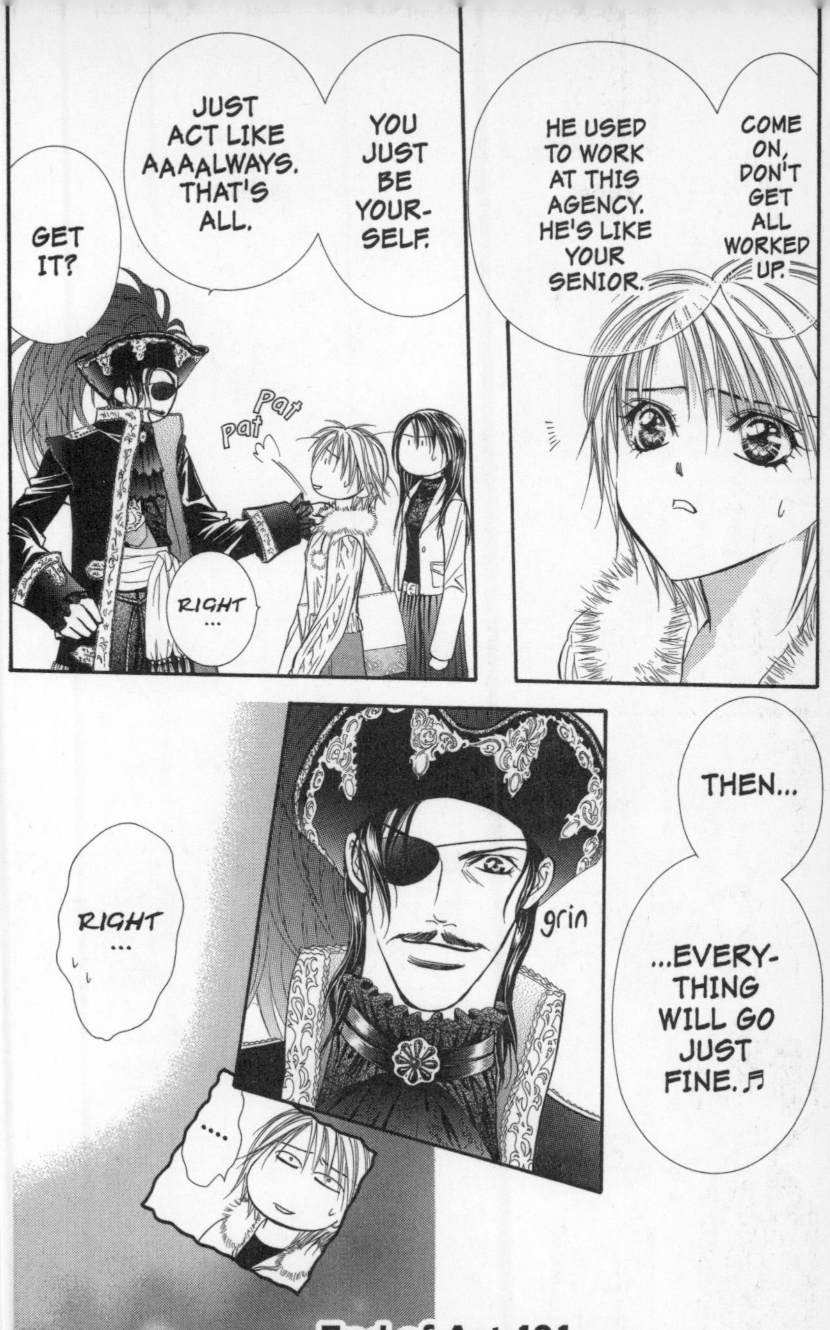
COME ON, DON'T GET ALL WORKED UP.
HE USED TO WORK AT THIS AGENCY. HE'S LIKE YOUR SENIOR.
YOU JUST BE YOUR-SELF.
JUST ACT LIKE AAAALWAYS. THAT'S ALL.
GET IT?
Pat pat
RIGHT ...
THEN...
...EVERY-THING WILL GO JUST FINE. ♬
grin
RIGHT ...
....

End of Act 101

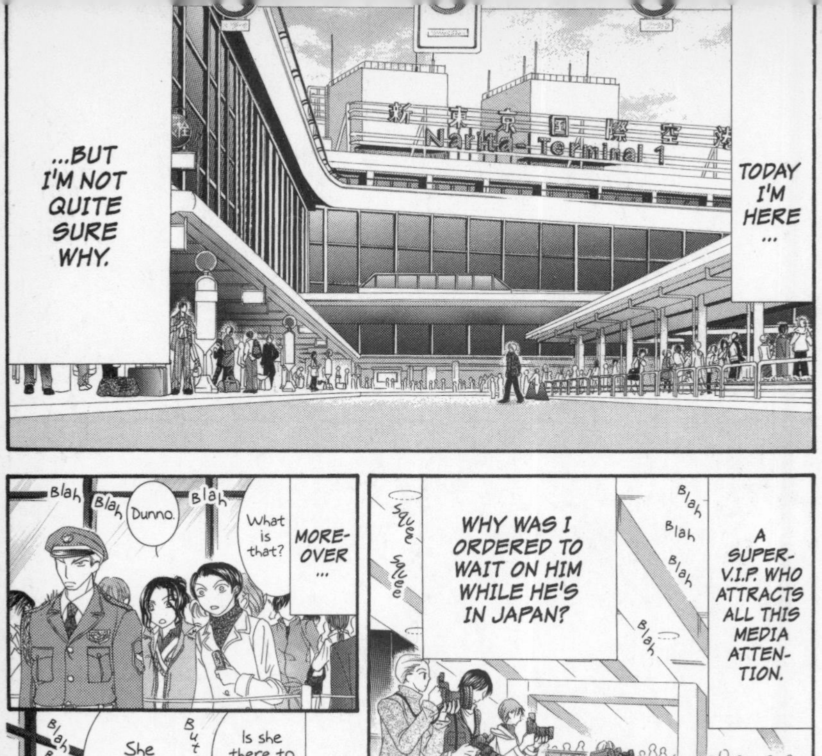
新東京国際空港
Narita-Terminal 1
TODAY I'M HERE ...
...BUT I'M NOT QUITE SURE WHY.
A SUPER-V.I.P. WHO ATTRACTS ALL THIS MEDIA ATTENTION.
Blah
Blah
Blah
Blah
WHY WAS I ORDERED TO WAIT ON HIM WHILE HE'S IN JAPAN?
Squee
Squee
MORE-OVER ...
What is that?
Blah
Dunno.
Blah
Blah
... WHY AM I...
Is she there to welcome him?
But...
She doesn't go with the car behind her.
Blah
Blah
I mean ...
Look at her.

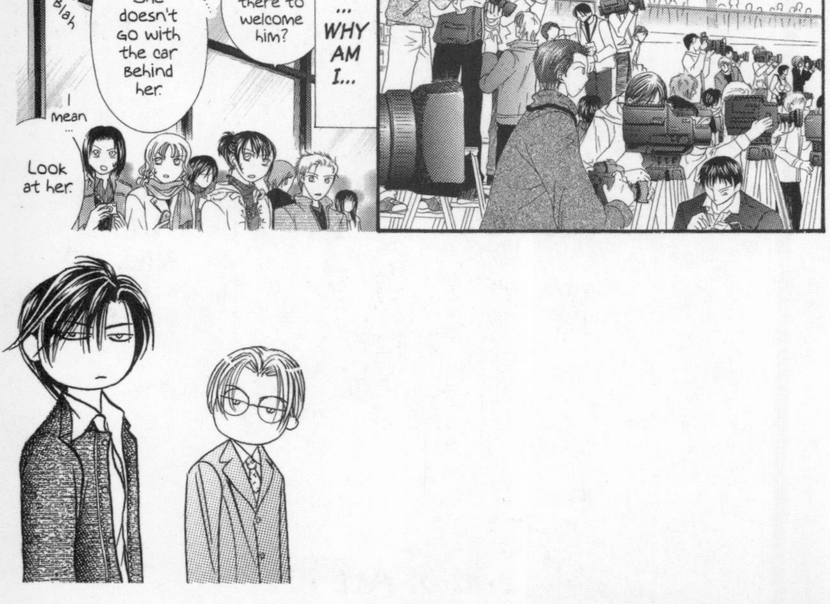

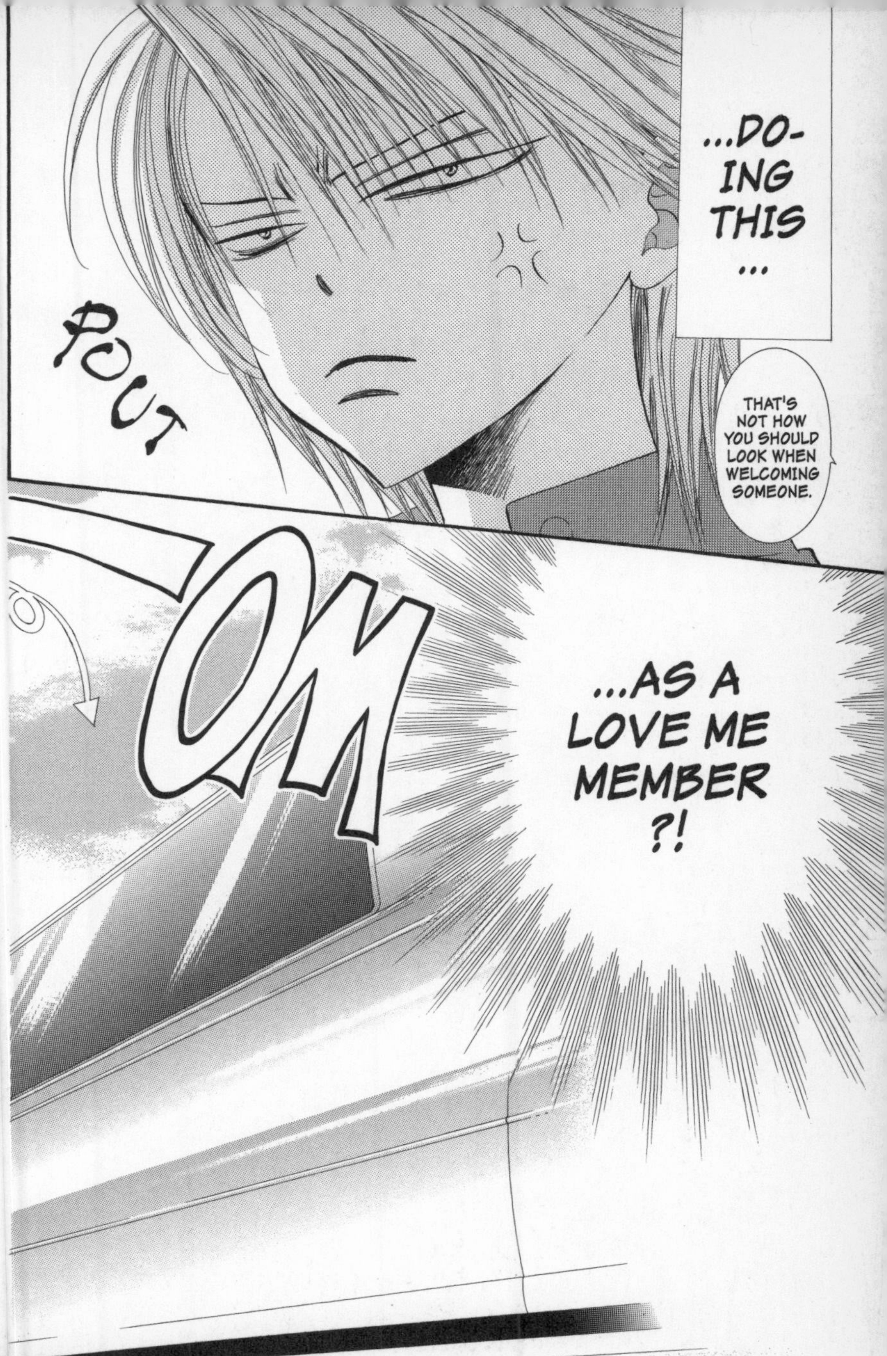
...DO-ING THIS ...
THAT'S NOT HOW YOU SHOULD LOOK WHEN WELCOMING SOMEONE.
POUT
...AS A LOVE ME MEMBER ?!
OM

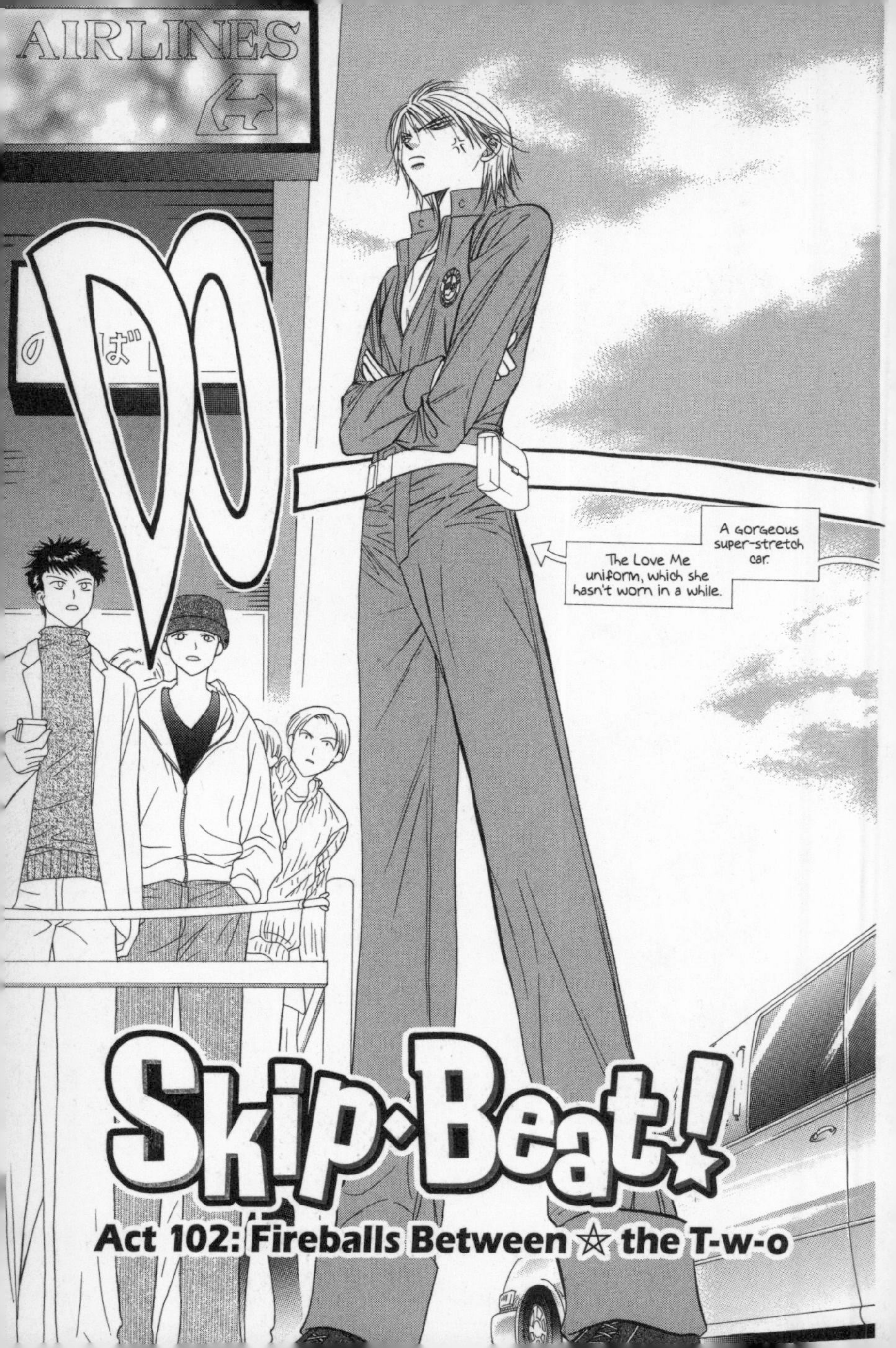
AIRLINES
DO
A gorgeous super-stretch car.
The Love Me uniform, which she hasn't worn in a while.
Skip·Beat!
Act 102: Fireballs Between ☆ the T-w-o

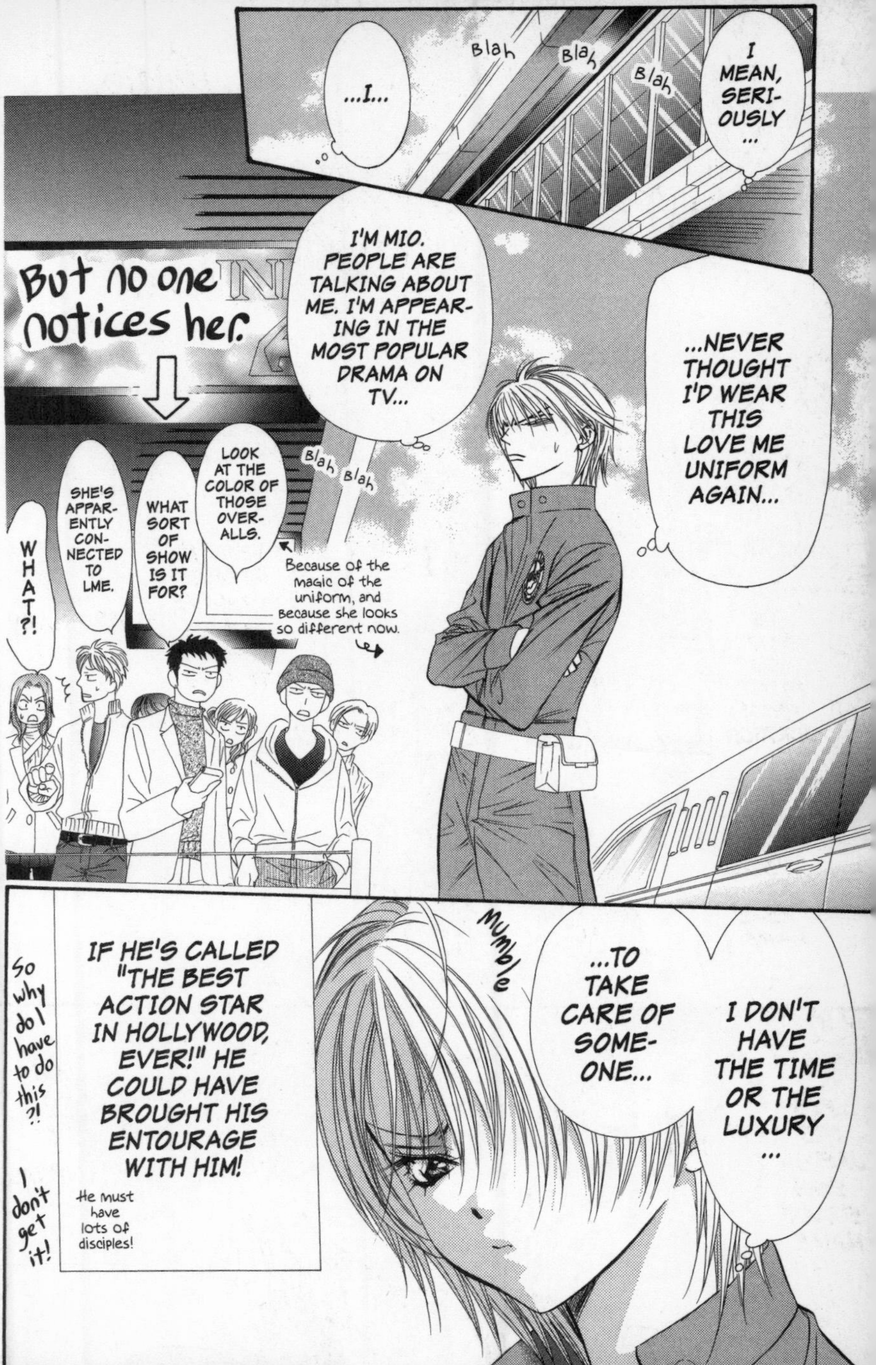

I MEAN, SERIOUSLY...
Blah
Blah
Blah
...I...
...NEVER THOUGHT I'D WEAR THIS LOVE ME UNIFORM AGAIN...
I'M MIO. PEOPLE ARE TALKING ABOUT ME. I'M APPEARING IN THE MOST POPULAR DRAMA ON TV...
Blah Blah
But no one notices her.
LOOK AT THE COLOR OF THOSE OVERALLS.
WHAT SORT OF SHOW IS IT FOR?
SHE'S APPARENTLY CONNECTED TO LME.
WHAT?!
Because of the magic of the uniform, and because she looks so different now.
I DON'T HAVE THE TIME OR THE LUXURY...
...TO TAKE CARE OF SOMEONE...
MUMBLE
IF HE'S CALLED "THE BEST ACTION STAR IN HOLLYWOOD, EVER!" HE COULD HAVE BROUGHT HIS ENTOURAGE WITH HIM!
He must have lots of disciples!
So why do I have to do this?!
I don't get it!

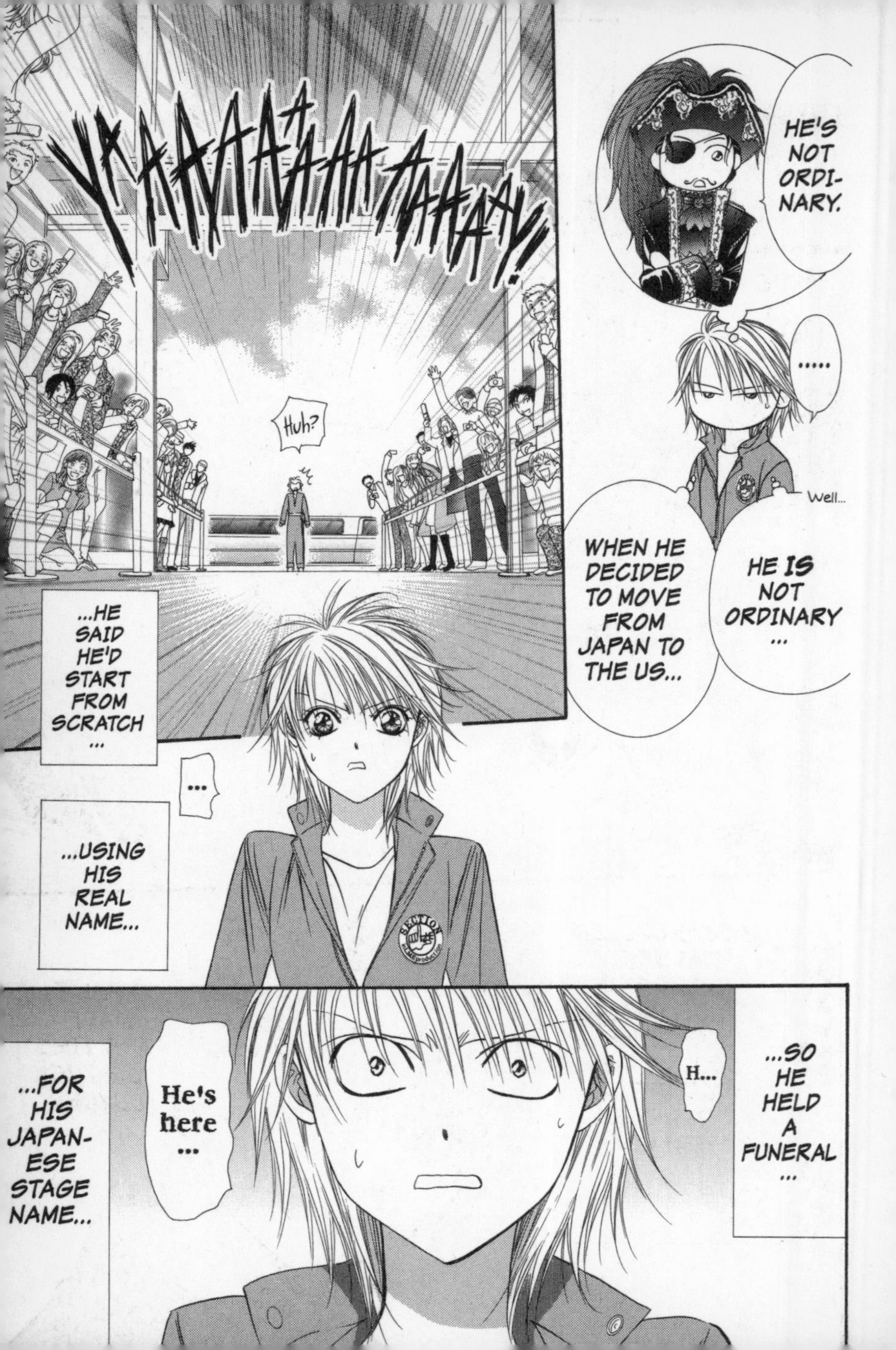
HE'S NOT ORDINARY.
.....
Well...
HE IS NOT ORDINARY...
WHEN HE DECIDED TO MOVE FROM JAPAN TO THE US...
YAAAAAAAAAAAAAY!
Huh?
...HE SAID HE'D START FROM SCRATCH...
...
...USING HIS REAL NAME...
...SO HE HELD A FUNERAL...
H...
He's here...
...FOR HIS JAPANESE STAGE NAME...

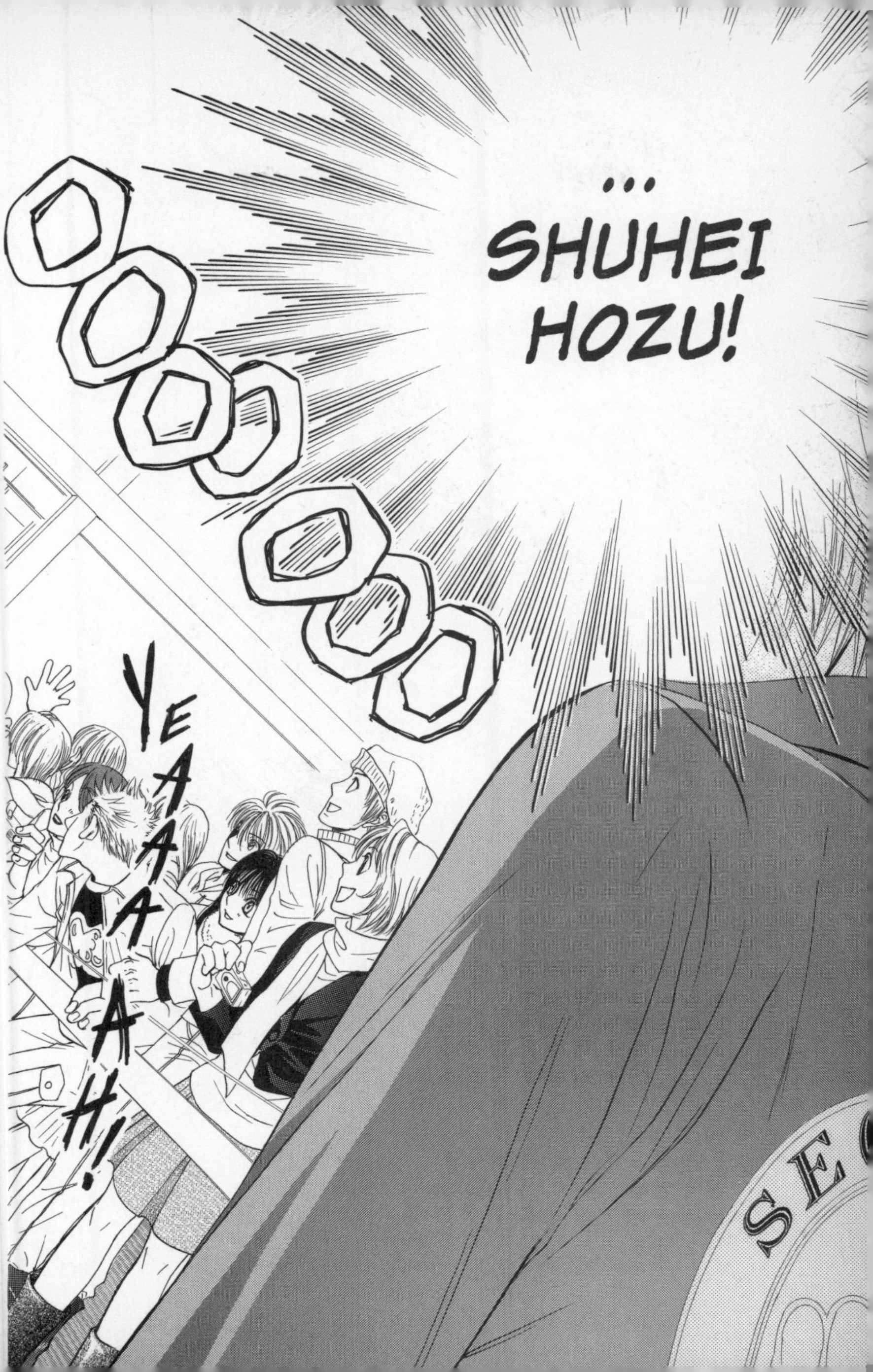
... SHUHEI HOZU!
OOOOOOO
YEAAAAAH!

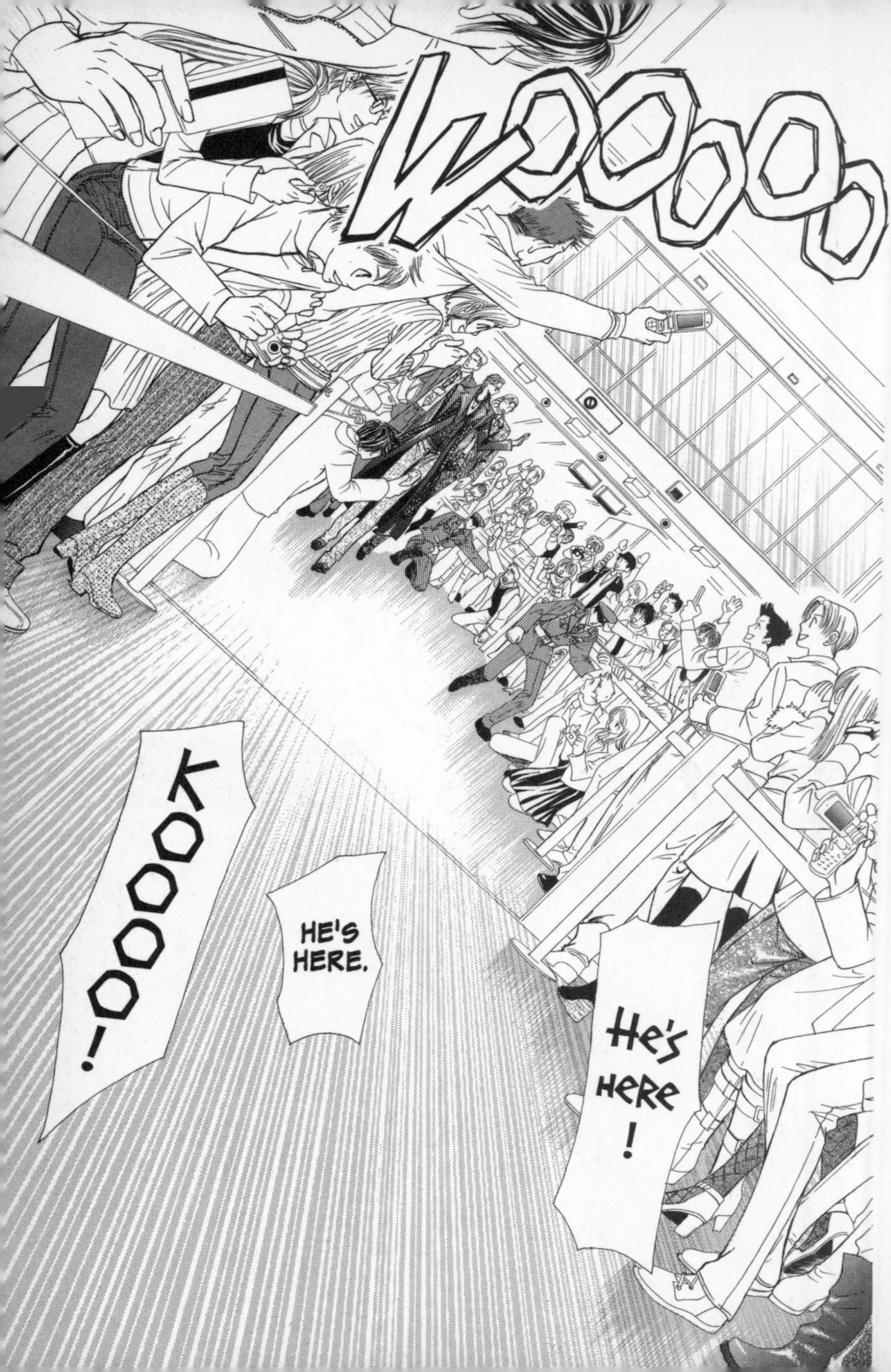
WOOOOOO
He's here!
HE'S HERE.
KOOOOO!

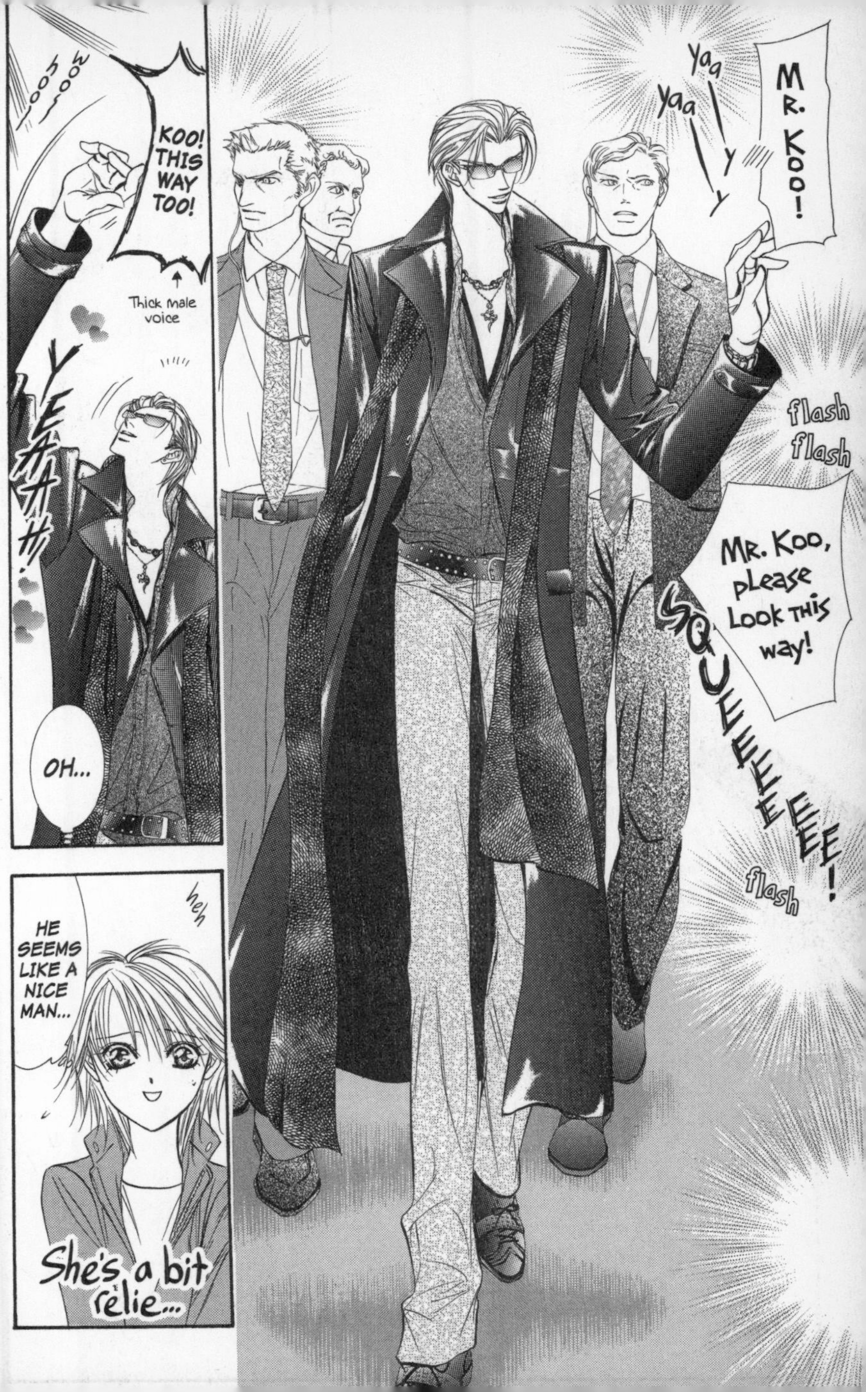
MR. KOO!
yaa yaa y y
flash flash
MR. KOO, please LOOK THIS way!
SQUEEEEEEE!
flash
KOO! THIS WAY TOO!
Thick male voice
YEAAH!!
OH...
heh
HE SEEMS LIKE A NICE MAN...
She's a bit relie...

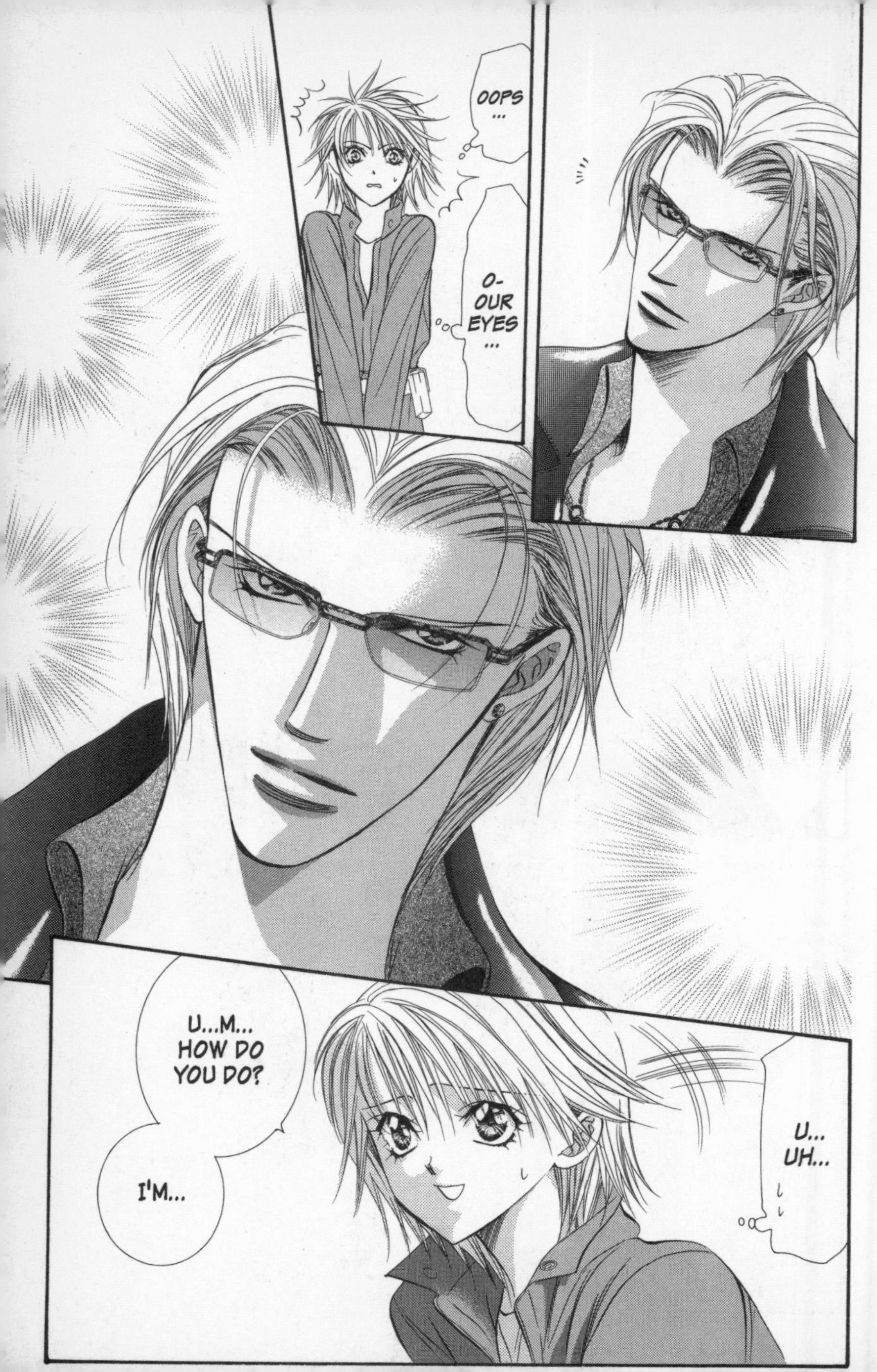
OOPS ...
O- OUR EYES ...
U... UH...
U...M... HOW DO YOU DO?
I'M...

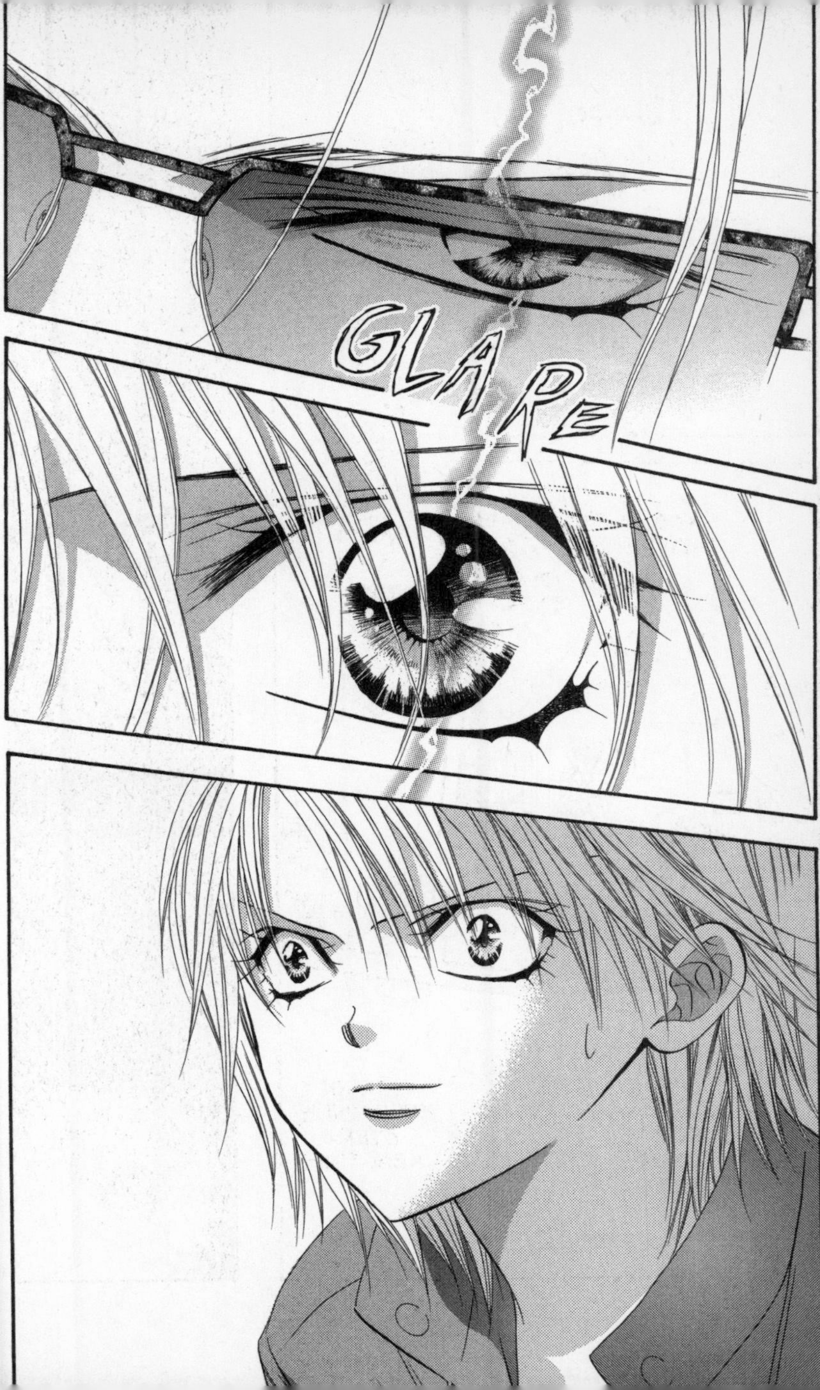
GLARE

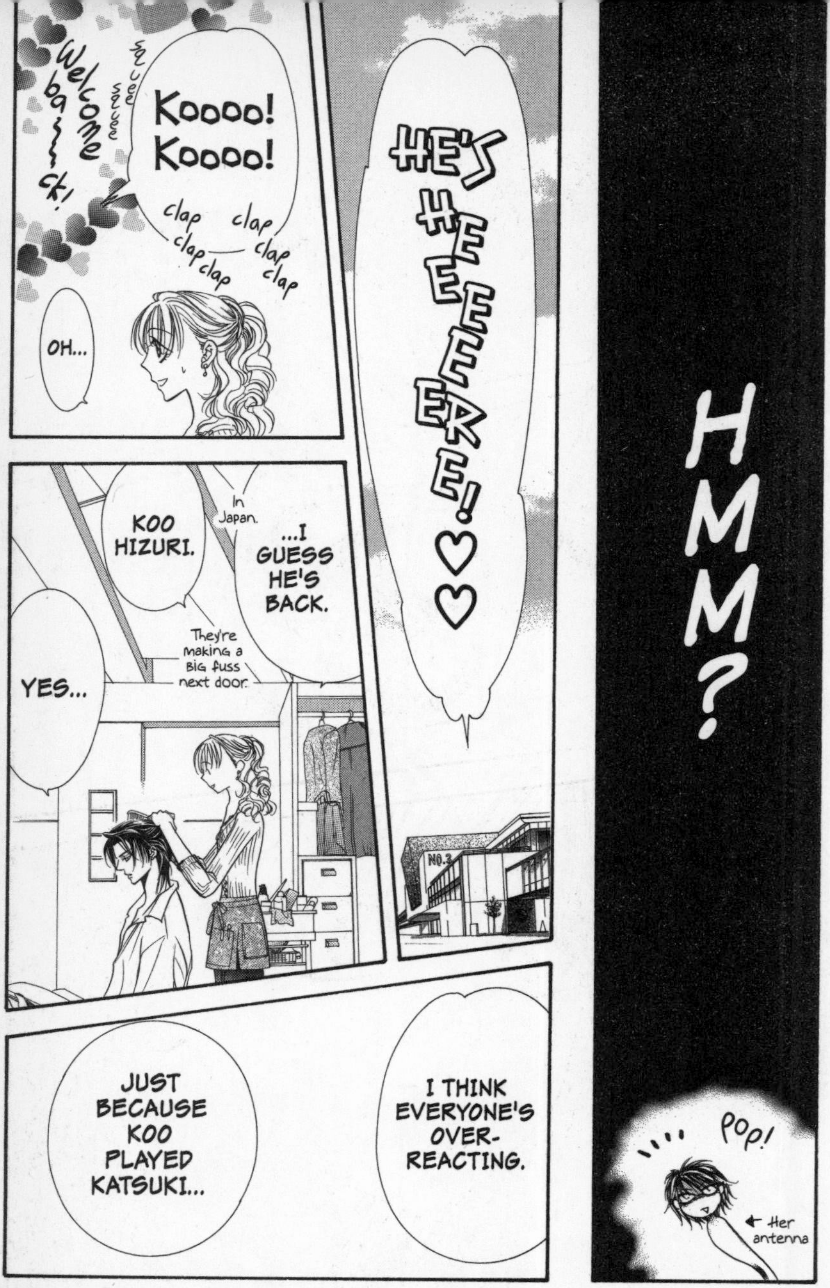
HMM?
Pop!
Her antenna
HE'S HEEEEERE! ♡♡
Koooo! Koooo!
squee squee
Welcome ba~~ck!
clap clap clap clap clap clap
OH...
In Japan.
...I GUESS HE'S BACK.
KOO HIZURI.
They're making a BIG fuss next door.
YES...
I THINK EVERYONE'S OVER-REACTING.
JUST BECAUSE KOO PLAYED KATSUKI...

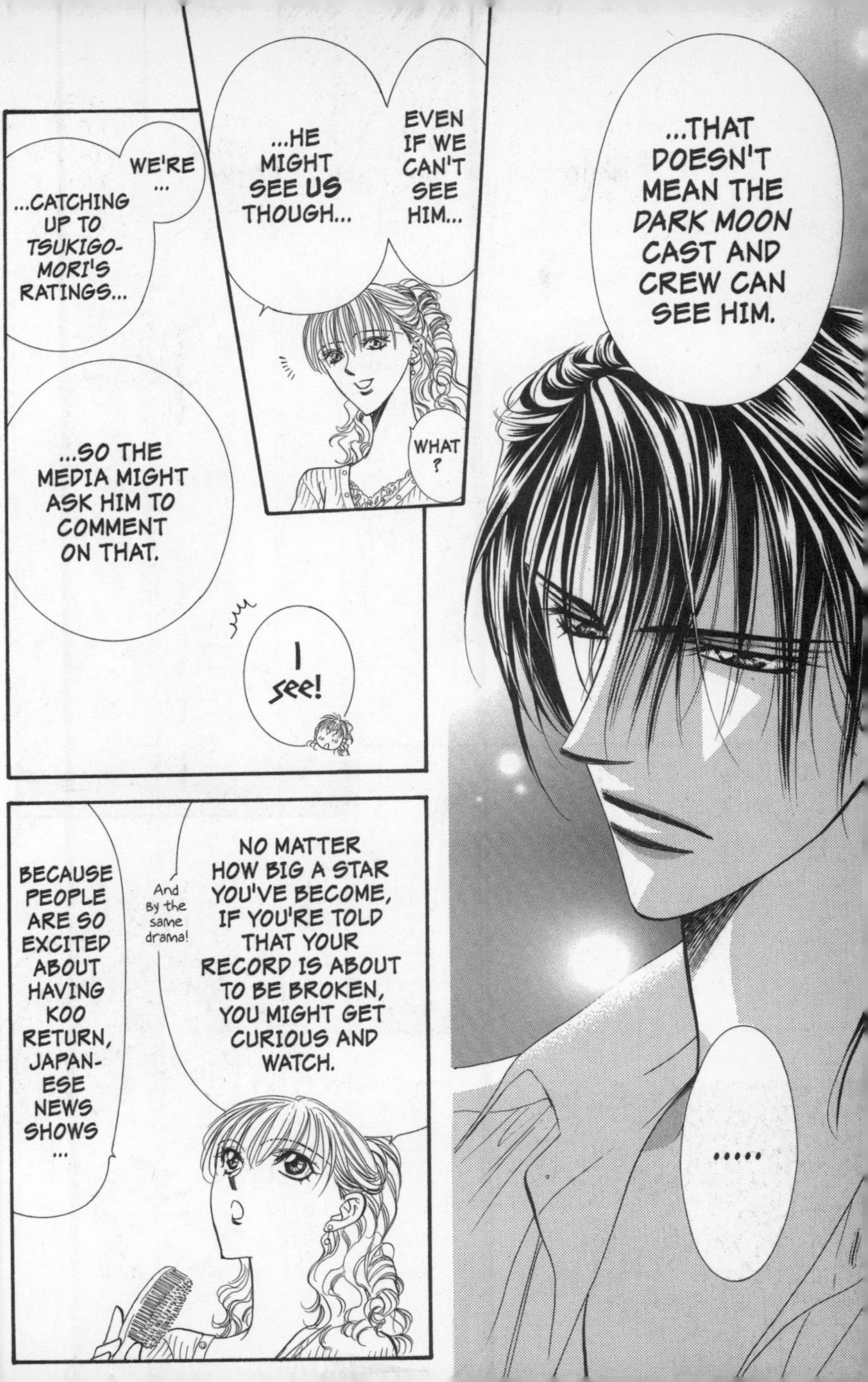
...THAT DOESN'T MEAN THE DARK MOON CAST AND CREW CAN SEE HIM.
.....
EVEN IF WE CAN'T SEE HIM...
...HE MIGHT SEE US THOUGH...
WHAT?
WE'RE ...
...CATCHING UP TO TSUKIGO-MORI'S RATINGS...
...SO THE MEDIA MIGHT ASK HIM TO COMMENT ON THAT.
I see!
NO MATTER HOW BIG A STAR YOU'VE BECOME, IF YOU'RE TOLD THAT YOUR RECORD IS ABOUT TO BE BROKEN, YOU MIGHT GET CURIOUS AND WATCH.
And by the same drama!
BECAUSE PEOPLE ARE SO EXCITED ABOUT HAVING KOO RETURN, JAPAN-ESE NEWS SHOWS ...

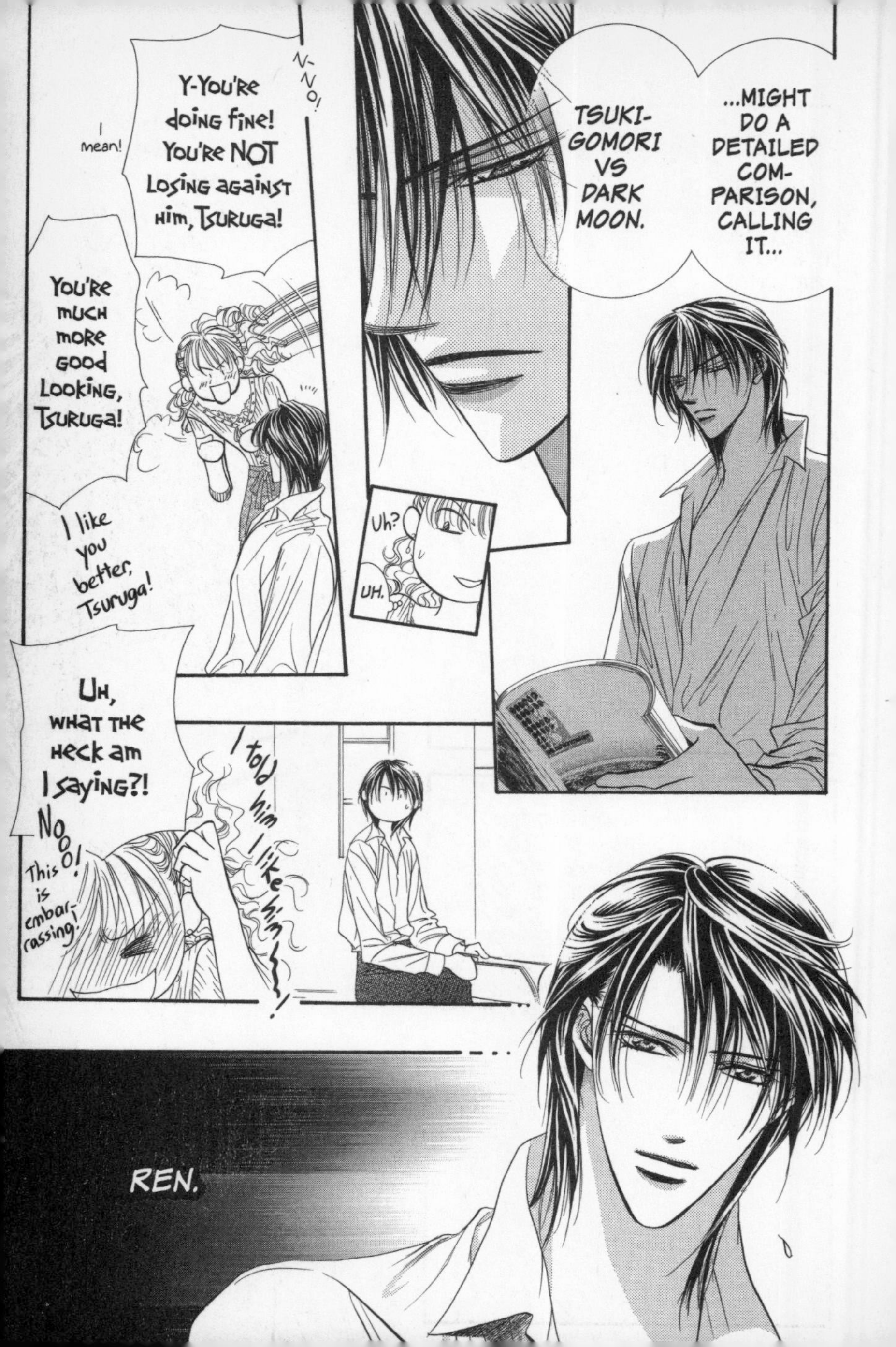

...MIGHT DO A DETAILED COM-PARISON, CALLING IT...
TSUKI-GOMORI VS DARK MOON.
Uh?
UH.
N-NO!
Y-You're doing fine! You're NOT losing against him, Tsuruga!
I mean!
You're much more good looking, Tsuruga!
I like you better, Tsuruga!
I told him I like him—!
Uh, what the heck am I saying?!
Nooo!
This is embar-rassing!
REN.

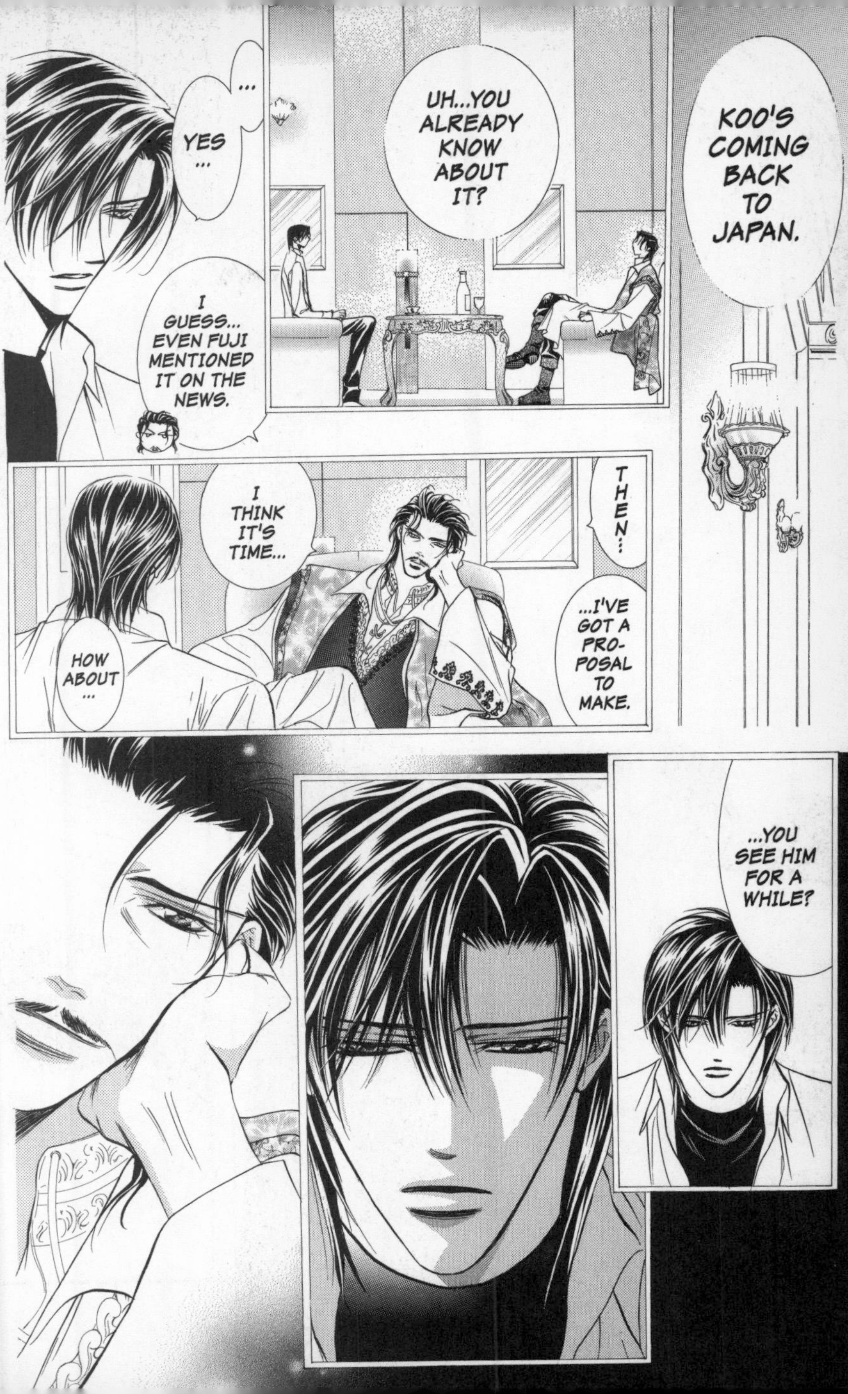
KOO'S COMING BACK TO JAPAN.
UH...YOU ALREADY KNOW ABOUT IT?
...
YES ...
I GUESS... EVEN FUJI MENTIONED IT ON THE NEWS.
THEN...
...I'VE GOT A PROPOSAL TO MAKE.
I THINK IT'S TIME...
HOW ABOUT ...
...YOU SEE HIM FOR A WHILE?

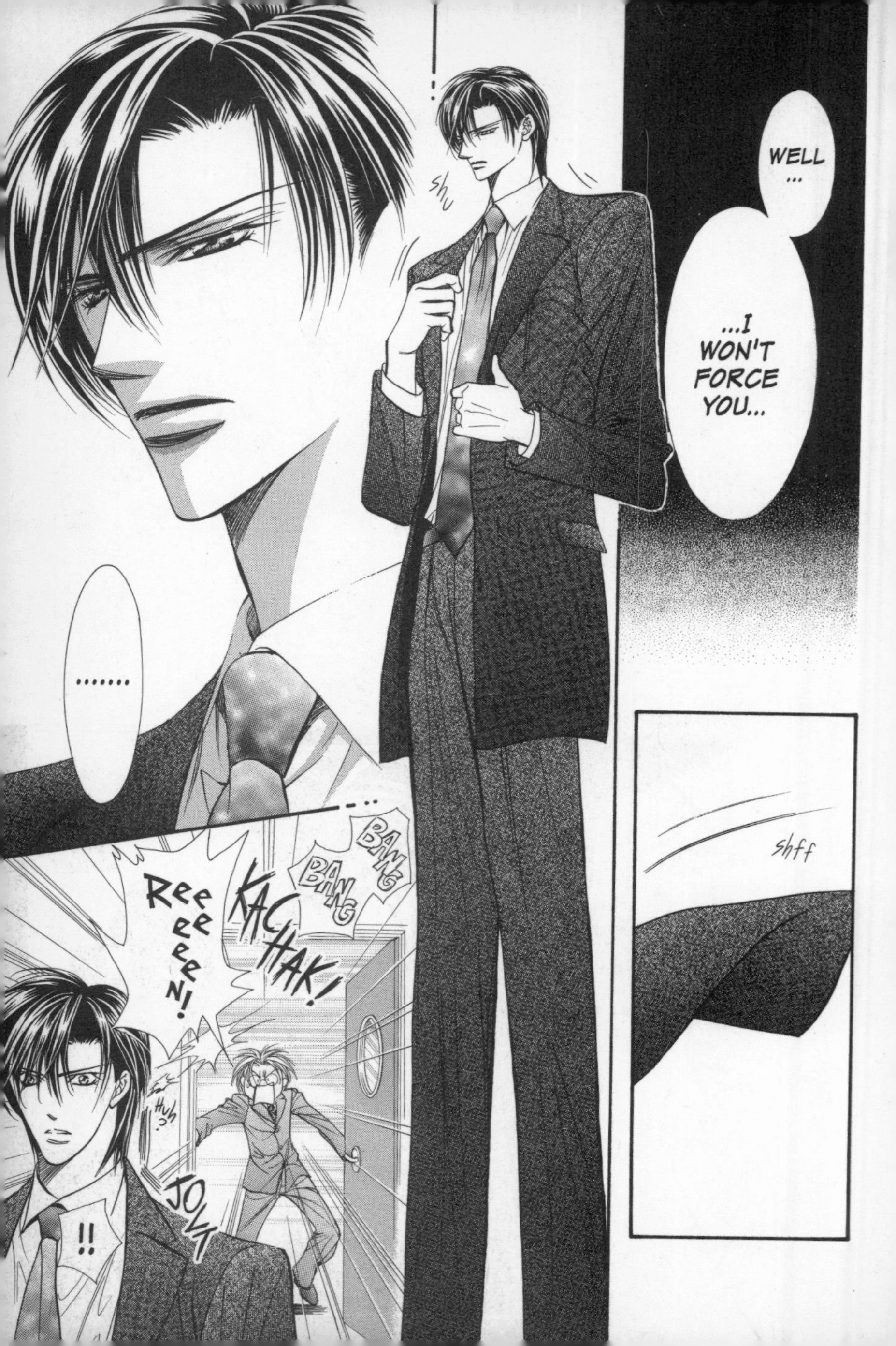
WELL...
...I WON'T FORCE YOU...
!
shu
shff
....
BANG
BANG
KACHAK!
Reeeeeeeen!
Huh?
JOLT
!!

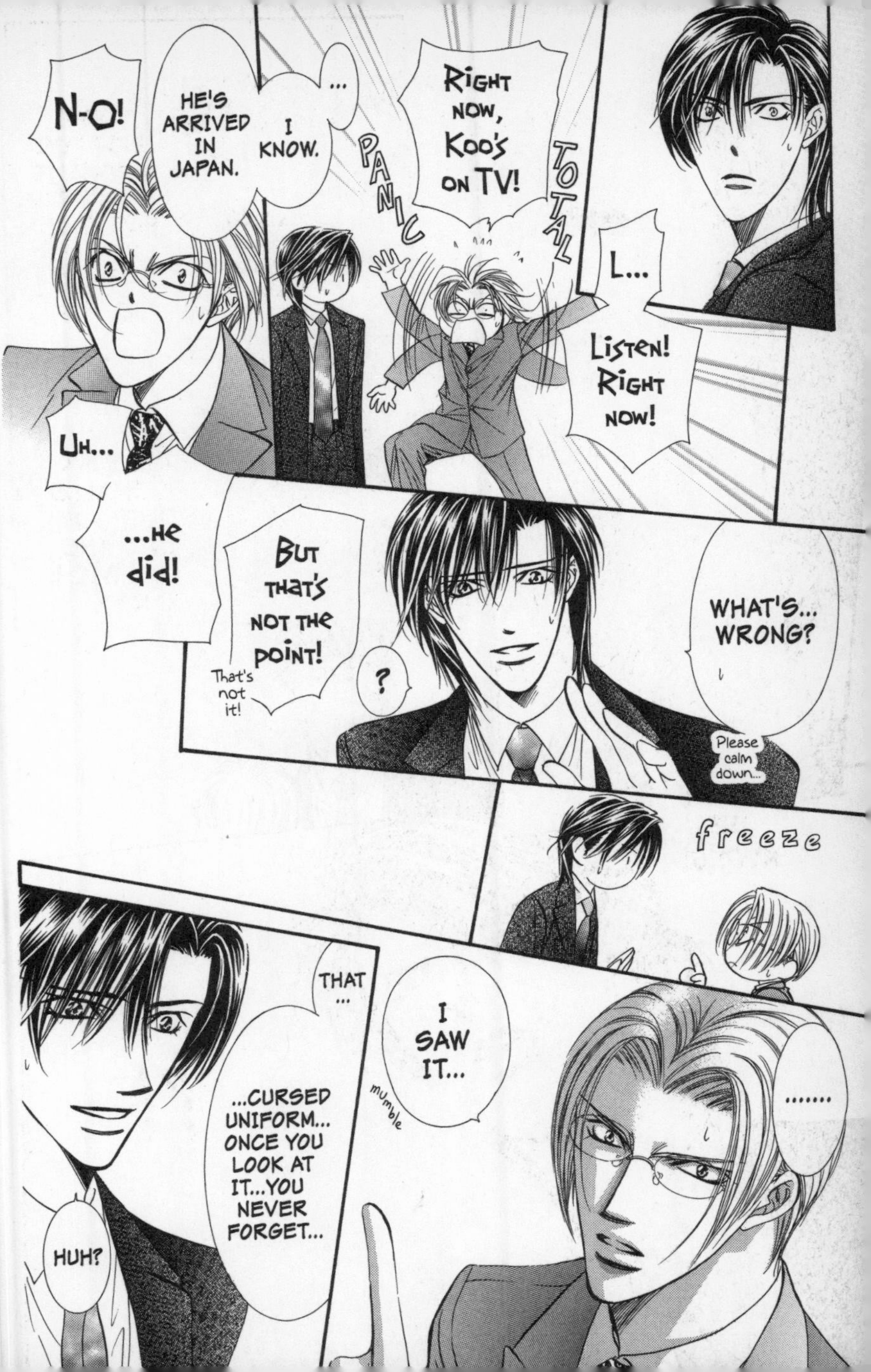
L...
RIGHT NOW, KOO'S ON TV!
TOTAL
PANIC
LISTEN! RIGHT NOW!
...
I KNOW.
N-O!
HE'S ARRIVED IN JAPAN.
UH...
...HE DID!
WHAT'S... WRONG?
Please calm down...
?
BUT THAT'S NOT THE POINT!
That's not it!
freeze
....
I SAW IT...
mumble
THAT ...
...CURSED UNIFORM... ONCE YOU LOOK AT IT...YOU NEVER FORGET...
HUH?

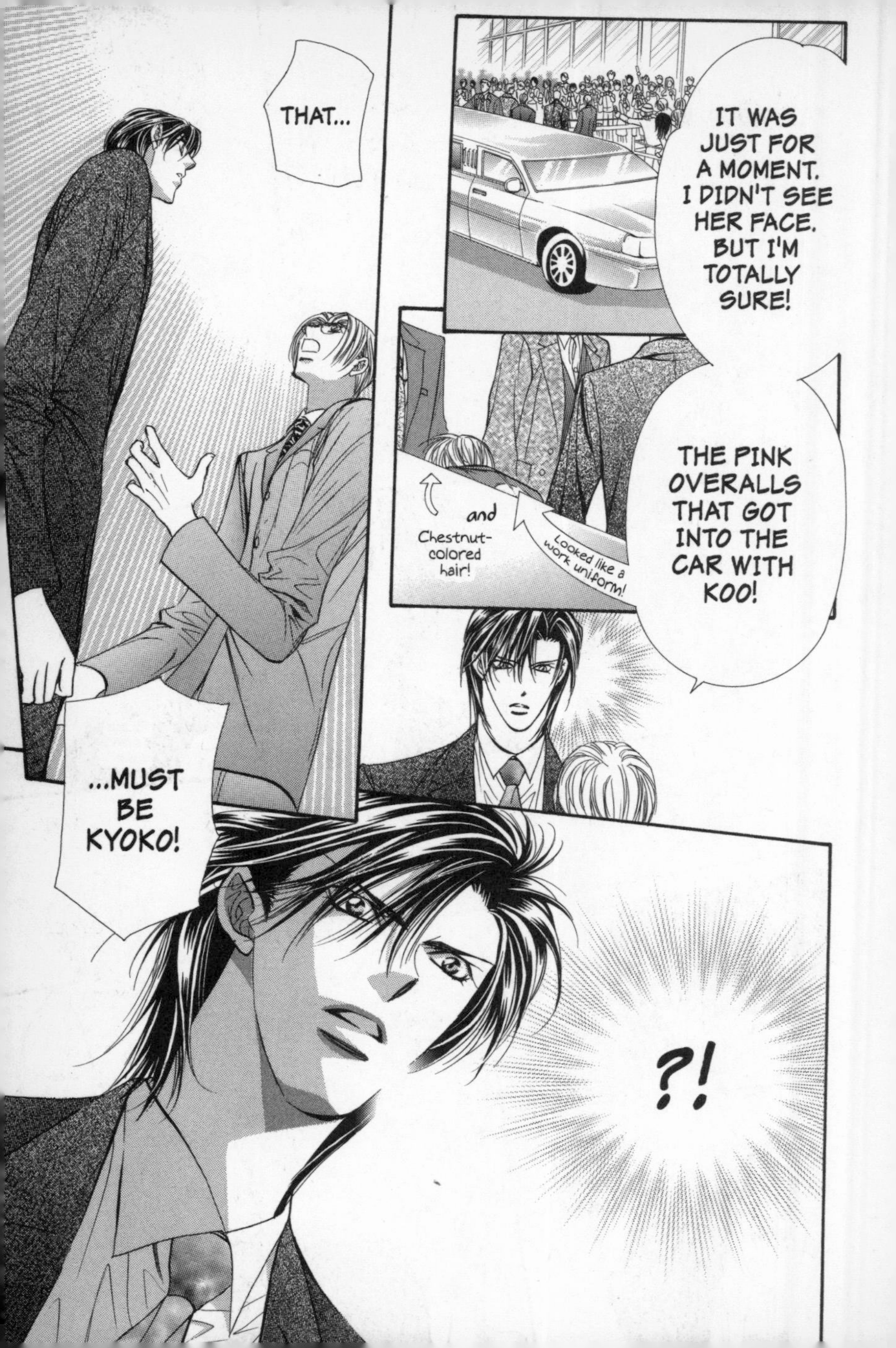
IT WAS JUST FOR A MOMENT. I DIDN'T SEE HER FACE. BUT I'M TOTALLY SURE!
THE PINK OVERALLS THAT GOT INTO THE CAR WITH KOO!
Looked like a work uniform!
and
Chestnut-colored hair!
THAT...
...MUST BE KYOKO!
?!

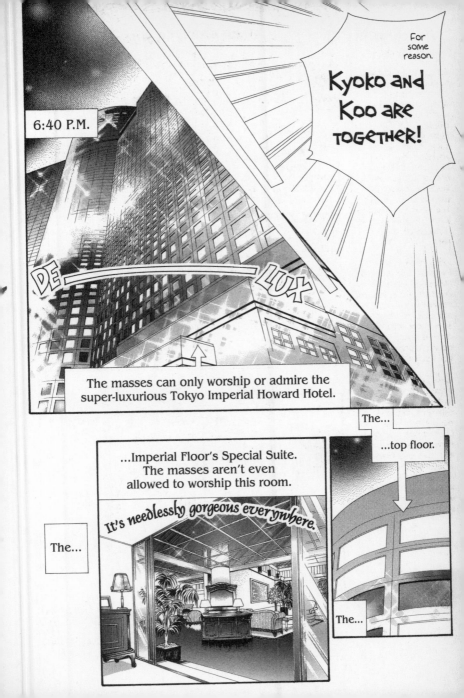

For some reason.

KYOKO AND KOO ARE TOGETHER!

6:40 P.M.

The masses can only worship or admire the super-luxurious Tokyo Imperial Howard Hotel.

The...

...top floor.

...Imperial Floor's Special Suite. The masses aren't even allowed to worship this room.

It's needlessly gorgeous everywhere.

The...

The...

100 chapters already...

After last volume's copy contest, I had a character popularity poll for the first time!! It was held to commemorate the 100th chapter. I was happy, but at the same time, I was surprised at the fact that I'd already drawn 100 chapters...because I don't feel I've drawn 100 chapters yet...anyway, I feel that I reached the 100th chapter very fast. (Compared to Kure-para... ꒰)

I feel...that it's because I was stretched to my limits with everything, and I had no breathing room (wry smile)...in any case, it's thanks to all my readers cheering on that I had the copy contest and popularity poll held.

Skip•Beat is different from my previous manga in that even after 100 chapters, the ending is nowhere in sight...But I'll continue to do my best so that the readers love this manga (and I'll work my hardest ||||) So I'll be happy if you can continue to watch warmly over this work. Thank you.

(Bow)
m(_ _)m

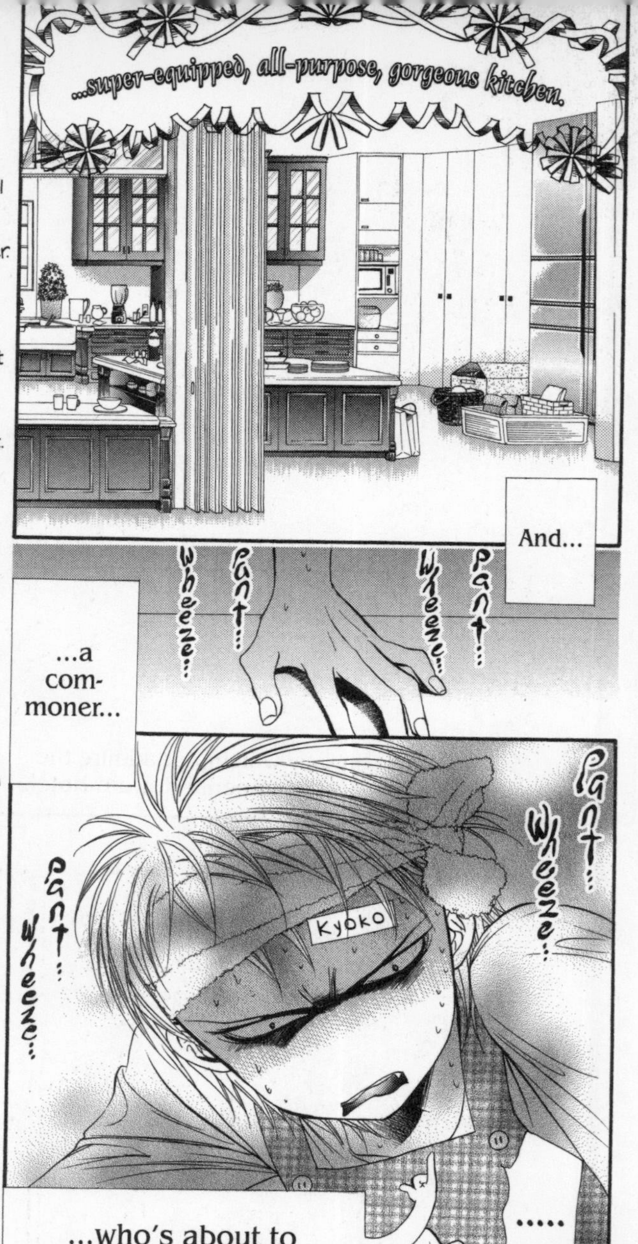
...super-equipped, all-purpose, gorgeous kitchen.
And...
Pant...
Wheeze...
Pant...
Wheeze...
...a commoner...
Pant...
Wheeze...
Kyoko
Pant...
Wheeze...
.....
...who's about to die any moment.

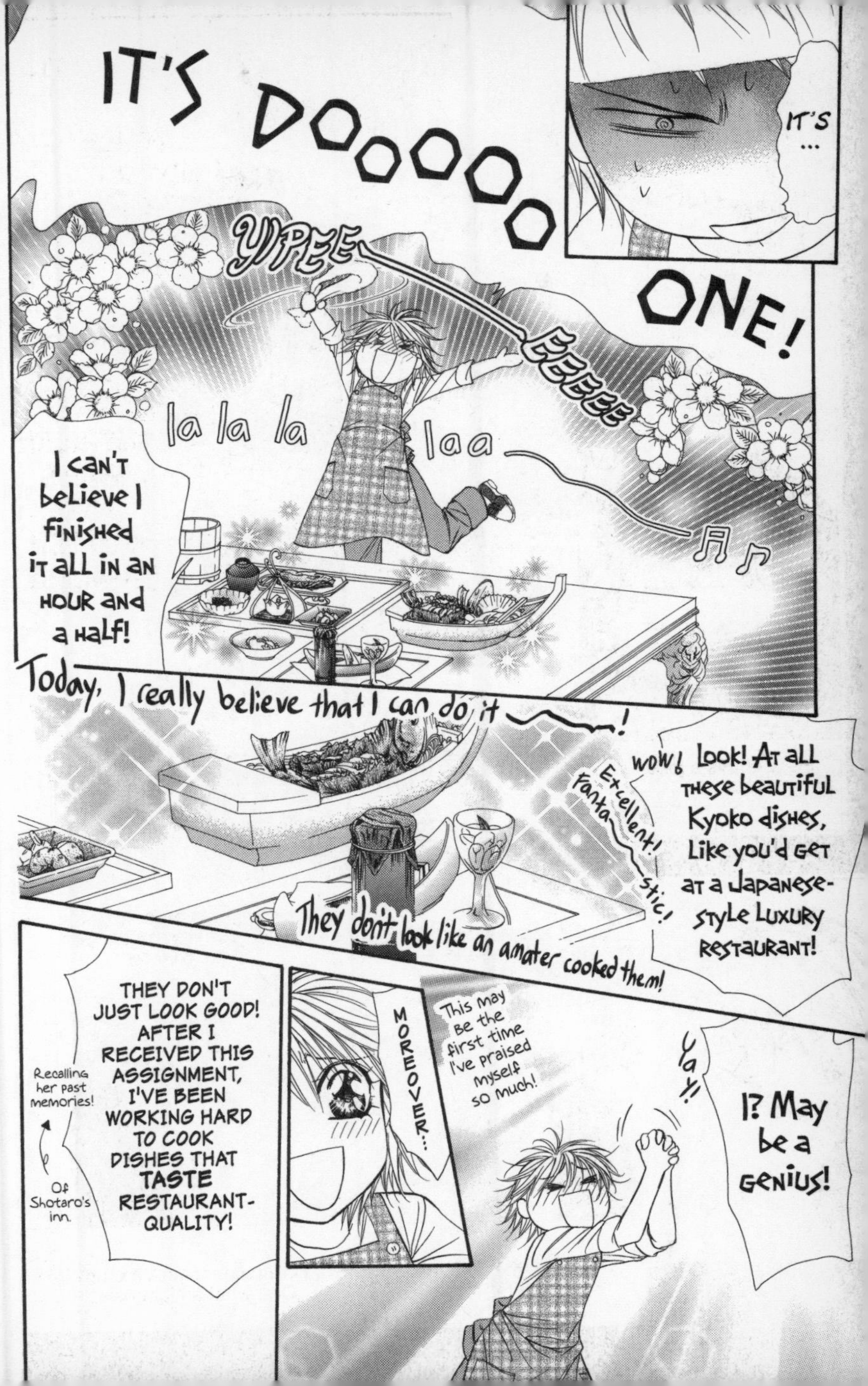
IT'S ...
IT'S DOOOOOO ONE!
YIPEEEEEEE
la la la laa
I can't believe I finished it all in an hour and a half!
Today, I really believe that I can do it!
Wow! Look! At all these beautiful Kyoko dishes, Like you'd get at a Japanese-style luxury restaurant!
Excellent! Fanta-stic!
They don't look like an amater cooked them!
Yay!!
I? May be a genius!
MOREOVER...
This may be the first time I've praised myself so much!
THEY DON'T JUST LOOK GOOD! AFTER I RECEIVED THIS ASSIGNMENT, I'VE BEEN WORKING HARD TO COOK DISHES THAT TASTE RESTAURANT-QUALITY!
Recalling her past memories!
Of Shotaro's inn.

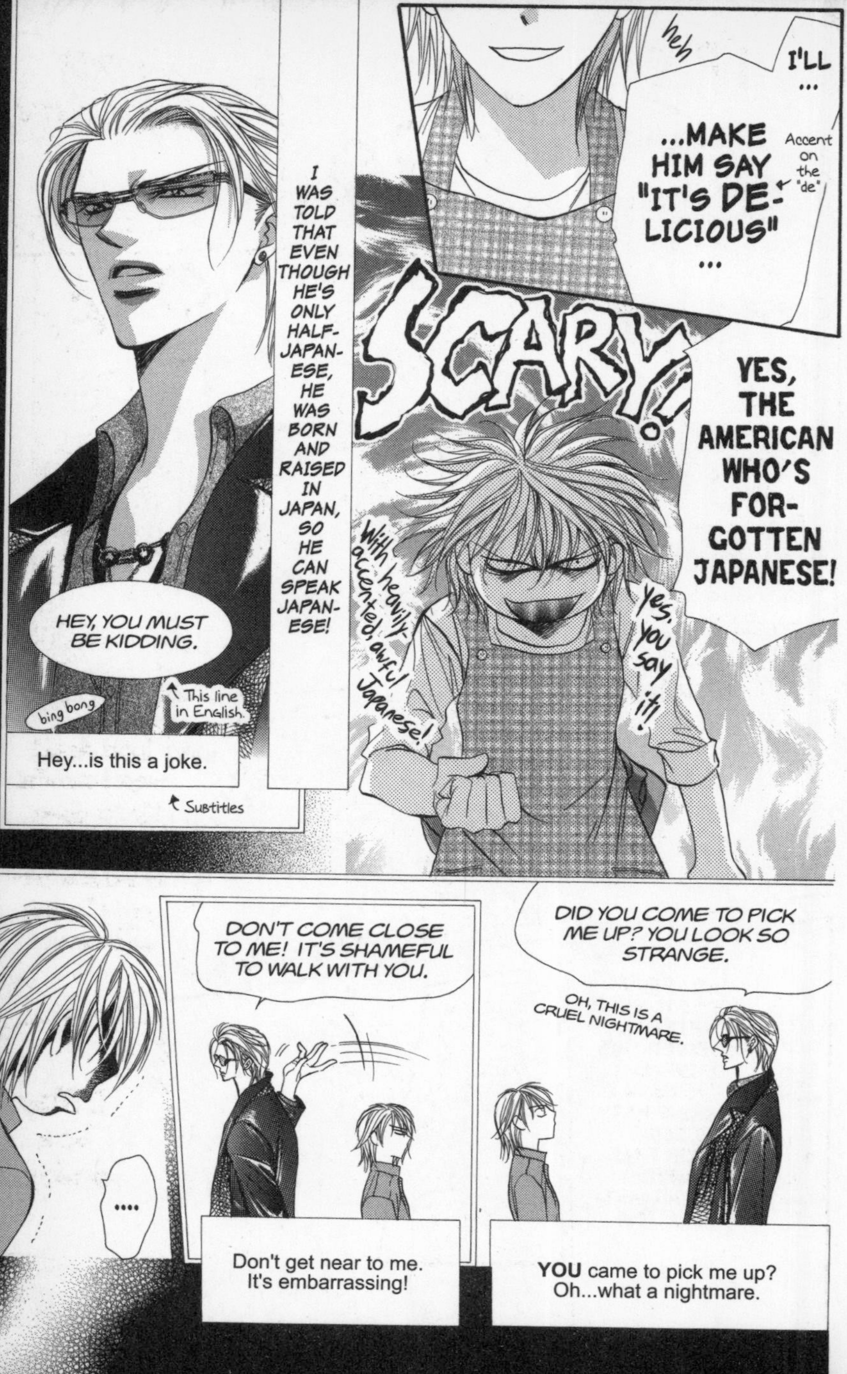

heh
I'LL ...
...MAKE HIM SAY "IT'S DE-LICIOUS" ...
Accent on the "de"
SCARY!
YES, THE AMERICAN WHO'S FOR-GOTTEN JAPANESE!
Yes, you say it!
With heavily accented, awful Japanese!
I WAS TOLD THAT EVEN THOUGH HE'S ONLY HALF-JAPANESE, HE WAS BORN AND RAISED IN JAPAN, SO HE CAN SPEAK JAPANESE!
HEY, YOU MUST BE KIDDING.
This line in English.
bing bong
Hey...is this a joke.
Subtitles
DID YOU COME TO PICK ME UP? YOU LOOK SO STRANGE.
OH, THIS IS A CRUEL NIGHTMARE.
YOU came to pick me up? Oh...what a nightmare.
DON'T COME CLOSE TO ME! IT'S SHAMEFUL TO WALK WITH YOU.
Don't get near to me. It's embarrassing!
....

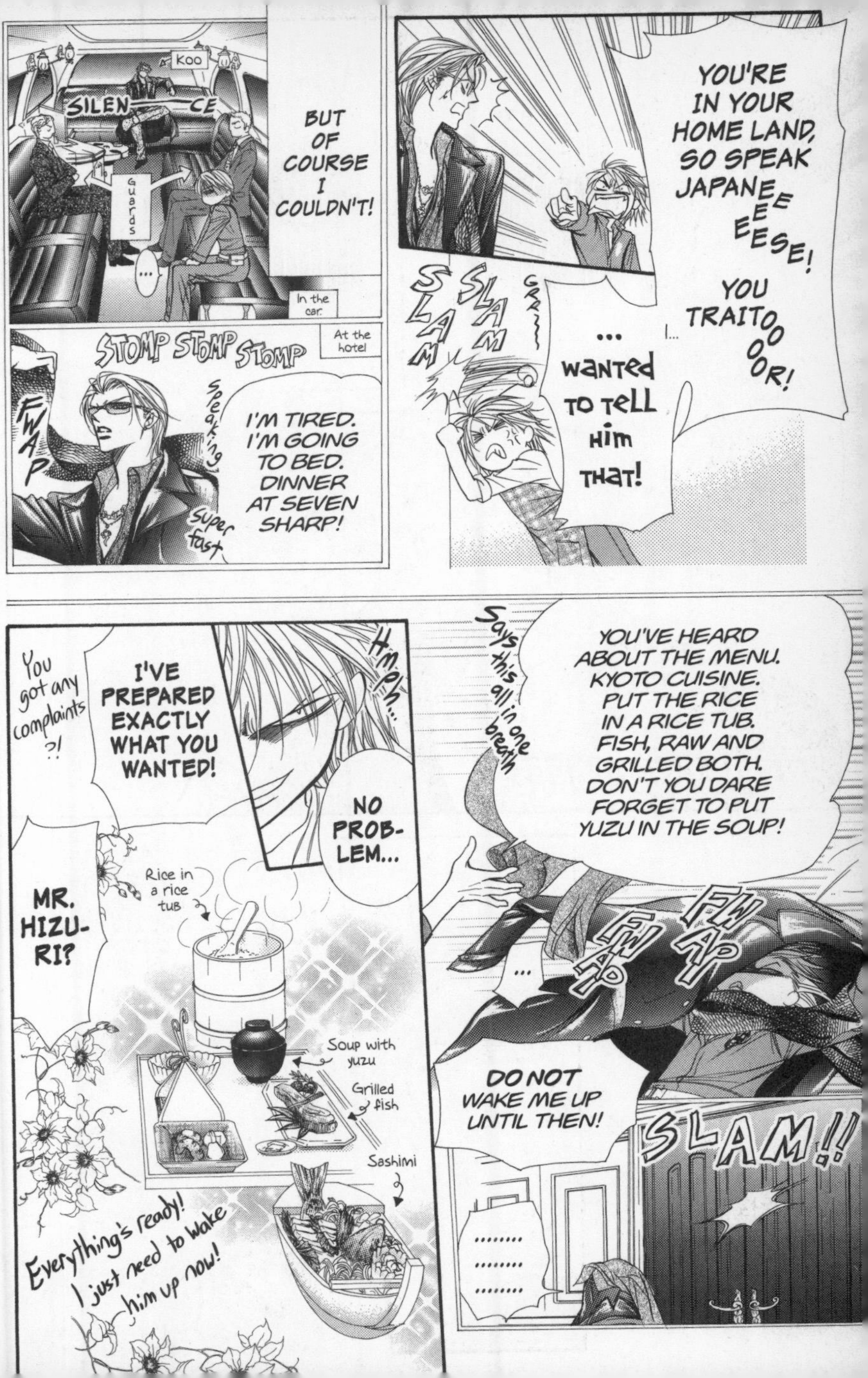
YOU'RE IN YOUR HOME LAND, SO SPEAK JAPANEEEEESE!
YOU TRAITOOOOR!
GRR
SLAM SLAM
I...
... WANTED TO TELL HIM THAT!
KOO
SILEN CE
BUT OF COURSE I COULDN'T!
Guards
...
In the car.
At the hotel
STOMP STOMP STOMP
FWAP
Speaking
I'M TIRED. I'M GOING TO BED. DINNER AT SEVEN SHARP!
Super fast
Says this all in one breath
YOU'VE HEARD ABOUT THE MENU. KYOTO CUISINE. PUT THE RICE IN A RICE TUB. FISH, RAW AND GRILLED BOTH. DON'T YOU DARE FORGET TO PUT YUZU IN THE SOUP!
FWAP FWAP
...
DO NOT WAKE ME UP UNTIL THEN!
SLAM!!
....
....
....
Hmph...
I'VE PREPARED EXACTLY WHAT YOU WANTED!
You got any complaints ?!
NO PROB-LEM...
MR. HIZU-RI?
Rice in a rice tub
Soup with yuzu
Grilled fish
Sashimi
Everything's ready! I just need to wake him up now!

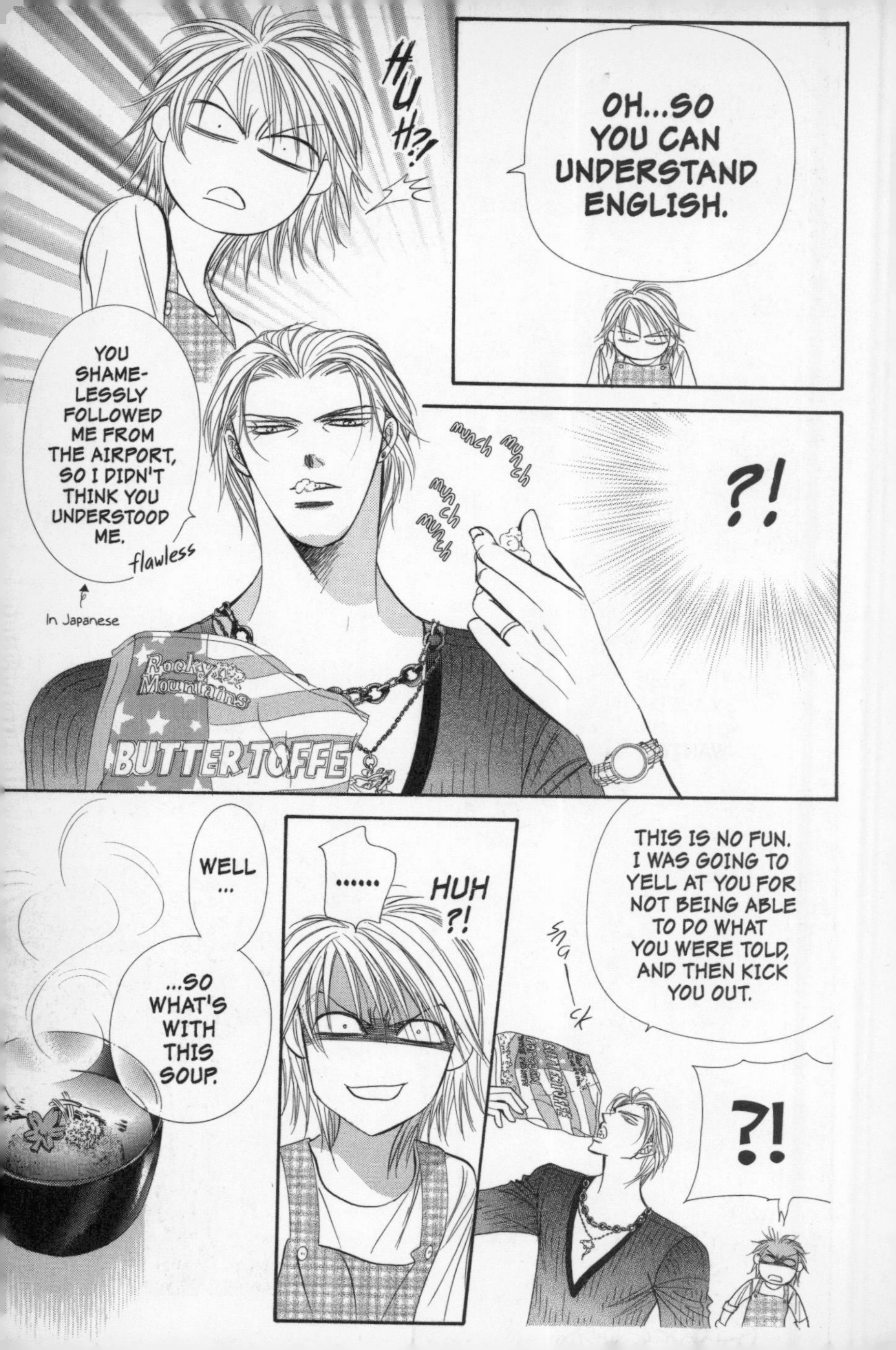
OH...SO YOU CAN UNDERSTAND ENGLISH.
HUH?!
?!
munch munch
munch munch
YOU SHAMELESSLY FOLLOWED ME FROM THE AIRPORT, SO I DIDN'T THINK YOU UNDERSTOOD ME.
flawless
In Japanese
Rocky Mountains
BUTTER TOFFE
THIS IS NO FUN. I WAS GOING TO YELL AT YOU FOR NOT BEING ABLE TO DO WHAT YOU WERE TOLD, AND THEN KICK YOU OUT.
sng—ck
?!
....
HUH ?!
WELL...
...SO WHAT'S WITH THIS SOUP.

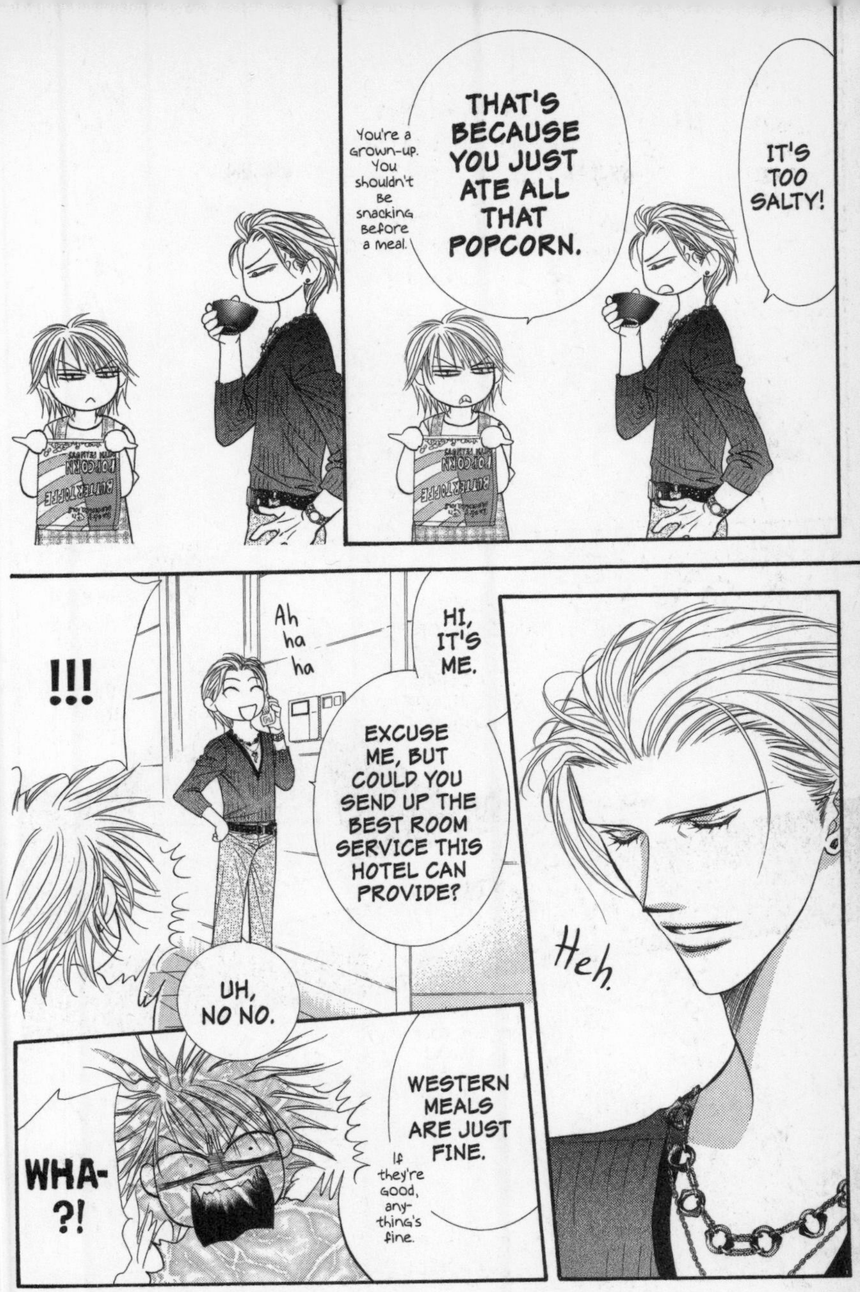
IT'S TOO SALTY!
THAT'S BECAUSE YOU JUST ATE ALL THAT POPCORN.
You're a grown-up. You shouldn't be snacking before a meal.
Heh.
HI, IT'S ME.
Ah ha ha
EXCUSE ME, BUT COULD YOU SEND UP THE BEST ROOM SERVICE THIS HOTEL CAN PROVIDE?
!!!
UH, NO NO.
WESTERN MEALS ARE JUST FINE.
If they're good, any-thing's fine.
WHA-?!

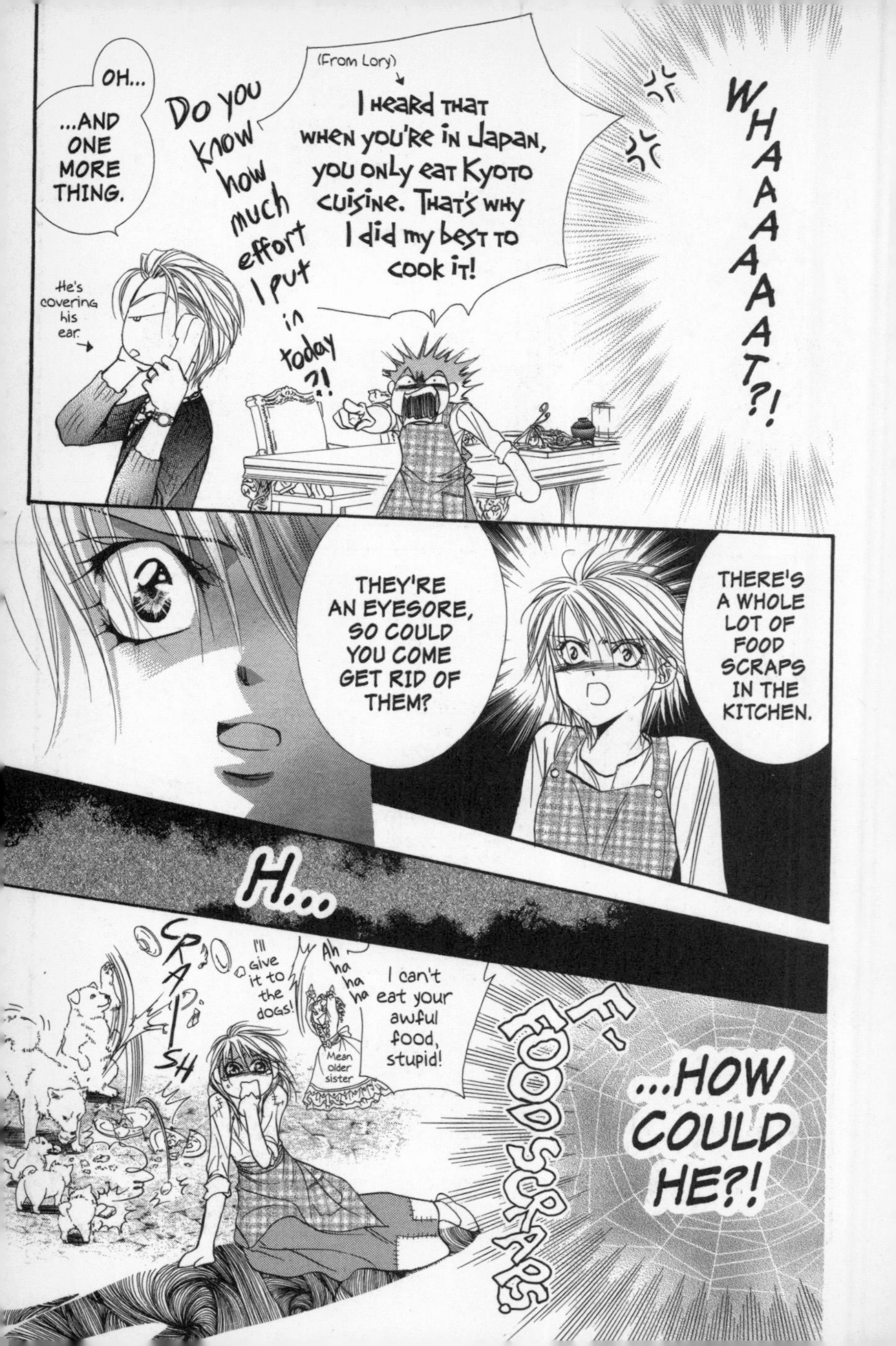
WHAAAAAAT?!
(From Lory)
I heard that when you're in Japan, you only eat Kyoto cuisine. That's why I did my best to cook it!
Do you know how much effort I put in today?!
Oh...
...and one more thing.
He's covering his ear.
There's a whole lot of food scraps in the kitchen.
They're an eyesore, so could you come get rid of them?
H...
...How could he?!
F-foodscraps?!
I can't eat your awful food, stupid!
Ah ha ha ha
I'll give it to the dogs!
Mean older sister
CRASH

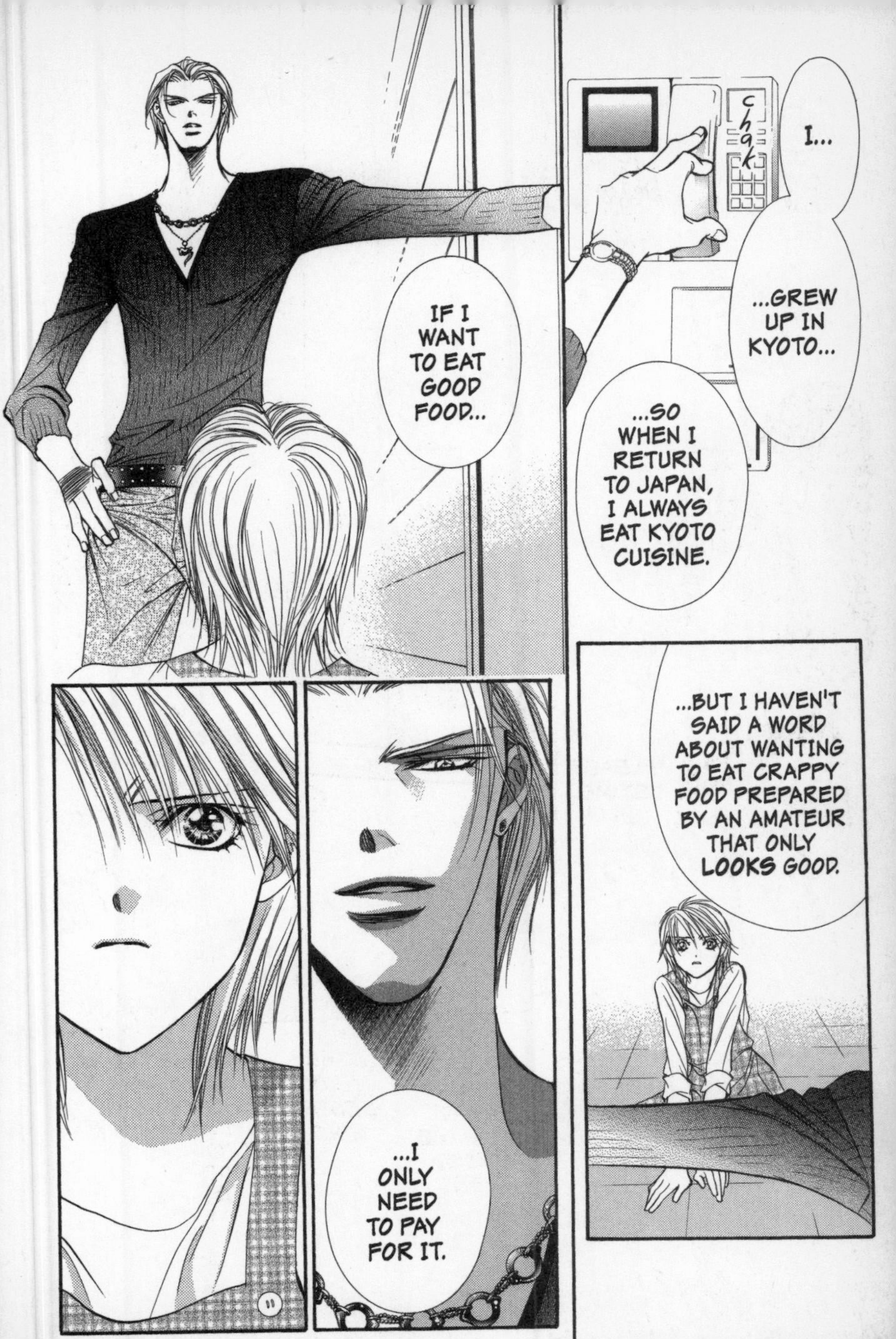
chak
I...
...GREW UP IN KYOTO...
...SO WHEN I RETURN TO JAPAN, I ALWAYS EAT KYOTO CUISINE.
IF I WANT TO EAT GOOD FOOD...
...BUT I HAVEN'T SAID A WORD ABOUT WANTING TO EAT CRAPPY FOOD PREPARED BY AN AMATEUR THAT ONLY **LOOKS** GOOD.
...I ONLY NEED TO PAY FOR IT.

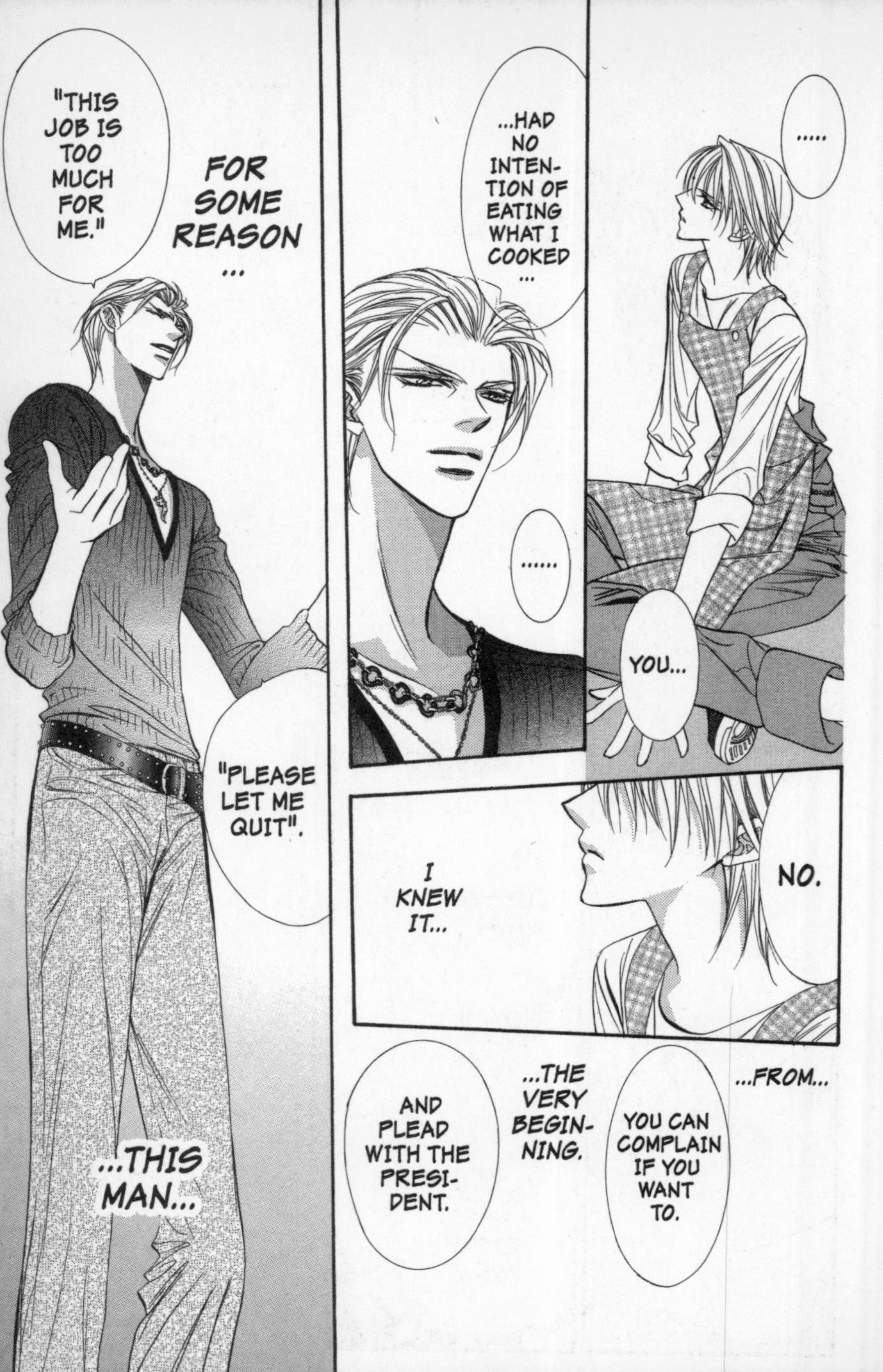
.....
YOU...
...HAD NO INTENTION OF EATING WHAT I COOKED...
......
NO.
I KNEW IT...
...FROM...
YOU CAN COMPLAIN IF YOU WANT TO.
...THE VERY BEGINNING.
AND PLEAD WITH THE PRESIDENT.
FOR SOME REASON...
"THIS JOB IS TOO MUCH FOR ME."
"PLEASE LET ME QUIT".
...THIS MAN...

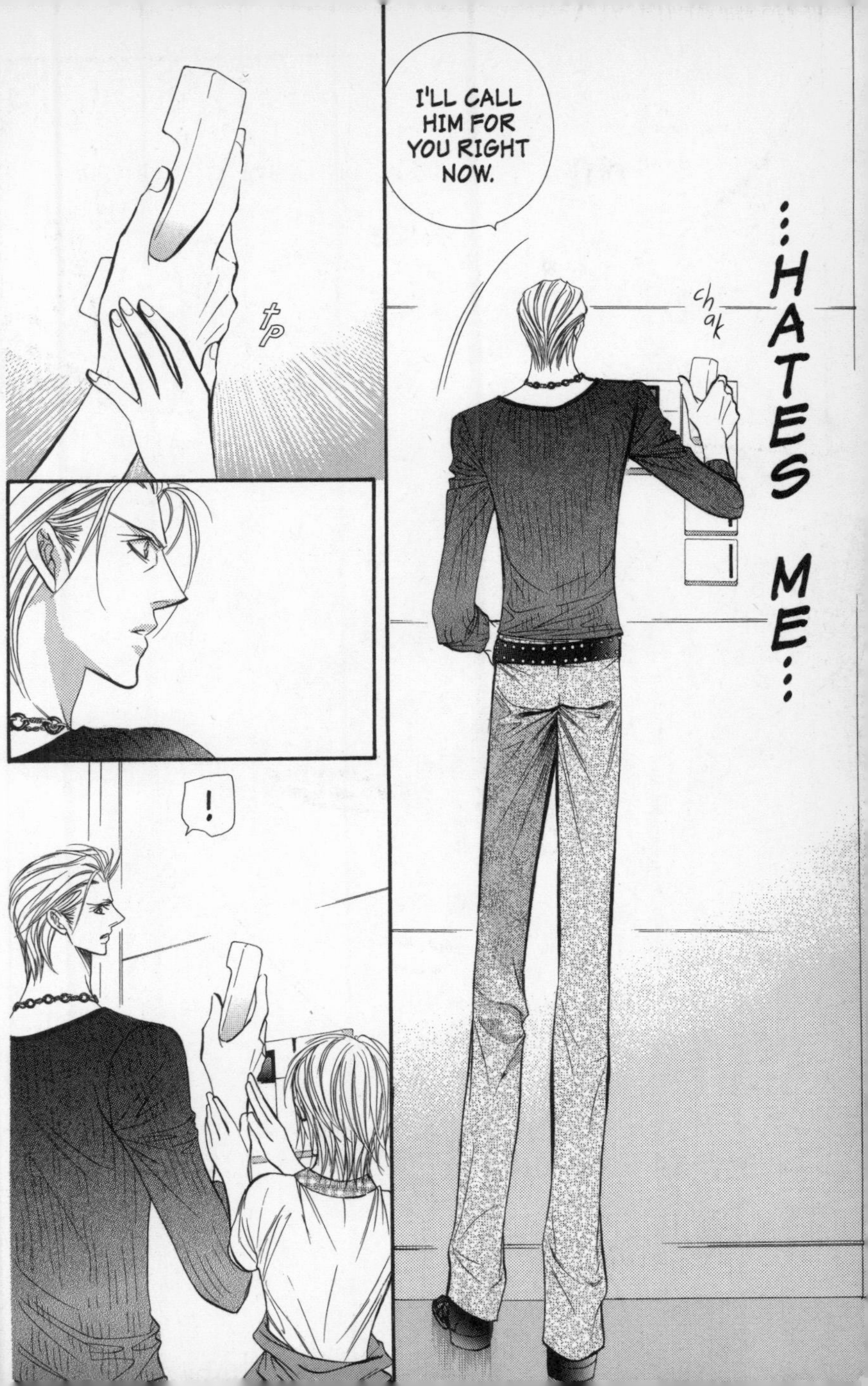
I'LL CALL HIM FOR YOU RIGHT NOW.
chak
...HATES ME...
tp
!

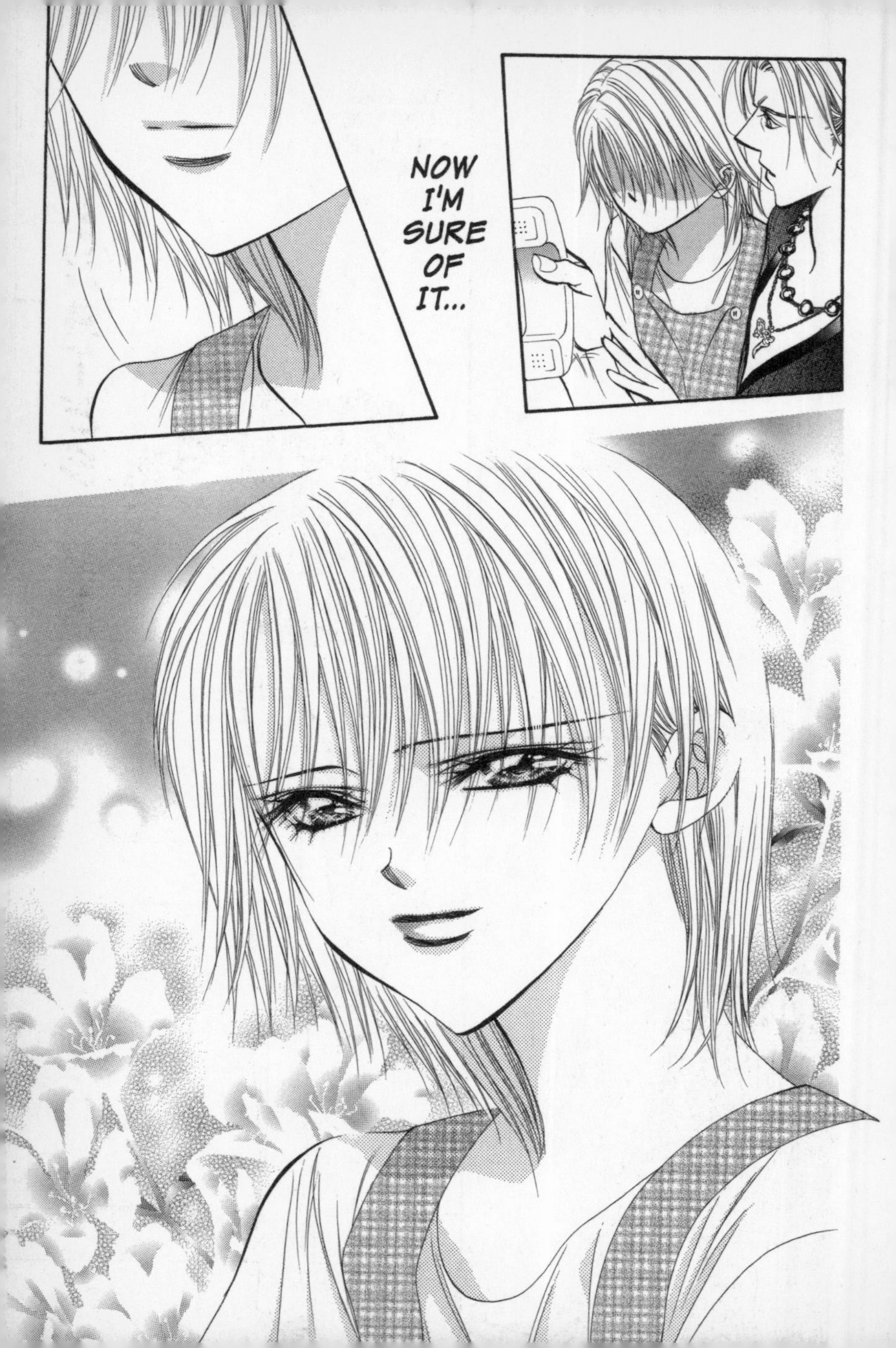
NOW I'M SURE OF IT...

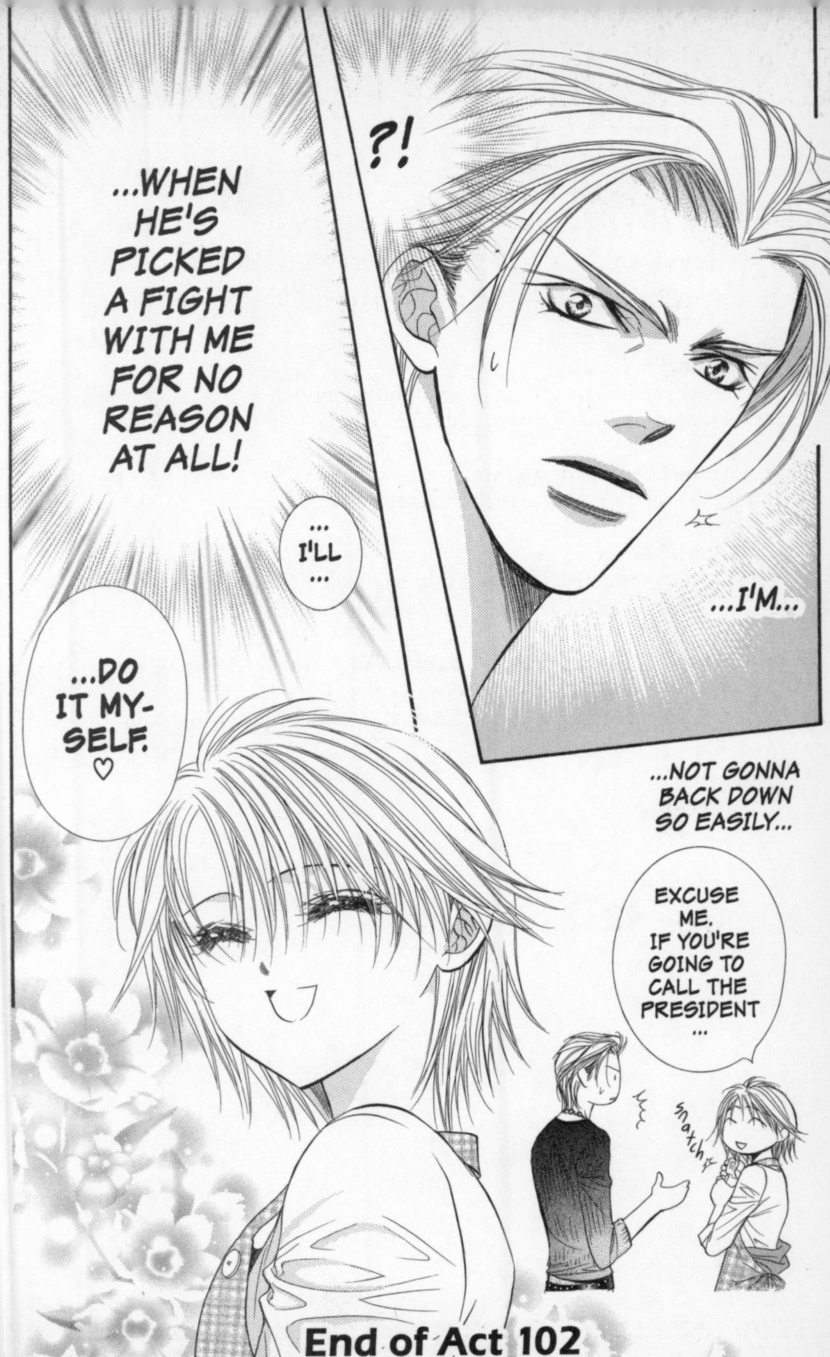
?!
...I'M...
...NOT GONNA BACK DOWN SO EASILY...
...WHEN HE'S PICKED A FIGHT WITH ME FOR NO REASON AT ALL!
... I'LL ...
...DO IT MY-SELF. ♡
EXCUSE ME. IF YOU'RE GOING TO CALL THE PRESIDENT ...
snatch

End of Act 102

Skip·Beat! End Notes
Everyone knows how to be a fan, but sometimes cool things
from other cultures need a little help crossing the language barrier.

Page 13, panel 5: Fujiko
A character in the *Lupin III* manga by Monkey Punch. She is a firearms
expert and an exceptionally talented thief.

Page 13, panel 5: Tallest mountain
A pun on the name Fujiko, which refers to Mt. Fuji.

Page 57, panel 4: Shota
Kyoko means a Sho fetish. Reino thinks she means Shotacon (or Shotaru
Complex), which is similar to a Lolita Complex, except with young boys.

Page 91, panel 1: Bussetsuma-ka-hannya-ha-ra-mi-ta-shingyokanji
This is the opening of Hannya Shingyo, or the Heart of Wisdom Buddhist
sutra. It is equivalent to having a Benedictine Chant as your ringtone.

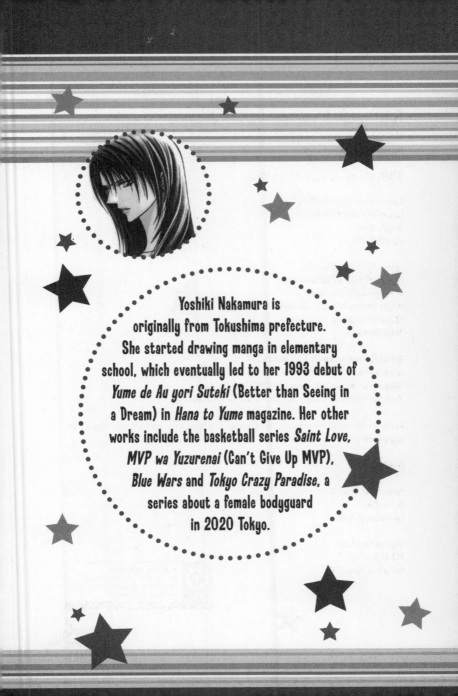

Yoshiki Nakamura is
originally from Tokushima prefecture.
She started drawing manga in elementary
school, which eventually led to her 1993 debut of
Yume de Au yori Suteki (Better than Seeing in
a Dream) in *Hana to Yume* magazine. Her other
works include the basketball series *Saint Love*,
MVP wa Yuzurenai (Can't Give Up MVP),
Blue Wars and *Tokyo Crazy Paradise*, a
series about a female bodyguard
in 2020 Tokyo.

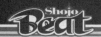

SKIP·BEAT!
Vol. 17
The Shojo Beat Manga Edition

STORY AND ART BY YOSHIKI NAKAMURA

English Translation & Adaptation/Tomo Kimura
Touch-up Art & Lettering/Sabrina Heep
Design/Izumi Evers
Editor/Pancha Diaz

Editor in Chief, Books/Alvin Lu
Editor in Chief, Magazines/Marc Weidenbaum
VP, Publishing Licensing/Rika Inouye
VP, Sales & Product Marketing/Gonzalo Ferreyra
VP, Creative/Linda Espinosa
Publisher/Hyoe Narita

Skip Beat! by Yoshiki Nakamura © Yoshiki Nakamura 2007.
All rights reserved. First published in Japan in 2007 by HAKUSENSHA, Inc., Tokyo.
English language translation rights arranged with HAKUSENSHA, Inc., Tokyo.
The stories, characters and incidents mentioned in this publication are entirely fictional.

Printed in Canada

Published by VIZ Media, LLC.
P.O. Box 77010
San Francisco, CA 94107

Shojo Beat Manga Edition
10 9 8 7 6 5 4 3 2 1
First printing, March 2009

store.viz.com

Tell us wha
about Shojo Beat Manga!

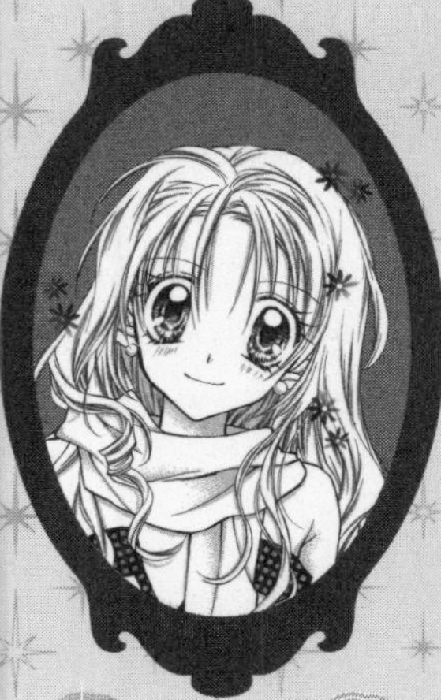

Our survey is now available online. Go to:

shojobeat.com/mangasurvey

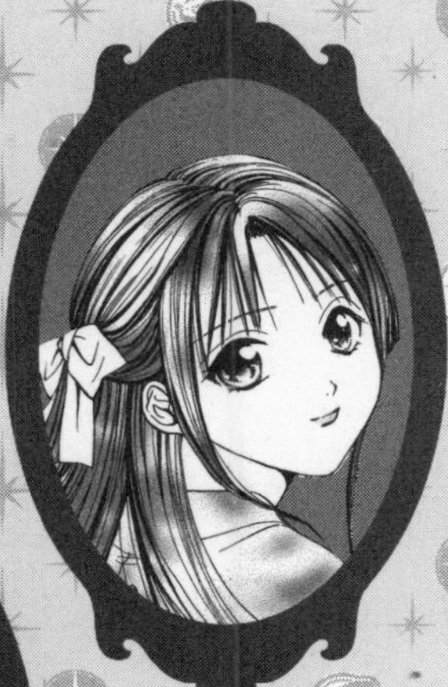

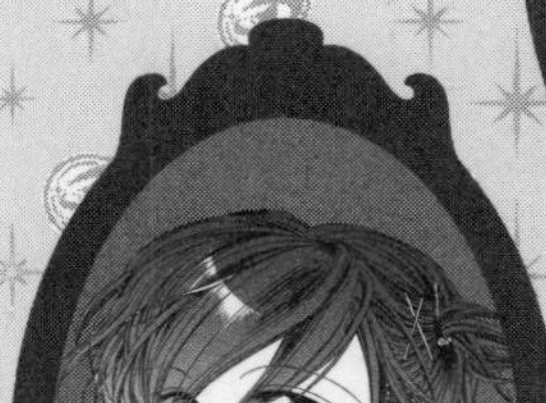

Help us make our product offerings better!

THE REAL DRAMA BEGINS IN...

Shojo Beat

MANGA from the HEART

VIZ media

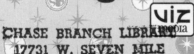